Admiral David Dixon Porter

THE CIVIL WAR YEARS

Admiral
DAVID DIXON
PORTER

Chester G. Hearn

NAVAL INSTITUTE PRESS   *Annapolis, Maryland*

Library of Congress Cataloging-in-Publication Data

Hearn, Chester G.
    Admiral David Dixon Porter: the Civil War years / Chester G. Hearn
        p.   cm.
    Includes bibliographical references and index.
    ISBN 1-55750-353-2 (alk. paper)
    1. Porter, David D. (David Dixon), 1813–1891.   2. Admirals—United States—
    Biography.   3. United States. Navy—Biography.   4. United States—History—
    Civil War, 1861–1865—Naval Operations.   I. Title.
    E467.1.P78H43   1996
    973.7'5'092—dc20
    [B]   95-49584

Printed in the United States of America on acid-free paper ∞

03 02 01 00 99 98 97 96   9 8 7 6 5 4 3 2

First printing

Frontispiece: Adm. David Dixon Porter in 1863 (Courtesy U.S. Naval Historical Center)

To Chet and Dana
and a good life together

Contents

Contents

Illustrations

Preface

Writing about the Civil War is a journey that has no end because each subject introduces the writer to another. For me, this has been true for three of the four books preceding my biographical work on Admiral David Dixon Porter.

While doing research for *The Capture of New Orleans, 1862,* I became fascinated with Porter's complex personality and his often turbulent relationships with his superiors and his peers. By the time I finished work on the New Orleans book, I was intrigued by how Porter, who appeared to have accumulated numerous powerful enemies, ever managed to become an admiral. Early in the war, Secretary of the Navy Gideon Welles questioned Porter's fidelity to the Union, and Pres. Abraham Lincoln, early in his administration, found himself drawn in to one of Porter's schemes. As a consequence, Porter, who was still a lowly lieutenant, entered the first year of the Civil War distrusted at the highest levels of government. How, then, could a naval officer rise to the grade of rear admiral and regain the trust of those who promoted him? The answer became plain. Lincoln, who once said of Gen. Ulysses S. Grant, "I cannot spare this man. He fights," found the same to be true of Porter.

Research on the New Orleans book introduced me to mountains of Porter's correspondence, and that which has not been transcribed is extremely difficult to read. At an early age Porter became a prodigious writer. His penmanship was deplorable, and I developed a deep admiration for James R. Soley, who published Porter's first biography in 1903. At the time, Soley did not have the full use of the *Official Records of the Union and Confederate Navies,* but he did a masterful job of reconstructing Porter's life from sheaves of scribbled archival material. Soley, however, documented nothing and left that research to others.

In 1937 Richard S. West Jr. published *The Second Admiral,* patterned to some degree after Soley's work but written in a more fluid and entertaining manner. West relied to some extent upon Soley, but he appears to have added sources and expanded on Porter's pre- and postwar careers. His documentation, however, is quite sparse, and only by redoing a considerable amount of archival and primary research can Porter's life, and especially his war years, be shaped accurately.

A third biographer, Paul Lewis, published *Yankee Admiral* in 1967. It is another undocumented biography, and as a secondary work it reads somewhat like an abridgement of Soley's and West's books.

What I found in my own research of Porter's life was enough interesting material to produce a thousand-page manuscript—something few publishers would be willing to accept. Had it not been for the Civil War, Porter would probably have resigned from the service as a lieutenant and become a full-time steamship captain. Because the war made Porter an admiral, it also made that part of his life the most interesting and the most meaningful. Porter's formative years, however, were shaped by his famous father, Commodore David Porter. Without that influence, amplified by embarrassing family problems, David Dixon Porter might not have been driven to become a great naval commander, and when the Civil War began, he grasped the opportunity.

In preparing this book for publication, I am indebted to Michael Musick and his assistants at the National Archives for helping me through the massive documents in Record Group 45, which contains not only Porter's papers but the papers of those men with whom he served and the logs of those vessels under his command. I found that much of this material is now contained in the *Official Records.*

I am also indebted to Mary Ison at the Library of Congress, where I found Porter's Letter Book and his "Journal," along with archival material on the men of the times who fought, argued, and, in many instances, bonded with Porter. If another writer was to develop a thesis on Porter's adversarial relationships, he or she could do much research here. Many of these documents were made available to me a few years ago when I was writing *The Capture of New Orleans, 1862,* and this is also true of the collections in the Henry E. Huntington Library and Art Gallery at San Mateo, California.

I am also grateful to Ann Hassinger at the United States Naval Institute for supplying me with articles published years ago in the Naval Institute *Proceedings,* along with other information I found helpful.

Not far from where I live is a small library in the town of Milton, Pennsylvania. The librarian, Susan Brandau, and her assistant, Mary Harrison, have become accustomed to my asking for information from all over the country. They are connected with the James V. Brown Library in Williamsport, Pennsylvania, where most of my requests land on the desk of Evelyn Burns, who does a magnificent piece of research in satisfying my inquiries. To all three of these ladies I am greatly indebted for more than ten years of combined research, as they have spared me much time by their able and collective help.

Bucknell University, in Lewisburg, Pennsylvania—a scant seven miles from my home augments my large personal library with books, magazines, and documents on microfilm. John Slonaker at the United States Army Military History Institute, in Carlisle, Pennsylvania, and the large holdings in the Pennsylvania State Library, in Harrisburg, have saved me many trips to more distant sources.

For those mentioned above, and for all of those I have failed to mention personally, I give my thanks.

Introduction

To understand the character of David Dixon Porter, and the influences that molded his behavior as well as his career, is to understand the special relationship he enjoyed with his father, David, who became one of the greatest captains of the War of 1812 and one of the most distinguished commodores of the U.S. Navy. To David Dixon, his father was a giant, an infallible deity, a man of great courage who walked the earth acclaimed and loved by an adoring public who appreciated him as a great fighter.

By the age of twelve, David Dixon had decided to become just like his father, and when the commodore was court-martialed in 1825, the father's disgrace became the lad's disgrace, and the boy consumed much of his life restoring the good name of the family. David Dixon never admitted that his thin-skinned father invited court-martial by publicly criticizing the secretary of the navy. In later years, when he wrote his father's biography, he devoted fifty pages to the apologia. The incident, however, soured David Dixon's attitude toward politicians, especially naval secretaries, an attitude that almost ended his Civil War career in the first week of the rebellion.

Long after the public had forgotten the commodore's court-martial, David Dixon still lived with it, and he developed many of his father's good attributes and some of his father's troublesome predilections. Father and son were much alike—both became great fighters but horrible politicians.

Had David Dixon Porter become a general instead of an admiral, dozens of books would probably have been written to celebrate his achievements and characterize his human fallibilities. But in the welter of wartime histories, the contribution of Admiral Porter has been overlooked even by some of the most sagacious historians of the war. As Richard R. West Jr. discovered in writing *The Second Admiral,* the policy of the Navy Department during the Civil War was one of censorship. Unlike the generals whose campfires were invaded by newsmen, Secretary of the Navy Gideon Welles, a onetime reporter himself, would not allow correspondents to accompany his commanders on expeditions. On rare occasions when they did, Welles would not allow anything to be printed without first having it screened and approved by the Navy Department.

Porter had the misfortune of cooperating with three powerful political generals—Benjamin F. Butler, Nathaniel P. Banks, and John A. McClernand—all of whom enjoyed free access to the press and who liberally attempted to transfer responsibility for their acts of ineptitude to the navy. All three were inimical toward Porter, and the relationship was mutual. An imbroglio with General Butler, a brilliant lawyer and shrewd politician, continued until the admiral's death, and Porter, like his father, was too much of a fighter to back away from an injustice—whether real or imagined.

Few Union generals fought as successfully as Porter in important campaigns, and the expeditions in which the admiral served could not have succeeded without his involvement. As a lieutenant in command of a mortar flotilla, he participated in one of the most significant Union victories of the war—the capture of New Orleans and the surrender of Forts Jackson and St. Philip. As an acting rear admiral and commander of the Mississippi Squadron, he captured Fort Hindman at Arkansas Post and cooperated with General Grant in destroying Grand Gulf and forcing the surrender of Vicksburg. His freshwater navy was the oddest assortment of gunboats ever assembled, and his unique methods of utilizing the vessels in the Mississippi watershed rank among the most imaginative and successful in naval history. After the Red River campaign, Rear Admiral Porter took command of the North Atlantic Blockading Squadron and, in the last naval battle of the war, cooperated with the Army of the James in capturing Fort Fisher—the most massive earthwork in North America.

The Civil War created 104 major generals, but only 7 rear admirals. Every admiral was a regular navy officer, but ninety of the major generals came from civilian backgrounds and many of them had political ambitions to satisfy. Porter showed little respect for President Lincoln's generals until he met Ulysses S. Grant and William Tecumseh Sherman, with whom he quickly bonded. Another exception was Alfred H. Terry, a volunteer general who knew how to fight and earned Porter's praise at Fort Fisher.

Admiral Porter never had political ambitions, and he disdained the profession with a passion. He was a great fighter who took great risks and sometimes made mistakes—but he had the most difficult assignments in the navy. He was the only lieutenant at the beginning of the war to rise to the rank of rear admiral. Compared with David Glasgow Farragut, who was—and still is—heralded by historians as the greatest admiral of the war, Porter commanded larger flotillas and was engaged in more important campaigns. Where Farragut's victories were largely his own, Porter's were mostly complex joint operations where one branch of the service could not succeed without the full cooperation of the other. On four occasions Porter received a congressional vote of thanks, more than any other officer serving in the U.S. Navy.

After the war, the admiral's numerous political enemies attempted to discredit him, and, like his father, Porter lashed back at his critics, throwing more fuel on fires cleverly kindled by his detractors. When he could not rely on the sword, he turned to the pen, often muddying the waters of his wartime career with angry rejoinders. Porter errantly blighted his brilliant wartime achievements by exposing his vulnerabilities to political adversaries—never realizing that by becoming an admiral he, too, had become a politician.

Some historians have misinterpreted Porter's career and distorted his Civil War accomplishments by relying too heavily on his postwar accounts. Like most admirals, Porter did not like criticism. Because of his sensitive personality and the rash methods he sometimes used in answering his critics, he often invited it. Although Porter was thought to have a photographic memory—his recall of details was extraordinary—he had a very human fallacy, that of rationalizing his own acts when confronted by adversity. At times, his keen insight and mental superiority were not enough to keep him from becoming embroiled with almost anyone who challenged him.

Despite the enormous naval accomplishments of David Farragut, General Grant considered Porter the greatest admiral of the Civil War, comparing him to Lord Nelson. This book is not written to validate Grant's statement or to glorify Porter. It is written to furnish a clear account of the admiral's Civil War years, leaving comparisons to the reader.

David Dixon Porter, however, was not only a unique and talented fighter. He was also an extremely colorful character with a marvelous sense of humor—often vibrant, occasionally careless and abrasive. He was a mixture of energy, creativity, ambition, courage, ability, and controversy. Those are the ingredients that make men who fight wars interesting—and David Dixon Porter possessed all of them.

This is his story.

Admiral David Dixon Porter

ONE

The Legacy

David Dixon Porter's association with the U.S. Navy began on the date of his birth, June 8, 1813, because his father, who was on a cruise in the frigate *Essex*, would want his sons to choose a career at sea. His brother, three-year-old William, had already muddied his feet on the banks of the river, and from their home overlooking the Delaware he had sat with his mother by the window of the old family mansion at Green Bank and watched as his father's frigate cleared for sea. At the age of twenty-two, Evalina Anderson Porter had grown accustomed to her husband's absence, and now, with David Dixon suckling at her breast, she stared furtively at the masts of British warships blockading the river below her home. Capt. David Porter had sailed from his anchorage off Chester, Pennsylvania, eight months ago, and she had heard nothing from him. After the British came up the river, she worried even more. When he sailed, she did not know she was pregnant, and with the captain gone when the baby came, she named the infant David Dixon, after his father and her sister-in-law, who was a Dixon in Norfolk. She knew the name would please the captain—if he ever came home.[1]

Seventeen months passed before she learned that *Essex,* after a glorious cruise, had been destroyed by two men-of-war in Valparaiso harbor. Six months later the captain escaped from a prison ship, rode home a national hero, and beheld for the first time his fifteen-month-old son.[2]

After the war, the captain received the new grade of commodore and moved to Washington to sit on the Board of Navy Commissioners with two famous peers, John Rodgers and Stephen Decatur. He purchased a 110-acre tract on the brow of a hill located a mile north of the scorched White House and began work on the family mansion. Meridian Hill, as he called it, was not ready until 1819, and by then his family had grown to five: William, Elizabeth, David Dixon, Thomas, and the infant Theodoric.[3]

David Dixon's fascination with the navy began on March 1, 1819, when the commodore packed the family into a carriage and drove them to the navy yard to witness the launching of the ship-of-the-line *Columbus.* The commodore, dressed in full regimentals, returned smart salutes from sentries posted at the gate, and in a light rain the Marine Band marched across the yard playing "The Star-Spangled Banner." Naval guns boomed a salute, and smoke enveloped the more than four thousand spectators. The commodore joined the official party, which included Pres. James Monroe and Secretary of the Navy Smith Thompson, but when Commodore William Bainbridge offered to take ten-year-old William on board *Columbus,* David Dixon made an impressive fuss and was added to the tour.

In later years he recalled the vibration of the vessel as she slipped into the Potomac, the sensation of seeing the crowd on shore drift away, and the thrill of knowing he was afloat. He marked this moment as the day he was launched into the U.S. Navy. Thereafter, the navy yard became a second home to the lad. He roamed the grounds and questioned the shipwrights, some of whom had served with the commodore. They filled the boy with droll stories of how his father had been captured and imprisoned by the Barbary pirates. David Dixon listened in rapt attention to their tales, and he wondered why his famous father had never mentioned them.[4]

Naval officers visited Meridian Hill to smoke cigars, drink whiskey, and reminisce, and the conversation always reverted to the war. David would sit with William and listen to men like Decatur, Rodgers, and

Bainbridge refight battles at sea in language rebuked by his mother. By then the boys could swear as well as a boatswain, but none of the visitors had a more lasting influence on the lad than his foster brother, Lt. David Glasgow Farragut, who had served as midshipman on *Essex* and fought beside his father.

In 1822, twenty-one-year-old Davy Farragut, having no real home of his own, married a Norfolk girl and honeymooned at Meridian Hill. The young lieutenant—who had already spent most of his life at sea—and the mischievous lad of nine formed a kinship that lasted as long as they lived. Farragut took the boy everywhere, but once during a concert David Dixon disappeared. The commodore spotted his son marching with the band as it paraded up Pennsylvania Avenue. Farragut captured the lad on the White House lawn, took full blame for the incident, and rescued him from a whipping by his father.

Commodore Porter lived in style until he depleted his prize money, and by 1822 his annual salary of thirty-five hundred dollars could not pay the bills at Meridian Hill. He applied for sea duty and asked for a command in the Caribbean to clean out the pirates who infested the islands. He also requested a midshipmanship for William, and the warrant arrived on January 1, 1823. David Dixon enviously watched his older brother go to sea and harangued his father for a commission for himself.[5]

Conditions in the Caribbean were turbulent. Countries like Mexico, Venezuela, and Santo Domingo had broken with Spain during the Napoleonic wars and established independent republics. Spain sent its navy to blockade rebel ports, and the new republics responded by commissioning privateers to capture Spanish merchantmen. The venture deteriorated when the raiders turned pirate and attacked American shipping. Lurid stories of massacred crews and torched vessels filtered back to American shippers, and when they called upon the government to eliminate the pirates, the forty-three-year-old commodore seemed to be the right man to command the West Indian Squadron. Naval secretary Thompson, however, cautioned the impetuous commander to refrain from actions that could provoke hostilities with Spain. The request was like asking a pot not to boil after lighting a fire under it.[6]

Porter's spring campaign in 1823 brought praise from the Navy Department and not a single complaint from Spain. The new secretary of the navy, Samuel L. Southard, rewarded the commodore by allowing him to expand the squadron for the 1824 campaign and approved his request to take his family on the cruise.

David Dixon came aboard the 32-gun frigate *John Adams* on December 10 and enjoyed the run of the deck. For five days he pestered the crew with questions, but after the flagship joined a squadron of schooners mustering at Norfolk the lad shifted his curiosity to *Sea Gull*. The galiot had been converted from a ferryboat to a steamer with her beams heightened to keep waves from washing over her decks and dousing her firebox. Though slow and cramped, *Sea Gull* was the first commissioned steamer in a navy on the brink of evolution. Her huge sidewheels, located amidships, occupied a third of her length. She carried two funnels, and her hold was filled with so much coal that her crew had little space to bunk. For several days David prowled the vessel, returning from each visit smeared with soot. The commodore ended his son's explorations and ordered his officers to subject the lad to the same discipline as a midshipman. David Dixon's unofficial naval training started in January 1824. The boy was ten years old.

On February 18 the squadron put to sea, cruised south to Puerto Rico, and stopped at Jamaica, St. Christopher, Santo Domingo, and St. Thomas. After two months at sea, Porter anchored at Key West, built a home for his family, and set men to work on building a navy yard. He intended to use the base for junkets into the pirate-infested shores of southern Cuba, but yellow fever struck the commodore and almost took his life. Evalina nursed her husband past the crisis and, by some miracle, kept the children healthy. Returning to Washington, David Dixon enjoyed a fascinating trip on *Sea Gull,* dividing his time between the engine room and the deck.[7]

David's unofficial midshipmanship lasted until he reached Washington, where his father enrolled him in Columbia College, a preparatory school with a dormitory housing ninety-two other youngsters. The school offered a typical nineteenth-century classical education—English, Latin, Greek, and mathematics. During his son's two years at school, the commodore sailed back to the Caribbean and became enmeshed in a diplomatic imbroglio at Fajardo, Puerto Rico. The affair would have a telling influence on the career of the boy whose father had ascended to heights of infallibility.[8]

When the commodore reached St. Thomas, he learned that pirates from Fajardo had robbed an American firm of five thousand dollars in merchandise. Lt. Charles T. Platt, commanding the schooner *Beagle,* had attempted to recover the stolen goods by applying to Fajardo's alcalde. The authorities horse-collared Platt, accused him of piracy, and threw him in the local guardhouse. Hooted and hissed out of the village, Platt returned to his ship and reported the incident. The commodore considered the insult an act of war, sailed to Fajardo, seized the town, and demanded an apology. The alcalde complied, and Porter reported the incident to the Navy Department.

Andrew Jackson's seizure of Florida still nettled the Spanish government, and Secretary of the Navy Southard feared that Porter's highhanded invasion of Puerto Rico might be more than Spain could bear. He laid the matter of the commodore's "invasion" before the cabinet, and they unanimously agreed that the matter must be investigated by a court of inquiry.[9]

Porter arrived in Washington on March 1, 1825, and felt no need to justify his action before a court of inquiry. The following day two congressmen ignited the commodore's temper by writing accusatory editorials. With his personal honor at stake, he ignored advice from his friends and wrote Southard, demanding that a board meet quickly and that he be cleared or dismissed from the navy. Spain, however, never registered a complaint. Southard had been tempted to let the matter drop until the commodore shifted his attack to the Navy Department.

Irritated by Porter's insubordinate attitude, Southard ordered the court of inquiry and named James Barron to the board. Porter rebelled. In 1807 he had sat on a court that tried Barron, and Porter had voted against him. Now, with the situation reversed, he accused Southard of salting the court with antagonistic officers. When the trial began, the court asked Porter if he objected to any of the judges. He dodged the question but attacked Southard, berating the secretary's character and condemning his motives for holding the hearing. The judges found Porter's remarks objectionable, cleared the courtroom, and ordered him to retract his attack on Southard. Porter refused, stomped out of the room, and forced the court to proceed with its deliberations without him.

Porter did not heed advice from anyone, and while the court of inquiry attempted to maintain a sense of decorum, the commodore continued his attack on Southard and defended himself by writing a pamphlet. Porter published the document at his own expense and dedicated it to the new president, John Quincy Adams. In it he lobbied for the removal of Southard and the vindication of himself.

When Southard ordered the commodore court-martialed, the trial drew national attention. Porter had two friends sitting as judges— James Biddle and John Downes. The other three he considered ene-mies—Jesse D. Elliott, James Barron, and Judge Advocate Richard Coxe. Porter attended few of the sessions. Instead, he spent his time appealing to the public and demanding the removal of their imprudent naval secretary. Ignoring warnings from his closest friends, Porter fol-lowed a path of self-destruction.

Out of respect for the commodore's past service, the court ruled with leniency, suspending Porter from active duty for six months. The suspension was merely intended to provide time for him to cool off. The court exonerated him from the charge of misconduct at Fajardo and praised him for upholding the honor of the nation and her navy. Biddle and Downes saved him from demotion, but the verdict did not appease Porter. Feeling disgraced by his enemies, he retired to Mer-idian Hill to brood for six months in sullen silence. "I shall see my sus-pension through," he declared stiffly. "That done, my commission goes instantly into the President's hands."[10]

The twelve-year-old lad witnessed his father topple from the pinna-cle of national recognition to the depths of sullen despair. Without un-derstanding how his one great hero brought humiliation upon himself, the boy empathized with his father and never faltered in his conviction that the commodore had been wronged. He vowed to eradicate the dis-grace blackening the family name. His father's enemies became his enemies, and because the commodore never forgave two friends who sat on the court-martial, they, too, became the enemies of the son. And long before the Civil War raged across the land, David Dixon would serve under four of these judges.

No event in David's life had a more lasting effect on his personality and character than witnessing his father's pain. He had modeled his own behavior after the commodore's—the good attributes along with the bad—and his father's disgrace became his own. The calamity intensified the lad's determination to become a naval officer and redeem the family name, but now he knew there were enemies other than those you fought in mortal combat. He developed a loathing for politicians, but the archvillain of all was the powerful secretary of the navy. How a young man who planned a career in the navy expected to function while seething with so much hatred for the system was a question the lad had not asked himself.

In the spring of 1826, after six months of suspension, the commodore kept his promise and resigned from the navy. He needed money but expected no help from those he had condemned. He stunned the Navy Department and his friends by becoming the general of marine for the Republic of Mexico. An annual salary of twelve thousand dollars represented financial salvation for the ex-commodore. He departed for Veracruz in late April with David, twelve, and Thomas, ten. For the lad with a passion for the sea, his career was about to begin in his father's Mexican navy.[11]

Evalina Porter remained at Meridian Hill with Elizabeth, Theodoric, Hambleton, and her newborn twins, Evalina and Henry. The mansion still swarmed with servants, and the general had borrowed heavily to keep them. When he departed for New York to join his flagship, the brig-of-war *Guerrero*, he hoped to augment his hefty salary with Spanish prizes. To accompany him, the general signed on friends and named his twenty one-year-old nephew, D. Henry Porter, *Guerrero*'s captain. Henry had already spent half his life in the navy, and when he resigned his commission to serve under his uncle, he was considered by superiors a rash but determined officer who would either die young or reach high rank. The general ignored his eldest son's application and told William to stay with the U.S. Navy and await developments.[12]

The 22-gun *Guerrero*, built in the East River shipyard of Henry Eckford, looked sleek and shiny in her fresh coat of black paint as she rocked at her moorings. In late April she stood for sea. David Dixon watched excitedly as the crew made sail for the Gulf of Mexico. The Spanish government already knew of the ex-commodore's enterprise and dispatched the man-of-war *Hercules* to intercept *Guerrero*. A day's sail from Veracruz, lookouts on *Guerrero* sighted *Hercules* standing in chase. David Dixon looked on eagerly as his father rolled out the guns, but *Guerrero,* undermanned and outmatched in firepower, put on her best heels and came to anchor under the guns of the great fortress at San Juan de Ulúa.[13]

With the fever season approaching, the general took the boys to Mexico City, and their aspirations for participating in a sea battle were shattered when their father enrolled them at a boarding school in Mexico City. While the general cast about to create a fighting force out of old hulks acquired by the Republic of Mexico, the boys learned to speak Spanish, play monte, and strum the guitar.[14]

Months passed before the general assembled a squadron of five vessels: the brig-of-war *Guerrero,* the frigate *Libertad,* and three small brigs, *Victoria, Bravo,* and *Herman.* He could not find crews, and the Mexican government sent him a company of mutinous soldiers. Porter translated Navy Regulations into Spanish, imposed the rules of conduct on the crews, and whipped the offenders. Since most Mexican officers came from politically influential families, Porter received numerous complaints from the government. In May 1827 he decided to remove the flotilla from Mexico and take it to Key West.[15]

In the summer of 1827, fourteen-year-old David Dixon became a midshipman on his father's flagship *Libertad,* and each day he visited the general's cabin for lessons in gunnery, navigation, and the elements of command. Awed by his father's knowledge, he began to appreciate the value of experience. He watched as the squadron sailed, returning later with their prizes, but *Libertad* remained in the harbor and kept a flotilla of Spanish blockaders busy watching her.

When the general armed the prize brig *Esmeralda* and gave command of her to Henry Porter, Midshipman David joined the crew for his next lesson—a short cruise under combat conditions. Henry took *Esmeralda* into Cuba's shipping lanes and sank four merchantmen before the undisciplined Mexican crew mutinied. Aided by two American officers, Henry shot two mutineers, put the others in irons, and returned to Key West. The episode became a sharp lesson in a commander's role at sea. His father had warned that a master loses control of his ship if he allows the slightest deviation from his orders. David now understood what his father meant.[16]

Early in 1828 Henry Porter brought David Dixon on board *Guerrero* and set a course for Cuba. The general wanted a few good prizes to expand his squadron. He salted the crew with a dozen officers and 186 seamen, the majority being handpicked Americans. On February 9 Henry captured two Spanish brigs, manned them, and sent them to Veracruz. The following day he chased a fleet of schooners into Mariel. Two armed brigs lay among them, and they all sought shelter behind a masonry fort armed with two long guns. *Guerrero* cleared for action and stood in close to shore. Shots from the fort, aided by faulty powder, fell short. Gunners on the Spanish brigs *Marte* and *Amalia* fired high, sending shot whistling through the tops, ripping the rigging and shredding sails. A lucky shot severed *Guerrero's* cable and set her adrift. She came about and resumed the attack, concentrating on the two armed brigs. Most of her shots missed the brigs and fell among the schooners.

David Dixon scrambled from one end of the vessel to the other, shouting the captain's orders to the gunners. Men lay wounded on deck, but as smoke from each broadside rolled back across the quarterdeck, crews shouted for ammunition. David dropped down the gangway to prod the Mexicans who carried up the shells, and when he came topside the captain sent him up the foremast to hurry the repair of the ropes. He toppled over when a spent ball struck him in the leg, but so great was the excitement of his first battle that he jumped back on his feet, feeling no sensation of pain.

He heard a crash and looked up as both topgallant masts snapped, falling into the shrouds and fouling the sails. David glanced apprehensively at the captain, who reassured him that the enemy was on the verge of surrender. But another shot split the port cable and again set *Guerrero* adrift. Men scurried aloft to repair the sails, but the sound of gunfire had carried to Havana, and *Lealtad*, flagship of the Spanish Caribbean fleet, bore down on the crippled *Guerrero*.

One look at the huge *Lealtad* convinced Henry Porter that what remained of his twenty-two guns were no match for the powerful Spaniard. Rigging what sails he could, he put out to sea, crossed *Lealtad's* bow, and raked her with a broadside. Using superior seamanship, Porter maintained a lead, tacked frequently, and fired his broadsides. When the Spaniard's foremast toppled into the mizzen, *Guerrero* sped away.

At dark *Lealtad* was barely in sight. A prudent skipper would have offered a prayer of thanks and sought safety—but not Henry Porter. He wanted the two armed brigs and the fleet of panic-stricken merchantmen trapped in Mariel's harbor, and he suspected to find them still there. If he sailed to Key West, *Lealtad* would follow and blockade the harbor. But if he doubled back and eluded the Spaniard, he could capture the brigs and scuttle the schooners. Then, by manning the brigs, he could attack *Lealtad* with all three vessels.[17]

David Dixon listened to his cousin's plan but took no part in the council. "I was too young," he later lamented, "to recognize the risks we were taking, and too inexperienced to know what needed to be done to overcome them." But he watched the captain persuade the others, bring *Guerrero* about, and set a course for Mariel.[18]

The night was black enough to cloak the captain's plan, but he failed to give *Lealtad* enough sea and ran under her guns. A broadside toppled *Guerrero's* mainmast. Porter came about and made a futile effort to reach Key West, but *Lealtad* systematically poured in broadsides, raking the stricken brig from stem to stern. With his decks in shambles, his masts down, and his carronades disabled, Porter surrendered.

Guerrero's colors had been shot away twice and run back up, and when Porter struck, *Lealtad* continued to fire. At close quarters the Spaniard switched to grape, and a hail of death swept the decks of the defenseless brig. Henry Porter lurched backwards, and David Dixon caught him by the armpits. He took one look at the gored body and knew his cousin was dead. When he searched for help, his horror intensified, for bodies lay everywhere, ripped apart by flying metal.

For four hours *Lealtad* stood off and made repairs before sending boats to collect *Guerrero's* prisoners. As each hour passed, David's hatred of the enemy's brutality festered, and when a boarding party came to take him, they snatched his cousin's body and unceremoniously pitched it over the side.

Lealtad towed her prize into Havana, and when Spanish authorities discovered they had captured the son of David Porter they offered him a gentlemen's parole. This entitled the boy to take up residence in Havana and enjoy life on the island until his father arranged his parole. He rejected the offer, choosing to stay with the crew and share the hardships of life on board a filthy prison ship in Havana harbor.[19]

For six months he suffered conditions more barbaric and inhumane than he ever imagined possible. In the stifling hold he watched thirty-one of his ninety-two shipmates perish. Not once did he fill his lungs with a breath of fresh air or see the sun. He had no fresh water to wash his clothes, and only two watery bowls of slop with stale bread to sus-

T W O

A
Matter of
Money

Midshipman Porter received orders to report to Capt. Alexander C. Wadsworth on the frigate USS *Constellation*, the flagship of Commodore James Biddle's Mediterranean Squadron, but Biddle and Wadsworth, both distinguished officers, had served on the board that had suspended his father from active service. Now at age sixteen, two years older than any other midshipman, Porter speculated on what miseries he might suffer serving under two of his father's enemies.

Grandfather Anderson sensed David's antipathy toward his father's so-called enemies and escorted him to Washington. He introduced him to the new secretary of the navy, John Branch, who bore no resemblance to Southard, the mean-spirited executive who had court-martialed his father. They visited Commodore Daniel Tod Patterson, his father's successor on the Board of Navy Commissioners, and David spent a pleasant evening relating his experiences in the Mexican navy, but he could not take his eyes off the Patterson's youngest daughter, George Ann. After four days of social indoctrination, Anderson considered his grandson's hostile attitude adequately modified, drove him to *Constellation*, and bid him farewell.[1]

tain him through each day of incarceration. When starving men began to rob the weak of their food, David Dixon joined a self-appointed group who maintained order.[20]

When the general finally negotiated his son's release, he sent the fifteen-year-old boy home through New Orleans. On his trip up the Mississippi, Vicksburg card sharks stripped him of his stage fare home. Thirty-five years later, when Porter returned to bombard the Mississippi town with 13-inch mortar shells, he would remember the gamblers who pilfered his small treasure and hope they were still there.

He eventually reached Pittsburgh and, with help from an old gentlemen, secured enough money to ride atop a stage to Chester. At Green Bank his mother greeted him with sad news. Thomas had died of yellow fever, and Meridian Hill had been auctioned for a third of its value to cover the family's debts. But his father would not come home. The Mexican government owed him thousands of dollars he would never collect. The elder Porter was a stubborn man, and he could not leave behind his last hope of financial salvation.[21]

Retired congressman William Anderson listened to the boy's account of the fight with *Lealtad* and knew his grandson belonged in the U.S. Navy. Anderson's warrant to the Navy Department resulted in a deadlocked debate between the commodore's friends and foes. Pres. Andrew Jackson, an admirer of the elder Porter, ended the debate and signed the warrant himself, and on February 2, 1829, David Dixon received his appointment as midshipman. He had already seen more action at sea than most of the lieutenants who would supervise his naval education. This portended problems for the ambitious young veteran, and David Dixon, who was rapidly growing into his father's shoes, had already begun to manifest some of the Porter characteristics that made great warriors—but horrible politicians.

Wadsworth, perhaps the strictest disciplinarian in the navy of 1829, noticed that Porter quickly established himself as the leader of the midshipmen. He also observed that since Porter joined the crew, his midshipmen had become an unruly lot of pranksters. Satiric sketches of the frigate's officers mysteriously appeared on the bulkheads in the midshipmen's mess. Occasionally a poem, written in Byronic style, poked fun at the lieutenants educating the boys. Porter's peers loved him, but Lt. Hiram Paulding, the frequent brunt of David's pranks, confined him to quarters during a three-day stay at Malta. Instead of letting the matter drop, Porter continued the pranks, and Paulding cited him for insubordination. Wadsworth entered a permanent black mark on Porter's record, and when David Dixon's warrant came up for annual renewal the captain refused to sign it.

Shocked by the rejection, Porter knew his naval career would end if Wadsworth did not sign the warrant. His father was home at the time and told his son to appeal to Biddle, but he warned that a commodore seldom overrules the decision of his captain. Contrary to the lad's opinion, Biddle bore no grudge against the elder Porter but rather admired him. He convinced Wadsworth to sign the warrant, not because Porter deserved it but because he was the son of a distinguished navy hero. The elder Porter advised his son to be grateful and take his career more seriously—he might not be so lucky the next time.

David Dixon returned to the Mediterranean and served on *Constellation* for another year. He became a model student and earned the respect of the same lieutenants he had harassed. When the frigate returned to New York in December 1831, Porter's transformation so impressed Biddle that in his report to the Navy Department he wrote, "Midshipman Porter will become an officer worthy of the name he bears."[2]

David found his father at home and, through the efforts of Pres. Andrew Jackson, reconciled with the government. Jackson so admired the old sailor that he created the post of chargé d'affaires at Constantinople. Before leaving for Turkey, Porter convinced his son that cruises were fine but, if a young man wanted to succeed in the navy, he must study mathematics, a course not taught to midshipmen. The eighteen-year-old budding officer, now a wiry, dark-haired man, five feet, six inches tall and charged with energy, obtained a leave of absence and enrolled at Chester Academy.[3]

Porter learned that Patterson had been given command of the Mediterranean Squadron, and he recalled the pleasant evening spent at the commodore's home. He also remembered George Ann, the Pattersons' attractive young daughter. On April 30 he wrote Secretary of the Navy Levi Woodbury requesting duty on the frigate *United States,* Patterson's flagship. Woodbury was not accustomed to accepting requests from midshipmen, but the Porter name carried influence in the Jackson administration and he approved the request.

When David Dixon reached the Brooklyn Navy Yard, he learned that Georgy would be coming on board. Ignoring a scourge of cholera infesting Manhattan, he rode into the city and spent most of his accumulated wages on a new uniform and a year's supply of bear grease to make his hair shine. His new blue coat with its gold-laced collar, his tight-fitting buff trousers, and his shiny boots made him the nattiest-looking midshipman on the commodore's flagship.

Carefully storing his new clothes, he watched for the arrival of the Pattersons. Because he could not keep a constant vigil, he bribed a friend to watch at the gangway. When the long-awaited moment came, he dressed in his new clothes and smeared his hair with grease. By then the crew knew Porter's intentions, and as the boatswain piped the Pattersons aboard they all watched with amusement as David Dixon drew his new dress sword, saluted smartly, and stood rigidly at attention. As Georgy came on board, she flushed with pleasure.[4]

Unlike his cruise under Wadsworth, Porter's tour on *United States* remained one of the most pleasant experiences of his life. The commodore ran a tight ship, but the food was splendid and the morale high. Unlike *Constellation,* Porter found himself surrounded by officers who admired his father, but instead of strutting about like some young peacock, he made every effort to uphold his father's high standards of propriety. On occasion he failed. The presence of Georgy turned his head, and he found every excuse to be with her. The commodore encouraged the relationship as long as Porter broke no rules. When in port or touring ashore, the Patterson girls always had escorts, but Georgy had only one, and when the flagship stopped at Constantinople to visit the elder Porter, both parents admitted to a match brewing.[5]

Midshipmen, however, could not afford marriage. Nobody understood that better than Georgy's father, who had spent his life in the navy. During the cruise, the commodore's motives for writing two letters of commendation to the Navy Department in praise of Porter's performance may have been driven not only by the young man's superior skills but also by the incentive to raise his grade and compensation.

During the summer of 1833, social events on board *United States* flowed with a romantic profusion of balls, dinners, and starlit nights, and when Midshipman George M. Bache announced his engagement to Elizabeth Patterson the crew expected David and Georgy's to be announced next. But on Porter's pay of $33.33 a month there could be no wedding. The commodore attempted to cool down the romance by creating new duties for his midshipmen and ordered the chaplain to establish a school to teach them mathematics, navigation, and foreign languages.

Two people in love, however, could not be separated for long on a vessel the size of a frigate, especially when they both conspired to meet where the commodore least expected to find them—right in his afterlounge. Patterson enjoyed the habit of snoozing after his evening meal and retired to his quarters to do so. Porter timed the daily nap, climbed over the vessel's side, and entered the afterlounge through the port gallery window. The nightly rendezvous continued unabated until one evening when the commodore rose prematurely from his slumber and caught the pair behind one of the stern ports.

"Young man," he growled, "how did you enter this cabin contrary to my orders, sir, to the sentry?"

"The orderly is not to blame, sir," Porter admitted. "I came over the mizzen chains and through the gallery window."

"Mr. Porter, when you again visit my family you must come in by the cabin door like a gentleman."[6]

The commodore submitted to the inevitable when the pair confessed they had become engaged. Marriage, however, had to wait until the eager suitor could afford it, and when the commodore shifted his flag to the ship-of-the-line *Delaware* in February 1834, Midshipman Porter came with him.

In October, David Dixon traveled to Baltimore to take his examinations for passed midshipman. Patterson assured the Navy Department that Porter would pass his tests with ease. The examination lasted three days, but David Dixon did not distinguish himself, ranking tenth in a class of twenty.[7]

In 1835, a passed midshipman faced the most difficult of all obstacles—promotion during a period of peace. What Porter needed was a war, and at the age of twenty-two his prospects looked grim. He toiled for six months at the Philadelphia Navy Yard, performing clerical duties on the old familiar steam galiot *Sea Gull,* her engines now rusted and her hull rotting. He watched officers of all ranks resign from the navy to seek civilian occupations, but despite the gloomy prospects he could not think of leaving the service.

Weakened from long hours on *Sea Gull's* cramped and dimly lit quarters, malaria infested his body, and when he went home to recover he found Green Bank in disrepair. With the commodore gone, his mother had not kept up the property, and the cost of hired help had grown beyond her means. When he recovered, the Navy Department could find no work for him at the Brooklyn Navy Yard and placed him on the waiting list. Then in March 1836, Commodore Patterson returned from the Mediterranean to take command of the Washington Navy Yard. Deeply distressed, David Dixon went to see Georgy.[8]

After the long separation, the couple wanted to marry at once, but the Pattersons objected. Their daughter had always lived in comfort, and with Porter's base pay of fifty dollars a month she would be reduced to poverty. With an assignment at sea, his pay would increase by twelve dollars—still not enough to provide for a wife. Porter offered to release her from their engagement, but Georgy hotly refused and said she would wait for as long as it took.[9]

With new hope, Porter sought work in a naval occupation and spent his days in Washington pulling strings. Now twenty-three, he made an imposing appearance. He stood erect, giving his tightly knit frame the impression of inner and outer strength. Beneath his mat of slick black hair was a darkly handsome face covered by a well-groomed beard. His dark brown eyes flashed when he spoke or twinkled when he told one of his many droll stories ridiculing some pompous officer. He was careful around Georgy, however, to not say anything she might repeat to her father.

In Washington Porter had a chance meeting with Benjamin F. Sands, a former classmate, who urged him to go to the Navy Department and ask for a berth with the Coast Survey. Porter knew nothing about the work but learned there were vacancies for twenty passed midshipmen. The main attraction was not the work but the compensation—regular pay at $50.00 a month, sea pay at $12.50, and survey pay of $30.00 a month—almost double what he currently earned.

The Coast Survey fell under the purview of the Treasury Department but used naval officers for the work. Too many vessels had been damaged as they entered the harbors of Boston and New York, and European shippers had avoided the American trade. Porter applied to Prof. Ferdinand R. Hassler, an eccentric and tyrannical Swiss scientist who convinced the Treasury Department to name him superintendent. Porter's expertise in mathematics impressed Hassler, and one month after Georgy promised to wait "for as long as it took," David Dixon began his new assignment on the survey schooner *Jersey*. He would be gone six to nine months a year and knew the routine would become tedious, painstaking, and hazardous, demanding endless hours of work taking soundings off mosquito-infested swamps along the New Jersey coast. Commodore Patterson, however, assured Porter that if he saved his money for three years, he could marry Georgy.[10]

By adjusting to Hassler's idiosyncrasies and autocratic supervision, Porter obtained an important education. Hassler amused Porter, and the two men got along well. The professor had been ejected from several European countries because he publicly scorned monarchies. After he came to America, he annoyed innkeepers by bringing his own imported wines and cheeses into their dining areas. He needed spectacles but loathed them, and discovered that a jolt of snuff stimulated his vision. When he examined sketches prepared by his staff, they often came back smudged with tobacco. Porter praised Hassler's scrupulous regard for accuracy. He discovered the importance of precise planning, benefiting from this experience throughout his career by developing an ability to make complex calculations quickly in his head. He also became an expert at charting channels and moving heavy vessels through seemingly impassable shoals.[11]

In winter the surveyors worked in two houses leased by the professor, and they all lived at the Washington Navy Yard, a two-minute walk from the Patterson home. Porter spent his evenings with Georgy and saved two thousand dollars. Three years elapsed, and the commodore gave up his daughter.

On March 10, 1839, David Dixon Porter married George Ann Patterson. Commodore Porter, now minister to Turkey, attended the wedding with his wife and younger children—all but Theodoric, who was a third lieutenant in the army and smitten with malaria at Baton Rouge, Louisiana. Two lines of naval officers crossed swords over the aisle to the altar, and at three o'clock the rector of St. John's Episcopal Church pronounced David Dixon and George Ann man and wife. Washington newspapers gave the wedding a big spread, making it the social event of the month, but for the newlyweds a series of misfortunes lay but months away.

Porter returned to the Coast Survey and, while working off Long Island, learned from Georgy of the death of her father. Forced to move from the navy yard, she and her mother rented a small home in Washington. Then news came from David's mother—the commodore had departed for Turkey with his finances in disorder. She had been forced to borrow five hundred dollars from an aged uncle against her silver plate, and Porter felt obligated to rescue her from financial embarrassment.

More problems followed. Midshipman Hambleton Porter died of yellow fever and was buried at sea. Henry Ogden Porter, a junior midshipman, developed a drinking problem and faced dismissal from the navy. William, Porter's older brother, brought scandal to the family by impregnating an immigrant servant girl. When word of the affair reached Constantinople, the commodore disinherited William and transferred the right of priority to David. William, rather than admit his mistake and appeal to his father for forgiveness, lashed out at David Dixon. The controversy flared into a hateful sibling rivalry that continued unabated for over a decade.[12]

In the winter of 1840 Georgy gave birth to a daughter, Georgianne, and the playful infant comforted the newlyweds. But four years of drawing maps under poor light had strained Porter's eyes, and four seasons in swamps had broken his health. His promotion to lieutenant was a year overdue. Constant headaches and regular bouts of fever made him irritable, and Porter developed a disaffection for the navy.

His distress surfaced one wintry day at the worktable when he picked a meaningless quarrel with Lt. Stephen C. Rowan, a colleague who had joined the navy the year David Dixon went to Mexico. Rowan, a high-spirited and redheaded Irishman, was Porter's age but stood many numbers above him on the navy roster. A scuffle ensued and friends broke it up, but Porter was in a foul mood and challenged

Rowan to a duel. Benjamin Sands carried the challenge to Rowan and discovered that the lieutenant had already appointed his second. The seconds, being good friends of both parties, dallied for two days exchanging delicately worded overtures of peace. No duel had been fought since James Barron killed Stephen Decatur in 1820, and although the navy's Code of Honor had not been repudiated, an officer participating in a duel was certain to be dismissed from the service. Saner minds prevailed and both parties exchanged veiled apologies. Because the affair was kept secret, Porter's lieutenancy arrived on March 6, 1841, and for a man who would eventually become an admiral, David Dixon owed Midshipman Sands a debt of gratitude.[13]

Bored by another year of toil with the Coast Survey, Porter applied for sea duty as a line officer, and in the spring of 1842 he finally received orders to report to the frigate *Congress* as second lieutenant and navigation officer. The transfer to the Mediterranean Squadron came at a propitious time. When *Congress* stopped at Constantinople, Porter saw his father for the last time. The commodore, weak from angina pectoris, lived long enough to invest his son with control of his affairs in America, including his claims against Mexico. Commodore Porter died a year later.[14]

David Dixon returned home to more family problems. His second daughter, Nina, had been born, and Georgy was bedridden with an unknown malady. His brother William was again in trouble—this time with the navy. He had invented a novel but unpredictable explosive shell that killed several workers at the Washington Navy Yard, and in an effort to exonerate himself he used the newspapers to shift blame to his superiors. William's reaction resulted in a court-martial for insubordination. David Dixon expressed no sympathy for his brother when he wrote his distressed mother, "He must lie in the bed he has made for himself."[15]

Evalina Porter reached new depths of financial despair, and William, disregarding his father's wishes, persisted in trying to gain control of the estate. After the commodore's death, William used his middle name, David, in an attempt to intercept his father's mail. The post office could not distinguish one David from another and delivered half of William's mail to David Dixon, who wrote his mother, "Somehow his plans all come to our knowledge. It would astonish him to know how much of his correspondence I have on file."[16]

Despite his own financial problems, Porter obtained a three-months' leave to settle the commodore's estate. On behalf of his father's service in the War of 1812, he applied in his mother's name for a naval pension. The Navy Department declined, claiming the commodore's resignation and subsequent employment by the Mexican government disqualified him. Then, in sorting through a packet of the commodore's papers, he discovered an old note. During the period of his suspension, the elder Porter had borrowed several thousand dollars from Commodore John Downes to settle an account with the Navy Department. Evalina explained that the naval debt was no more than a technical claim, but in a fit of anger the commodore had foolishly borrowed money to pay it. Downes, a wealthy man, had never pressed for payment, and the commodore, who was then about to take command of the Mexican navy, expected to earn thousands of dollars in prize money. So David Dixon, twenty years later and with his own family seriously ill, wrote his mother on October 16, 1845, and assured her that he would shoulder the debt.[17]

For Porter, who was now thirty-two, life seemed to have taken a turn for the worse. He was a junior lieutenant with no assignment, a bedridden wife, two sick children, a mother in a crumbling mansion, a bereft mother-in-law, and thousands of dollars of debt. With no one to turn to for help, he felt as imprisoned by his father's debt as the boy who twenty years earlier had suffered months of misery on board a Spanish prison ship in Havana's harbor.

What Lieutenant Porter needed was a war.

THREE

Twenty Years of Indecision

For David Dixon Porter war came slowly, but in January 1846 Capt. Arthur A. Bowen unexpectedly invited him to the Navy Department and asked if he was satisfied with his present work. The question surprised him. Officers were seldom asked their opinions of their assignments. Bowen explained that high-ranking officers had recommended Porter for a secret mission of great importance, but he then apologized for being unable to discuss the details. Porter agreed to accept the assignment, whatever it was, but if war came with Mexico, he asked to participate in it.[1]

On March 8, 1846, he was summoned to the office of Secretary of State James Buchanan, who needed to send an emissary to the Republic of Santo Domingo, which had broken away from Haiti and established a separate government on the eastern half of the island of Hispaniola. Santo Domingo had asked for recognition and applied for American loans, but President James K. Polk remained skeptical. Buchanan informed Porter that the mission involved a voyage to the new republic to assess its political and social stability, its economy, and the suitability of the Bay of Samana as a future naval base.[2]

Knowing that Commodore David Conner's Home Squadron stood off Veracruz, and that Commodore John D. Sloat's Pacific Squadron had been given orders to take San Francisco if war with Mexico commenced, Porter hoped to complete the Santo Domingo mission and get back to Washington before the fighting started. On March 15, 1846, he packed his bags, kissed the family good-bye, and departed for Pensacola.[3]

For Lieutenant Porter, nothing ever happened the way he planned it. When he reached Pensacola, the vessel assigned to him had been sent on other duty. Twenty days later he climbed aboard the brig *Porpoise* and sailed slowly to the old city of Santo Domingo, on the south side of the island. Porter went ashore to speak with President Santana, who was ill, and wasted twelve days entertaining local officials while waiting for an audience. Santana finally granted permission for the survey to be conducted, and Porter spent the next two weeks cruising the coast, taking soundings, and sketching a map of the harbor.

On May 19 he started on the last leg of his inspection—a lengthy journey through the tropical interior to the port town of Puerto Plata, on the north side of the island. His task was to assess the country's economy, and he took nothing with him but a change of clothes, a guide, a hammock, and a string of horses. Unacclimated to the sweltering heat of the interior, Porter sweated over rugged mountain trails and through rain forests lush with giant mahoganies and thick with snakes, scorpions, and stinging insects. Daily downpours flooded valleys, turning uncharted streams into impassable rapids. He lost count of the number of times he forded the same river, and in swimming the horses he ruined his watch, damaged his paper money, and lost his food. Breadfruit and bananas grew everywhere, but meat was almost nonexistent.

In the valleys vegetation clogged narrow pathways, and Porter cut through it with a machete. Twelve to fourteen hours each day, he and his guide plodded through uninhabited jungles, arriving on occasion at some uncharted village to sleep and wait for dawn. The natives spoke Spanish, and Porter found he could communicate without difficulty. He lost three horses, one being pushed over a waterfall by the guide, so he beat the guide and discharged him. Natives led Porter from village to village until he reached the heights above Puerto Plata and began his descent. When he rode into the town on June 19 he was unrecognizable. Insect bites covered his body, his legs had swollen to twice their normal size, and he was so badly bruised that he could scarcely walk—but he carried the information the State Department wanted.

At Puerto Plata he rejoined *Porpoise* and found the crew in a state of excitement. The United States had gone to war with Mexico, and General Taylor's army was engaged in a battle with a large Mexican force under Santa Anna. Porter forgot his discomforts and hurried home, anticipating active duty. The Home Squadron would be bearing the brunt of the war in the Gulf of Mexico, and he wanted to be there.[4]

He reached Washington in July and submitted his report to Buchanan, but joy and grief greeted his homecoming. Georgy presented him with a son, David Essex Porter, but the War Department delivered the remains of Lt. Theodoric Porter, killed in action at Matamoros, Mexico. The loss of Theodoric staggered him, and he wanted to get into the fight. Forced to take a brief leave, he conveyed the body to his mother's home at Chester. Evalina, hardened to tragedy, displayed little emotion, so Porter hurried back to Washington and argued that his past service with the Mexican navy qualified him for duty in the Gulf. Secretary of the Navy John Young Mason told him that the Home Squadron had more officers than it needed and sent him to the Naval Observatory in Washington, D.C., another scientific post, to study stars and apply the research to improve navigation.[5]

Determined to get into the action, Porter spent his idle hours contriving schemes to destroy Mexico's land-based naval defenses. He remembered the ancient fortress at San Juan de Ulúa and wrote Mason that it could be blown up by imbedding hundred-pound kegs of powder in the soft coral foundation and exploding them from a distance by using galvanic batteries connected to the powder by wires. Mason filed the proposal, and Porter, who volunteered to participate in the venture, returned to his confinement at the observatory.[6]

Hampered by recurring headaches and discouraged by the navy's disinterest in his proposals, Porter considered resigning, but his debt to Downes and the need to provide for his family prevented it. With three children and a wife accustomed to living comfortably, he was dependent solely on the navy for income.

By November 1846 disease had decimated the blockading force off the hot, virulent coast of Mexico, and the navy ran short of men.

Hoping sailors from the South would tolerate the Gulf climate better, the navy decided to recruit in New Orleans and sent Porter to open an office. Since New Orleans brought him closer to the action, he kissed the family good-bye and hurried south. Setting up shop near the levee, he advertised for seamen, but the response was anemic. War had brought prosperity to the town. Shippers competed for manpower and paid higher wages than the navy. Applicants bargained for enlistment bonuses, but all Porter could offer was the speculative prospect of prize money. Most men turned away. Two months passed before he received orders from Conner to close the office at New Orleans and bring his recruits to Veracruz. Porter chartered a steamer, embarked three hundred volunteers, and joined the Home Squadron off Veracruz.[7]

Conner assimilated Porter into his command and assigned him as first lieutenant on the side-wheeler *Spitfire,* a small gunboat under Comdr. Josiah Tattnall, a tough-minded fighter tired of inaction. Conner, although a first-rate sailor, had nothing to show for nine months of cruising off Mexico's coast. In the meantime, Taylor's army defeated Santa Anna at Palo Alto and Resaca de la Palma, and Commodore Robert F. Stockton captured California and claimed the territory for the United States. Tattnall, who found Porter to be a smart, imaginative officer, celebrated when Matthew C. Perry arrived and relieved Conner. With Perry came a flotilla carrying ten thousand soldiers under the command of Maj. Gen. Winfield Scott. Now, Tattnall declared, there would be action.[8]

Veracruz lay in a harbor surrounded by high walls and battlements built on the same soft coral as the fortress of San Juan. Two small works guarded the half-mile-wide entrance to the harbor—Fort Concepción on the north sea face, Fort Santiago on the south—making the city inaccessible to enemy vessels. Scott wanted to occupy the town and use it as a supply center, but he thought wooden-hulled vessels would be hammered to pieces if they came within range of San Juan. Moreover, coral reefs cluttered the narrow entrance to the harbor, and any vessel going aground would be destroyed.

Scott decided to land his force south of the city and approach it from the flank. On March 10, 1847, *Spitfire, Vixen,* and five small schooners stood into the beach, anchored in line, and covered Scott's landing. An unseasonably strong norther forced the fleet to sea, and for three days

The fortresses of Veracruz, Mexico, 1846 REPRINTED FROM JAMES R. SOLEY, *ADMIRAL PORTER*

Scott's army subsisted off what they carried on their backs. When the seas calmed, artillery went ashore, followed by mortars and six heavy naval guns. Hundreds of sailors came off the ships to help lug the guns over dunes and into position. Resistance stiffened, forcing Scott to lay siege to the town.

On March 22 Perry sent Tattnall's squadron to engage the batteries at Fort Santiago. *Spitfire* anchored in line about a mile below the city but beyond range of San Juan. Porter took command of the bow gun and poured in a steady, well-directed fire. The thundering of guns, the clouds of smoke, and the crash of shells exhilarated him. After seventeen years in the navy, he was finally in combat.[9]

The day's fighting only made him want more. With eight oarsmen and the ship's gig, he sounded the south channel. At nightfall, unnoticed by sentinels, he worked up the harbor, passing within a few yards of the batteries. At 2:00 A.M. he returned to *Spitfire* and worked all night charting the channel. While Porter labored, Tattnall held a council of war with his squadron to resume the engagement at dawn. Stripped for action and loaded with fresh ammunition, *Spitfire* and *Vixen* attached hawsers to the armed schooners and steered for the harbor.

Instead of anchoring in the spot prescribed by Perry, Tattnall lobbed shells into Fort Santiago and continued up the harbor, routing Mexican batteries along the sea face. As the squadron nosed into the channel leading to Veracruz, the guns of San Juan de Ulúa opened. Shots splashed nearby, wetting the decks of *Spitfire.* Porter assured Tattnall that Mexican gunnery was notoriously inaccurate, and as they entered the harbor all six vessels opened on the giant fortress. Astonished by Tattnall's unauthorized attack, men of the Home Squadron lined the decks of their vessels to watch and cheer, and Mexican gunners, dumbfounded by the attack, deserted shore batteries and fled to Veracruz.

From a distance, Perry observed Tattnall going up the harbor. Smoke from a hundred guns filled the harbor, and Perry frantically signaled *Spitfire* to withdraw. Porter did not look at the flagship, and Tattnall, expecting a recall, ordered his officers not to look. The squadron held its position in the harbor and exchanged gunfire with San Juan until an officer sent by Perry arrived with orders for Tattnall to withdraw. As *Spitfire* came about, Scott's troops applauded the squadron, and when the vessels returned to the fleet, Perry accepted Tattnall's weak apology that he and his officers had been too busy to see the commodore's signal. Scott praised the attack and sent letters of congratulation to Tattnall and Porter. Perry later learned that Porter had taken *Spitfire's* gig into the harbor the previous night. He then realized the scheme had been premeditated and in defiance of his orders, but the act of courage infused the fleet with so much enthusiasm that Perry decided against disciplinary action. He took no more chances, however, and kept Tattnall and his squadron with the fleet.[10]

Porter would have grown restless had Veracruz not capitulated six days later. Perry was not surprised when Scott invited Tattnall and Porter to attend the surrender ceremonies. The pair had won a little praise for the otherwise undistinguished Home Squadron.[11]

A few days later Perry came on board *Spitfire* to lead a flotilla of barges carrying a force of marines up the Tuxpan River. Five batteries of Mexican artillery lined the cliffs above the town of Tuxpan, and when they opened on the barges Porter manned the pivot gun and drove them away. Perry landed the marines, took the town, and praised Porter's gunnery.[12]

Six weeks passed before Porter had an opportunity to participate in another campaign. With General Scott advancing on Mexico City, Perry led a flotilla south to the mouth of the Tabasco River, bringing with him three brigs, four steamers, and 1,050 marines. With Tattnall detached, Perry gave Porter temporary command of *Spitfire,* and on June 14 the flotilla started its ascent, towing the brigs and the transports. They ran through an ambush, entered Devil's Bend, and came under fire from artillery. Perry pressed forward until he reached obstructions ten miles below Tabasco and called a halt.

At daybreak on July 16, Perry sent a detail upriver to study the obstructions, but the effort abruptly ended when guerrillas opened fire and wounded an officer. Leaving his vessels below the obstructions, Perry ordered the shore shelled to clear out snipers. He then disembarked and, with ten fieldpieces, prepared to attack Tabasco by land. As the marines began cutting their way through dense chaparral, Porter took *Spitfire* upriver for a look at the obstructions.

Here was an opportunity to test his theory on using submerged explosives triggered by galvanic batteries. With Capt. George W. Taylor, a submarine expert, Porter set drums of powder under the obstructions, stood off, and activated the spark. In a thunderous roar, tons of water, mud, and debris flew into the air. Porter eased upriver to assess the damage, found the logs loosened, and cleared a passage the width of his vessel. All four steamers beat through the opening and, with Porter in the lead, raced upriver.

Much to the surprise of the enemy, who had discovered Perry's advance, four steamers ran by their fort and began shelling it from the rear. Porter collected eighty-six volunteers—seamen, engineers, and coal passers—and attacked with small arms. Scaling the walls of the earthwork, they drove half the defenders out of the garrison and captured the others. The attack occurred so unexpectedly that not a blue jacket was killed or wounded. Porter returned to *Spitfire,* steamed up to Tabasco, and forced the town's surrender. Two hours later Perry's detachment stumbled into town exhausted, but the commodore appreciated a nice piece of work when he saw it and rewarded Porter with a fine commendation and permanent command of *Spitfire.*[13]

For the first time in his thirty-four years, Porter commanded a warship of the U.S. Navy, but it would not last. General Scott captured Mexico City, and Porter returned to Washington. A letter he had written to Georgy before leaving the Gulf of Mexico arrived a few days later. "Had I been stationed elsewhere," he stated glumly, "I would have fared better. It is true that I won a small measure of attention, but my achievements contributed little to the winning of the war, and soon will be forgotten, I fear."[14]

Porter wanted duty afloat and command of a steamer, but the navy began selling its vessels to commercial shippers and reverting back to sailing ships, which were less costly to operate. Reassigned to the Coast Survey on January 10, 1848, Porter penned his resignation. After learning he would have command of the schooner *Petrel,* he changed his mind and spent the next few months sailing around New York Harbor to prepare for a summer survey of Hell Gate and Buttermilk Channel.

Shippers on the northeastern seaboard recognized the importance of Porter's survey and followed his progress with interest. The shortest route for carriers coming to New York was through Hell Gate. Hundreds of vessels made the passage each week, and dozens of them ran upon shoals. Hell Gate, the graveyard of international shipping, threatened to stifle the growth of America's greatest city. Porter spent six weeks marking the channel and during that time counted fifty ships aground. Officials in the Treasury Department considered his work so important that they asked for daily reports, and New York's Chamber of Commerce published Porter's progress in the daily newspapers.

Buttermilk Channel, lying between Governors Island and Brooklyn, had not been used by deep-draft vessels because a safe route had never been found, but in ten days Porter located one. The discovery delighted the navy because the new channel gave warships access to commercial facilities at the Atlantic dock. What astonished Secretary of the Treasury R. J. Walker was Porter's statement that Buttermilk Channel could be used immediately, as it required no dredging or blasting.

New York shipping interests pronounced Porter a genius, but Walker was skeptical. He challenged Porter to a trial trip on a revenue cutter, and on September 22, accompanied by a delegation of shippers, members of the New York Chamber of Commerce, and dozens of doubtful harbor pilots, *Jefferson* steamed into Hell Gate for the test. Porter considered *Jefferson* a good choice because she was heavy, clumsy, and slow to respond to her helm. He turned his charts over to the cutter's captain and pilot and told them to follow the markings. The vessel steamed through Hell Gate and back without incident.

The captain then ran down East River to Buttermilk Channel. With the tide ebbing and a stiff northwesterly blowing, conditions were not ideal for a trial, and anchored in the middle of the channel was a lumber ship with planks protruding from both sides. Porter told the pilot to follow the markings and they would pass through. Leadsmen took soundings as the vessel steamed through the channel, and as they cleared into the river Secretary Walker extended his hand and complimented Porter warmly and, later, officially. New York newspapers did more and hailed him as a hero.[15]

John L. Aspinwall, of the banking firm of Howland and Aspinwall, acknowledged Porter's feat by offering him command of the U.S. mail steamship *Panama*. The discovery of gold in California had created a huge western market, and the fastest way to get there was by sea. Aspinwall wanted vessels in the Pacific to sail the short leg between San Francisco and the Isthmus of Panama, and because the navy had reverted to sailing ships, Porter sought experience on the fast steamers owned by private interests. But the offer presented a problem. He was still an officer in the navy, and Georgy had just given birth to Carlisle Patterson, their fourth child. Porter went to Washington to convince Secretary Mason that the navy would benefit from allowing him to command *Panama*. Mason liked the idea, as he had an appropriation before Congress for the construction of four steamers.[16]

On February 15, 1849, Porter put to sea, loaded stem to stern with passengers, mining implements, camping equipment, and merchandise. Four days out an engine failed, forcing him back to New York. Passengers grumbled, but Porter expedited the repairs and stocked up with parts. Soon off again, he overtook scores of windjammers during the nonstop voyage around stormy Cape Horn and up the Pacific to California. On June 4, 1849, he docked at the busy port of San Francisco and turned *Panama* over to the Pacific Mail Steamship Company. The agents were delighted to get the vessel so quickly and conveyed Porter to the Chagres River. In the heat of summer he hiked across the Isthmus, and when he reached New York an agent from the shipping firm of Law and Roberts greeted him at the dock and offered him command of *Georgia*, a powerful mail steamer not yet commissioned.[17]

Eager to accept, Porter hurried to Washington to obtain approval from William B. Preston, the new naval secretary. Preston temporized on a technicality—naval officers could not be assigned to a vessel subsidized with public funds until government inspectors approved her. Porter argued that red tape should be set aside to enable him to supervise the installation of *Georgia's* double engines. Preston closed the discussion and told Porter to reapply after the inspection. Stomping home in a state of agitation, Porter collapsed. Disabled by malaria, he lay in bed for weeks and was still recovering on December 14, 1849, when his third son was born. He named the boy Theodoric, in memory of his brother.[18]

When Law and Roberts notified Porter of *Georgia's* acceptance by the government, Preston could no longer find reason to deny Porter's request. On January 26, 1850, temporary civilian David D. Porter stowed his baggage in the captain's cabin and took command of *Georgia.* His passengers and crew were about to receive a shock. Although he observed the amenities of a passenger ship, Porter manifested few similarities to the ordinary sailing master. The crew learned a lesson in naval discipline, and the passengers, through hell or high water, got from one place to another in record time.

If the Mexican War foreshadowed Porter's combativeness, his years with the mail service exposed other traits. His drive to excel could have caused trouble with his employers. Instead of sailing into port like most vessels, he arranged to have tenders meet him off the harbor to transfer mail and passengers. Complaints flowed into Law and Roberts, but Porter ignored them because he believed the greatest value of a steamship was its speed, and he set out to prove it. Wasting time in port did not fit his plans, and for a while his employers wondered whether Porter belonged in the mail service. One traveler complained that Porter "had a wicked way of dumping passengers and mails into fishing smacks . . . outside the bar, leaving them to make their way in as best they could," but others admitted that no steamship brought them to their destination faster than one commanded by Porter.[19]

During his tenure on *Georgia,* Porter kept the Navy Department informed of the ship's performance and of the laxity of civilian crews. After clapping an engineer in irons for not keeping a log, Porter asked that junior officers in the navy be transferred to *Georgia* for training. Preston sent him three midshipman: Robert W. Shufeldt and Francis A. Roe, who ten years later fought for the Union; and James D. Bulloch, who during the Civil War built three Confederate cruisers in England. Thereafter, *Georgia* achieved recognition as being the most efficient steamship in the mail service, if not the very best on the Atlantic coast.

Law and Roberts, who had prematurely regarded Porter as a martinet, discovered that *Georgia's* bills for fuel and repairs were the lowest in the fleet and her profits the highest in the industry. They imposed Porter's navy standards on all their skippers and soon had the most efficient steamships in the service. Law and Roberts became the benchmark in the mail service until other shippers discovered the reasons why. The American carrying trade, which had become lackadaisical, soon surpassed British competitors in performance and for ten years enjoyed a brisk business around the world. Much of the change can be credited to Porter, who spent most of his time on deck or in the engine room and little of it in his cabin.[20]

Porter, however, could not keep out of trouble and, like his father, provoked an incident with Spain. In the summer of 1852, while commanding the steamer *Crescent City,* he put into Havana on a routine run. Spanish officials came on board in search of Porter's purser, a man named Smith. They claimed that Smith had visited the island before and condemned the governor for jailing more than a thousand Cuban patriots. Smith denied the charges, and Porter relayed the information to the Spanish investigators.

When *Crescent City* returned in September, soldiers came aboard to conduct Smith, who was quite old, to the governor-general to deny the charges in person. Porter again spoke with the purser, who repeated he had done nothing wrong. Porter ordered the Spaniards off his ship and sent a letter to the governor suggesting he look for Smith elsewhere. Without waiting for a reply, he sailed for New York.

On October 3 *Crescent City* returned to Havana with Smith still on board, and this time Spanish officials were furious. When Porter would not give up Smith, they ordered the vessel out of the harbor and refused to accept her passengers or her mail. A Spanish gunboat came abeam to enforce the governor's decree. Porter left an account with the American consul, mounted cannon fore and aft, snubbed the gunboat, and sailed to New Orleans. When he docked at Canal Street, every newspaper in America contained a report of the incident in Havana. New Orleans hailed Porter as a hero, politicians stumped for war and annexation, and angry demonstrators staged torchlit parades. But Porter had his own plans, and after loading mail and passengers he steamed down the river to the Gulf.[21]

On October 14, an hour before dawn, Porter slipped by a Spanish man-of-war off Morro Castle and piloted *Crescent City* through Havana's treacherous channel. At sunrise the captain of the port experienced an unpleasant shock when he noticed the steamer moored at her usual berth. He came alongside and asked if Smith was still aboard, and Porter replied he was. Since *Crescent City* was already inside the harbor, the captain informed Porter his ship would not be molested but no passengers or mail could be landed. Porter, wishing to give the impression he was in no hurry to leave, set the crew to painting the ship's hull. The governor, intent on settling his differences with Smith, dispatched two gunboats with orders to detain *Crescent City* in the harbor.

Late in the day Porter met with the American consul and an agent for Law and Roberts. He gave them a sharply worded letter of protest for the governor, bid them good-bye, and hoisted anchor. Ignoring the two gunboats, he steamed out of the harbor, firing a salute to the American flag flying from the staff on the consulate lawn.

At New York, thousands turned out to greet him, but the State Department was bewildered by the incident and sent two warships to Havana to investigate. Ordered to Washington, Porter explained the situation. The State Department took the easy way out, one acceptable to Madrid, and induced Smith to write a denial of the charges against him.

Porter resumed command of *Crescent City* but for the next seven months fought recurrent bouts of malaria. Forced to take a year's leave of absence, he considered returning to active duty, but when Georgy gave birth to Elizabeth he could not support the family on lieutenant's pay.[22]

Unsure of his future, he was pleasantly surprised when in 1854 the Australian Steamship Company offered him command of *Golden Age,* a new steamer that looked more like a riverboat than an ocean vessel. He went to the New York yard where she was being built and listened to skeptics scoff at her blunt prow, towering cabins, and huge paddles. He ignored how she looked topside, went to the engine room, and studied her massive machinery. Confident of her power, he obtained leave from the navy and on *Golden Age*'s maiden voyage set a new record for crossing the Atlantic. Loading at Liverpool, Porter rounded the Cape of Good Hope, sped across the Indian Ocean, and arrived at Melbourne in an astonishing fifty-six days, beating the old record by thirty. An instant celebrity, he drew crowds wherever he went, and newspapers around the world hailed his achievement. Folks in Melbourne and Sydney called him Yankee Doodle and placed bets on how much time he would shave on his next run. In one trip he carried twelve hundred passengers. For the first time in his life, forty-one-year-old David Dixon Porter tasted with gratification what he had sought since his youth— fame and recognition.[23]

The owners of *Golden Age* paid him handsome bonuses and begged him to accept permanent employment, but his eldest daughter, Georgianne, was desperately ill, so he hurried home. To get away from the foul summer weather of Washington, he moved the family to East 33rd Street in New York City, but it was too late to save his daughter. Grief still hung heavy on the family when Georgy gave birth to her seventh child, a fourth son, Richard Bache.

With Lieutenant Porter back in the United States, the Navy Department belatedly recognized the value of the man and in the summer of 1854 placed him on active duty. Navy doctors took one look at him and ordered him to bed. Porter recovered slowly. In March 1855 he started pestering the department for an assignment. He had lost time in grade. Brother William had been elevated to commander, and David Dixon coveted promotion even more than the extra money it brought him.[24]

He seemed to attract assignments nobody else wanted. Secretary of War Jefferson Davis, intrigued by the use of camels in the arid regions of the world, thought the animals might prove useful for transporting supplies in Texas and New Mexico. With thirty thousand dollars to finance his experiment, Davis applied to the navy for assistance. The department gave Porter command of the storeship *Supply* and sent him to Tunis with Maj. Henry C. Wayne to buy and bring back a herd of camels.

Porter assembled all the information he could find on camels and designed a special stable for carrying them across the ocean. Neither the sultan of Constantinople nor the bey of Tunis was anxious to sell his animals, and Porter spent two years on the project. While Major Wayne negotiated with the sultan, Porter went to the Crimea and visited the massive fortress at Malakhov. He walked aboard a huge ironclad floating battery used by the French and was so impressed by its impregnability that he built one in miniature. The French and British had improved underwater explosives, and Porter copied them, tested them, and sent lengthy reports to the Navy Department. When he finally returned home in 1857 with his last load of camels, Davis was no longer secretary of war and incoming Pres. James Buchanan wanted nothing to do with the project. The camels were turned loose in Texas, and Porter's reports lay dormant until 1861.[25]

For the next three years he settled into a dreary life of sitting on court-martial hearings. Congress finally agreed to pay his mother a pension, and in 1857 the Navy Department assigned him to duty at the Portsmouth Navy Yard. He moved the family to a rented home and remained there for two years. New Hampshire's climate agreed with him, but Nina died, and Georgy, having lost two daughters, succumbed to bouts of melancholy. Porter considered life boring, his career stifled by the absence of promotion.

On April 14, 1858, the Pacific Mail Steamship Company approached him with an attractive offer. The owners planned to operate a huge steamer on the Pacific coast and asked Porter to command her. By naval standards, the pay was spectacular. The vessel had not been started, giving him eighteen months to accept or reject the offer. "I don't think it suits me sitting down so quietly here," he wrote brother-in-law Bache. "I suppose if I was to be appointed I should be cursed to death by every other fellow in the Navy (I should like that), and . . . by the time the ship was constructed I should be denounced everywhere as a damned villain."[26]

While waiting for the steamer to be launched, Porter joined a board of officers inspecting all the navy yards on the Atlantic seaboard. Inertia existed everywhere he went. None of the gunboats being built by the navy compared with the warships he had seen in the British and French fleets. Dry docks were in disrepair, and ships were being laid up because there was no money to repair them. The only facility capable of reconditioning steam engines was at Washington, and every class of vessel, from ship-of-the-line to dispatch sloop, lay rotting in the yards. Morale among officers and enlisted men had deteriorated, and civilian employees took no pride in their work. If Porter wondered beforehand why advancement came so slowly, or why assignments at sea were so few, he saw all the reasons firsthand. With the opportunity to join the Pacific Mail Steamship Company ripening in his pocket, Lieutenant Porter kept his options open.[27]

In 1860 he received command of the Coast Survey schooner *Active,* but he accepted it without enthusiasm. During his years in Portsmouth, nothing had changed in Washington. Senior naval officers still thought in terms of sail-driven vessels—not the modern fleet of steamers envisioned by Porter.

In late autumn, Porter began to prepare for his long trip to the West Coast. The national election came and went, and Abraham Lincoln won the hotly contested presidency. Southern senators like Jefferson Davis stepped up the debate in Congress, and Porter kept his ears open. Secession could mean war, and the postponement of *Active*'s survey delighted him. During the camel mission he had established a warm relationship with Davis, and they often talked about the building crisis. There was no question in Porter's mind—the South would fight to defend its separation from the Union. At a gathering at the senator's home on December 20, 1860, to celebrate the secession of South Carolina, Davis turned to Porter and with a twinkle in his eye offered him command of the Southern navy. "Thank you," Porter replied, "but I am going to the California goldmines, and when the South and the North have done quarreling, and all you seceders have come back and taken your seats in Congress, I will join the navy again."[28]

On the day South Carolina seceded, Porter leaned toward accepting the Pacific Mail Steamship Company's offer, but he made no decision. Over the next several weeks, with secession building across the South, he watched an outpouring of old friends like Josiah Tattnall resign their commissions and return to their Southern homes. At the Navy Department nobody knew who to trust, and with the whole country turned upside down, forty-seven-year-old David Dixon Porter shifted about Washington waiting for the explosion.

For twenty years he had been a lieutenant, but now was a time to be patient—and to watch.

FOUR

Intrigue at the White House

As the year 1861 broke damp and cold over the muddy streets of Washington, Isaac Toucey, the republic's twenty-third naval secretary, waited in his office for instructions from President Buchanan. Toucey, from Connecticut, and Buchanan, from Pennsylvania, shared the conviction that if South Carolina wished to secede, the federal government had no authority to stop it. Toucey supported most of Buchanan's opinions, and in cabinet meetings he usually sat quietly while the vacillating president thrashed through the opinions of other members. Such was the case in early January when Secretary of War Joseph Holt and Gen. Winfield Scott convinced the president to reinforce Maj. Robert Anderson at Fort Sumter in Charleston Harbor. At Buchanan's bidding, Toucey hired *Star of the West,* an unarmed merchant vessel, for the task. A few days later he detached USS *Brooklyn* and ordered her to support the operation. On January 9, 1861, South Carolinians fired on *Star of the West* as she entered Charleston Harbor. She backed off and, without unloading so much as a cracker, returned to New York. *Brooklyn* arrived off Charleston three days later and found *Star* gone. Southerners in Buchanan's cabinet promptly resigned, and Mississippi seceded from the Union. Using the intrusion as an excuse, Florida, Alabama, Georgia, Louisiana, and Texas followed.[1]

Actions as sophomoric as this dismayed Porter, and he questioned the future of the U.S. Navy. Although he had accepted the assignment with the Coast Survey, he still hesitated to leave Washington. It was commonly believed that Toucey sympathized with the South. During his final weeks in office the secretary issued no orders to put the navy in a state of readiness, and by blithely accepting the resignations of officers who wished to take their commissions south he drew sharp criticism and the censure of Congress.[2]

Porter watched the antics from his home in Georgetown, and by the time of Lincoln's inauguration on March 4, 1861, civil war seemed inevitable—at least from his perspective. The first weeks of the new administration resembled the last months of the old, and when Lincoln named fifty-eight-year-old Gideon Welles as naval secretary, Porter was unimpressed by the short-bodied, thin-legged man who seemed to quietly sit in the background, thoughtfully stroking his long, silver beard. In this, a time of crisis, Porter could not understand why Lincoln would appoint a small-town politician from Connecticut who for most of his life had been a Democrat.

Welles, however, was more than a small-town politician. His editorials in the *Hartford Evening Post* had swung voters to Lincoln, and when the president named him to the cabinet, few remembered that Welles had served as chief of the Bureau of Provisions and Clothing during the Mexican War, a post customarily held by a senior naval officer. Despite lobbying efforts by old salts to have him removed, Welles proved to be a man of good judgment who took calculated risks, cut red tape, and drove hard bargains with contractors. Although his appointment was resisted by Republican leaders in New England, Welles brought more experience to the office than any of his predecessors. Lincoln eventually discovered that "Grandfather Welles," as he comically called him, had an innate knack for evaluating key personnel. More importantly, Welles concentrated on his job and brought to the cabinet a balanced approach to the problems facing the nation—an attribute deficient in other cabinet members.[3]

While the Lincoln administration parleyed with emissaries from the South who asked for peaceful recognition but demanded Forts Sumter

President Abraham Lincoln COURTESY U.S. ARMY
MILITARY HISTORY INSTITUTE

and Pickens, Porter discussed the issue with his next-door neighbor, army Capt. Montgomery C. Meigs. They believed that if the government acted swiftly, Pickens could be occupied and the Pensacola Navy Yard recaptured. Meigs suggested a joint operation to General in Chief Scott, and on April 1, as Porter was enjoying his last meal with his family, Secretary of State William H. Seward, who at the time appeared to be running the government, sent a carriage to Porter's home with a summons to come to his office. "Leaving my dinner unfinished," Porter recalled, "I jumped into the carriage and drove at once to the Secretary's office."

On arriving, he was surprised to find the lean and lengthy secretary unceremoniously reclined on a sofa with his knees up and fingering through a document. Without changing his position so much as to shake Porter's hand, Seward asked if Fort Pickens could be saved. Porter replied that it could, and as he sketched out his plan Meigs entered the room and joined the conversation. Seward nodded approvingly and asked both men to accompany him to the White House to see the president.[4]

Lincoln's first four weeks in office had not gone well, and his hopes of placating the South through mildness only seemed to resonate a lack of resolve and encourage more threats and violence. With most Southern forts now in the possession of the secession states, Lincoln considered the situations at Pensacola and Charleston grave. Gustavus Vasa Fox—a former naval officer gifted with intelligence, and a personal friend of Porter's—had already proposed a mission to relieve Fort Sumter. Lincoln hesitated, fearing that another effort to reinforce Major Anderson would widen the breach and lead to war, and if he approved the expedition, sympathizers in the Navy Department would pass the news to friends in the South. Seward, however, considered Fort Pickens more important than Sumter, and since an expedition to Florida had not been discussed in the Navy Department, he believed it could be conducted secretly. Knowing of Lincoln's interest in the scheme, Seward decided the time had come to discuss Fort Pickens.[5]

Porter recalled that "Lincoln . . . seemed to be aware of our errand [and] opened the conversation." The president listened intently as Porter and Meigs explained how, with one large steamer and six companies of soldiers with artillery, they could make Fort Pickens impregnable. Since the fort commanded the inlet to Pensacola Bay, Porter believed the navy yard, now occupied by Floridians and located across the channel, would become useless to the Confederacy. He suggested using USS *Powhatan* for the mission, as she had been recently decommissioned. Lincoln thumbed through a stack of papers listing the vessels designated for the Sumter expedition but found no mention of *Powhatan.* Seward urged that Porter be given command of the warship but urged that the mission be kept secret.

"But what," Lincoln inquired, "will Uncle Gideon say?"

"I will make it all right with Mr. Welles," Seward replied, cautioning against leaks in the Navy Department. "This is the only way, sir, the thing can be done."[6]

Before the meeting ended, Porter retired to a separate room and penned four orders for Lincoln to sign, placing himself in command of *Powhatan,* relieving her commander, Capt. Samuel Mercer, and ordering Commodore Samuel L. Breese at the Brooklyn Navy Yard to arm and provision the vessel for an undisclosed mission. In the letter to Breese, Porter added, "She is bound on secret service, and you will under no circumstances communicate to the Navy Department the fact that she is fitting out."[7]

Lincoln signed the letters, but he turned to Seward and said, "See that I don't burn my fingers."[8]

Breese had taken leave, and Capt. Andrew Hull Foote commanded in his place. Foote was amazed when he received Lincoln's orders, for in his other hand he held an urgent telegram from Welles that read, "The Department revokes its orders for the detachment of the officers of the *Powhatan.* . . . Hold her in readiness for sea service."[9]

Seward could have prevented the confusion had he "made it all right" with Uncle Gideon, but he enjoyed the self-appointed privilege of functioning as Lincoln's major-domo. He regarded Welles as a petty politician from Connecticut placed in a position far beyond his abilities. Seward especially enjoyed dabbling in the affairs of the army and navy. Unfortunately, his meddling in the Fort Pickens expedition eventually caused weeks of turmoil and almost ended Porter's naval career.

In some respects, Welles was remarkable for his insight into a person's character. He knew of Porter's relationship with Jefferson Davis and believed Porter would remain with the Coast Survey rather than enter a war to fight his friends, but he also knew Porter was ambitious, audacious, and adventuresome. Welles considered him careless in his statements and given to intrigues, which fit his surreptitious involvement in the Fort Pickens affair. "As a lieutenant," Welles declared, "he was entitled to no such command as the *Powhatan,* a fact of which Mr. Seward, who had little knowledge of details, was ignorant, but the trust flattered and gratified the ambition of Porter." But Welles, who always tried to salvage some good from a bad situation, philosophically admitted that by detaching *Powhatan* from the Sumter mission, Seward had extricated Porter from Southern influences "and committed him at once, and decisively, to the Union cause"—and Welles was right.[10]

Welles's suspicion of Porter's loyalty also emanated from the lieutenant's close association with Capt. Samuel Barron, a Virginian whose father had been a judge at the elder Porter's court-martial. Over the years, Porter and Barron became close friends. Lincoln accidently signed an order placing Barron in charge of the Bureau of Detail. The president learned of the "accident" when Welles protested, claiming Barron could not be trusted. Lincoln scanned the order bearing his signature and did not recognize it as being among a stack of letters Seward

Secretary of the Navy Gideon Welles NATIONAL ARCHIVES

had asked him to sign, but he admitted it must have been in the same pile. He examined the letter more closely and noticed it had been written by Porter, copied by Meigs, and included with those he signed later. He told Welles to consider it canceled, confessing he did not know Barron and would not have signed the order had he read it.

Lincoln then recalled that when Seward brought Porter to his office, each had spoken of Barron favorably. Two weeks later Barron resigned and went south. Welles, who believed the whole scheme had been hatched by Seward, enjoyed the satisfaction of reporting Barron's defection. The president, however, believed the attempt to thrust Barron upon the Navy Department was the fault of Porter, who he felt had flattered Seward, a vain man, into accepting the idea. Thereafter, Lincoln watched Porter more carefully, but he kept his reservations mainly to himself.[11]

In the first month of the Lincoln administration, Porter had already become conspicuous. Welles questioned his loyalty, and the president suspected him of sneaking letters for signature into his official correspondence. Lincoln, however, was no slouch when it came to intrigues. He had ample opportunity to inform Welles of Porter's secret mission but said nothing. Had he done so, Welles would have convinced Lincoln to recall Porter on the premise that the lieutenant had cleverly plotted to steal a warship for his friends in the South. But that did not happen, and Porter, as directed by the president, took command of *Powhatan* and left Welles bewildered as to why one of his lieutenants had run off with the only warship available to relieve Fort Sumter.

Before Porter and Meigs departed on their secret mission, Seward gave them a draft for twenty thousand dollars to cover expenses. He also dispatched a message to Welles asking that Gwynn Harris Heap be detached from his clerical duties at the Navy Department for a State Department mission. Welles complied, never suspecting that Porter was behind the request and wanted the company of his brother-in-law as *Powhatan*'s paymaster.[12]

Urging Georgy to tell their friends he had left for the Coast Survey, Porter started for New York on the night of April 1. He brought with him his seventeen-year-old son, Essex, whom he had planned to take to California. Acquaintances he met on the train thought he was on the way to the West Coast, and Porter said nothing to change their minds.

In the meantime, Lincoln wondered whether he erred by not discussing the Pickens mission with Welles, but he still said nothing to the naval secretary. Instead, he confided the scheme to Scott, who assigned command of the mission to sixty-five-year-old Col. Harvey Brown, whose fighting instincts had drastically declined since the Mexican War. Porter never considered his role altered, however, because Lincoln's carefully crafted letter elevating Brown looked innocuously official, and the distribution was such that Porter may never have seen it.[13]

On the morning of April 2 Porter arrived at the Brooklyn Navy Yard and found Foote rather than Breese in charge. He spent three hours convincing Foote that he was not a rebel in disguise plotting with *Powhatan*'s officers to run off with the ship. Because of recent trouble, Foote had reason to suspect a plot afloat.

On March 28, when Welles ordered *Powhatan* to the Brooklyn Navy Yard for decommissioning, Mercer had deposited the vessel and granted shore leave for the crew. When Fox discovered *Powhatan* there, he persuaded Welles to reactivate her for the Sumter mission. Welles wired Breese, who was not there, orders to recall *Powhatan*'s crew. Foote received both the telegram and Porter within the same time frame. He thought it was strange that Welles made no mention of Porter. He read and reread Porter's orders from the president, suspiciously examining the Executive Mansion stamp.[14]

"I must telegraph to Mr. Welles before I do anything," Foote said, reaching for a blank.

"If you must telegraph," Porter cautioned, "send a message to the President or Mr. Seward." He reminded Foote that Lincoln's order specifically excluded the Navy Department from being informed of *Powhatan*'s mission.[15]

Meigs arrived and confirmed Porter's orders, and Captain Mercer, whom Foote had recalled from leave, joined the discussion and happily relinquished his command to Porter, warning him that the vessel was not fit for sea.

Foote mentioned nothing to Porter about the Navy Department wanting *Powhatan* for Fox's expedition, but he now realized the vessel was going somewhere and doubled her work crews. He distrusted Porter and, to keep an eye on him, invited the lieutenant to stay at his home. Porter liked the arrangement because he could watch Foote. By April 4 the pressure on Foote to confer with Welles drove him to stretch Lincoln's mandate for secrecy. He wired Welles a confusing message, hoping to prompt a clarifying response. "Captain Meigs has called on me with a letter, showing his authority from the Government to have certain preparations made and things placed on board vessels soon to go to sea, about which you are familiar; but as the orders do not come direct, I make this report; but as no time is to be lost, I am preparing what is called for and report my action."[16]

Welles read the telegram, assumed Foote was referring to the Sumter mission and that Meigs was part of it, and urged Foote to use haste in getting *Powhatan* to sea. Meanwhile, Foote learned of further correspondence from Welles ordering Mercer to use *Powhatan* in a four-ship expedition to Fort Sumter. Late on April 5, he made one last effort to provoke Welles's curiosity, this time sending two telegrams. The first read: "I am executing orders received from the Government through the Navy officer as well as the Army officer. Will write fully if possible today, certainly tomorrow. I hope the *Powhatan* will sail this evening." The other advised that *Powhatan* was ready for sea and would "drop down off the Battery at daylight to await your orders."[17]

Welles thought Foote's reference to "executing orders received from the Government" odd and wired back, "Delay the *Powhatan* for further instructions." Foote advised Porter, who replied, "I am with Captain Meigs and we are telegraphing Mr. Seward. Meigs thinks Mr. Welles' telegram is bogus. Would he . . . dare to countermand an order of the president? I will be at the yard at six o'clock in the morning."[18]

Late on April 5, Seward learned that Welles had issued separate instructions to Foote. Fearing the Fort Pickens plot would be delayed by conflicting orders, Seward stormed into Welles's rooms at Willard's Hotel at 11:00 P.M. and shook awake the drowsing secretary. Seward waved a telegram he had just received from Meigs, asked Welles why he was obstructing the expedition, and demanded a retraction. Seward's promise to the president to "make it all right with Mr. Welles" was about to be kept under less than harmonious conditions.

Welles wiped the sleep from his eyes and asked for an explanation. Seward said he "supposed it related to the *Powhatan* and Porter's command." Welles told Seward he was mistaken, that "Porter had no command, and . . . *Powhatan* was the flagship . . . of the Sumter expedition." A heated debate ensued, during which Welles got dressed and suggested they call on the president. On the way to the Executive Mansion, Welles knocked on the door of Capt. Silas H. Stringham's room, woke him up, and asked if he knew anything about *Powhatan* being diverted. Stringham said he did not, dressed, and joined the trio on their trek to the White House. The president had not retired but was astonished by the midnight visit. Thinking Seward had cleared the mission with Welles, Lincoln admitted *Powhatan* had been diverted, but only because the navy had decommissioned her. Welles went to his office and returned with a handful of dispatches showing his orders to Breese, Foote, and Mercer. Lincoln confessed the scheme and, turning to Welles, admitted that Fort Sumter was far more important than

Fort Pickens and directed Seward to "return the *Powhatan* to Mercer without delay." Welles suspected Porter of being the architect of the scheme and in the heat of the moment declared the lieutenant "absent without leave."

It was well past midnight before all retired to their rooms, but it was late morning before Seward deposited at the telegraph office the wire canceling Porter's mission. After a restless night's sleep, Welles blamed the muddle on Seward and hoped some good would come from it. Seward, not given to making apologies, admitted he had learned a lesson "from this affair, and . . . had better attend to his own business and confine his labors to his own Department." But the "affair" was alive and moving toward an unexpected conclusion—all because Seward wasted much of the day before wiring Porter new instructions.[19]

Early in the morning, Meigs departed with four companies of soldiers on the steamer *Atlantic* and waited for Porter off Staten Island. Mercer adhered to Welles's orders and took temporary command of *Powhatan*. At 2:30 she sailed with both Porter and Mercer on board, and by prior arrangement Mercer agreed to turn the vessel over to Porter "by order of the President" and disembark after exiting the channel.[20]

As *Powhatan* passed out of sight, Foote intercepted Seward's telegram: "Give the *Powhatan* up to Captain Mercer."

Foote, desperate to correct what he considered a gross error, sent Lt. Francis A. Roe to New York to hire a fast steamer, overhaul Porter, and bring back *Powhatan*. Roe acted quickly and reached Porter just before he entered the Narrows. Porter read the order and handed it back to Roe, grimly stating that it was too late to change his plans.[21]

When Roe overhauled *Powhatan*, Porter faced a difficult decision. If he turned about, he would desert Meigs, whose artillery was on *Powhatan*. Because of his connivance with Seward, Welles might be angry enough to dismiss him from the navy, so he disobeyed Seward's command on a technicality—he was acting on orders from Lincoln and not from Seward. So on April 6, Porter, in defiance of Seward's orders, and Mercer, in partial defiance of Welles's orders, committed *Powhatan* irretrievably to the Fort Pickens mission. Roe returned to Brooklyn with Porter's reply to Seward: "I received my orders from the President and shall proceed and execute them."[22]

Porter sent a letter of explanation to Foote, partly to apologize for implicating him in the scheme, but giving his reasons why he felt compelled to ignore Seward's order. "This is an unpleasant position to be in," Porter lamented, "but I will work out of it."[23]

Years later Porter admitted that after Roe departed, he gave orders for *Powhatan* to go ahead fast. "In an hour and a half," Porter recalled, "we were over the bar . . . steering south for an hour, and then due east, to throw any pursuers off my track (for I was determined to go to Fort Pickens)." Foote never forgot the episode and later reminded Porter, "You ought to have been tried and shot; no one but yourself would ever have been so impudent."[24]

The fault, however, lay not with Porter but with Lincoln and Seward. Both had much to learn about running government. Because of the president's connivance, Welles let the matter drop, but Porter had exposed himself and put his career in jeopardy. Now he must prove himself, but only Meigs knew that when Porter reached Fort Pickens he intended to bring on an engagement and recapture the navy yard. If the plan worked, there would be promotions in it for both of them.

Fort Pickens lay on the eastern entrance to Pensacola Bay and at the western tip of Santa Rosa Island, a slender spit of sand forty miles long running parallel to the mainland. Fort McRee, a small earthwork and water battery, lay across the channel to the west about one mile by water from Pickens. Just inside the looping entrance to the bay lay the Pensacola Navy Yard, now in the possession of Brig. Gen. Braxton Bragg. Two roads led north to the town of Pensacola, seven miles up the bay, and the others led west to Fort McRee and Fort Barrancas. When Florida seceded on January 9, Fort Pickens was little more than an unoccupied pile of bricks with a few old guns deteriorating on rotten mountings.[25]

Lt. Adam J. Slemmer occupied Fort McRee with Company G, 1st U.S. Artillery, and septuagenarian Capt. James Armstrong commanded the navy yard, located about two miles from Slemmer's batteries. Surrounded by a staff of Confederate sympathizers, Armstrong made no effort to hold the navy yard and on January 12 turned it over to the State of Florida. Slemmer, however, transferred his company—thirty-one volunteer seamen—and all the ammunition at Fort Barrancas to Fort Pickens. He spiked the guns along the western shore, took supplies

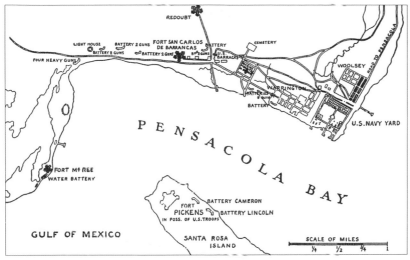

Map of Pensacola Bay and Fort Pickens REPRINTED FROM JOHNSON AND
BUEL, *BATTLES AND LEADERS OF THE CIVIL WAR*

from the navy yard, and went to work repairing the relics at Fort Pickens.
Slemmer sent a wire to Washington reporting his actions, and by the
beginning of February he had fifty-four guns mounted and enough supplies to last about five months. Florida troops occupied everything else.[26]

When the victorious Floridians called upon Slemmer to surrender,
he refused. Cut off from communication except by sea, he waited for
reinforcements. On February 8, *Brooklyn*, under Capt. Henry A. Adams,
arrived off Fort Pickens with eighty men under Capt. Israel Vogdes,
who had orders to go ashore and supersede Slemmer. But Adams had
orders from Toucey to remain outside the harbor. He kept Vogdes on
the vessel, and Slemmer, acting on prior orders from the War Department, refused to be superseded. For two months *Brooklyn* lay off the
fort, and Vogdes watched each day from the quarterdeck as Confederates lined the western shores with artillery.[27]

On April 6, the same day Porter and Meigs sailed from New York,
Welles learned that Toucey had stopped Vogdes from landing at Fort
Pickens. He dispatched Lt. John L. Worden by rail with orders for
Adams to assist Vogdes's landing "on the first favorable opportunity."

Having destroyed his dispatches near Atlanta, Worden reached *Brooklyn* on April 12 and reported the substance of Welles's orders. The following day Vogdes landed his company and took command of Pickens.[28]

Four days later, April 17, Meigs reached Fort Pickens, followed a few hours later by Porter. *Powhatan* had been delayed by storms, but Porter used the time to exercise the guns. On quieter days he suspended seamen over the side of the vessel to paint out the gunports and disguise the vessel as a mail carrier. He intended to pass Confederate batteries at Fort McRee, run by Barrancas and the navy yard, and force Bragg to wear himself out fighting Fort Pickens and the guns of *Powhatan*. But when Porter attempted to enter the harbor, Meigs climbed aboard *Wyandotte* to head him off. Porter had planned his attack back in the Brooklyn Navy Yard, and he sheered to run by *Wyandotte*. Meigs had supported the plan in Brooklyn, thinking then that when they reached Pensacola timorous old Colonel Brown could be coerced into agreeing with them. But when Brown arrived he notified Bragg of his intention to reinforce Fort Pickens and then gave his unsolicited promise to not act on the offensive. Meigs intercepted *Powhatan* and handed Porter a copy of Brown's order.[29]

Porter could not believe it. "I felt like running over Meigs's tug," he said, "but obeyed the order." He was so annoyed at having his attack stopped that he questioned Meigs on the validity of Brown's order. Meigs added an endorsement certifying Brown's directive as carrying the same weight as a verbal order from the president.[30]

Porter came to anchor twenty fathoms off the beach and positioned *Powhatan* so her broadsides could bear on the navy yard. He hoisted the Stars and Stripes, hoping the flag would draw fire and provide his gunners with an excuse to destroy the enemy's water batteries. His 11-inch pivot gun and all ten of the 9-inch Dahlgrens had been loaded with grape and canister and moved to port in expectation of a fight. Meigs's howitzers had been brought up from the hold and loaded with shrapnel. Angered by Brown's order, Porter asked the colonel to address him "more fully on the subject." Brown sent Porter extracts of reports he was preparing for General Scott that painted a grimly exaggerated picture of conditions at Fort Pickens, and he warned the lieutenant against "a voluntary provoking of hostilities."[31]

Porter reluctantly obeyed the order, but when a flotilla of tugs and barges loaded with Confederate soldiers came down from Pensacola and made for the fort, he assumed they mistook *Powhatan* for an unarmed supply vessel and intended to board her. A warning shot from the 11-inch pivot gun sent them scurrying back up the bay.

Troubled by the unimpeded flow of Confederate supplies into Pensacola, Porter waited until Meigs moved all his artillery to Fort Pickens before asking Captain Adams for permission to blockade the harbor. A number of fat prizes had snubbed him as they passed, but Adams objected to a blockade without orders from Washington. Porter offered to assume the responsibility but Adams still said no, allowing that foreign vessels could be turned away but not seized as prizes. "There was in all this business an inanity of which I never conceived," Porter lamented. "The commanding officer of Fort Pickens had no orders at all that I am aware of, except to hold the fort, and not draw the fire of the enemy."[32]

On April 28 a civilian claiming to be a Union man was caught examining the batteries at Fort Pickens. Colonel Brown questioned him, and because "Joe," as he was called, did not want to go back to the mainland, Brown sent him to *Powhatan*. When Joe shredded some paper and threw it in a spitbox, Porter had the pieces pasted together. The note read: "I spent a couple of days at Pensacola previous to my departure for Texas. I want to see a besieged fortress once in a lifetime. Everything goes finely here. Hope to hear of surrender of Fort Sumter today; next Pickens, and then Washington." By then Sumter was a bygone conclusion, having been bombarded by Brig. Gen. Pierre G. T. Beauregard on April 12 and evacuated by Major Anderson on the 14th. A constable from Pensacola came to the fort and showed Brown a trumped-up warrant for Joe's arrest. When the colonel complied, Porter considered the release an act of stupidity, as the spy had seen every inch of Fort Pickens's defenses.[33]

The army held no patent on what Porter considered acts of stupidity. Adams summoned Porter to the flagship to ask about a floating dock the Confederates were moving toward the fort. Porter found Adams and Brown at supper and waiting for an explanation from Bragg, who replied that the dock had gotten adrift and the men were bringing it

back to Pensacola. Four hours later it "accidentally" sank in the channel. Neither Adams nor Brown thought the sinking an accident, but,
Porter reflected, "our senior offices thought they had done their duty by
inquiring of Bragg what he intended to do, and, after seeing him carry
out his intentions, they sat quietly down to dinner. Colonel Brown filled
up some more sandbags, and Bragg mounted an extra gun; they were
like two schoolboys daring each other to knock off chips from their
shoulders and playing a farce at war."[34]

A dispatch arrived from Welles announcing the blockade of Southern ports, effective April 19, and with it an order to Porter: "The President has notified this Department that the special duty to which you
were assigned having been executed, the *Powhatan,* under your command, until further orders will constitute a part of the Gulf Blockading
Squadron, and you will report to the senior officer present." Porter read
the order with relief—Welles had forgiven him. By then, however, a
month had passed since Lincoln's proclamation, and Porter lamented
over the number of enemy vessels he could have captured had Adams
permitted him to operate under his own responsibility.[35]

Adams notified Bragg of the blockade, demanding that all foreign
vessels leave within two weeks. Bragg was already aware of the blockade, calling it an "act of aggressive war" and "a virtual acknowledgment
of our national existence and independence." Bragg retorted by closing
the harbor "to all boats and vessels of the United States," an act Adams
had already accomplished by keeping Porter and other Union vessels
out of the bay. Weeks passed. Bragg kept his eye on Fort Pickens, and
Brown, Porter observed, "never troubled Bragg. Neither of them committed an overt act. A more innocent war was never carried on."[36]

Lincoln's proclamation raised questions in his cabinet. On April 14
Welles argued that the government was engaged in putting down an in-
surrection, not a foreign war. The 3,549 miles of coastline to be block-
aded was not foreign territory but a part of the Union. He warned that a
blockade would encourage foreign powers to extend belligerent rights
to the South, and he feared this could lead to full diplomatic recognition. He urged Lincoln to close Confederate ports, not blockade them.
Once closed, any vessel attempting to enter a Southern port could be

seized in direct violation of municipal law and her crew criminally pros-
ecuted as smugglers. Seward was caught off guard by Welles's knowledge of international law, but he garnered enough support from the cabinet to convince Lincoln to dismiss the naval secretary's advice. As
Welles predicted, Britain, France, and other European powers pro-
claimed their neutrality, recognized the Union and the Confederacy as
belligerents, and permitted their citizens to trade with both entities at
their own risk.[37]

What Welles feared most now happened. The navy had ninety vessels in the department and only forty-two in commission. Twenty-seven
others, mostly sailing vessels, lay out of service in a half-dozen shipyards. Twenty vessels classed as unserviceable contained the navy's old
sailing frigates. A blockade could not exist unless enforced, and Welles
did not have enough ships. Twenty-seven of his best vessels were on
duty around the world, including seventeen steamers. The question
became where and how to deploy the vessels available. In the Gulf of
Mexico, the two most important ports were New Orleans and Mobile.
Key West, where Commodore Porter had once attempted to establish a
naval base, now became essential to operations in the Gulf and in the
Caribbean.[38]

While policy makers in Washington muddled over maps and charts,
Porter chafed for action. The war had started, but neither Adams nor
Brown seemed inclined to oust Bragg from the Pensacola Navy Yard.
Porter, writing his friend Fox, referred to them as "worn out men with-
out brains."[39]

On May 25 Capt. William W. McKean arrived off Fort Pickens in
the 12-gun screw steamer *Niagara* and superseded Captain Adams. The
new sixty-year-old commander from Philadelphia had been in the navy
for forty-six years and had attracted the notice of the Navy Department
when he purged all disloyal Southern officers from his command.[40]

Porter was glad to see anyone who could get him out from under the
suppressive restraint of Adams. McKean had orders to blockade Mobile
and New Orleans and, if necessary, to use every vessel to do it. Before
the day ended, McKean sent *Brooklyn*, under Comdr. Charles H. Poor,
and *Powhatan* to the Mississippi passes. Porter stopped at Mobile Bay

and notified Fort Morgan of the blockade. The garrison tantalized him by running up a huge Confederate flag. A smaller copy of the Stars and Stripes, union down, fluttered below it. Porter resisted the temptation of shelling the noisy garrison and went about his business.[41]

As the rickety old side-wheeler churned toward the Mississippi delta, Porter felt a sense of relief. Welles had not shown vindictiveness by depriving him of the command of *Powhatan,* but he needed to find a way to distinguish himself—and earn a little prize money in the process.

The
Chase

On May 29, as *Powhatan* churned toward Southwest Pass, the watch sighted a sail. Porter recognized her as a schooner on course for New Orleans and ordered her overhauled. Two officers boarded the vessel and learned she had recently been stopped by *Niagara* and warned away from the Southern coast. Porter seized her as a prize, and when he reached Southwest Pass he sent her to New York with a dispatch for Welles. "The present allowance of crews is for peace," Porter wrote. Without more men, he could not afford to take prizes.[1]

Porter anchored *Powhatan* off the bar and sent a boat to Pilottown to inform the authorities that the river was under blockade and foreign vessels must leave within fifteen days. Merchant ships were already streaming down from above, as Gov. Thomas O. Moore wanted the river cleared and the channel blocked at Fort Jackson. Pilottown officials asked if Porter would allow their tugs to draw outbound neutrals over the bar. He agreed, providing they extended the same courtesy to American vessels. At the time, only two of the delta's four passes were under blockade, and Porter later learned that some of the tugs, after hauling Northern vessels over the bar, took them to another pass and towed them to New Orleans as prizes. For two weeks a wild scramble ensued at Southwest Pass, and dozens of vessels grounded and became entangled.[2]

Mixed among the merchantmen making their way through the pass were a perplexing number of ships owned by New Orleans shippers but commanded by Americans sailing under provisional registers provided by the town's English consul. Porter spoke to the consul, who assured him that everything was legal and that Great Britain would take responsibility for infractions of international law. Porter was not satisfied and searched suspicious vessels for guns. Confederate privateers operating off the delta had already captured a half-dozen small prizes, and Porter was determined to end the abuse.[3]

Many pilots working the passes remembered Porter from the fifties, when he commanded *Crescent City* and made regular trips up the river. Some still had roots in the North and became a useful source of information. They warned that Capt. Lawrence Rousseau's naval committee had converted riverboat facilities at New Orleans and Algiers into shipyards. Five vessels were being fitted out for sea, among them two steamers, *Sumter* and *McRae,* both fast packet vessels confiscated by the State of Louisiana. Porter wrote Welles, "Commander Raphael Semmes, formerly of the U.S. Navy, commands the *Sumter* and Commander Thomas B. Huger, formerly a lieutenant in the U.S. Navy, commands the *McRae.* . . . [They] cannot get out of this pass," he added, "but they can get out of two other passes where there is no vessel blockading."[4]

Porter knew Semmes, having shared quarters with him on *Porpoise* during the 1846 mission to Santo Domingo. They had met again at Veracruz, where Semmes commanded *Sommers.* Porter remembered Semmes as having no particular taste for his profession but having a fondness for literature and law. Porter thought of him as "indolent and fond of his comfort"—a man of little energy. A few weeks later he would change his mind.[5]

The four passes of the delta pointed outward much like the claws of a giant bird, with its leg serving as the river and its ankle joint as Head of Passes. Pass à l'Outre, at the eastern outlet to the Gulf, was usually the deepest. Southwest Pass lay on the opposite side of the delta, thirty miles to the west. Between were two shallow passes—Northeast Pass,

Map of the Mississippi River from Fort Jackson to the Gulf of Mexico REPRINTED FROM *OFFICIAL RECORDS OF THE UNION AND CONFEDERATE NAVIES*

which branched off Pass à l'Outre, and South Pass, which divided near the Gulf. The smaller passes accommodated light-draft vessels but could not be trusted for routine navigation. Porter was in error when he advised Welles that *Sumter* could get out of a shallow pass, as she drew too much water, but light-draft vessels moved through them freely.

From the west side of the delta, the other approach to New Orleans was up Atchafalaya Bay to Berwick or up Barataria Bay to the rail junction of the Berwick's Bay and Texas Railroad, where goods could be transported to Algiers and barged across the river to New Orleans. Since his arrival at Southwest Pass, Porter had noticed an increase of sails going up both bays and complained to Welles that he had no coal and could not chase vessels "in plain sight."[6]

Poor, commanding *Brooklyn* off Pass à l'Outre, faced a similar problem. He could not leave his post to chase sailing ships entering Lake Pontchartrain, where schooners still enjoyed a brisk trade at New Orleans. Both Porter and Poor felt hamstrung by blockade duty. Each of them could watch one of the delta's four outlets, but they could not chase a sail without opening the pass.[7]

Welles placed Flag Officer William Mervine in command of the Gulf Blockading Squadron, which extended from Key West to the mouth of the Rio Grande, and assigned the squadron sixteen vessels: *Massachusetts, Brooklyn, Colorado, Niagara, Mohawk, Crusader, Huntsville, Water Witch, Mississippi, R. R. Cuyler, Montgomery, Massachusetts, South Carolina, Wyandote, Powhatan,* and the sloop of war *St. Louis.* He promised to send more vessels as soon as they could be commissioned. Some of the ships had just been purchased and fitted out for blockade duty; others were old and barely serviceable.[8]

Mervine, a septuagenarian, did not arrive in the Gulf until June 23. He had fought in the War of 1812 and in the Mexican War and had served the navy for fifty-two years. In 1861 he had been on waiting orders, which may have been the best place for Welles to have kept him, but at this stage of the war seniority still carried weight. It took Mervine six weeks to reach Fort Pickens. He blamed the delay on a breakdown of *Mississippi's* condensers and other misfortunes he attributed to saboteurs rather than to poor sailing.[9]

Once the outpouring of neutral vessels cleared Southwest Pass, life on *Powhatan* lapsed into a dismal daily drudge. The torrid heat of late June brought afternoon downpours and vicious thunderstorms. Evening winds blowing off the flat, marshy delta sent clouds of mosquitoes out to the vessel. In early morning, dense fog blanketed the flats and enveloped *Powhatan,* wetting the decks and obstructing vision to the extent that Porter could not see from one end of the vessel to the other.

Men perched in the crow's nests stretched their necks above a veil of fog for the telltale sign of smoke from a steamer slipping to sea. Porter looked for ways to keep the crew busy, but off Southwest Pass there was nothing but boredom and days on end of perpetual misery.

On June 21 Semmes brought the 520-ton *Sumter* down to Head of Passes and, with the side-wheeler *Ivy*, Lt. Joseph Fry, to do his scouting, primed the crew to run the blockade. Because of *Sumter's* thirteen-foot draft, Semmes had two choices—Southwest Pass or Pass à l'Outre. *Sumter* carried a 68-pounder in pivot and four 32-pounders in broadside, and, being a steam-propelled fully rigged bark, she could develop ten knots under steam and sail. Semmes had spent two months converting her from a packet ship to the Confederacy's first high-seas commerce destroyer. Now he was anxious to get to sea.[10]

Porter noticed that *Ivy* made frequent stops at Pilottown's telegraph station and suspected she was scouting and relaying information upriver to Semmes. Porter sent a boat detail up the pass, and on June 21 they found *Sumter* anchored at the Head. Porter took soundings but found he could not get *Powhatan* over the bar, so he fitted out a detail to go up the river at night, seize the telegraph station, cut the wire, and lie in wait for *Ivy*. He assigned the mission to Lt. Watson Smith and gave him thirty-five picked men for the enterprise. *Ivy* never returned, but three days later a mail steamer came down the pass and nosed against the bank opposite to where Smith lay hidden. Smith concealed sixteen men in an old deck boat and started across the river, but the skipper of the steamer smelled trouble and departed under a full head of steam, thereby dashing Porter's hopes. He had wanted to get into the river with two hundred men, board *Sumter*, take her back up the river, and destroy the shipping and shipyards at New Orleans.[11]

For nine days Semmes ranged between Southwest Pass and Pass à l'Outre, waiting for Porter or Poor to make a mistake. Porter would not allow himself to be drawn off the bar as long as *Sumter* was in the river, but on June 30 Poor left his station to chase a sail standing for South Pass. Semmes seized the moment and came bounding out Pass à l'Outre.

Poor stood about eight miles away when *Brooklyn's* lookout spotted *Sumter* moving. Poor came about, set all sail, ordered full steam, and began the chase. Semmes put on his best heels, but *Brooklyn* closed to four miles. Just when Semmes began to think he had made a mistake, an afternoon squall beat across the Gulf, shrouding both vessels. As the storm passed, *Brooklyn* surged out of the downpour, closing rapidly. The wind shifted, favoring *Sumter* and forcing Poor to furl his sails. Semmes eased away, and after three and a half hours Poor gave up the chase. *Brooklyn* had been within range for more than thirty minutes, and Semmes thought it odd that Poor never fired a shot. After *Brooklyn* came about, Semmes sent his men into the rigging to give three cheers. The first Confederate raider was loose and on a course for Cuba.[12]

When Porter learned the details of *Sumter's* escape, he credited Semmes with executing a bold and dashing escape, but he criticized Poor, citing an old navy axiom that you never give up the chase until the enemy is out of sight.[13]

Porter, however, was conscious of Poor's predicament and wrote Mervine, asking that another vessel be added to each of the passes, thereby enabling one vessel to cruise while the other stood guard. He also suggested that instead of trying to blockade four passes, a few gunboats be sent to Head of Passes to block the main stem of the river. "I am an old cruiser in this river," he wrote, "and know every inch of the ground. I assure you that an expedition up the river is an easy thing for vessels not drawing over 16 feet, and I do believe the people would return their allegiance if they had any guarantee of protection."[14]

Mervine, however, had no vessels to spare, and those he had were breaking down. *Powhatan,* Porter wrote, "is destitute of everything. We can not raise a tack, scarcely a nail to repair damages with. We have not an ounce of paint on board, nor whitewash. The ship is actually going to ruin for want of her wood being covered." He needed parts for the machinery, planks to repair his boats, and rope to replace sails, bowlines, braces, and halyards. Porter's letter reflected his distaste for inactivity. He hated the stifling climate and wanted to be at sea.[15]

If Porter expected relief from the hot, torpid days of blockade duty, he did not get it, and when news of *Sumter's* depredations filtered back to Washington, Welles began to understand the consequences if he permitted another enemy cruiser to put to sea. By July 6, Semmes had captured eight vessels off Cuba. Welles tapped the Gulf Blockading Squadron for three vessels to search for Semmes and added six more from the Atlantic Blockading Squadron. *Niagara* made a futile dash around Cuba, but Semmes, knowing the risks of staying in one place too long, had departed.[16]

~oast of Venezuela and on July 25 captured the
~d, two days later, the bark *Joseph Maxwell*.
the agent he had placed in charge of his
~emines sent *Abby Bradford* to New Orleans, cau-
~aster Eugene Ruhl to take care when approaching the
~d to avoid the blockaders. While the Union navy searched for
ɔumter in the Caribbean, Semmes cruised the coast of South America.[17]

When a supply vessel dropped off a mailbag on July 4, Porter found a letter from his friend Gus Fox, who was now the assistant secretary of the navy and Welles's right-hand man. Fox offered an advancement in grade to the first officer who captured a fort. Speaking for himself, Porter replied:

> I think it better to wait until I get the one which has been due me for *five* years. After I get that, it will do to try and earn another. . . . A man don't associate down here with alligators, sand flies, mosquitoes and snakes for nothing, he soon gets his eye teeth, and gets wide awake— take a fort indeed! I don't think it likely that any body will take any- thing down here unless it is the fever. . . .
>
> I will let you know when I take a fort. I have my eye on one now, but I must get my Commander's Commission first, and then I will look out for the next peg.
>
> This blockade is the greatest farce on earth. I wish the country well rid of her troubles and old fogies.[18]

With commerce on the river ended, the flow of reliable information from New Orleans ceased, but in Washington rumors trickled into the Navy Department. One described modifications to the steamer *Enoch Train,* whose upper works had been replaced with timbers two feet thick and covered with one-inch iron plates. The body of the vessel was humped like a turtle to deflect shot and shell. Welles thought the ves- sel might do serious damage to his blockade and warned Mervine that it carried "sharp irons" on the bow meant to "stave a hole" through a ship. Welles doubted the reliability of his information but wanted Mervine to inform the blockaders.[19]

To occupy the crew, Porter maintained active boat patrols, and on July 16 an armed detail captured a party from New Orleans who claimed to be refugees fleeing the Confederate draft. The defectors talked freely of how the blockade had put an end to privateering. They

USS *Powhatan,* Porter's first command in the Civil War COURTESY U.S. NAVAL HISTORICAL CENTER

referred to the *Enoch Train* as "a poor concern without speed" and said that nobody expected much of her. According to the informants, New Orleans was already "very tired of the war and would be glad to see it over." Porter advised Mervine, "There is no danger to be apprehended from the boat with the iron horn." As he blotted his report, the Confederate army won a signal victory near a town in Virginia called Manassas, and the builders of the "boat with the iron horn" now had a name for their ugly creation.[20]

If such a vessel existed, *Powhatan* was vulnerable. For two months Porter had waited for parts. His boilers sprang new leaks whenever he raised steam, and some of the castings on the machinery had hairline cracks and would split if the engines were pressed. Without parts, Porter complained, "we will soon be obliged to let our fires go out."[21]

Porter, who had been searching for a way to get to sea, received his parts just in time to take advantage of an unexpected opportunity. On August 13 lookouts sighted a brig standing for Barataria Bay, and for the first time in weeks Porter stood in chase, capturing *Abby Bradford* with her prize crew on board. Prizemaster Ruhl not only neglected to throw

Semmes's dispatches over the side, he also forgot to avoid the passes. Porter made copies of Semmes's reports and sent them to Welles. He interrogated the crew and induced one of the sailors to give an accurate account of Semmes's problems and his likely location. Porter learned that *Sumter* could carry only eight days' coal and wrote Welles, "He is in a position now where he can't escape. He is out of coal and out of credit." Porter's assessment of Semmes's problems was quite accurate, but catching him was another matter.[22]

In his dispatches to Confederate Secretary of the Navy Stephen R. Mallory, Semmes gave only a bare outline of *Sumter*'s activities—facts already known by Welles. And because *Abby Bradford* had not been adjudicated in an admiralty court, she was technically a recapture, for which Porter would receive no prize money. But Porter was after bigger game. He steamed over to Pensacola to speak with Flag Officer Mervine. On the trip to Pensacola, he penned a note to Welles:[23]

> [Semmes's] plan is to sink, burn, and destroy all that is not very valuable, and no pirate that ever swam the ocean had such an opportunity for doing damage, for he can do it with impunity. . . . There are hiding holes [in Samana Bay] known to Semmes where a hundred prizes might be concealed. There are places around Isle of Pines where the devil himself would not find vessels unless he knew the locality. I have been all through them and know them well, and so does Semmes. If he gets pushed hard he can find shelter among the reefs on the Mosquito Banks. No one would think of following him there.[24]

On the evening of August 14 *Powhatan* arrived off Pensacola and came abeam *Susquehanna*, Mervine's flagship. The flag officer listened to Porter's scheme and replied, "Why, man alive. I was just going to send for you to come up and help me capture Ship Island. The enemy have mounted six guns. . . . I think our two ships can clean them out." But Porter prevailed by using the same reasoning as in his letter to Welles, and Mervine, who was not happy about weakening his blockade, released him to go after Semmes.[25]

Five days later Porter stopped at Cienfuegos to pick up *Sumter*'s trail. He learned that Semmes's tenth prize, *Joseph Maxwell*, had been refused entry and was run aground by her crew off the southern coast of Cuba. Porter believed Semmes would hide among the trading routes of the Caribbean, and he wrote Welles suggesting that two steamers be deployed between Cuba and Haiti and that two more be sent to the Spanish Main to cover ports where Semmes might stop for coal.[26]

After sharing his thoughts with Welles, Porter headed for Puerto Cabello, Venezuela, where *Joseph Maxwell* had been captured. He stopped at Kingston, Jamaica, but he did not feel welcome. British authorities sympathized with the South and inflated the price of coal. Great Britain's proclamation of neutrality applied equally to her colonies, but local officials were inclined to grant favors to the belligerent who produced the most cotton. By then Welles had added four warships to the chase, but none of them had seen *Sumter.* Semmes, it seemed, left no trail.[27]

On August 29 Porter dropped down to Curaçao, where Semmes had stopped on July 16 for repairs. Gov. J. D. Crol had denied *Sumter* entrance, but Semmes baffled him with a long litany of international law and convinced island officials of his right to the port. Once inside St. Anne's harbor, Semmes ingratiated himself with the governor. *Sumter* had been shaken by storms after leaving Cienfuegos and needed extensive work. The governor allowed Semmes to buy a new topmast, repair his boilers, paint the ship, and purchase coal and supplies.[28]

After condemning Crol for aiding *Sumter* and discussing the matter with the American consul, Porter believed Semmes might return to Cienfuegos to look after his prizes. At St. Anne's he read in an old newspaper that Semmes had coaled at Trinidad on July 30 and intended to cruise down the Spanish Main to Pernambuco, Brazil, but Porter preferred to follow his own hunches. It was now August 30, which meant that Semmes could be anywhere, but *Sumter's* presence at Trinidad was Porter's best lead, so on September 1, after disputing with Dutch officials the legality of coaling "pirate" Semmes, he cleared for sea.[29]

Porter sailed northeast, hoping to find Semmes zigzagging his way back to Cienfuegos, but he found not a trace. He doubled back to St. Thomas, hoping to pick up *Sumter's* trail. A schooner informed him that *Sumter* had stopped at Paramaribo, Suriname, to coal, and that a freighter sent by Semmes to Demerara for fuel had been seized at British Guiana. Porter filled his bunkers and on September 7 set a course for the coast of South America. Knowing Semmes would not be found where he was last reported, Porter stopped at Martinique for information. Picking up not so much as a clue, he headed for Barbados and on the 10th entered the port of Bridgetown and saluted the British flag. He spoke briefly to American consul Edward Trowbridge, who had been in contact with his counterpart at Paramaribo and confirmed that Semmes had been there but had sailed. Porter departed in pursuit, and as the rickety *Powhatan* plowed down the Windward Islands he divided his time between the pleasant breezes of the quarterdeck and the stifling racket in the engine room. He was closing the gap on *Sumter,* but with day and night being of equal length he feared passing her in the dark.[30]

On September 5 Porter stopped briefly at Suriname and learned from consul Henry Sawyer that Semmes had entered the port on August 18, made repairs, and sailed on August 31. When he departed, Semmes slyly suggested that he would cruise to the northwest. Porter suspected him of intentionally planting misinformation, but he sped up the coast to Demerara to confirm his suspicions, pushing the boilers with every ounce of steam they could carry. Sawyer warned Porter to not be fooled by a merchant vessel, as Semmes could disguise *Sumter* by lowering her smokestack. This meant Porter would have to stop every three-masted vessel. Nonetheless, he left a message for Welles: "I will follow her as long as my engine [holds] together."[31]

Powhatan, spewing clouds of black smoke, churned up the coast of South America and on September 13 stopped at the lightship off Demerara to ask if *Sumter* had been seen. The tender said no and re-peated what Porter already knew—she had been in the Suriname River. Porter doubled back and hailed the lightship off Paramaribo. They had not seen *Sumter* since August 31. With so many Union warships hunt-ing her in the Caribbean, Porter now believed Semmes had sailed down the coast of Brazil and would take *Sumter* as far south as Cape St. Roque, six hundred miles below the equator. Knowing Semmes must use his sails to conserve coal, Porter calculated he could gain about fifty miles a day on her. If his boilers stood the strain, he felt he could catch her. Semmes had a two-week lead, but Porter now had hope of over-hauling the wily Confederate—provided *Sumter* was headed, as he sus-pected, to Brazil.

The chase began on September 13, but one of *Powhatan's* boilers cracked a day after leaving Suriname. The sea was smooth, however, and Porter pressed forward, intending to stop at Maranhão, Brazil, for it was there Semmes would stop for coal. If Porter was right, *Powhatan* could be off the port in time to catch *Sumter* as she returned to sea.[32]

Despite problems with the machinery, Porter managed to get five pounds of steam out of the ruptured boiler. *Powhatan* paddled day and night, swishing down the coast of Brazil, consuming coal at an unheard-of rate but generating only eight knots. The chief engineer pleaded to slow her down, but Porter pressed ahead. Under the circumstances he made good time, arriving off São Luís, Maranhão, on the 21st. Fog shrouded the channel, and all the pilots had gone inshore to wait for it to clear. Porter could not wait. He sounded his way into the harbor, only to learn that Semmes had coaled and departed five days earlier. The man who had led *Sumter* out of the harbor approached Porter and said, "You must have had the devil for a pilot. Even the little *Sumter* struck coming in and came near leaving her bones." She did leave one of her bones, the false keel, which started her to leaking. Semmes had spent ten days making repairs and departed with fifteen of his crew in chains. Had Porter not lost the efficiency of a boiler, he may have caught Semmes near the equator.[33]

Outside of the Confederacy, Brazil remained the largest slave-holding country in the Western Hemisphere, and Porter's reception at São Luís, the first Brazilian port below the equator, was cold. Semmes had livened his stay by making proslavery speeches to a neosecessionist party who treated him to banquets and provided for his needs. William H. McGrath, the American consul, had tried to detain *Sumter* and interfere with her repairs, but the governor ignored him. Semmes had no money, but J. Wetson, a friendly Texan domiciled in Brazil, loaned him two thousand dollars to purchase a load of coal.[34]

Porter regarded Brazil as being in defiance of international law and, instead of paying the governor a customary courtesy call, sent him an angry two thousand–word complaint. He described Semmes as a ruthless pirate who destroyed vessels and cargoes owned by innocent shippers, a man who wantonly forced neutrals to act against their will and whose treatment of prisoners was a disgrace to mankind. He also disclosed one of Semmes's deceits in a convincing manner. The Confederate commander had informed the governor that the South possessed the larger part of the warships formerly belonging to the U.S. Navy and that the North "could not even fit out a ship . . . to pursue him." The governor had not seen a Union warship, and when *Powhatan* paddled into port he had never seen one so big. Porter's angry letter, combined with *Powhatan*'s heavy guns, convinced Brazilian officials to make amends, and when Porter demanded facilities to repair his boilers the governor consented.[35]

After forfeiting a week for repairs and coaling, Porter made one last effort to track down *Sumter*. From the pilot who had guided her out of the harbor, he learned that *Sumter* had sailed to the northeast, and Porter surmised she would eventually double back to the Windward Islands or Brazil for coal. He also learned that *Sumter*'s journals overheated, slowing her speed to six knots under steam. When she lost her false keel on the bar she also lost her ability to hold the wind, and now any good sailing vessel could beat her. Porter also suspected she leaked. "Close hauled in a fresh breeze," he declared, "with sails and steam, she could not overtake a smart sailing craft. . . . They are short of money, without which they can't run much longer, as Confederate scrip is not at par, even in Brazil."[36]

On September 28, after assessing *Sumter*'s deficiencies, Porter resumed the chase, but Semmes was not to be stopped. On the 25th he captured the brig *Joseph Park*, six days out of Pernambuco and en route to Boston. At the time, *Sumter* lay about 750 miles east of French Guiana.[37]

As Porter predicted, Semmes began easing westward, and on the 30th *Sumter* drifted in a calm sea about five hundred miles east of Cayenne, having barely moved for five days. *Powhatan*, sailing from Maranhão on the 28th, steered north, bending slightly to the west. At 8:00 P.M. *Sumter*'s lookout reported a steamer's red light moving across the eastern horizon. Semmes ordered all lights screened, batteries cleared for action, and the boilers fired. Moments later the light disappeared. Semmes noted in the ship's journal, "It was only a meteor or a setting star on a hazy horizon."[38]

Porter, however, ran almost straight up the forty-fourth longitude and, traveling at ten knots, could by the 30th have been quite close to *Sumter*. For more than a week, *Powhatan* zigzagged off the Windward Islands, staying in the track of vessels bound from the East Indies, the Pacific, and Brazil. On the night of October 5 the lookout reported a dim distant light, and Porter went in chase. The light vanished, and Porter found no further trace of it.

He sailed into St. Thomas for coal and on October 10 spoke to the captain of *Spartan,* a British brig Semmes had boarded five days earlier. The captain gave his position at the time as 47°25' W longitude and 9° N latitude. Porter quickly checked his log and found he had passed within seventy-five miles of *Sumter.* Years after the war, Semmes and Porter compared records and agreed that on October 5 *Powhatan* had passed within forty miles of *Sumter* and had perhaps been as close on September 30. Had it not been for darkness, *Sumter* may not have captured another seven prizes, and Semmes, a year later, may never have captained the most dreaded of all Confederate commerce raiders—the famous CSS *Alabama.*[39]

For Porter, the ten thousand–mile chase had come to an end. He enjoyed the excitement of the hunt, much as his father had fifty years earlier when he commanded the frigate *Essex.* He could be pleased with his effort but not with the results. The age of steam had brought a new dimension to commerce raiding. Wind and seamanship no longer determined the outcome of a chase. He had not destroyed *Sumter,* but he had nearly destroyed *Powhatan.* She could not stand the strain, and he took her back to Pensacola. When he arrived on October 25, his friends greeted him as commander. Porter attributed his promotion not to Welles but to the lengthy letter he had sent his friend Fox.[40]

Other changes had occurred. Mervine had been replaced by sixty-one-year-old Captain McKean, a man Porter considered a healthier and more energetic commander. Of more interest, Capt. John Pope had taken two steamers and two sailing vessels into the Mississippi to blockade and fortify the river at Head of Passes, a scheme Porter had once suggested to Mervine. On October 12 the Confederate ram *Manassas* led a small flotilla of gunboats down the river and chased Pope's squadron back to the Gulf. In naval circles the ignominious retreat was dubbed "Pope's Run," and the captain sensibly asked to be relieved. When Porter heard the story he recognized the ram as the same vessel described to him in July by the captured boatload of defectors.[41]

Having little appetite for blockade duty, Porter prepared a report of *Powhatan's* deficiencies, referring to her boilers as "unfit" and the vessel "rotten throughout." He wanted action and another command. "Her planking won't bear calking," Porter declared, "and above the water you can run a knife through the seams. The bottom is covered with barnacles which is the only thing that keeps the oakum from washing out. But for her condition," Porter added, "there would be no more efficient ship afloat." McKean ordered Porter to take the vessel to New York for repair.[42]

Before departing, Porter acquainted himself with the details of Pope's Run. He considered the occupation of Head of Passes the only effective way to blockade the Mississippi and believed its possession by the Union navy crucial to the ascent of the river. Pope had blundered by failing to post picket boats upstream and by including in his four-ship squadron two old sailing vessels that could not maneuver in the river. When *Manassas,* which could barely stem the current, ran down the river, rammed the USS *Richmond,* and stove in several planks, Pope panicked and led a predawn retreat back to the Gulf. In the squadron's haste to get to sea, *Richmond* and *Vincennes* grounded on the bar. Pope signaled the squadron to "retire from action," but Comdr. Robert Handy misread the message, abandoned ship, and appeared on the deck of *Richmond* with the American flag wrapped around his body. Handy had lit a fuse to the magazine before leaving the vessel and expected *Vincennes* to blow up, but the quartermaster snipped the fuse the moment Handy left the hold. When the vessel failed to explode, Pope sent Handy and his crew back to defend her. A pair of Confederate gunboats lobbed a few shells at the two grounded vessels and departed upriver. For Porter, Pope's Run ranked as one of the most disgusting affairs in the history of the U.S. Navy, but the citizens of New Orleans naturally considered it "the most brilliant and remarkable exploit on record."[43]

Porter arrived at New York on November 9, and by then his thoughts had shifted from the chase of *Sumter,* which he wanted to forget, to a collection of ideas dating back to those tiresome, sweltering days off Southwest Pass. Pope's ridiculous disaster at Head of Passes reminded him of the importance of capturing New Orleans. Porter constantly thought about it as he steamed up from the Gulf, and by the time he tied to the wharf at the Brooklyn Navy Yard he had conceived a plan to control the lower Mississippi.

But would anybody listen?

Porter Picks a
Flag Officer

On November 7, two days before *Powhatan* tied up at the Brooklyn Navy Yard, Flag Officer Samuel F. Du Pont proved a point that would alter the old naval axiom that wooden vessels could not pass heavy fortifications without paying a horrible price in ships and casualties. With seventeen wooden warships and twelve thousand men in transports, Du Pont entered Port Royal Sound and captured two earthworks guarding the entrance to the harbor: Fort Beauregard at Bay Point and Fort Walker on Hilton Head. The flotilla steamed inside the harbor at 9:00 A.M. and for the next six hours circled between the two forts, firing broadsides at one and then at the other. The defenders, with forty-one guns bearing on the channel, found it difficult to hit moving targets, and at 2:00 P.M. they abandoned Fort Walker. Fort Beauregard's garrison fled an hour and a half later. Much to the surprise of the Navy Department, Du Pont's squadron suffered only slight damage and thirty-one casualties.[1]

Porter arrived in Washington on November 12, about two hours after the news of Du Pont's great naval victory hit the streets. He bought a paper and read the headlines as he rode toward his home in Georgetown. By engaging two forts lying nearly opposite each other, Du Pont had put to test Porter's own theory on how to capture New Orleans. However, there was a difference. The two forts guarding Port Royal Sound were modest earthworks compared with the strength and fire-power of Forts Jackson and St. Philip, which lay seventy miles below New Orleans and twenty miles above Head of Passes. The Mississippi River was also narrower than Port Royal Sound and carried a four- to five-knot current. The Louisiana forts, one on each side of the river, were so arranged to enable them to concentrate their fire across a three-and-a-half-mile stretch of river. Any intruder attempting to run the gauntlet could come under fire for as long as thirty minutes.[2]

Porter had not been home since April 1, but he was so anxious to take his plan to the Navy Department that he spent little time with his family. Georgy wanted to know why he had not written to her since July; Tod had grown an inch; Carlisle was at the Naval Academy, which had been moved to Newport, Rhode Island; and sixteen-year-old Essex, who had returned with his father on *Powhatan,* found a commission awaiting him in the Army of Virginia.[3]

Concerned about his relationship with Welles, Porter excused himself from the family reunion and took a carriage to the Navy Department, housed in a three-story brick building on grounds just west of the White House. He hoped Welles would give him an audience, but after diverting *Powhatan* from the relief of Fort Sumter he wondered if the secretary would listen to him. Welles had a good memory of the bothersome incident and noted, "Commander D. D. Porter returned with the steam frigate *Powhatan* from an irregular cruise on which he had been improperly sent."[4]

Porter had not been inside the Navy Department since the outbreak of the war, and he found it humming with activity. Welles left word he was busy and could not see him. Porter noticed that "Fox was not communicative; [William] Faxon eyed me askance; [Capt. Henry A.] Wise was jocose, but knew nothing, and old Commodore Joe Smith said, 'Well, you didn't run away after all!' and I wandered about like a cat in a strange garret." Porter decided to wait in the anteroom to Welles's office and fell into a conversation with two senators from the Naval Affairs Committee, James W. Grimes of Iowa and John P. Hale of New Hampshire. He related his experiences on the lower Mississippi and said he had a plan to capture New Orleans. Impressed by Porter's ideas, the senators escorted him in to see Welles, who listened with interest and invited Fox to join the meeting. "The Secretary of the Navy, much to my surprise, received me kindly," Porter recalled, "and listened attentively to all I had to say. When I had concluded he suggested we should all go to the President." So for the second time since the outbreak of the war, earlier as a lieutenant and now as a commander, Porter made a trip to the seat of government that culminated in a high-level strategy session with the president.[5]

Porter was fortunate that neither Welles nor Lincoln manifested any resentment, for he had manipulated both of them. His timing was also good, because they were euphoric over Du Pont's victory. Porter, however, did not know that plans to capture New Orleans were already under consideration at the Navy Department, but Welles and Fox were especially interested in hearing Porter's views because the commander had spent several years navigating the lower Mississippi.

Porter understood the difficulties of blockading New Orleans from the Gulf. Having spent more than two months there, he advised against trying to seal off the Mississippi passes and all the inlets, lakes, and bays bordering the delta where shallow-draft schooners continued to operate. Instead, he advocated the capture and occupation of New Orleans as the only effective method to curb the trade and relieve the blockading squadron for duty elsewhere. Because the city was surrounded by swamps and not easily reached by land, a strong naval force would be needed to open the river by getting above Forts Jackson and St. Philip. Porter claimed the heavily casemated works could be passed if first neutralized by an overpowering forty-eight-hour bombardment of 13-inch mortar shells. He suggested mounting the mortars on schooners, towing the vessels upriver, and placing them in range of the forts. Once the city fell, the forts would be isolated and compelled to surrender. Porter felt the mission could be successfully conducted with a few thousand soldiers, enough to occupy the town and garrison the forts. Welles seemed to favor the proposal, but Fox remained silent. The president, however, warmed to the project and suggested that Welles, Fox, and Porter discuss it with Maj. Gen. George B. McClellan, who had recently replaced General Scott as commander in chief and would be obliged to supply the troops.[6]

Welles remembered the occasion differently:

The Navy Department, having decided to make a naval attack on the forts and the city, was glad to avail itself of [Porter's] recent observation, and of whatever information he possessed in regard to the river and the forts. He was therefore questioned and soon taken into our confidence. He entered with zeal into the views of the Department but expressed great doubts whether the forts could be passed until reduced or seriously damaged. This he said might be effected by a flotilla of bomb vessels with mortars which could in forty-eight hours demolish the forts or render them untenable. Commander Porter's proposition was a departure from the original plan of the Navy Department, and was strongly objected to by Assistant Secretary [Fox].[7]

Postmaster General Montgomery Blair corroborated Welles's version of the meeting. He recalled that Fox, his brother-in-law, discussed capturing New Orleans by ascending the river from the Gulf rather than attacking it from upriver as the War Department favored, and that Porter was included in the council at Fox's suggestion. Welles had held several secret sessions on methodology, and according to Blair, Porter did not conceive the plan but contributed to it.[8]

Brig. Gen. John G. Barnard, U.S. Engineers, had warned Fox that New Orleans should not be attacked from the lower Mississippi unless the forts were reduced. Barnard had spent many years before the war improving the works and possessed detailed knowledge of their strength. Porter was unaware of Barnard's recommendation until this meeting, but he provided a novel approach to solving the problem by suggesting the use of mortar boats. Fox, however, credited Welles, not Porter, with the original plan.[9]

If Porter had conceived the idea, he made no mention of it in his previous correspondence with either Fox or Welles. More than likely, Porter's thoughts coincided with those of the department's at a time when everybody was celebrating Du Pont's victory and anxious to organize another coup de main. Porter had no appetite for blockade duty, and during his pursuit of *Sumter* he had ample time to formulate a strategy. There is no record of the expedition being discussed with Lincoln prior to Porter's involvement, but the idea of reducing the forts

Asst. Secretary of the Navy Gustavus Vasa Fox
NATIONAL ARCHIVES

with a flotilla of mortars, a weapon usually associated with land-based siege operations, seemed to solve the key obstacle in approving the project. The Navy Department wanted the mission approved, and when Lincoln said "We will go and see General McClellan and find out if we can't manage to get some troops," Welles arranged the meeting.[10]

On the night of November 15, Welles, Fox, and Porter rode to the home of General McClellan on the corner of H and 14th Streets just as Lincoln arrived in his carriage. They retired to a sitting room and closed the door, and Welles explained the plan. McClellan reacted skeptically. He doubted whether wooden warships would get beyond Fort Jackson, although they might survive the fire from Fort St. Philip if Jackson was disabled. He considered Jackson—with its heavy casemated guns— one of the strongest forts in the country, capable of disabling any number of vessels attempting to pass it. The general also envisioned a request for fifty thousand troops, too large a number to spare from an army he was organizing for operations in Virginia. Welles explained that the navy would take responsibility for capturing the forts and the city and asked for only ten thousand troops to hold them. McClellan then showed more interest, giving effusive approval to Porter's mortar flotilla as "absolutely essential for success." From the general's point of view, if the mortars destroyed Jackson and the expedition succeeded, the army would be assured a share of the credit, as the navy would not carry a force large enough to occupy the forts. Fox, however, tenaciously held to his contention that "steamers could pass the forts without reducing or even bombarding them," but McClellan and Porter prevailed on the premise that the mortar flotilla would render assistance "and be of no detriment to the expedition." When the meeting ended, McClellan agreed to supply 12,500 troops, including 2,500 raw recruits Maj. Gen. Benjamin F. Butler was raising in Massachusetts. Lincoln approved the final adoption of the plan, and Welles enjoined the others to work out the details in extreme secrecy. He asked that the name "New Orleans" not be mentioned in the department.[11]

Although the decision to attack the Crescent City from the lower Mississippi became one of the foremost tactical decisions of the war, it was hurriedly conceived and dangerously incomplete. By all military standards, the land force committed by McClellan was inadequate if the enemy improved the city's defenses. Rumors of ironclads being built at New Orleans had already trickled into the Navy Department, and the Port Royal victory could not be compared to conditions at New Orleans. The objectives were different. Port Royal was merely a harbor. New Orleans was the largest and greatest city of the South, the gateway to the Gulf of Mexico, the center of commerce on the river, and the epicenter of Confederate wealth. McClellan's and Welles's notion that a naval expedition with a few thousand soldiers could capture New Orleans contained all the pitfalls of a military fantasy, and its success would have little to do with Union military might.

To do it at all required a flag officer, and Welles did not have any idea of whom to select. His profile of the ideal commander included requirements such as "courage, audacity, tact, and fearless energy, with great self-reliance, decisive judgment, and ability to discriminate and act under trying and extraordinary circumstances." Welles quickly discarded McKean, the present commander of the Gulf Squadron, who was ill and needed to be replaced.[12]

Porter, of course, was not even considered, but he had the satisfaction of learning that the department had chosen him to command the mortar flotilla. Two days later Welles sent him to Philadelphia and New

York to select from the schooners owned by the government "those suitable as bomb vessels" and, if necessary, to purchase more and modify them "as you may suggest."[13]

The decision to capture New Orleans, combined with the command of the mortar flotilla, not only elevated Porter's self-esteem but drew heavily upon his well-known endurance. He faced a huge task and had little time to get it done. Mortars had to be cast and machined in Pittsburgh, where other military demands had swamped the town's foundry capacity. Schooners had to be acquired, decks dropped and reinforced, and mortar carriages built and installed. Thousands of 13-inch shells needed to be cast and stowed on the vessels, and, to tow the schooners, a squadron of armed shallow-draft steamers had to be fit for service in the river. Instead of being chastised for past indiscretions, Porter saw his suggestions adopted and his career enhanced by a unique command, so he threw himself into the work with great energy.

With Porter gone, Welles returned to the task of naming a flag officer. Closeting himself with Fox, he set Nelsonian standards and combed the seniority list of active captains. The likeliest candidates—Goldsborough, Wilkes, and Du Pont—could not be spared, and Welles disqualified many others for their age or undistinguished records. After culling through the list, Fox recommended David Glasgow Farragut. Welles retained a favorable impression of Farragut from the Mexican War, and Fox liked him because, after Virginia seceded, he had cleared out of Norfolk and professed his loyalty to the Union. Welles made a few discreet inquiries and decided that Farragut had "a good but not conspicuous record. All who knew him gave him credit of being a good officer, of good sense and good habits."[14]

Farragut had another distinctive feature—he and Porter were foster brothers, which Fox considered an asset. This relationship, however, led to another round of debate as to who chose Farragut to lead the expedition. Before Welles made a decision, he wanted to test Porter's reaction because, he said, "As Porter himself was to take a conspicuous part in the expedition, it had an important influence."[15]

According to Porter, Fox mentioned several names to him, among them Farragut's, who stood thirty-seventh on the list of active captains. Porter compared the men above Farragut to the "old fogies" in the Gulf who had forgotten that their first duty was to fight. He reminded Fox that Farragut had fought under his father. The comment carried weight because Fox considered the elder Porter the greatest commodore who ever lived. Of all active captains, Farragut had probably seen the most fighting, he was still energetic, and his keen mind was ideally suited to cope with the unfamiliar conditions he would be confronted with in the river. Porter made the point that the other older officers might not want command of the mission because they had not been consulted about the expedition, but Farragut would not haggle over such trivialities. Porter believed Farragut was the right man for the job and said so. Because of this private conversation with Fox, Porter believed he had influenced Welles to consider Farragut.[16]

What actually happened back in the Navy Department was quite different. Welles still pondered his options. Wanting Farragut's resolve confirmed before making a commitment, he asked Fox to have Porter, who was in New York, sound out Farragut's "ideas, feelings, and views" on the war. Welles believed Farragut would speak freely to his foster brother, and, if the captain passed the loyalty test, he authorized Porter to ascertain Farragut's views on a naval attack "as was proposed by the Navy Department, without advising him of our object or letting him know that the Department had any purpose in [the] inquiries."[17]

Porter, who enjoyed intrigue, must have felt a little like the fox being let into the henhouse. In mid-December he met with Farragut at the Pierpont House in Brooklyn and left the only record of the meeting: "I found Captain Farragut the same active man I had seen ten years before. Time had added grey hairs to his head, and a few lines of intelligence, generally called 'crows' feet,' round his eyes. Otherwise he seemed unchanged. He had the same genial smile that always characterized him and the same affable manner which he possessed since I first knew him when I was quite a child and he a married man."[18]

As a loyalty test, Porter asked Farragut what he thought of those officers who defected to join the Confederate navy. Farragut replied, "Those damned fellows will catch it yet!" He admitted some reluctance to fight against his wife's relatives, who still lived in Norfolk, but short of doing so, he wanted a command at sea where he could best serve his country. Porter reported the conversation to Fox, who then wired back asking if Farragut thought New Orleans could be captured. Porter took the message to Farragut, who answered in the affirmative. Fox then asked Farragut if he thought *he* could take it, and Farragut replied he could and, "if furnished with the proper means, was willing to try."[19]

Welles ordered Farragut to Washington, and Fox met him at the train station the morning of December 21 and took him to Montgomery Blair's home for breakfast. The tight-lipped circle of conspirators had barely changed in number since the mid-November meeting in McClellan's sitting room. Porter was not at the Blair breakfast table when Fox briefed Farragut on the plan and asked, "What is your opinion of it?" Farragut replied, "It will succeed." Later in the morning Farragut met with Welles and repeated his convictions, and Fox assured him that "more vessels would be added to the expedition."[20]

Commenting on Porter's mortar flotilla, Farragut said, "I would not have advised this, as these vessels will be likely to warn the enemy of our intentions, and I do not place much reliance upon them. But some of them have already been procured, and they may be more efficient and of greater benefit than I anticipate. So I willingly adopt the flotilla as part of my command."[21]

After the war, Blair admitted that "Porter was given a command in the expedition to bring his influence to bear on Farragut in carrying out the programme, into which he entered warmly." Porter never knew how close he came to losing his flotilla, but Farragut eventually agreed with Welles that the mortars "might render assistance and be of no detriment to the expedition," so they remained.[22]

A more compelling question is whether Farragut would have been chosen to command the squadron had Porter not been in the right place at the right time and providing persuasive influence. Porter never mentioned to Welles or Fox that Farragut's brother's family lived in New Orleans, his sister in Pascagoula, Mississippi, and that he might have to fight the husband of his wife's sister, Comdr. John K. Mitchell. If Welles knew of these relationships, he never shared it with his critics, and on January 9, 1862, he officially assigned Farragut command of the West Gulf Blockading Squadron—from St. Andrew's Bay in West Florida to the Rio Grande.[23]

Farragut's promotion to flag officer brewed a strange and unofficial correspondence between Porter and Fox, both of whom possessed an appetite for intrigue. The pair had much in common, although Fox, at forty, was eight years younger than Porter. He had left the navy in 1856 to become an agent for Bay State Mills, and his elevation to assistant secretary of the navy came through a sequence of events that began

Adm. David Glasgow Farragut, Porter's foster brother
COURTESY U.S. ARMY MILITARY HISTORY INSTITUTE

with Blair, his powerful brother-in-law, who had drawn him into the Fort Sumter crisis. Had Porter not sailed off to Fort Pickens with *Powhatan*, Fox would have used the vessel for his emissarial mission to Charleston. The peacekeeping attempt failed, but Lincoln appreciated Fox's efforts and offered him command of a warship. Fox preferred work in the Navy Department, and on August 1, 1861, Lincoln, over Welles's initial objections, created the post of assistant secretary. Welles needed an experienced and diplomatic administrator, and he soon found Fox indispensable.[24]

Gus Fox and David Dixon became friends long before the war start-ed. They spent many long evenings at the Porter home on Gay Street drinking whiskey punch and criticizing their superiors. They influenced each other to the extent that after Fox resigned from the navy, Porter might have followed had he not been offered command of a mail steamer. For many years they kept in touch, and but for the barrier of rank Fox would have preferred Porter as commander of the New Or-leans expedition. After Welles chose Farragut, Fox made his doubts known to Porter, thereby spawning a secret pact wherein Porter agreed to inform Fox whether Farragut was functioning up to expectations once the squadron reached the Gulf. So much for foster brotherhood.[25]

On the day of Farragut's promotion to flag officer, Porter had neither time nor reason to write letters to Fox. He was too busy telegraphing orders to Pittsburgh for twenty giant mortars—"chowder pots," as the gunners called them—and thirty thousand 13-inch shells. Somewhat to his chagrin, he discovered that Captain Foote had filled the foun-dries with work. Foote, the former acting commandant of the Brooklyn Navy Yard, still remembered Porter as the man who "stole" *Powhatan.* He was as determined as Porter to have his orders filled and posed a serious obstacle to the troublesome commander. Foote was rushing gunboats to Brig. Gen. Ulysses S. Grant for an attack on Forts Henry and Donelson, but Porter badgered the foundries with so many demands that Foote's requirements fell behind schedule.[26]

Porter had the gun carriages installed by the time the mortars arrived. By February 3 he had fitted out twenty-one schooners and five steam-ers with ammunition, provisions, medical supplies, hawsers, and tools of every description. He needed two vessels to complete his flotilla: the flagship *Harriet Lane,* a small steamer built for the revenue service, and the gunboat *Octorara,* which was still under construction. Welles watched Porter with keen interest and admitted he had never seen any-body with more "energy, great activity, [and] abundant resources." Years later he referred to it as a Porter characteristic.[27]

On February 11 Porter kissed his family good-bye, joined his flagship *Harriet Lane* in the Washington Navy Yard, and sailed to rendezvous with his flotilla at Key West. *Octorara* remained behind, delayed by work at the Brooklyn Navy Yard. Of the twenty-eight vessels under his command, all the schooners and six of the seven steamers were at sea.[28]

Lt. Jonathan M. Wainwright commanded *Harriet Lane,* and he had no idea he was going to the Gulf until a day before he sailed. Space on the vessel was dominated by the machinery required to drive the huge paddle wheels, and when Wainwright greeted Porter on the gangway he said, "I don't see how we shall be able to store that trunk in the cabin, but I must contrive some way." Porter replied, "Put it in the maintop and get underway at once." Wainwright protested. He needed another day to coal, supplies had not been shipped, and two officers and the cabin steward were still on shore leave. "We'll leave without them," Porter replied, and twenty minutes later the vessel headed down the Potomac. He was one week behind Farragut and anxious to catch up.[29]

Harriet Lane's five guns—three 9-inch smoothbores and two 24-pounder howitzers—occupied much of the deck. The vessel's greatest asset was her speed, and to get to sea Wainwright had to run Confederate batteries strung along a sixty-mile stretch of the Potomac River. As *Harriet Lane* passed Cockpit Point, artillery fire whizzed across the river and knocked out the rim of the port wheel. Another shell passed through the smokestack and exploded. Porter withheld fire, convinced the gunners would only waste ammunition. Three more shots skittered across the deck before the vessel cleared the battery. Porter lost three days at Hampton Roads making repairs and coaling. He wrote Fox, warning that "the *Merrimac* [CSS *Virginia*] will be out this week," and then he was off to the Gulf.[30]

Harriet Lane showed her speed on the trip to Key West, plowing through storms off Cape Hatteras without missing a beat. She stopped at Port Royal, dropped off messages to Du Pont, and filled her bunkers. Off St. Augustine she chased and captured the schooner *Joanna Ward,* a Confederate vessel showing Spanish colors, and Wainwright sent her back to New York as a prize. When Porter eased into Key West on February 28, he found the mortar flotilla waiting at anchor.[31]

Porter spent a few days at Key West organizing the squadron into three divisions, placing them under Lts. Watson Smith, Walter W. Queen, and K. Randolph Breese. He sent them out to maneuver and had barrel targets floated to give the gunners a little practice before sailing. Porter expected to be called into action as soon he reached the delta, and he was beginning to feel the weight of his commitment to demolish the forts in forty-eight hours.[32]

On February 12 Farragut and his flagship USS *Hartford* had stopped at Key West, where he found some of the mortar schooners, but he did not find Porter. He sailed to Havana three days later and observed huge quantities of Confederate cotton, rice, and turpentine being exchanged for British arms and ammunition. After leaving Havana he stopped again at Key West, noted Porter was still absent, and sailed for Ship Island off the coast of Biloxi, Mississippi.[33]

Since December the foster brothers had seen little of each other, but Porter knew what to expect. Farragut wanted the attack to be a surprise, giving the enemy no opportunity to improve their defenses. The plan sounded simple. From Ship Island Farragut would bring seventeen warships into the river and hold them at the Head of Passes. Porter would follow with the mortar boats, stringing them along the shore below the Head while engineers from the Coast Survey worked up to the forts, staked out the flotilla's position, and established firing coordinates. Porter would tow the schooners into position along the bank below Fort Jackson and in forty-eight hours disable the batteries. A barrier chain below the forts, supported by hulks, would be cut the night before the attack and the way opened for Farragut's warships to run the gauntlet and invest New Orleans from the river.

Porter sailed from Key West on March 6 and seven days later brought the mortar flotilla to anchor off Ship Island. He learned that Farragut could not get his heavier vessels over the bar. "We arrived here before the flag-officer was ready for us," Porter wrote Welles. "I regret to say there is no coal here at present, and . . . but one day's allowance for these steamers." In his first letter to Fox he added a little flavoring: "Farragut is zealous (they say) and will try to get them all over if he bursts his boiler, but I don't think they will lighten the ships much by merely scraping the outside blisters off."[34]

If Porter sounded skeptical, he had reason. There would be blisters of a different kind before Farragut got his squadron over the bar and into the river.

SEVEN

Porter's Bummers

When Porter came to anchor off Ship Island on March 11, 1862, he found the harbor cluttered with transports, supply vessels, a few of Farragut's warships, and most of the mortar flotilla. General Butler had not arrived, but three of his brigades had landed and pitched their tents on the flea-infested island. When Porter last passed Ship Island, it had been a flat, narrow strip of sand a half-mile wide and seven miles long inhabited mostly by gulls. The island lay about fifty miles east of Lake Pontchartrain, fifty miles west of Mobile Bay, and about seventy-five miles north of Pass à l'Outre. The Confederates had occupied the island and thrown up light fortifications but were driven away in September 1861 by a few shots fired from the USS *Massachusetts*. After that, Union blockaders moved in and established the most important base west of Florida.[1]

Farragut arrived off Ship Island on February 20, and as long as he remained there he kept the enemy guessing as to where he intended to strike. By land and by water, Mobile and Galveston seemingly offered better targets than New Orleans, and by maintaining an active blockade off all three ports Farragut concealed his intentions for nearly a

Comdr. David Dixon Porter, commanding the
mortar flotilla COURTESY NAVAL IMAGING CENTER

month. When Porter reached Ship Island, Confederate spies at Biloxi
were reporting a large assemblage of Union troops, supplies, and warships and predicting an attack on Mobile.[2]

Although Farragut did not enter the delta in force, he sent *Brooklyn*,
under Capt. Thomas T. Craven, into the river with a team from the
Coast Survey to take soundings and mark the channel off Pass à l'Outre.
Brooklyn grounded and had to be pulled off by *Hartford*. After three days
of toil neither vessel could get over the bar, so Farragut steamed around
the delta to Southwest Pass. *Brooklyn* drew only sixteen feet of water,
but the absence of traffic coming through the pass had allowed the
channel to fill. *Brooklyn* grounded at Southwest Pass but got off the bar
and into the river. Craven steamed up to Head of Passes and seized the
telegraph station. He cut the lines to New Orleans and ordered up all
the vessels that could get over the bar. When *Hartford* came up a few
hours later, *Kineo, Kennebec,* and *Winona* were already there.[3]

Fleet Capt. Henry H. Bell led the vessels upriver for the fleet's first
reconnaissance. Bell's gunboats chased two small steamers as far as

The Jump, but to avoid attention he kept out of sight of Forts Jackson and St. Philip. Pope's squadron had tried a similar tactic in the fall, so nobody in New Orleans considered the intrusion an imminent threat—although it caused consternation.[4]

But Farragut was not the same hapless commander as the orchestrator of Pope's Run. On March 5 he issued a general order with detailed instructions on how to prepare for action after entering the Mississippi River, and the order contained the words of a man who meant business. He stripped the sloops of superfluous spars and rigging and ordered guns mounted on the poop, forecastle, forward, and aft. He had every vessel trimmed by the head, so if she touched bottom she would not swing head downriver. If a ship became disabled, she was to fill her sails and back stern first. "No vessel," Farragut added, "must withdraw from battle under any circumstances without the consent of the flag-officer."[5]

Seeing how well everyone adhered to those orders had to wait until the first Confederate fire raft drifted downriver, but before that happened Farragut had other problems to solve. Not all of his fleet had arrived, and those that had were running out of coal. The army loaned Farragut eight hundred tons from their supply at Ship Island, a gesture Welles regretted as he did not want to be burdened by obligations to Butler. *Pensacola* arrived on March 3 with her commander, Capt. Henry W. Morris, reporting the engine in "lamentable condition." He carried a letter from Capt. James Alden reporting that *Richmond* had struck a Florida reef and lost part of her false keel before getting off. Despite the sorry condition of *Pensacola*'s engines, Farragut told Morris to run her into the river. Three days later *Richmond* arrived from Key West with *Kennebec*, under Lt. John H. Russell. *Colorado* (Capt. Theodorus Bailey) and *Mississippi* (Capt. Melancton Smith) were already off the passes, having provided the mainstay of the Gulf Blockading Squadron before Farragut's arrival.[6]

With his fleet at hand, Farragut grew impatient waiting for Porter and on March 4 left him a note: "You will find me at Pass à l'Outre or on the Mississippi, anxiously awaiting your arrival." A day later he wrote Fox: "The moment Porter arrives with his mortar fleet I will collect my vessels, which are pretty close around me, and dash up the river; but I do not wish to make a display until I am ready." But the dash up the river had another obstacle to surmount—mud.[7]

Colorado drew twenty-three feet, *Mississippi* and *Pensacola* eighteen each, and Farragut sent them back to Ship Island to be lightened. On March 17 he took the gunboat *Winona* to Ship Island to oversee the operation, and there he found Porter, who with Alden and Bailey convinced him that *Colorado* could not be stripped enough to float her over the bar. Crews began to lighten *Pensacola* and *Mississippi* of everything but the coal to carry them back to Southwest Pass. They would still have to be pulled through more than a foot of mud, but Porter said he could do it with his steamers.[8]

While Farragut agonized over lost time, news of the war drifted into headquarters at Ship Island. On March 9 two ironclads, USS *Monitor* and CSS *Virginia,* had fought to a standoff at Hampton Roads, Virginia, but not before the latter destroyed USS *Cumberland* and USS *Congress,* two of the Union's old wooden sailing warships. Rumors of two Confederate ironclads on the stocks at New Orleans worried Farragut. He felt an urgency to get to those vessels before they were finished, and every day he lost could make a difference.[9]

Not all the news was bad. In mid-February, far upriver, Forts Henry and Donelson had fallen to General Grant, and by the end of the month Nashville had surrendered, putting both Kentucky and western Tennessee under Union control. The losses alarmed the Crescent City. "There is a great fear of everything at New Orleans," Farragut reported. "I think they are becoming very much demoralized, and there could not be a better time for a blow to be struck by us."[10]

The March 6 edition of the *New Orleans Daily Delta* confirmed Farragut's belief, describing an instantaneous soaring of prices and the refusal by many shopkeepers to accept Confederate money without deep discounts. Speculators had bought up all the mourning goods in New Orleans because they expected the city to soon be "filled with grief and wailing"—not because of Farragut's fleet but because of Grant's penetration of northern Mississippi.[11]

Porter towed his flotilla through Pass à l'Outre and waited for Farragut's lightened vessels. On March 18 *Clifton* and *Westfield* arrived, and Porter put them to work. By the end of the day, all twenty-one mortar schooners lay at anchor off the abandoned village of Pilottown.[12]

On March 20 General Butler and his wife arrived at Ship Island with the 31st Massachusetts. Farragut met with the bald-headed, cross-eyed

Maj. Gen. Benjamin F. Butler at Ship Island
REPRINTED FROM JOHNSON AND BUEL, *BATTLES
AND LEADERS OF THE CIVIL WAR*

general the evening of March 24 and observed that Butler did not have any "plan of operations, but simply to follow in my wake and hold what I can take." Farragut underestimated the general's ability to create a tempest out of a little wake. The general, however, performed an unexpected and remarkable role that saved Farragut days, perhaps weeks, of delay. Instead of ballasting his transports with stones, Butler had loaded them with coal. When he offered it to Farragut, the flag officer reminded the general that army regulations prohibited the transfer of supplies to the navy. "I never read the army regulations," Butler replied, "and what is more I shan't, and then I shall not know if I am doing anything against them."[13]

Farragut returned to Head of Passes on the gunboat *Miami* to find Porter and his steamers hard at work off Southwest Pass. On March 24 Captain Alden got *Richmond* over the bar. After two unsuccessful attempts to enter Pass à l'Outre, *Richmond* had come around to Southwest Pass and, with help from Porter, crossed the bar. For Porter the real struggle had just begun. *Pensacola* and *Mississippi* still lay off the pass, and neither vessel could get into the river without help.[14]

A month had passed since the beginning of the Union buildup at Ship Island. From headquarters in New Orleans, Maj. Gen. Mansfield Lovell, who commanded the Confederate army in Louisiana and southern Mississippi, began to suspect trouble in the delta. The War Department had consistently warned him to prepare for an attack from Foote's flotilla above Memphis. Jefferson Davis and his advisors maintained the notion that wooden warships could not pass Forts Jackson and St. Philip. They still believed Farragut intended to attack Mobile and that the gunboats in the delta were merely a feint. Lovell did not agree with Davis, but when he attempted to rush reinforcements and heavier guns to the forts, Davis withdrew them and sent them north. To add to the depletion of Lovell's army, Secretary of the Navy Mallory, at Davis's bidding, sent Commodore George N. Hollins's fleet upriver to watch Foote, leaving no organized naval force at New Orleans to support the forts or contest the Union's presence in the delta. Farragut could not have wished for better circumstances, but he was not aware of Lovell's weaknesses, and he constantly worried that *Louisiana* or *Mississippi*, the two ironclads being built at New Orleans, would come down the river and dismantle his plans.[15]

Speed became as essential as watchfulness, and Porter shouldered the task of tugging the remainder of Farragut's squadron over the bar. First came *Pensacola*, 230 feet long and lightened but still drawing eighteen feet. Four of Porter's steamers, working in unison, could not slide her through the mud. *Mississippi*, with her huge paddle wheels, proved even more obstinate, and both vessels hung on the bar while a gale blew hard against the best efforts of the tugs.

On March 28 Farragut expressed his frustration: "We are still tugging at the *Pensacola* and *Mississippi* to get them over the bar, and I am much disheartened by the many trials without success, but live in the hopes that a southerly wind will raise the tide on the bar a few inches higher."[16]

Porter carried the lion's share of the nasty work. He lived with the job day and night, and as each day passed he blamed Morris of *Pensacola* and Smith of *Mississippi* for doing nothing to help. "I really don't know where the officers have been brought up," he confided to Fox. "They go wandering about here as if this river was deep all over. . . . Neither skill nor energy has been displayed in the management of [*Pensacola*]; there are too many 'can't do this' and 'can't do that' to expect much from her."[17]

After days of failure and frustration, Porter leveled his criticism at Farragut, whom he imagined to be listlessly waiting at Head of Passes for some miracle to bring his ships inside. Since Fox had encouraged Porter to spy on his foster brother, Porter seized the opportunity and penned a scathing letter to his co-conspirator:

> I never thought Farragut a Nelson or a Collingwood; I only consider him the best of his rank and so consider him still; but men of his age in a seafaring life are not fit for the command of important enterprises, they lack the vigor of youth. . . . I know you and the Secretary will feel chagrined when I tell you that the *Mississippi* is still on the bar, and likewise the *Pensacola*; the former half a mile inside and the latter hanging to two of the Mortar Steamers waiting her chance. . . . The obstacles are serious, and time has been lost, and a mistake of any kind can ruin us. I have not spoken six words to Farragut, so anxious have I been to get the ships over, and all my time has been spent on the bar.
>
> What his plans are I don't know. He talks . . . much at random at times and rather underrates the difficulties before him, without fairly comprehending them. I know what they are and appreciate them, and as he is impressible [I] hope to make him appreciate them also. . . . I have great hopes of the Mortars if all else fails. . . . The Flag will be urged to move at once, the moment we get the bar clear of ships; there will be nothing to prevent it except for the want of coal, which is a great stumbling block.[18]

On April 4 *Mississippi* scraped over the bar and paddled up the channel. She had dug herself deep in the mud by slashing her wheels on the bottom and creating a suction on the bar. *Pensacola* followed four days later, but to get her across Porter had to careen the vessel on her side until her prop came out of the water. Morris aggravated the situation when he insisted on taking her into the river without Porter's help and drove the vessel into a sunken hulk a hundred yards from the main channel. Both vessels anchored at Head of Passes, but the work had only begun. Neither vessel had coal, and all their guns, ammunition, and equipment had been removed. "I am at last able to announce that the *Mississippi* and *Pensacola* are over the bar," Farragut advised Welles, "thanks to the Tugs and the exertions of Captains Porter and [William B.] Renshaw and [Charles H.] Baldwin of the *Westfield* and *Clifton*. We had a strong Southerly wind yesterday, which raised the tide, and they brought the *Pensacola* over by main force."[19]

Porter was not so gracious, and on April 8, the same day Farragut penned his praises, Porter wrote Fox, "Again I say [Farragut] is physically and mentally the best of his rank, except perhaps Du Pont, Goldsborough and Foote. He is full of zeal and anxiety, but has no administrative qualities, wants stability, and loses too much time in talking." Perhaps to comfort the Navy Department, Porter added, "Everyone likes him personally" and "if I get all my shells here shortly, I think the game is ours." To his private journal he confided, "I assert that without my aid [*Mississippi* and *Pensacola*] would not have succeeded in getting across. Farragut never once thanked me publicly or privately." Farragut was more grateful than Porter realized, and even if the vessels had not been stuck in the mud for two weeks they would have been stuck in the river waiting for coal.[20]

Supplies arrived on April 8, and Porter moved the bomb boats upriver. He strung the flotilla along the bank above Head of Passes and put the bummers through gunnery practice while Farragut reconnoitered upriver.[21]

The original chain barrier below Fort Jackson had been swept away by a buildup of debris carried by unusually high water. Brig. Gen. Johnson K. Duncan, commanding Forts Jackson and St. Philip, reconstructed the barrier by stringing eight schooners across the river and tying them together with a heavy chain. The masts had been removed from the hulks, but the ratlines and cables had been left to trail astern to entangle the enemy's propellers. A severe windstorm on April 10 and 11 broke the cable again, scattering the hulks. Duncan had it repaired a few days later, but rather poorly.[22]

Clearing the way—the deck on one of the mortar schooners COURTESY U.S. ARMY MILITARY HISTORY INSTITUTE

Farragut knew the barrier had to be broken before his attack, and because breaking it would put the volunteers directly under the guns of Fort Jackson, he decided to give the bummers a few days to disable the fort's guns.

Reducing the forts was a more difficult task than Porter had anticipated. Before the war, General Barnard had spent many years strengthening the works. In a letter to Farragut, he described Fort Jackson as a bastioned pentagon, with fronts of 110 yards, built of brick and in good condition, with scarp walls twenty-two feet high and surrounded at the bottom by a wet ditch. Two curtains casemated for eight guns each bore on the river. The parapets of the two waterfronts contained twenty-two channel-bearing guns, with sixteen guns in barbette mounted on each of the other parapets. A covert way with two branches faced the channel and mounted another eight to nine guns. Barnard estimated that as many as 111 guns could be brought to bear upon the channel, and at the time he departed from the fort it contained 87 guns, although 20 of them covered the flanks. Below the fort had been added a water battery, which Barnard believed held as many as twenty-five guns, but Duncan had only been able to obtain eight. A bombproof had been built in the center of the fort to accommodate four to five hundred men, and most of the guns had been sheltered from attack.

Fort St. Philip lay seven hundred yards above Fort Jackson and on the opposite side of the river, which at that point was seven hundred yards wide. Built by the Spaniards, St. Philip was very old and had grown into an irregular quadrilateral work of about 150 by 100 yards. Barnard believed the fort mounted seventy-two channel-bearing guns —many with furnaces nearby to heat shot. From a point in the river one and a half miles from the lowest battery at Fort Jackson to a point one and a half miles from the uppermost battery at Fort St. Philip, Barnard believed that Farragut's ships would be under fire from as many as 125 guns for as long as thirty minutes. Most of the forts' guns, however, were short-range smoothbores, enabling Porter to move his mortar flotilla in range of Fort Jackson but not Fort St. Philip. The bummers could concentrate their fire on Jackson and stay out of range of most of Duncan's guns.[23]

Porter had brought a detail from the Coast Survey with him, and on April 13 Ferdinand H. Gerdes and four assistants took *Sachem* upriver and began five days of laborious work under fire from roving sharpshooters. They staked out an anchorage for each bomb boat and laid out firing coordinates. While Gerdes's crew worked, Porter cruised the river to drive away snipers and draw the fire of the forts. On April 18 Gerdes presented Porter with a detailed map of the river from The Jump to the parapets and water batteries at Fort Jackson and Fort St. Philip. It showed the position of the hulks, the chain across the river, and every distinguishing object along seven miles of the river.[24]

On April 15 Porter towed three schooners into position three thousand yards from Fort Jackson for a test. After firing several rounds, he wrote, "I found the range satisfactory and had no reason to doubt the durability of the mortar beds and foundation. I received but little encouragement from anyone about the success of the mortars, it having been confidently predicted that 'the bottoms of the schooners would drop out at the tenth fire.' "[25]

On April 16 Farragut moved the fleet upriver and asked Porter to begin the bombardment. The thirteen-man mortar crews had been busy drilling for days, ramming home 20-pound powder charges, cutting fuses, loading 216-pound shells into the chowder pots, and firing at targets placed in the swamps. As the gun went off, the crews stood on tiptoe with their mouths and ears open to lessen "the shock of the discharge and the concussion on the ear." After firing the first shell, Acting Master George W. Brown, commanding the schooner *Dan Smith,* surveyed the deck and found the mortar had jumped off the turntable, "driving the rear of the carriage into the water-ways, and listing the vessel about 10 degrees." The concussion shook doors off their hinges, and the bummers lost another day adding breechings to the chowder pots.[26]

When the boats started up the river on the morning of April 18, their masts had been camouflaged with a latticework of bushes and small trees to blend with the foliage at their firing posts alongshore. The schooners anchored under the lee of a thickly wooded, vine-choked rise where they could lie unseen along the west bank and lob shells into Fort Jackson. The woods were just low enough to allow observers in the tops to give a fair account of where the projectiles landed without being seen from the fort. Smoke rising from the mortars gave gunners in the fort something to shoot at, but the trajectory had to pass through an impenetrable jungle of woods and vines. Porter, however, placed one of his three divisions on the east bank of the river, where there was no protection, and he soon discovered he could not keep it there.[27]

At daybreak on April 18, Porter's steamers towed the schooners upriver, four at a time, and the bummers edged into position along the banks and anchored by the markers set by the Coast Survey. The day had come for Porter to deliver on his promise to Welles, and his forty-eight-hour clock began to tick. So also might he have remembered his last words to Fox when he wrote, "I have great hopes for the Mortars." William C. Holton, a seaman on *Hartford,* watched the bummers file smartly into position and declared, "They looked very pretty as they ranged along the shore in line of battle, with their flagship, the *Harriet Lane,* at their head."[28]

Porter had divided his flotilla into three divisions at Key West, and this order had not changed. Lt. Watson Smith commanded the seven schooners of the first division: *Norfolk Packet, Oliver H. Lee, Para, C. P.*

Williams, Arletta, William Bacon, and *Sophronia*. He posted his vessels along the west bank and ahead of Lt. K. Randolph Breese's third division, which consisted of the schooners *Horace Beals, John Griffith, Sarah Bruen, Racer, Henry Janes, Dan Smith, Sea Foam,* and *Adolph Hugel*. Lt. Walter W. Queen's second division occupied the exposed east bank and contained the schooners *T. A. Ward, M. J. Carlton, Matthew Vassar, George Mangham, Orvetta,* and *Sydney C. Jones*. All the vessels lay in line and within a boat's length of each other. Smith's first division was about 2,850 yards from Fort Jackson and 3,600 yards from Fort St. Philip. Queen's second division lay along the eastern shore, 3,680 yards from Fort Jackson. Fort St. Philip was in range for Smith's and Queen's divisions, but Farragut wanted to concentrate the first day's firing on Fort Jackson.[29]

As each schooner anchored at her post, five gunboats—*Cayuga, Iroquois, Kennebec, Sciota,* and *Wissahickon*—steamed above the flotilla to draw the fire of the forts. The mortars opened, first one and then another, until a hail of shells, fired from each boat at ten-minute intervals, rained down upon Fort Jackson. Acting Master Amos R. Langthorne of *C. P. Williams* was among the first to get into position and opened at 8:00 A.M. from the western shore. *Sea Foam,* far to the rear, did not get into action until six hours later.[30]

At 9:00 A.M. General Duncan's observers began their count, and when the bummers ceased fire ten hours later, 2,997 shots had been tallied. Porter had positioned his bomb boats well. Duncan's gunners complained of being unable to elevate their guns and of the inferiority of their powder. Although Queen's division lay in sight along the eastern bank, Duncan discovered he could barely reach them with his best guns. "Even our nearest gun," he lamented, "a 10-inch seacoast mortar, would not reach his boats with the heaviest charges." Instead of concentrating on Porter's schooners, Fort Jackson's gunners shot at Farragut's roving gunboats.[31]

Had Duncan's batteries been more attentive, they might not have shifted their long guns away from Queen's exposed schooners. Commander Bell, who occupied a ringside seat at the commencement of the bombardment, recorded the "enemy firing beautifully and with effect. Struck two or more mortar boats and shot falling close to them and beyond [the] farthest vessel from the fort."[32]

Mortar schooners engaging Fort Jackson REPRINTED
FROM JOHNSON AND BUEL, *BATTLES AND LEADERS OF
THE CIVIL WAR*

Queen's schooner, *T. A. Ward,* lay at the head of the division and about thirty-nine hundred yards from Fort Jackson. Soon after he opened, a shot from the fort ripped through the deck and plunged into the water six inches above the waterline. Porter ordered Queen to drop downriver three hundred yards, taking with him the next three vessels. Moments later, another shot passed through the port bow of *George Mangham* and lodged in the mortar bed.[33]

Porter watched the bombardment from the deck of *Harriet Lane,* keeping one eye on his gunboats and the other on Fort Jackson. Queen's division drew the heaviest fire, and to distract the enemy, Lt.

John Guest took *Owasco* to within twenty-eight hundred yards of the fort and in less than three hours fired most of his 11-inch shells. Porter came on board and ordered him to withdraw. Later, seeing that Queen's division was still suffering from enemy fire, Porter asked Farragut for permission to move the schooners across the river. At 6:00 P.M. the bummers ceased fire, and in the morning Queen transferred his division to the west bank.[34]

Queen withdrew with regret. He could see flames leaping from inside Fort Jackson and knew there was damage. Unlike the divisions on the western shore, his men could watch the trajectory of each shot, follow it into the fort, and make adjustments quickly. Although the two divisions on the western shore were closer to the fort, observers in the tops had a difficult time following the shells. The discharge stunned them, listed the vessel over, and then enveloped the spotters in a cloud of smoke. If they were then able to pick out a descending shell, they could not be certain who shot it. Referring to the firing from the fort, Queen admitted that the "shot came around us in immense numbers, yet not one man was even wounded during the first day's engagement." The only casualty occurred in Smith's division on the opposite shore when the schooner *Arletta* took a shot that knocked the trucks off the mortar and wounded a seaman.[35]

The fire inside Fort Jackson grew intense, spreading from the men's quarters to the bombproofed citadel, and at 5:00 P.M. Duncan brought the gunners down from the parapets to help put it out. "When the enemy ceased firing," Duncan declared, "it was one burning mass, greatly endangering the magazines, which at one time were reported to be on fire. Many of the men and most of the officers lost their bedding and clothing. . . . The mortar fire was accurate and terrible, many of the shells falling everywhere within the fort and disabling some of our best guns."[36]

Had Porter not ceased fire at 6:00 P.M., and had he kept Queen's division on the eastern bank for another day, he may have realized his promise to Welles. One more shell, properly placed, might have exploded the magazine and ended Duncan's resistance. His men were badly demoralized, but during the night they extinguished the fire and repaired most of the guns, and by morning the fort was almost as strong as before.

Porter realized his mistake too late. In his report to Welles two weeks later he wrote, "Had I known the extent of the fire I should have proceeded all night with the bombardment, but the crews had had nothing to eat or drink since daylight. . . . A little after sunset I ordered the firing to cease, and made the only mistake that occurred during the bombardment." Several years later he was less honest when he wrote an article for *Century Magazine* and said, "During the night, in order to allow the men to rest, we slackened our fire, and only sent a shell once every half hour." The bummers fired no shells that night, but should have.[37]

On the night of April 18, as the powder-smeared bummers crawled below deck to catch a few winks before morning, Porter still had twenty-four hours to keep his promise to "Grandfather" Welles.

EIGHT

Farragut Scores a Victory

On Good Friday, April 18, word of Porter's bombardment spread rapidly through the streets of New Orleans. Curious churchgoers joined nervous crowds gathering on Canal Street or outside the St. Charles Hotel where General Lovell and Governor Moore occupied suites. Anxious for news, people posted themselves at the levee to listen for the sound of gunfire fifty air miles away. The *New Orleans Bee* discounted the public's concern, cautioning against "such a high degree of anxiety." The widely read *Daily Delta* felt differently and warned, "New Orleans is in serious peril. It is well for our citizens to know these facts and to look at them squarely—to face them like men. . . . The defense of the river should at this conjuncture be the paramount object of their concern. Upon its defense hangs the fate of New Orleans and the Valley of the Mississippi"—a matter Jefferson Davis and Secretary Mallory seemed to have overlooked. Prodding General Lovell and Commander Mitchell to take action, the *Delta* added, "Let not history look back with scorn upon the puny efforts of New Orleans to defend herself."[1]

Porter's bombardment created anxiety in the Crescent City, and workmen doubled their efforts to mobilize the town's two ironclads.

Louisiana had been launched on February 6, but she had no motive power and not all of her guns were installed. *Mississippi* was afloat but unfinished, looking much like a huge raft stacked with lumber. The salvation of New Orleans depended upon activating the ironclads before Farragut passed the forts, and Porter felt a heavy commitment to make the passage as bloodless as possible.[2]

After the first day's bombardment, night settled along the river, but Porter remained restless. Fire rafts drifted down from above, lighting up the river, but they all went aground before they reached the schooners. Two rafts lit up the eastern bank near one of the hulks supporting the chain. Porter saw them burning and sent Julius H. Kroehl, a submarine specialist, upriver to examine the obstruction and prepare to blow it up the following night. At midnight Kroehl took two boats up to the barrier and observed that each hulk contained two chains—one fastened to the bow, which faced upstream, and the other amidships. He worked across the river, hulk by hulk, until the moon rose. Then he returned to the fleet and reported himself ready to break the chain. Porter was satisfied. If the forts were silenced on schedule, Farragut would not have to worry about the chain.[3]

At 6:30 A.M. on April 19 the bummers reopened on Fort Jackson, and two hours later Commander Bell sent a message down to Farragut asking for gunboats to draw the enemy's fire away from the mortars. Every time a gunboat nosed around the bend, both forts opened on her. *Oneida* worked in closer, and a shot from her pivot gun knocked down the flagstaff in Fort Jackson. Porter's heart skipped a beat when he heard cheers, looked up, and saw the flag down. A few minutes later another was hoisted, and *Oneida,* for her insolence, took two 10-inch shots near her pivot gun, wounding nine men.[4]

After watching the glow of fires raging inside Fort Jackson late into the night, Porter was both surprised and dismayed at the intensity of the enemy's gunfire. At 10:00 A.M. a shot from the fort crashed through the trees, struck the quarterdeck of *Maria J. Carlton,* snapped a beam, plowed through the magazine, and plunged out the bottom, wounding three men. The schooner filled and sank. Late in the day a shell burst near *Norfolk Packet*'s masthead, wounding the carpenter's mate and damaging the rigging, but the rest of the flotilla survived the day without serious damage.[5]

Fort Jackson's artillery had little success penetrating the dense woods screening the bomb boats, but the bummers wasted much of their ammunition. Porter stepped up the firing, and some of the boats lobbed shells at five-minute intervals. The smoke and concussion made it impossible for spotters to follow the shots, and many of them landed outside the fort. Bad fuses added to the problem, and shells exploded before they reached the target. At midday Porter stopped trying to time the bursts and ordered the bummers to insert full-length fuses. To those inside the fort the effect resembled an earthquake. The projectiles descended twenty feet into the soft, wet ground and exploded, lifting up great geysers of earth. The bursting shells buried a few men but did little damage to the parapets.[6]

At 4:00 P.M. the bummers went into rotation, each division firing in turn until midnight. But there was no flag of surrender flying from the staff at Fort Jackson, and Porter's forty-eight hours expired. He was surprised by Duncan's resistance, but had he been able to see inside the fort he would have been encouraged. Duncan reported the interior "very much cut up." Seven guns had been disabled, two of them in the important water battery.[7]

On Ship Island, sixty miles away, Sarah Butler heard the faint rumble of distant artillery, but she could not imagine the sound carrying all the way from the lower Mississippi, where she knew her husband was. She penned her thoughts to her daughter Blanche: "I think the firing must be at Mobile, some vessels, maybe, trying to run the blockade."[8]

The same rumble of artillery, whether heard or imagined, jarred the nerves of New Orleans. Fresh signs of panic gripped the city. The *True Delta* attempted to rally public support, warning that "the hour is quickly approaching when the question will be solved whether or not New Orleans will be a conquered city. The issue is now to DO or DIE. Who will be so craven as to falter?" The question was probably directed at General Lovell, from whom the public expected more protection than he had the means to deliver.[9]

Farragut, concerned by the intensity of artillery fire still coming from Fort Jackson, decided to give Porter more time. Fort St. Philip had escaped punishment and remained undamaged. At 4:00 A.M. on Easter Sunday, April 20, the bummers opened from the third division, followed at two-hour intervals by the rest of the flotilla, and once again shells crashed upon the parapets of Fort Jackson.[10]

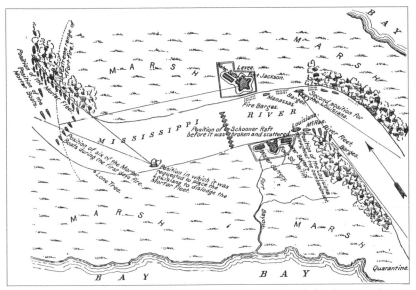

Diagram of the bombardment of Forts Jackson and St. Philip from April 16 to April 24 REPRINTED FROM *OFFICIAL RECORDS OF THE UNION AND CONFEDERATE NAVIES*

Porter began to doubt the efficacy of his mortars when a mud-bespattered civilian in a red cap and shirt appeared alongshore and hailed *Norfolk Packet*. The skipper listened to his tale and took him to Porter. The man claimed to be a Pennsylvanian working with Dan Rice's traveling show when he was impressed into the Confederate army and sent against his wishes to Fort Jackson. There he stole a skiff, crossed the moat, and, by following flashes from the mortars, made his way through the swamps. The deserter described a scene of immense destruction inside Fort Jackson, claiming hundreds of shells had smashed casemates, ripped up parapets, burned buildings, threatened magazines, and cut the levees. Porter greeted the news with some doubt, but he was eager to believe it. He took the man to *Hartford* and deposited him with Farragut. "After bombarding the fort for three days," Porter admitted, "I began to despair of taking it, and indeed began to lose my confidence in the mortars," but after questioning the deserter "we went to work with renewed vigor and never flagged to the last."[11]

Farragut was anxious to get up the river before the bummers consumed their ammunition, and after listening attentively to the deserter's story he signaled his commanders to *Hartford* for a conference. Earlier, General Butler had come on board and paced the deck of *Hartford* waiting for Farragut to put the fleet in motion.[12]

Porter returned upriver, but he had formulated his own plans for the capture of the forts. Farragut, however, had drafted orders before calling the meeting and laid out neatly detailed charts for everyone to digest before asking for comments. Porter had campaigned behind Farragut's back and found a few senior officers who agreed with him. One of them, Comdr. James Alden, volunteered to propose Porter's plan at the conference. Midway through the council Alden asked permission to read it, and Farragut agreed to listen.

Porter's proposal agreed with Farragut's plan in three aspects—that the barrier chain across the river not be cut until the time of attack, that the attack be made at night, and that the effort be supported by mortar fire. Porter, however, was concerned about the safety of his flotilla and feared that Farragut considered them expendable. Conscious of the schooners' vulnerability if the Union fleet passed the forts and left them behind, Porter suggested the forts be captured first. He knew of the enemy's three ironclads—*Manassas, Louisiana,* and *Mississippi*—and, if left alone, he envisioned the destruction of his flotilla. He suggested that, if Farragut chose to pass the forts rather than capture them, some of the schooners be towed through the gauntlet and taken upriver to support the attack on New Orleans.[13]

Farragut's plan, however, consisted of one objective—getting past the forts as quickly as possible and with minimum damage. Porter's notion of anchoring the fleet off Fort Jackson was a recipe for disaster unless the forts had been sufficiently disabled and were unable to defend themselves, which, at the time of Farragut's conference, was not the case. Porter also suggested waiting for Butler to bring up two thousand infantry to flank Fort St. Philip, for it had not been damaged. When Alden finished reading Porter's proposal, he folded it and returned it to his pocket. Commander Bell suggested that Porter's proposition be given to Farragut as part of the conference record, whereupon Alden handed it to Farragut.

Unlike Porter, Farragut saw no harm in leaving the bomb boats behind. If the fleet reached New Orleans, the forts would be isolated and forced to surrender. Although he could not be certain of the strength of the Confederate navy, he had seen nothing to fear, including ironclads, as deserters had spoken of their unreadiness. He saw no reason to wait for Butler to flank Fort St. Philip and believed the forts would be less inclined to settle for a siege if they were isolated from New Orleans. He agreed with Porter that the attack be made at night and advised his officers that plans were already afoot to break the barrier.[14]

Farragut summarized the conference by issuing a general order: "The flag-officer, having heard all the opinions expressed by different commanders, is of the opinion that whatever is to be done will have to be done quickly, or we will be again reduced to a blockading squadron without any means of carrying on the bombardment, as we have nearly expended all the shells and fuzes and material for making cartridges." He praised some of Porter's suggestions without adopting them and settled the role of Butler's participation by saying, "The forts should be run, and when a force is once above the forts to protect the troops, they should be landed at Quarantine from the Gulf side by bringing them through the bayou, and then our forces should move up the river, mutually aiding each other, as it can be done to advantage."[15]

Late on the night of April 20, Commander Bell, who also served as Farragut's fleet captain, took two gunboats, *Pinola* and *Itasca*, to the barrier chain and broke it. Kroehl, Porter's explosives expert, joined the mission, but when his petard failed to explode, sailors from the gunboats climbed aboard the hulks and knocked away the bits holding the chain, which then dribbled into the river.[16]

The Confederates cut loose several fire rafts, and at 2:30 A.M. one drifted among Farragut's fleet, causing great confusion as crews worked to weigh anchor and get out of the way. As the raft passed *Hartford* and *Richmond,* a strong wind kicked up flames that towered mast high. *Kineo* collided with *Sciota* and became entangled, and both vessels drifted into *Mississippi. Sciota* caught fire, and when *Iroquois* attempted to pull off the raft she collided with *Westfield.*[17]

The episode embodied some of the manifestations of the panic that had precipitated Pope's Run, but there was no Confederate navy to

follow up the one-raft attack. On April 11 Secretary Mallory had recalled Commodore Hollins for the transgression of responding to a plea
from Lovell to bring his flotilla back to the city to help drive Farragut
out of the river. Had Mallory listened to Hollins rather than to Davis,
Farragut may have had his own "run" to contend with in the early hours
of April 21. Mallory could not have contrived a better way to ensure the
success of Farragut's effort than relieving Hollins two weeks before the
Union attack.[18]

While Farragut refined his tactics, the bummers resumed their bombardment of Fort Jackson, and Duncan continued to demonstrate a
show of resistance. Meanwhile, tugs towed *Louisiana* downriver and
cast her loose above Fort St. Philip. Duncan greeted the arrival of the
ironclad "with extreme pleasure" and urged that she be positioned
below St. Philip. *Louisiana*'s engines were inoperable and Mitchell
refused, but Duncan insisted she be moved because without her he had
no way of engaging Farragut's vessels before they rounded the bend and
came in sight of Jackson's water battery. Duncan also wanted *Louisiana*
below because her gunners would have a clear view of Porter's mortars.
Mitchell would not cooperate, and as the night of Farragut's attack
approached, relations between Duncan and Mitchell could not have
been worse.[19]

By April 21 the bummers were having their own problems. Porter
reported them "overcome with fatigue." He had seen his "commanders
and crew lying fast asleep on deck with a mortar on board next to them
thundering away and shaking everything around them like an earthquake." The schooners had lost their camouflage, and *Para,* the head-
most vessel, had been struck in her upper works. A shell tore through
Norfolk Packet's deck, another shredded her rigging, and a third wounded a man. Porter moved three of the schooners farther back.[20]

On April 22 Duncan transferred everything afloat to Mitchell, including his own River Defense Fleet of lightly armed steamers commanded by quasi-military riverboat captains. If he hoped the gesture
would induce Mitchell to move *Louisiana* below Fort St. Philip, he was
disappointed, and Fort Jackson suffered another day of heavy bombardment. With shells battering the fort day and night, his men, jaded and
threadbare, began to manifest signs of resignation.[21]

Farragut also tired of the bombardment, and when Porter came
aboard looking frazzled, Farragut said calmly, "We are wasting ammuni-

tion and time. We will fool around down here until we have nothing left to fight with. I'm ready to run those forts now, tonight."

Porter asked for another day, and Farragut replied, "Allright, David. Go at 'em again and we'll see what happens tomorrow."[22]

On April 23 Duncan moved two heavy rifled guns into a makeshift water battery below Fort St. Philip. The guns annoyed the head of Porter's column until one of the schooners dropped a shell into the battery and disabled it. At the time, Porter thought the battery had only run out of ammunition and expected more trouble from it. He went upriver to find Farragut, and, according to B. S. Osbon, Porter looked "downcast but still anxious to continue the bombardment."

Farragut offered to "demonstrate the practical value of mortar work" and, turning to his signal officer, said, "Mr. Osbon, get me two small flags, a white one and a red one, and go to the mizzen topmasthead and watch where the shells fall. If inside the fort, wave the red flag. If outside, wave the white one." To Porter he said, "You recommended Mr. Osbon to me, so you will have confidence in his observations. Now go [to] your vessel, select a tallyman, and when all is ready, Mr. Osbon will wave his flags and the count will begin."

Osbon climbed into the crow's nest and situated himself to get the best view of Fort Jackson. "It kept me busy waving the little flags," he recalled, "and I had to watch very closely not to make a mistake. On the deck, 'way aft, Farragut sat, watching the . . . flags and occasionally asking for the score. The roar became perfectly deafening, and the ship trembled like an aspen." When the tally sheet was footed up, the "outs" had it by a large majority.

When Porter returned to *Hartford,* Farragut handed him the tally sheet and said, "There, David, there's the score. I guess we'll go up the river tonight."[23]

Porter admitted the men could not hold out much longer, and Farragut issued orders for the fleet to move that night, but at the last moment he was forced to delay it as repairs were made in the aftermath of the fire raft attack.[24]

On the afternoon of April 23 Farragut visited each ship to ascertain that every commander understood his orders. He had divided his seventeen warships into three divisions and placed Capt. Theodorus Bailey in charge of the first, himself in charge of the center, and Bell in charge of the third. Bailey would lead the first division's eight vessels

through the broken obstructions. Once he cleared, Farragut would follow with *Hartford, Brooklyn,* and *Richmond.* Bell, with the last six vessels, would fall in behind *Richmond* and, after passing the barrier, press
with every ounce of steam to get above Fort St. Philip. Farragut knew
the guns of both forts bore upon the center of the river, and he cautioned his commanders to stay close to Fort St. Philip. What Farragut
overlooked was an eddy that ran upriver adjacent to the fort, an eddy
strong enough to fool some commanders into thinking they had been
turned around in the smoke of battle and were steaming in the wrong
direction.[25]

Farragut placed Porter's flotilla below the barrier, but he gave him
plenty to do. At 2:00 A.M. Porter would bring *Harriet Lane, Westfield,
Owasco, Clifton,* and *Miami* around the bend and anchor just below
Fort Jackson's water battery. The old sailing sloop-of-war *Portsmouth*
and her sixteen 8-inch guns had been towed up from the passes and
attached to Porter's squadron. As soon as Bailey's first division came
under fire, Porter was to engage the water battery with all six gunboats
and the entire mortar fleet.[26]

Mitchell had twenty-two vessels above the forts to dispute Farragut's
passage, but his entire squadron contained only thirty-three guns,
mostly 32-pounders. *Hartford's* 9-inch guns could throw more weight
than Mitchell's squadron, and most of *Louisiana's* guns had been mis-
mounted and could not be fired. The task of repulsing Farragut depended mainly on the marksmanship of the gunners in the forts. Duncan
had repaired most of his artillery, and Porter's seven-day bombardment
had not so much as scratched Fort St. Philip. Duncan expected to be
attacked that night, as he had seen Union boats setting white markers
along the bank of the river below St. Philip. He urged Mitchell to keep
the river lit up with fire rafts, but at midnight the river was still cloaked
in darkness and covered by a slight mist. Mitchell seemed determined
to ignore every request made by his army counterpart.[27]

At five minutes before 2:00 A.M. Farragut signaled the fleet to move
into position. Porter crept forward but stopped when he observed confusion in the rear of the flag officer's column. *Pensacola,* commanded by
Captain Morris, reported her anchor snagged. "Damn that fellow!" Farragut grumbled. "I don't believe he wants to start."[28]

Mortar schooners engaging the water battery the night of Farragut's attack
REPRINTED FROM JOHNSON AND BUEL, *BATTLES AND LEADERS OF THE CIVIL WAR*

Other vessels muddled in the darkness as they fell into formation. At 3:00 A.M. Porter moved quietly forward, keeping to the shadows on the western bank. He waited, watching for Bailey's division to pass to starboard. Forty minutes elapsed before he saw the outline of *Cayuga* leading the division to the broken barrier. Capt. William B. Robertson's artillery opened at the water battery, its lurid flashes spewing great clouds of smoke across the river. "Not a torch had been applied to a single fire-raft," Robertson declared, "and not one of them had been started from their moorings." Porter replied with a broadside from *Harriet Lane,* and in an instant all hell broke loose on the lower Mississippi.[29]

The Union column steamed ahead, their broadsides silent. Men lay flat on the deck as shells whistled through the tops. Salvos roared from Forts Jackson and St. Philip, and a dense, acrid smoke rolled down the river. Riding at the head of the column, *Cayuga* sheered to starboard and fired her port guns at Fort Jackson, and as she came abeam Fort St. Philip she fired the others. Young Lt. George H. Perkins steered *Cayuga* close under the walls of St. Philip, and for fifteen minutes gunners battered the old bastion with grape and canister. Smothered by smoke and blinded by the flash of guns, Perkins kept the wheel steady. Carried along by the eddy off St. Philip, he suddenly emerged from the smoke and found himself in the midst of Mitchell's fleet. "After passing the last battery and thinking we were clear," he recalled, "I looked back for some of our vessels, and my heart jumped into my mouth, when I found I could not see a *single one*. I thought they all must have been sunk by the forts. Then looking ahead I saw eleven of the enemy's gunboats coming down upon us, and it seemed as if we were '*gone*' for sure."[30]

But the other sixteen vessels of Farragut's fleet were still encased in smoke and working their way up the river. Porter watched as they crossed through the break in the barrier, but as each became swallowed in the smoke he could only see the flash of their broadsides or catch an occasional glimpse of a spar. *Hartford* unfurled the Stars and Stripes as she disappeared "into the black folds ahead, through which the flash and thunder came back incessantly." Had he been on *Hartford* he would have heard Farragut remind Osbon that ships did not fly colors at night. Osbon, who had an answer for everything, replied, "Flag Officer, I thought if we were to go down, it would look well to have our colors flying above the water." Farragut had no time to reply as shells ripped through the tops. Thinking Farragut had ordered out the colors, *Brooklyn* and *Richmond* followed suit, presenting the enemy with not one, but three tempting targets.[31]

As *Brooklyn* approached the barrier, she sheered to fire a broadside at Jackson's water battery but collided with *Kineo,* the seventh of the eight gunboats in the first division. Farragut had intended to hold the center division back until the first cleared the barrier, but he moved *Hartford* ahead prematurely and drew *Brooklyn* and *Richmond* into the path of Bailey's division.[32]

The stacking up of Bailey's vessels had been caused by *Pensacola* under Captain Morris, the second vessel in the first division. Instead of running at full speed as ordered, Morris hesitated in the smoke, fumbled about firing broadsides, and stacked up the rest of the fleet behind him. The stalling of the first division explains why Perkins, when *Cayuga* got above the forts, saw no vessel behind him and believed the fleet had been destroyed. After *Brooklyn* collided with *Kineo,* Captain Craven became disoriented, smashed into a hulk west of where the chain had

Farragut's fleet passing the forts, April 14, 1862 REPRINTED FROM JOHNSON AND BUEL, *BATTLES AND LEADERS OF THE CIVIL WAR*

been cut, steamed toward Jackson, and collided with an unlit fire raft. In the confusion *Brooklyn's* anchor tore loose and snagged on the bottom, leaving her in plain sight of Jackson's guns. From his ringside seat by the barrier, Porter observed *Brooklyn* in trouble and steamed over to give assistance. He told Craven to pass under Fort Jackson and go up the river. Craven did so, but after he got above he observed *Hartford* grounded and in flames under the guns of Fort St. Philip. He swung *Brooklyn* across the river to offer aid but was rammed by *Manassas*. By the time Craven reached the other side, *Hartford* had backed off the bank and gone upriver.[33]

Because of delays caused by *Pensacola*, Bell's third division did not get under way until the first dull streaks of dawn broke dimly on the eastern horizon. *Sciota* and *Iroquois* followed behind *Richmond* and quickly disappeared into the smoke, but *Kennebec*, commanded by Lt. John H. Russell, struck one of the hulks and became entangled with a raft. After freeing himself Russell attempted to get above the forts, but by then it was daylight. Driven back by Duncan's artillery, he steamed downriver and joined Porter's flotilla.[34]

Pinola passed the forts safely, but the last two vessels, *Itasca* and *Winona,* never had a chance. A 42-pounder from Fort Jackson struck *Itasca's* boiler and set her adrift. Her commander, Lt. Charles H. B. Caldwell, eased through the barrier and brought her to anchor beside *Harriet Lane.* By the time *Winona,* commanded by Lt. Edward T. Nichols, got untangled from a collision with *Itasca,* sunlight fell upon the river, and every gunner in the forts concentrated his fire on her. With three men killed and several shots through his hull, Nichols came about and joined Porter.[35]

Of seventeen warships running the gauntlet, fourteen met at dawn off the village of Quarantine. Artillery fire from the forts had been high, ripping through the tops of the squadron. Every vessel suffered damage, but only *Varuna* could not make the trip to New Orleans. Sunk by *Governor Moore,* under Lt. Beverley Kennon, she lay on the bottom with only her topgallant forecastle above the water.[36]

Porter could not see the naval battle above the forts—he could only hear the guns. Farragut's warships decimated Mitchell's squadron with little loss in Union lives. The feared *Louisiana* never became a factor in the fight, but she still lay above Fort St. Philip, undamaged but for a small hole in her deck, and for all Porter knew, *Manassas* could be somewhere upriver and still armed and dangerous. As skies brightened, he could see the smoke of ships burning above Fort St. Philip. He could not tell whose vessels they were, but wreckage floating down the river contained nothing familiar. At dawn Porter signaled the squadron to retire. The mortars ceased fire, and the gunboats dropped below the bend in the river, joined by *Itasca, Kennebec,* and *Winona.* Having three of Farragut's gunboats gave him comfort, but everything had become uncommonly quiet. Porter wondered—was it over, or must he now face the ironclads?[37]

For the answer, he did not have long to wait.

Surrender
of the Lower
Mississippi

The answer to one of Porter's questions came at 7:00 A.M. on April 24. His bummers were eating breakfast when the guns of St. Philip opened. Some wondered if Farragut had returned to enfilade the fort from upriver—or was it a crippled Union vessel adrift? Porter sent a gunboat to investigate, but back it came in a hurry. "The celebrated ram *Manassas* was coming out to attack us, and sure enough," Porter declared, "there she was apparently steaming alongshore ready to pounce upon the defenseless mortar vessels." Two gunboats opened on her, but Porter soon learned the ram could harm no one, as she was on fire and slowly sinking. "Her only gun went off, and emitting flames through her bow port, like some huge animal, she gave a plunge and disappeared under the water." Soon three more Confederate gunboats, all smoldering wrecks, drifted by. The gunfire from St. Philip remained a mystery until a few days later, when the Louisiana Artillery admitted firing seventy-five times at the sinking ram.[1]

Porter, feeling more comfortable about his situation, sent *Owasco*, commanded by Lt. John Guest, under a flag of truce to demand the surrender of Forts Jackson and St. Philip. At the broken barrier, two shots from Jackson plunged into the water off *Owasco's* bow. Guest sheered across the river, only to have a shot from St. Philip pass over-head and splash abaft. He withheld fire and returned to *Harriet Lane,* commenting that the forts "did not seem willing to receive a flag of truce." An hour later a boat from Fort Jackson came down the river and apologized for the firing. Guest met the boat and asked permission to go up to the fort with Porter's demand. This was refused, but the officer of the boat agreed to take the terms back to his commanding officer. Guest waited above the barrier for an answer, and an hour later Lt. Col. Edward Higgins, who was nominally in charge of Fort Jackson, replied that the demand was "inadmissible."[2]

Porter put the bummers to work, and for two hours they lofted shells into Fort Jackson. At 5:30 P.M., however, he believed *Louisiana* had crossed to Fort Jackson under her own steam, and he sent most of the schooners to Pilottown.[3]

The answer to another of Porter's questions arrived on April 25, when Comdr. Charles S. Boggs came around from Quarantine Bay on one of Butler's steamers with a message from Farragut. "We had a rough time of it," he wrote, "but thank God the number of killed and wounded was very small. . . . We have destroyed all but two of the gunboats, and those will have to surrender with the forts. I intend to follow up my success and push for New Orleans and then come down and attend to the forts; so you hold them in statu quo until I get back." Farragut's men had cut the telegraph wires at Quarantine, so he added, "I think if you send a flag of truce and demand their surrender, they will do it, for their inter-course with the city is cut off." Then, in a sincere gesture of apprecia-tion toward his foster brother, Farragut wrote, "You supported us nobly."[4]

Porter replied, "You left at the forts four steamers and the [*Louisiana*]; they are mounting guns on it, and 1,000 men are at work on it. She is unhurt and moves about with the stream. How fast she is, I don't know. One of the steamers is ironclad on the bow. The *McRae* is also at the fort. I sent a summons to surrender, but it was politely declined."[5]

Although *Louisiana* had steam, she could not navigate. Duncan wanted her moved to the opposite shore, as he expected Farragut to attack the forts before going to New Orleans. Because so few of his guns could bear upriver, he wanted the ironclad positioned just below the upper bend, where she could fire upon the Union vessels before they rounded into sight. Duncan had reason to worry because Farragut had left some of his gunboats at Quarantine, and periodically one came down the river to reconnoiter. Mitchell would still not cooperate with the army, but now it made little difference because Lovell had evacuated New Orleans and left the city in the hands of Mayor John T. Monroe.[6]

Porter could not divine Duncan's intentions, and his communications with New Orleans were no better than the general's. The first rumor of the city's surrender reached Duncan on April 26, when Mitchell returned from Quarantine after going up under a flag of truce. Mitchell claimed that Butler's troops had landed in the bay and would soon invest Fort St. Philip. Since there had been no firing that day, Duncan suspected the rumor was true, but he still had nothing official. Neither did Porter, but at 4:00 P.M. the smoldering wreckage of the CSS *Mississippi* drifted down the river and produced grave apprehensions for the defenders in the forts. Assuming New Orleans had been captured, Porter sent another demand to Higgins to surrender.[7]

Porter was not being quite honest with Higgins, as New Orleans had neither surrendered nor chosen to defend itself. When Lovell pulled his troops out of the city, he left no military organization behind to capitulate. New Orleans reverted to civil authority, and Mayor Monroe stubbornly refused to acknowledge the capture of the town by lowering the flag flying over city hall. This ceremony did not take place until the 29th, when Commander Bell, with a battalion of marines, marched to city hall and forcibly lowered the flag. On May 1 General Butler, who was never on time for any engagement, arrived with part of his occupation force. Although New Orleans came into Farragut's possession on April 25, 1862, the city never officially surrendered.[8]

On April 27 Higgins rejected Porter's second attempt to bargain for the surrender of the forts. Higgins, however, showed a willingness to consider a "proposition for a surrender" if he received official information from his own authorities that the city had been captured.[9]

Duncan, who coauthored Higgins's replies, observed growing dissension among the defenders of Fort Jackson. The men in the parapets had a clear view of all the wreckage floating down the river—partially submerged hulks, empty barges, charred bales of cotton, and all sorts of debris. Through all the days of Porter's bombardment they had stood by their guns, and on the morning Farragut ran the gauntlet they endured the blistering fire without flinching. Now they were tired and discouraged. Duncan knew his men, typifying them as "mostly foreign enlistments, without any great interests at stake in the ultimate success of the revolution. A reaction set in among the men during the lull of the 25th, 26th, and 27th," Duncan declared, "when there was no other excitement to arouse them than the fatigue duty of repairing our damages." The general's couriers, dispatched to New Orleans on the 24th and 25th, never returned, and to the soldiers this looked like a bad omen.[10]

On the afternoon of the 27th Duncan gave the men a "pep talk," praising their courage, urging them to "be vigilant and stand by your guns, and all will yet be well." With darkness came an uncommon quiet, but at midnight Fort Jackson's garrison revolted, seized the guards and posterns, turned the fieldpieces on the interior of the fort, and started to spike the guns. Others just gathered up their arms and walked away from the fort. Duncan attempted to reason with those who stayed, but the men were convinced "the city had surrendered, and that there was no use in fighting; that the enemy were about to attack by land and water on three sides at once, and that a longer defense would only prove a butchery." The general sent a detail of officers to the ramparts to keep the men from spiking the remaining guns, but the mutineers repulsed them with musket fire.[11]

Duncan erroneously believed the mutiny had also infested Fort St. Philip. He called the garrison together and allowed those to leave who refused to fight. He needed to know how many would stay, and half of the command walked out the gates and into the swamps. Duncan knew it was only a matter of time before Porter discovered what had happened, and rather than wait he decided to send a flag of truce and secure the lenient terms Porter had offered on the 26th. He wanted to confer with Fort St. Philip, but he could not get across the river because the deserters had taken all the boats.[12]

Early in the morning Mitchell crossed from St. Philip and told Duncan he had gotten *Louisiana*'s engines running and would go upriver to shell Butler's force at Quarantine. Capt. M. T. Squires, commanding Fort St. Philip, argued against it and urged Duncan to surrender. Higgins penned a brief note to Porter, accepting the terms offered on the 26th but warning that "we have no control over the vessels afloat."

While Duncan and Higgins waited for a reply, Mitchell returned to *Louisiana* and held a council with his officers. They unanimously agreed to destroy the ironclad, reasoning that her unreliable engines, combined with only ten days' provisions, made her surrender inevitable by the simple process of blockade. "With the most painful regret," Mitchell agreed to have her set on fire.[13]

Mitchell's decision came at the time when *Harriet Lane,* accompanied by three gunboats flying flags of truce, came to anchor between the forts. As Duncan and Higgins retired to Porter's cabin to consummate the surrender, Mitchell's men set *Louisiana* on fire and, with a fuse to her magazine, cast her loose. With curls of black smoke streaming from her gunports, the ironclad began her final voyage downriver.

Oblivious to Mitchell's activity, Porter and his staff sat with Higgins and Duncan at a table on *Harriet Lane* as *Louisiana* drifted toward them. They were discussing surrender terms when an officer called Lieutenant Wainwright to the deck. Wainwright returned to the cabin and angrily reported the ironclad in flames and drifting toward the squadron, which was anchored at thirty-yard intervals.

"This is sharp practice," Porter said to Duncan, "but if you can stand the explosion when it comes, we can."

Porter sent Wainwright topside with orders "to hail the vessel next to him and pass the word to each of the others to veer to the end of their chains and be ready, by using steam, to sheer out of the way." Porter then handed the pen to General Duncan and Colonel Higgins, "who coolly signed their names in as bold a hand as if they were not momentarily in danger of being blown up. Then we all sat quietly awaiting the result. In a few moments an explosion took place that fairly shook us all out of our seats and threw the *Harriet Lane* over on her side . . . *Louisiana* had blown up before reaching the flotilla." Duncan condemned the act, denying any responsibility for the actions of Commander Mitchell.[14]

Porter went on deck but saw no sign of the ironclad. He then learned she had been caught in an eddy, drifted back toward Fort St. Philip, and "blew up with a force which scattered fragments in all directions, killing one of their own men in St. Philip. Had it occurred near the vessels," Porter declared, "it would have destroyed every one of them. This, no doubt, was the object of the archtraitor who was the instigator of the act."[15]

After signing the surrender, Porter sent Commander Renshaw to Fort Jackson and Lieutenant Nichols to Fort St. Philip. "The rebel flag was hauled down, and the stars and stripes once more floated over the

property of the United States. The sun never shone on a more contented and happy looking set of fellows," Porter recalled, "than those of
the prisoners in and about the forts. Many of them had not seen their
families for months."[16]

After disarming the prisoners, Porter devoted his attention to Mitchell, who was a mile upriver with two small steamers. One shot from
Harriet Lane's pivot gun whistled over Mitchell's head before he lowered his flag. Wainwright went on board and was greeted by the Confederate commander, who demanded treatment as prisoners of war.
Wainwright replied that none of the officers would be paroled but "held
as prisoners to answer for violating the sanctity of a flag of truce."
Mitchell then appealed to Porter in an attempt relieve his officers "from
the odium of having set fire to the _Louisiana,_ and thus endangering the
Union vessels while under a flag of truce."[17]

Mitchell, however, not only lost his appeal but was soundly condemned by Duncan's officers for his uncooperative behavior. Porter for-
warded Mitchell and his officers to Farragut, who sent them to Boston
Harbor, where they spent the next four months confined at Fort Warren.
Released in August, Mitchell had nothing nice to say about Farragut
or Porter, referring to them as "servile and degraded tools, well fitted
for carrying out the infamous policy of an unprincipled and despotic
Government."[18]

After his release, Mitchell demanded a court of inquiry, and on December 5, 1863, Flag Officer Samuel Barron exonerated the disgruntled commander, praising him for doing "all in his power to sustain the
honor of the flag and to prevent the enemy from ascending the Mississippi River." By then Vicksburg had fallen and the lengthy congressional investigation of the Navy Department had ended, giving Secretary of the Navy Mallory a vote of confidence he deserved no more than
Commander Mitchell.[19]

When Forts Jackson and St. Philip surrendered, Butler was with
Farragut off New Orleans, but his troops were below Quarantine and
slogging through the swamps toward the rear of St. Philip. Another unit
crossed the river to attack Jackson. Neither force got far before being
inundated with deserters who told them the forts had surrendered to
Porter. During the capitulation Porter sent _Clifton_ to Head of Passes to

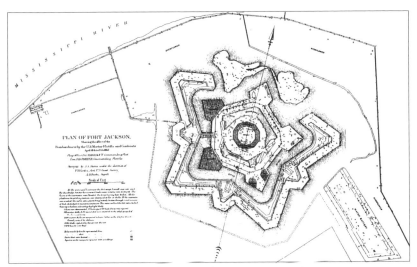

Sketch of the effect of Porter's bombardment on Fort Jackson REPRINTED FROM *OFFICIAL RECORDS OF THE UNION AND CONFEDERATE NAVIES*

bring up Brig. Gen. John W. Phelps's 30th Massachusetts and 12th Connecticut infantry regiments. Phelps arrived in time to witness the lowering of the Confederate flag and relieve the navy of more than two hundred prisoners. After the excitement ended, Butler came down the river, assigned the 26th Regiment Massachusetts Volunteers to garrison the forts, packed the others up, and took them to New Orleans. On May 1 Butler's army took possession of the Crescent City. The fighting had ended, but Butler's nine-month conflict with the town's populace had just begun.[20]

Another skirmish precipitated by Butler took place more by accident than by design, and this one involved Porter. After the forts surrendered, Porter inspected Fort Jackson to assess the effect of his seven-day bombardment. In his report to Welles, he wrote:

> Never in my life did I witness such a scene of desolation and wreck as [Fort Jackson] presented. It was plowed up by XIII-inch mortars; the bombs had set fire to and burned out all the buildings in and around

the fort; casemates were crushed and were crumbling in, and the only thing that saved them was the sand bags that had been sent from New Orleans. A day's bombardment would have finished them. The levee had been cut by the XIII-inch bombs in over a hundred places and the water had entered the casemates, making it very uncomfortable if not impossible to live there any longer. It was the only place the men had to fly to out of the reach of the bombs. . . . The accuracy of the fire is perhaps the best ever seen in mortar practice.[21]

Porter reported eleven guns dismounted, the magazine damaged, the drawbridge over the moat broken to pieces, and the causeways blown to rubble. The water battery, which contained six heavy guns, had been smashed by more than 170 bombs. Despite the damage, casualties were surprisingly light, with fourteen killed and thirty-nine wounded. Of Fort Jackson's seventy-four guns, only eleven had been disabled. Having been spared from the bombardment, Fort St. Philip sustained little damage until Farragut's fleet advanced, which in passing disabled four of the fort's fifty-two guns.[22]

Butler, who was miffed at not being included at the surrender, claimed the forts were "as defensible as before the bombardment—Saint Philip precisely so, it being quite uninjured." Had Butler's statement applied solely to Fort St. Philip, Porter might not have reacted, but the general stated neither fort had been damaged, which directly contradicted Porter's report. This led to a rift in relations between the two commanders. After claiming he could disable the forts in forty-eight hours and then failing, Porter had felt a little better after examining the effectiveness of the bombardment. Then Butler, who had contributed nothing to the expedition but some coal, with one sentence discredited Porter's claims. General Phelps, who spent more time at Jackson than Butler, considered the bastion "very much injured" and "in a great state of disorder," with everything knocked apart and flooded with water. Since Butler attached Phelps's report to his own, he must have read it, which suggests that Butler's criticism of Porter's hard work was not accidental but intentional.[23]

Porter sent Gerdes and his surveyors into Fort Jackson to prepare a sketch of the damage, which depicted a scene much like modern-day carpet bombing. After Gerdes completed his inspection he wrote, "I can not understand to this minute how the garrison could have possibly lived so long in the enclosures. The destruction goes beyond all description. The ground is torn by the shells as if a thousand antediluvian hogs had rooted it up."[24]

Nobody thought to settle the argument by examining carpenters' reports. By eliminating Mitchell's weak defense from the equation, firing from Fort St. Philip caused more than half of the damage sustained by Farragut's squadron, but its guns could throw only half the metal of Fort Jackson. Without Porter's bombardment, it is conceivable that an undamaged Fort Jackson could have repulsed enough Union warships to alter the outcome of the campaign.[25]

Butler, while demeaning Porter's bummers, hurried to New Orleans and provided correspondents with grossly embellished tales of how his men had captured the forts. Before the first official report reached Washington, newspapers hit the street in praise of Butler's great victory, overshadowing Farragut's capture of New Orleans and Porter's capture of the forts. Farragut paid little attention to Butler's claims, but Porter screamed foul. In reply to a letter of praise from Fox, Porter sarcastically grumbled:[26]

> *Butler* did it all!!! So I see it by that blackguard reporter of the Herald who acted as Farragut's Secretary and Signal Officer [Osbon], and who had his nose everywhere. If you could have seen the trouble I had getting old Butler and his soldiers up to the Forts . . . you would laugh at the old fool's pretensions. But he actually asserts that it was his presence (30 miles off) which induced the forts to surrender, and this Herald fellow tries to make it appear so, and says that no harm was done to the forts and that they were as good as new.

Butler could not help noticing Porter's reaction. He had stirred up a hornet, which no doubt amused him, for Butler was a major general and Porter a lowly commander. The pair, however, had not seen the last of each other—a matter Butler failed to enter into his assessment of the fiery naval officer.

By sullying Porter's performance, Butler was giving the commander a dose of his own medicine. Porter had sent reports to the Navy Department criticizing Farragut for procrastination and indecisiveness. When

Farragut decided to leave the mortar flotilla below the forts, Porter chafed because he believed the order would deprive him of taking a fort and advancing, as Fox had promised, one grade to captain. Now, after capturing two forts, he regretted the statement and asked Fox to delete it from his report. He also asked if the statement that he "urged the Flag Officer to go up in the ships" could be deleted because "it won't do in a public despatch to say so."[27]

Welles refused to alter Porter's report. In his opinion, Farragut never needed urging from anyone. Porter learned and profited from the experience, but it did not change his attitude toward Butler. Both men spent much of their lives attempting to convince the public the other was a liar when in reality nobody really cared.[28]

Porter, however, distinguished himself in the lower Mississippi, and nobody in the Navy Department disputed his fighting instincts. Welles sized him up as a troublesome subordinate, prone to rashness and exaggeration, but a tough-minded fighter who got the job done. The navy needed men like Porter—Welles knew it and praised him:

> The important part which you have borne in the organization of the Mortar Flotilla and the movement on New Orleans has identified your name with one of the most brilliant naval achievements on record, and to your able assistance with the flotilla is Flag-Officer Farragut much indebted for the successful results he has accomplished. To yourself and the officers and seamen of the Mortar Flotilla the Department extends its congratulations.[29]

Three months later Porter received his first resolution of thanks from the U.S. Congress—and it would not be his last.[30]

On to Vicksburg

The citizens of New Orleans celebrated May Day by greeting the paroled defenders of Forts Jackson and St. Philip with an outpouring of anger as they disembarked from transports at the foot of Canal Street. "Some were killed," wrote Lt. Francis A. Roe of *Pensacola*, "some stoned, all jeered and hooted through the streets. Several persons were hung . . . for professing Union and national sentiments."[1]

After Farragut's marines restrained the crowd, General Butler and his staff strode down the gangplank to a musical rendering of "Yankee Doodle" and marched into town. "On landing," Butler declared, "we were saluted with cheers for 'Jeff. Davis' and 'Beauregard' and the last man heard to call for cheers for the rebel chief has been sentenced by the provost judge to three months' hard labor." The general billeted his troops in the city's fine public buildings and for his headquarters took possession of the elegant St. Charles Hotel. In his May Day debut, Butler wasted no time imposing martial law on a public who came to despise him.[2]

Porter arrived on *Harriet Lane*, accompanied by *Miami*, *Westfield*, and *John P. Jackson*. From the deck of *Richmond*, Captain Alden orchestrated a chorus of three cheers for Porter, which the commander returned in kind. In the lower Mississippi Porter had not endeared himself to many of Farragut's skippers, and of them, Alden remained a friend.[3]

Porter joined Farragut and found him puzzling over his next move. Welles's orders, dated January 20, still applied, and the flag officer had a dilemma. The instructions read: "If the Mississippi expedition from Cairo shall not have descended the river, you will take advantage of the panic to push a strong force up the river to take all their defenses in the rear. You will also reduce the fortifications which defend Mobile Bay and turn them over to the army to hold." At the same time, Welles demanded "a vigorous blockade at every point," and Farragut did not believe he could deliver on all three objectives at the same time.[4]

Forts Morgan and Gaines, at the entrance to Mobile Bay, were heavily armed, although not nearly as strong as Forts Jackson and St. Philip—which meant that Farragut would have to return to the Gulf. He had misgivings about leaving Butler without naval support and decided the best way to protect the army was to ascend the river and join forces with Flag Officer Charles H. Davis, who had recently replaced the ailing Foote, at Memphis. Farragut doubted whether he could get all of his heavy vessels to Memphis, which meant he would have to be supplied from New Orleans, forcing Butler to occupy the rebellious towns along the river with troops he could not spare. Farragut's lighter gunboats had been damaged and needed repairs, and even if some of them did reach Davis, he doubted if they would be of much use.[5]

At this indecisive moment, Porter entered Farragut's cabin and, seizing another opportunity to utilize the mortar flotilla, urged him to deploy it in demolishing Vicksburg. Farragut, facing dual problems, decided to keep his warships in the river and send Porter to Ship Island, where an expedition could eventually be organized to capture Mobile. Farragut cautioned Porter not to enter Mobile Bay, as he had received information that two Confederate ironclads were operating off the city. He told Porter he had decided to go to Vicksburg, force the town's surrender, return to the Gulf, and then capture Mobile. There was still a small Confederate naval force operating on Lake Pontchartrain and a small fort on Barataria Bay, and he gave Porter the task of mopping up all the resistance on Butler's flanks.[6]

"Carefully as the project of capturing Vicksburg was planned," Porter recalled, "it was not executed. Why, I do not know. I presume Farragut delayed his advance from New Orleans until he could secure the necessary troops. . . . I urged pushing on to Vicksburg, instead of which I was pushed on to Ship Island, a delightful retreat where General Butler used to send rebellious women who hooted at the Union flag."[7]

Farragut discovered that capturing Vicksburg was no easy task. On May 3 he sent Captain Craven upriver with *Brooklyn, Sciota, Winona,* and *Itasca* to occupy Baton Rouge. Craven passed the town without capturing it and continued up the river to Union Point, twenty miles below Natchez. *Itasca* broke down and *Sciota* ran short of coal. Comdr. Samuel P. Lee, with orders to go to Vicksburg, came up with *Oneida, Pinola,* and *Kennebec* but found Craven in no condition to make the trip. All seven vessels turned about and on the afternoon of May 7 anchored above Baton Rouge. On the morning of May 9 Lee started back upriver with the gunboats, and Craven dropped down to Baton Rouge, where he found Comdr. James S. Palmer anchored off the city in *Iroquois* and waiting for the mayor's answer to his surrender demands. A few hours later Farragut came up with *Hartford* and *Richmond.*[8]

Annoyed that Craven had detained Lee's squadron, Farragut took all eleven warships and two transports carrying about fourteen hundred troops upriver and on May 24 arrived three miles below Vicksburg, where he found conditions much worse than at New Orleans. The swift current made navigation difficult, but what troubled him were the strong Confederate batteries terraced on bluffs two to three hundred feet above the river, which could be approached from below only head-on or in line ahead because of a bend in the river. He decided to leave six of the gunboats below Vicksburg and, because the river had fallen, send the heavier vessels and the transports back to Baton Rouge for supplies. Vicksburg presented a more complicated challenge than Farragut anticipated.[9]

During the first week of May, Porter marked time at Ship Island waiting for word from Farragut. When none came, he took his gunboats and the schooner *Sachem* to the bar off the entrance to Mobile Bay to range in his mortars and plant buoys for Farragut's vessels "to run in by when they arrive." The gunboats exchanged shots with the forts, but *Clifton* ran aground under the guns of Fort Morgan while taking soundings. She got off before suffering serious damage, and when a storm struck, Porter sent all the vessels but *Harriet Lane* back to Ship Island.

On the evening of May 9 he cruised eastward, hoping to capture a prize, but at 2:00 A.M. the watch reported a light glowing in the sky above Pensacola Bay. Porter ordered steam, and as he entered the bay at 9:00 A.M. he discovered the navy yard, Fort McRee, and the naval hospital in flames. He anchored off Pensacola and communicated with Brig. Gen. Lewis G. Arnold, who had sent a lieutenant to town to demand its surrender. The mayor admitted that the sudden evacuation had been prompted by a rumor of Union gunboats running into Mobile Bay. "A thousand rebels . . . encamped 5 miles outside of Mobile," Porter reported, "had destroyed everything that time would permit." Porter spent the balance of the day shuttling thirteen hundred troops and two pieces of artillery from Fort Pickens to Pensacola.[10]

Because all of Farragut's recent correspondence with the Navy Department had spoken of ascending the river to Vicksburg, Welles was amazed to hear that Porter had just buoyed the entrance to Mobile Bay and was now at Pensacola. "Somebody has made a most serious blunder," Fox wrote Porter, "in persuading the Flag Officer to go at [sic] Mobile instead of obeying his instructions to go up the Mississippi River. We have sent out [three] steamers in all haste to require him to proceed at once, and cut off Beauregard. . . . It seems extraordinary how Farragut could have committed this terrible mistake." Fox probably suspected Porter of being the unknown "somebody" who had urged the flag officer to "blunder."[11]

At Pensacola Porter's new flagship arrived, and he transferred his flag to the more spacious 6-gun side-wheeler *Octorara,* 193 feet long and fresh from the New York Navy Yard. In April he had complained, "I have not slept in a bed since I left home; I have all kinds of writing to do, have no clerk, and have to go around and borrow one. Every man should have a little privacy at times, but I have not a place where I can retire to shift my clothes when wet. I can stand as much as any man, but if this can be rectified, I should be very much pleased." And so he was, writing in May, "I am delighted with the *Octorara.* She is the easiest boat I ever was in. . . . I never enjoyed so much comfort."[12]

Welles continued to fret over Farragut's activities. After the Union fleet entered the Mississippi in early April, the military situation had drastically changed. Grant's army drove deep into western Tennessee and on April 7 eked out a victory at Shiloh. Thereafter, Maj. Gen. Henry W. Halleck came down from St. Louis to whip General Beauregard and elbowed Grant into the role of second in command. He then stifled Sherman, who might otherwise have taken independent action against the Confederate army encamped at Corinth. As a consequence, the fighting dragged through the month of May, with Halleck advancing fourteen miles in fourteen days, entrenching as he went. Halleck's slow pace alarmed Lincoln, who expected Beauregard to be easily defeated, but what alarmed him more was the rumor that the rebels were crossing the Mississippi and escaping into Arkansas. If Halleck allowed Beauregard to withdraw, the Confederates could set up across the river and continue the war indefinitely. Flag Officer Davis's flotilla had been checked above Memphis, and the only means of hindering Beauregard's westerly withdrawal was for Farragut to come up the river and stop him.

Because dispatches between Washington and New Orleans took as long as three weeks to reach their destination, one of the first reports to reach the Navy Department was Porter's message written on May 10 intimating that Farragut planned to attack Mobile. This caused great consternation in the White House because Welles remembered that his original orders had mentioned Mobile. At the end of May, just when it became crucial to block Beauregard's retreat, word reached Welles that Farragut had gone to Vicksburg earlier in the month but had returned to New Orleans. Welles naturally suspected that Farragut intended to leave the river and transfer operations to Mobile Bay. Why else would he have sent Porter there to set buoys?[13]

On May 19 Welles dispatched three fast steamers with an urgent message to Farragut: "The President of the United States requires you to use your utmost exertions (without a moment's delay, and before any other naval operations shall be permitted to interfere) to open the river Mississippi and effect a juncture with Flag-Officer Davis."

Farragut had indeed returned to New Orleans, but not at the urging of Porter—his guns could not be elevated to reach Vicksburg's upper batteries. To add to his worries, he expected the Confederates to launch CSS *Arkansas,* a powerful ironclad being built at Yazoo City. He asked Porter to send "six to ten" mortar boats to New Orleans, promising that

Butler would have tow vessels waiting. The general also planned to send enough men upriver to take Vicksburg "in the rear or on the flank" while the navy bombarded the town from the front.[14]

Charles Lee Lewis, Farragut's biographer, suggests that Butler, who was still smarting over Porter's capture of the forts, urged Farragut to bring the mortars upriver, thereby preventing Porter from grabbing more laurels by taking possession of Mobile Bay. Knowing that Porter was quite capable of provoking an unauthorized attack made Farragut more uneasy, and if he had not needed the mortars to reach Vicksburg's heights he may have asked for them anyway.[15]

Porter promised to bring the schooners to Pass à l'Outre immediately, but he cautioned against Butler's drawing troops from New Orleans because, he said, "If Beauregard is whipped at Corinth, his hordes will work down in this direction [and] seize Baton Rouge." He also warned that if the river fell as expected, Union ships would be stranded upriver and unable to support Butler if Beauregard attacked New Orleans. Porter knew the river well and his concern was genuine, but underlying his warning lay a different strategy. "Mobile is so ripe now that it would fall to us like a mellow pear, while we, I fear, will fall . . . before the difficulties above in the river. . . . If we miss taking Mobile now, we won't get it."[16]

Farragut, who was well aware of the problems, promised Welles he would ascend the river without delay, bringing with him five thousand of Butler's troops. He denied any insinuation by the department of having forgotten his orders and blamed delays on repairs and on the scarcity of supplies.[17]

Conscious of Farragut's original orders from Welles, Porter wrote Fox: "No one was more surprised than myself that Farragut had received orders to go up the River. . . . When Farragut wrote to me to come up with the Bomb Flotilla, I thought this some wild scheme got up by himself and Butler . . . but when I saw his orders I said: 'Go ahead fast, and I will be with you before you are half way there.'"[18]

Porter took his entire command to Pass à l'Outre, where he expected to be met by Butler's tow vessels. Instead, he found the delta clogged with merchant vessels, some departing loaded with cotton and others waiting for a tug to bring them inside. Tugs were plentiful, but none of them were assigned to Porter, so he used his own vessels to tow the schooners to Fort Jackson. He implored Butler for assistance and received a courteous answer, but no help. "I little knew then the system of red tapism," Porter complained, "or I don't think I should have had anything to do with the Army, or that portion of it which, through the naval exertions, now occupy New Orleans. I found that the captain of the fort had entire control of the towboats . . . but [they] were engaged in towing private vessels having no connection whatever with the Government." Porter recognized several of the tugs as prizes the navy had turned over to the army. "They are burning up Government coal," he protested, "for which the Government derives little benefit." A month had passed since Butler had taken possession of New Orleans, but Porter quickly sized up the situation:

> I don't hesitate to say there has been a deliberate attempt made to deceive and trifle with me, and whosoever's fault it is, it should be made known. We have traitors enough to fight against without finding them holding office under our Government at posts of honor which have for a moment become so lucrative that the holders thereof fear to miss the golden opportunity, and intend to make hay while the sun shines . . . . When the army was without transportation almost every steamer belonging to the flotilla was engaged in placing the troops where they were required, for which they obtained very little thanks, and only enabled the army to put forth pretensions they were no way entitled to claim.[19]

Farragut had departed for Baton Rouge, and Porter missed him. He needed towage, so he applied to Butler: "The mortar fleet is all here and will proceed up river with all dispatch the moment I can obtain towage. I never like to send a boy on a man's errand, so instead of six mortars I bring nineteen. I can tow thirteen with what vessels I have, and if you will let me have two tugboats . . . I can get up with all before the flag-officer."[20]

On June 13, with all of his gunboats and fifteen of his schooners, Porter began the four hundred–mile journey to Vicksburg. Although the army had not brought up his supply vessels, and his men were on half rations, he was anxious to leave the sweltering city where a fetid atmosphere swarmed with insects and caused much illness. Four of the boats left a few days later, towed not by Butler's promised steamers but by

Farragut's vessels. For Porter, who was forced to make many stops to purchase fresh provisions, the trip upriver was slow and torturous. At each stop dozens of slaves slipped on board seeking freedom and employment, and Porter gave them jobs as coal heavers and laborers.[21]

Between New Orleans and Vicksburg the river was an unbroken series of S-curves and devil's elbows flowing to all points on the compass. From New Orleans to Baton Rouge the land lay below the levee, and a sailor in the tops could look down from the masthead at weathered shacks and see slave women carrying all sorts of articles on their heads. From time to time a musket cracked, fired by a sniper behind the levee who would scamper out of sight. Baton Rouge, situated on a hillside forty feet above flood stage, marked the beginning of a long ridge of bluffs that rose gradually along the east bank of the Mississippi until they reached the Yazoo River north of Vicksburg, where the hills reached a height of 250 feet. Along this three hundred–mile stretch, Confederate militia and small cavalry detachments with mountain howitzers made sudden appearances on the bluffs and fired a few rounds at passing Union vessels before dropping out of sight.

On June 20, seven days after leaving New Orleans, Porter arrived below Vicksburg and reported to Captain Craven, the senior officer present. Most of Farragut's squadron was there, but *Hartford* had gone aground below Natchez. Brig. Gen. Thomas Williams came up with Butler's transports and on the 21st pulled the flagship off. On the 25th Farragut came to anchor seven miles below Vicksburg and found Porter there with sixteen schooners and the gunboats *Octorara*, *Harriet Lane*, *Miami*, *Westfield*, *Clifton*, and *Jackson*. Of Farragut's flotilla, *Brooklyn*, *Richmond*, *Iroquois*, *Sciota*, *Wissahickon*, *Oneida*, *Kennebec*, and *Winona* lay close to the west bank. *Pinola* was still several miles below and towing the last of Porter's mortar boats.[22]

When General Lovell evacuated New Orleans, he sent his guns to Vicksburg. Because Farragut lost two months getting his fleet upriver, the Confederates moved with speed and terraced the Vicksburg hillside with an arsenal of artillery tiered from the water's edge to the crest of its highest hill, fifteen hundred yards from the river. Above Vicksburg the Mississippi made a sharp, dramatic bend at De Soto Point, and artillery emplaced on the banks held a commanding diagonal sweep along the shank of the horseshoe. Upper batteries could pour a destructive plunging fire into passing ships, rake them, and have little fear of return fire. Thirty guns bore on the river, including two 10-inch Columbiads. With few exceptions, Porter's chowder pots were the only Union guns that could reach Vicksburg's upper batteries.[23]

To the men on board the gunboats, Vickburg's defenses presented a demoralizing prospect, and they began to grumble about life on the Mississippi. The river fell, vessels went aground, food ran short, coal supplies dwindled, and the weather became so hot that crews worked at night and slept during the day, but they were driven half-mad by swarms of mosquitoes—and then malaria took its toll.

The summer malaise affected Porter, and he wrote Fox, "I would be very much pleased if the Department would relieve me from this command or all connection with the Gulf Squadron. I have no reasons to assign, and am willing to serve anywhere else in a yawl boat." What motivated Porter's unofficial letter is unclear. It may have emanated from the feeling of being stifled by Farragut or Butler, but two months had passed since the surrender of Forts Jackson and St. Philip, and he probably expected the promotion Fox had promised to the man who "takes a fort." No further mention had been made of the offer. Though a commander, Porter had a larger command than most captains, and he probably felt unappreciated.[24]

Porter, however, had never ingratiated himself with Farragut's commanders, and he especially disliked Captain Craven, of *Brooklyn,* whom he viewed as an inept martinet. When Craven sent a boat to *Octorara* to gather up the blacks in the mortar flotilla, Porter declined, as he had hired most of them to fill vacancies. He explained the situation to Craven and refused to give them up without a written order. The reply irritated Craven, who complained to Farragut that he wished to have no more dealings with Porter. Craven would get his wish sooner than he expected.[25]

For Farragut, the military situation had changed since his first excursion to Vicksburg. Beauregard evacuated Corinth on May 29, forcing the abandonment of Fort Pillow on June 4. Two days later Flag Officer Davis's squadron defeated the Confederate navy above Vicksburg, and Memphis fell. Farragut could now be supplied from upriver if he ran another gauntlet. Porter, however, would be forced to keep his squadron below the city, but supplies could be carted across the peninsula from

Young's Point. And on the way upriver, General Williams had stopped at Grand Gulf, destroyed the town, and driven off six hundred militia, but he left the cannon on the heights untouched. The only unpleasant news to greet Farragut's arrival below Vicksburg came from a deserter who claimed the ironclad CSS *Arkansas,* mounting twenty guns, was nearing completion up the Yazoo and would be down in a week.[26]

When Butler's transports reached Vicksburg, it became obvious to Farragut that Williams's force was no match for the ten thousand gray-clads Maj. Gen. John Breckinridge kept nearby. It also became obvious to Farragut, who had hoped to capture the town by threat, that his vessels would be mauled by Vickburg's batteries if they stood off the town and engaged in an artillery duel. Nonetheless, he felt compelled to pass the city's batteries, join forces with Davis's command, and map out a strategy for coercing the town's surrender.[27]

To support Farragut's movement, Porter ranged his mortars along both banks of the river. Breese had not come up because of delays in getting *Sea Foam* off a bar, so Porter divided the squadron into two divisions instead of three, giving Watson Smith command of nine vessels and Queen command of eight. Porter placed Smith's division along the east bank, about 2,500 yards from Vicksburg's main batteries and 2,200 yards from the water battery. He moved Queen's division to the exposed west bank but seven hundred yards further away and well concealed by brush. The mortars filed into position on the night of the 26th and opened at daylight with a furious bombardment. The bummers did little physical damage to the batteries but drove the enemy into their bombproofs.[28]

Farragut intended to move that night, giving Porter the day to soften up the enemy's artillery. The attack, however, was delayed when the bummers discovered defects in their fuses and asked for time to solve the problem. Finally, at 2:00 A.M. on the 28th, two vertical lights hoisted to *Hartford's* mizzen put the fleet in motion.[29]

At 3:15 A.M., with colors flying, the squadron steamed upriver. Because she had the best chase guns, *Richmond* took the lead, followed by *Hartford* and *Brooklyn.* In a second column, eight gunboats ranged along the west bank. *Iroquois* and *Oneida* edged ahead of *Richmond* so their fire would not be blanketed by the larger vessel. *Wissahickon* and *Sciota* slipped into the interval between *Richmond* and *Hartford;*

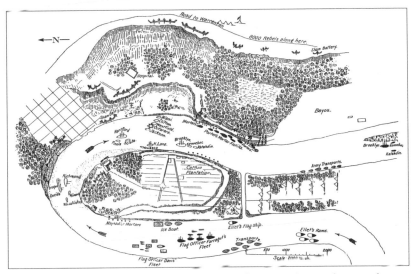

Map of Vicksburg environs and the passage of Farragut's squadron on the morning of June 28, 1862 REPRINTED FROM *OFFICIAL RECORDS OF THE UNION AND CONFEDERATE NAVIES*

Winona and *Pinola* wedged in between *Hartford* and *Brooklyn;* and *Kennebec* and *Katahdin* brought up the rear. To some, Farragut's plan seemed to be unclear, and his explanations to questions asked by his commanders may have been sloppy. One officer, Captain Craven of *Brooklyn,* who was next in age and seniority to Farragut, believed the flag officer wanted the Vicksburg batteries silenced before passing above the city.[30]

At 4:00 A.M. the squadron hove into sight below the city, and Porter, bucking a three-knot current, opened with every gunboat and every mortar. Vicksburg's water battery engaged *Richmond,* and minutes later a cloud of smoke covered the river. Batteries tiered on the bluffs targeted on flashes from the gunboats. Gunners on *Richmond* had the best view of the fight, and Alden reported that "at 4:30 a.m. the hills were one line of blaze from the rebel batteries. We could not see for smoke. Broadside after broadside we fired into them and their shots came crashing through our bulwarks, brains and blood flying all over the deck." Men on *Hartford* could hear enemy shells thudding into the hull and tearing through the tops, and when the vessel broke for a moment into the clear, Bell watched mortars and shells land in "a perfect hailstorm against the slopes where no guns are," and lamented, "It was provoking." *Hartford* knocked out one of the batteries on the ridge, but for most of the fight the gunners fired blindly at flashes on the hillside produced by exploding shells.[31]

Porter's seven gunboats moved into position about a thousand yards below the city and fired rapidly at the guns mounted near the wharf and at a heavy battery by a hospital located midway up the bluff. The artillery on the hill, commanded by Lincoln's brother-in-law, Capt. David H. Todd, energetically replied. From the deck of *Octorara* Porter could clearly see *Richmond* and four gunboats pass to port, their broadsides smashing into the shore with grape, shrapnel, and canister. The untouched upper batteries answered with a furious fire, and Porter heard shells splash among his flotilla. At last *Hartford* hove into sight, moving slowly with two gunboats off her port quarter and firing through a screen of smoke at exploding mortar shells. As the trio slowly passed, Porter looked for *Brooklyn* through the thin gauze of dawn but could not find her among the passing fleet.[32]

Octorara's wheel ropes suddenly jammed, and Porter lost control of his steerage. Before falling back to make repairs, he hailed *Miami* to close the range to six hundred yards. Drifting downriver, *Octorara* fell under *Brooklyn's* line of fire, and a shell burst off the port side. The next blast from *Brooklyn* spewed the deck of *Clifton* with grape. Porter hailed *Clifton, Westfield,* and *John P. Jackson* and attempted to get them out of *Brooklyn's* line of fire by ordering them forward. This put the gunboats closer to the enemy's guns, where for several minutes they became stationary targets. With *Octorara's* ropes repaired, Porter took her back upriver. *Jackson,* which had moved to the front of the squadron, received a shot in the wheelhouse that carried away the helmsman's leg. Porter sent *Clifton* to help her, and as she was passing a line to the disabled steamer a shot struck her boiler, killing six men and scalding a dozen others. Several of the injured jumped overboard, and one drowned. With both vessels adrift, a shot tore into *Westfield* and landed butt end on her engine frame. *Octorara* managed to run a line to *Clifton* and towed her out of the action, and Porter, thinking *Brooklyn* had passed upriver during the action, signaled the squadron to withdraw. It was not until he fell back that he noticed *Brooklyn* and her two gunboats were still below the bend and drifting backwards with their bows facing upstream.[33]

At 5:00 A.M. the sun rose red in a tinged, smoke-smeared sky. *Hartford* rounded De Soto Point and came to anchor about four miles upriver and below the city. Lt. Col. Alfred W. Ellet of the Ram Fleet was there and waiting, but when Farragut looked below he did not see *Brooklyn, Kennebec,* or *Katahdin.* He feared they had been lost and sent a messenger across the bend to look for them. Hoping *Brooklyn* was still afloat, he directed the message to Captain Craven. "What is the difficulty?" he asked. "I hope your ship is not disabled and that your casualties have not been great." Craven, who disliked Porter, replied:[34]

> Thank God there is nothing the matter with either of the three vessels below. After you left us, and Porter stopped throwing his shells, the rascals who had been thoroughly driven from their guns . . . returned, and I was trying to silence the only two guns remaining in action, it seemed as if a thousand new hands had come to demolish us. I laid the *Brooklyn* under the heights for about an hour and a half, and . . . after expending nearly all my rifle shells, obliged to give it up. Should you desire Porter to keep up a demonstration upon the hills, please write to him, for it is too evident he does not like to receive instructions from myself.

Farragut rejected Craven's excuse for not following orders and asked for a full report. He recalled two other occasions when Craven seemed to hold back and suspected the reason had nothing to do with Porter.[35] Craven changed his story, this time blaming Porter's gunboats for blocking his passage, thereby forcing him to stop his engines and enabling the enemy to concentrate their fire on his ship. Farragut became more suspicious when Craven reported only slight damage and no casualties. After he read the account, it also became clear why *Kennebec* and *Katahdin* withdrew, as both vessels had been guiding on *Brooklyn.* What angered Farragut most was Craven's assertion that his retreat complied with the flag officer's instructions to withdraw if Vicksburg's batteries had not been silenced.[36]

Furious, Farragut accused Craven of disobeying orders and fabricating invalid reasons for failing to follow the fleet. As for Porter's gunboats, he distinctly remembered passing them at 4:00 A.M. "We were moving as slowly as possible," he said, "waiting for the *Brooklyn* to come up. The gunboats of the Mortar Flotilla were on our starboard quarter firing at the time (and they did it in handsome style, too), because they knew where the batteries were and we did not." Farragut accused Craven of purposely failing to run by the batteries, and on July 1 Craven asked to be relieved. Farragut complied and that evening transferred Comdr. Henry H. Bell to *Brooklyn*.[37]

Bell accepted the command with mixed feelings, as he and Craven were close friends. To his diary he confided, "This is a heavy blow to me and interferes with my calculations for getting free of the river, as there is every prospect of the fleet summering between its steep banks, smitten with insects, heat intolerable, fevers, chills, and dysentery, and inglorious activity, losing all the fleet has won in honor and reputation. I incline to the belief that persons in the mortar fleet have been instrumental in establishing this state of things in the Gulf fleet." Bell's relationship with Porter was no better than Craven's, so on the night of July 1 he "went to bed with a heavy heart," blaming Porter for the "bad state of feeling" everywhere.[38]

Porter had nothing to do with Bell's "bad state of feeling" and summed up everyone's feelings in his report to Farragut: "It is to be regretted that a combined attack of army and navy had not been accomplished. Such an attack would have resulted, I think, in the capture of the city. Ships and mortar vessels can keep full possession of the river . . . but they cannot crawl up hills 300 feet high, and it is that part of Vicksburg which must be taken by the army."[39]

Porter sent a detachment of marines ashore who worked to within twenty-one hundred yards of the enemy's batteries. Attacked by two regiments, the marines retreated and asked the gunboats to spray the woods with grape. Returning to the woods, the marines found dozens of enemy soldiers hopelessly stuck in a marsh. Porter questioned the mud-streaked defenders, and they told him that if two hundred Union soldiers had gone into the woods at that time, both regiments would have surrendered because they had thrown away their arms and become "perfectly helpless." Porter sent five howitzers ashore, posted fifty pickets, put crews to work digging earthworks, and established a beach-head a short distance below the city. Convinced there were six thousand Confederates defending Vicksburg, he kept the detail ashore and waited for the army. Had he known that Vicksburg was defended by only a brigade, he may have tried to take it himself.[40]

A campaign begun with high hopes now showed visible signs of having accomplished nothing. Farragut, however, who was never easily moved to effusing compliments, wrote Welles: "It gives me great pleasure to say that nothing could exceed [Porter's] perseverance in getting to the scene of his labors, or the steadiness with which his officers and men have carried on his work of demolition. Porter's service has been hard upon his officers and crew, but they have performed it well, willingly, and unflinchingly."[41]

Porter always praised his officers, crediting them with standing in the face of battle under all conditions and competing with their fellow officers for the flotilla's "post of honor," which meant becoming the lead vessel, the one most likely to be sunk. "They know no weariness, and they really seem to take delight in mortar firing, which is painful to those even accustomed to it. It requires more than ordinary zeal to stand the ordeal. Though I may have at times been exacting and fault-finding with them for not conforming to the rules of the service (which requires the education of a lifetime to learn) yet I can not withhold my applause when I see these men working with such earnest and untiring devotion to their duties while under fire."[42]

It came as no surprise to either Farragut or Welles that Porter's bummers had difficulty, at times, "conforming to the rules of the service." In Porter, they probably had the least conforming officer in the navy to lead and train them. And when the expedition began to show signs of failure off Vicksburg, Welles began to consider other options, but his decision had nothing to do with Farragut.

Porter took advantage of his extraordinary relationship with Fox, ignored the so-called "rules of the service," and on June 30 penned a letter to the assistant secretary: "I will not call this a battle we have fought," he declared, "it was a useless sacrifice of human life." He blamed Butler for supplying too few men and criticized Williams for showing no initiative with his infantry. "I had reconnoitered the ground and drawn maps of it but Williams *declined* the glorious movement." Had he assaulted the main forts, "he would have had a complete success, without scarcely the loss of a man." Porter then stretched a point by claiming he could destroy the forts in "24 hours," although he had not, and praised the mortar fire as "terrible" with "almost every shell falling into their works," which was not true. He supported Farragut but accused Craven of bungling the attack and firing into the mortar flotilla. "Save me from my friends," Porter declared, closing the letter by adding, "We are living on half rations . . . but we are outsiders and not expected to eat—I have an infirmity of temper which never permits me to forget nor to forgive, and the only pleasure I have is in knowing that a day of *Reckoning* will come."[43]

Williams would not have gotten far with his troops, and if Porter had asked the defenders of Vicksburg for an honest assessment of damage they would have told him that "no gun was disabled, no battery injured, and only thirteen were killed or injured."[44]

For Porter, though, a "day of reckoning" was not far off.

An Unexpected Surprise

After Farragut passed the Vicksburg batteries, he received a visit from Lt. Col. Alfred W. Ellet, who commanded the War Department's Ram Fleet. In March 1862, Alfred's brother Charles Jr. had convinced Secretary of War Edwin M. Stanton that he could convert nine old steamboats into a fleet of river rams. Although the boats were lightly armed, they were fast, shallow-draft vessels with reinforced bows and made good transports. Their test came on June 6, 1862, when, through Ellet's efforts, Flag Officer Davis destroyed the Confederate fleet and captured the city of Memphis. The only casualty in the Ram Fleet was Charles, its commander and originator. He died two weeks later, and the command shifted to his brother, forty-one-year-old Alfred, and it was he who met *Hartford* on the morning of June 28.[1]

Farragut expected to see Davis, whom he had communicated with earlier, but not a vessel from the upper squadron was there. Short of supplies, Farragut considered returning to New Orleans, but Ellet offered to take another message to Memphis to ask if Davis intended to bring down his fleet.

In a letter to Halleck, whose army was still at Corinth, Farragut asked for infantry to flush out the troops defending Vicksburg. To Welles he wrote, "I passed up the river this morning, but to no purpose. I am satisfied it is not possible for us to take Vicksburg without an army force of twelve to fifteen thousand men. General [Earl] Van Dorn's division is here and lies safely behind the hills. The water is too low for me to go over 12 or 15 miles above Vicksburg."[2]

Davis arrived on the morning of July 1, bringing with him the ironclads *Louisville, Benton, Carondelet,* and *Cincinnati,* eight mortar vessels, thirteen transports, and an enormous array of tugs hauling coal and provisions. Cheers from both fleets shattered the morning quiet. It was Farragut's introduction to the "curious" river ironclads. He told his wife they looked "like great turtles," and he was amazed that they drew less than eight feet of water. He and Davis clasped each other warmly—two old friends who never expected to share a reunion on the Mississippi. Farragut had carried out his orders to clear the river and connect with the upper fleet, but Vicksburg still stood, defiant and impregnable. The two flag officers discussed strategy while Porter's mortars thundered from the other side of the bend.[3]

Fifty-five-year-old Charles Henry Davis had risen in the navy rapidly, earning his lieutenancy in 1827 after serving as a midshipman for only three years. Later he graduated from Harvard, returned to the navy, and quickly displayed exceptional intelligence for scientific work. He rose to the rank of commander in 1854, a time when other navy men were on the wait list. After participating in the attacks on Hatteras Inlet and Port Royal, Davis replaced Foote, and on June 6 his squadron, with help from Ellet's rams, destroyed or captured all but one vessel of the Confederate River Defense Fleet at Memphis. When he greeted Farragut on July 1, he wore a long handlebar mustache and a wisp of whiskers under his bare chin. Coming aboard *Hartford,* he gave Farragut one of his rare smiles, and when the reunion ended Davis returned to his more scholarly demeanor and waited for Farragut to suggest a plan.[4]

Farragut could suggest nothing until he heard from Halleck, who in his deliberative style replied evasively from Corinth on July 3 that because of his "scattered and weakened" condition he could do nothing until he concentrated his forces. "This may delay the clearing of the river," he said, "but its accomplishment will be certain in a few weeks." Welles was delighted to learn that Farragut and Davis had joined forces, but six months later he confided to his diary, "Halleck was good for nothing then, nor is he now."[5]

Davis's mortar boats anchored above the city and began to shell the enemy's upper batteries, joined intermittently by Porter's bummers below. For eight days the two mortar units took turns bombing the town. The defenders attempted to erect batteries to drive off Davis's boats but were driven off themselves. On July 4 both fleets fired a national salute. Porter disdained wasting ammunition and celebrated by lofting thirty-four shells at enemy positions. Firing slackened, but Porter kept his men laboring on earthworks. Finally, General Williams brought part of his force across from the peninsula and took command of the navy's makeshift fort.[6]

On July 8 Farragut received an urgent message from Welles ordering Porter to Hampton Roads with twelve mortar boats. Porter understood the order no better than Farragut, and he crossed the peninsula to speak with the flag officer. A few days earlier Davis had received information from Grant that Richmond had surrendered to McClellan, and everybody in the flotilla believed that when the news reached Vicksburg the town would capitulate. This now proved to be false. Instead, Gen. Robert E. Lee had taken command of the Confederate army after Gen. Joseph E. Johnston had been wounded, and, in battles known as the Seven Days, Lee had driven McClellan back to the James River. Before Porter departed, he received a message from Farragut promising that "the moment this place surrenders, we will be off to Mobile." But to Bell he wrote, "How strange to send nearly 2,000 miles for mortar boats. . . . I regret that this news should have arrived at this time, as it will cheer them up very much in Vicksburg"—and it did.[7]

On July 10 Porter started downriver, and three days later he stopped at New Orleans to write Farragut that news of his departure had spread down the Mississippi and rebels all along the river turned out to bid his bummers good riddance. He reported seeing numerous enemy vessels working between the mouth of the Red River and Natchez. Those he captured were laden with contraband for the Confederate army, and he took them to New Orleans. Before departing, Porter detached *Miami* and dispatched her to Farragut with messages and sent *Harriet Lane* and *John P. Jackson* back to the Red River to put a stopper in the enemy's flow of supplies. With the balance of his flotilla, he sailed on July 16 for Hampton Roads and arrived there ten days later.[8]

The trip home gave Porter plenty of time to think about his brief stay in the Crescent City. He wrote Fox:

> The people of New Orleans are eminently disgusted with Butler rule, and will kick out the traces the first chance they get. There is not a Union man from the mouth of the Mississippi to Vicksburg. New Orleans will either be in the hands of the Rebels in 40 days, or it will be burnt. Rest assured of that unless another man is sent in Butler's place. They are great fools for not wishing to keep him there, as he is supplying the Rebels with all they want by way of Pearl River (Salt, Shoes, Blankets, Flour, etc.) for which he charges license, which goes, God knows where! This is literally true.[9]

At Hampton Roads, another piece of news caught Porter's eye. Four days after he departed from Vicksburg, the ironclad CSS *Arkansas* ran down the Yazoo, exchanged broadsides with the Union flotilla, and anchored off the town. Farragut had engaged her with his wooden warships, but Davis stood off with his ironclads. When Porter heard what happened, he added a postscript to his letter to Fox: "I have just heard of the escape of the *Arkansas;* it is nothing more than I expected . . . there was one flag officer too many. I saw enough to convince me that Davis should not have been one of them, he deserves to lose his command." Later, when given the opportunity, Farragut would agree, but at the moment, with the river falling, he had little choice but to leave the Vicksburg area and return to deeper water.[10]

Porter also learned that Welles had pushed through Congress the greatest naval bill since the War of 1812. The measure created two new grades, commodore and rear admiral, and nine superannuated senior officers had been retired to make way for four active rear admirals: Farragut, Du Pont, Goldsborough, and Foote. Instantaneously, eighteen senior captains were appointed commodore and forty commanders made captain, but Porter was not among them. Capt. Henry A. Adams, one of the oldest men in the navy and the former senior officer off Fort Pickens, wrote Welles asking why he had been passed over, mentioning in his inquiry Porter's "theft" of *Powhatan.* Welles did not need a reminder from Adams, because every time the matter came up Seward recalled how Porter's junket saved Fort Pickens, but the navy's effort to relieve Fort Sumter failed. Then, during the New Orleans expedition, instead of following the line of command, Porter flooded Welles with reports that any other commander would have sent to the flag officer. Welles never answered them, except when it became his official duty to congratulate Porter on the surrender of the forts.[11]

With promotions being dispensed from the Navy Department, Porter fought a bout of intermittent fevers and in a sizzling heat wave traveled by stage to Washington. He stopped at his home in George-town and learned that the family had gone to Newport to escape the heat. Giddy with fever and shaking from chills, he went to see Welles, who seemed to be the only cabinet member in town. Despite the hun-dred-degree weather, the secretary greeted him genially, but, observing that Porter was ill, he asked him to return when he felt better. Porter sought promotion, but all Welles would tell him was that the mortars would probably be given to the James River flotilla. He refused to dis-cuss the matter further, wrote out a two-week leave, and sent Porter to Newport to recover. By the time he got there he could barely stand, and Georgy put him to bed and kept him there for three days.[12]

While Porter recovered at Newport he read the war news, and none of it sounded good. Farragut had returned to New Orleans, and Davis had gone to Helena, leaving the river from Helena to Baton Rouge in Confederate hands. Du Pont's combined attack on Charleston had failed as badly as McClellan's Richmond campaign. Lee's legions had mysteriously disappeared from the Peninsula, and Maj. Gen. Thomas J. "Stonewall" Jackson's corps had popped up along the road to Orange Courthouse. Nobody in Washington knew what to expect next.

Porter learned from Fox that his men had arrived at Hampton Roads, most of them sick. "The *Octorara* will not be ready under ten days so you have that length of time [to recover.] I will telegraph you when she is about ready." Hearing that Lincoln had just canceled all furloughs and still puzzled as to his status, Porter crawled out of bed to write his reply: "I was much surprised getting two weeks leave of absence. I did not expect more than ten days; two weeks is a great deal to lose in these times. I am pretty sick, but not sick enough to lie idle, and I hope you won't let anything go in without me and the Mortar fleet being there."[13]

Three days before his leave expired, Porter received a telegram ordering him to Washington. He arrived late but went straight to the Navy Department. Welles had gone home, but Fox was still there. He greeted Porter with bad news. Welles had given *Octorara* to Lt. George Brown, and the mortar schooners had been transferred to the James River flotilla and placed under Commodore Wilkes. Porter asked about his own assignment, but Fox said no orders had been cut. To Porter, the reasons were unclear, so he pressed Fox for an explanation. The assistant secretary replied that Porter had violated protocol on August 7 when he publicly criticized McClellan's competence during a billiards game at the Newport Club, and the statement rankled Welles when it was carried back to the Navy Department.[14]

Porter tried to see Welles in the morning, but Fox intercepted him and said the secretary had decided to send him to St. Louis as aide to Commodore Joseph B. Hull, an elderly officer who managed his activities by reveling in red tape. Fox explained that Hull needed a younger man to help inspect the construction of gunboats and deal with troublesome contractors. Porter left a note to Welles requesting active duty, and, with Fox's permission, he started back to Newport.

Porter decided that since the axe had fallen, he may as well see the president before returning home. With a war on, he could not imagine why Welles would want to punish him for a small transgression at a social gathering, especially after his part in the New Orleans expedition, but he could find no other reason for losing his command. When he entered the White House he found Seward with Lincoln, much like the situation that had gotten him into trouble with *Powhatan*—and, like the first meeting, he felt he had little to lose.

The president greeted him cheerfully and asked what he wanted. Porter stated his case and, referring to his dismal assignment under Hull, said, "I should fret my heart out there in a week suffering such an indignity; yet that's what the Navy Department proposes doing with me."

Lincoln seemed more interested in why Vicksburg had not been captured, and Porter's description of the town's fortifications, the sweep of the river, and the forbidding topography came as a revelation to him. He quickly grasped the importance of the fortress on the river, summoned a messenger, and said, "Go tell the Assistant Secretary of the Navy that I wish to see him at once." Porter did not want to be there for the meeting, so he asked the president if he could take leave to catch the train to Newport. Lincoln agreed, adding "you sha'n't go to St. Louis, you sha'n't resign, and you shall be at Vicksburg when it falls."[15]

Porter's illness lingered for a month, and as time passed his hope for reinstatement dwindled. When Lee destroyed Gen. John Pope's Army of Virginia at Second Manassas and moved into Maryland, McClellan came up from the Peninsula and resumed command of the Army of the Potomac, but when Porter received an offer from Fox to take temporary command of the Potomac flotilla he turned it down. He wanted nothing to do with McClellan and again asked for active duty.[16]

During the interregnum word reached Newport that William Porter, now a commodore, had dropped below Vicksburg in the ironclad *Essex* and defeated the CSS *Arkansas*. The press printed glorified accounts of the battle, elevating David Dixon's brother to national fame. Reporters attached to Butler's army scoffed at the achievement, declaring that *Arkansas* had been destroyed by her crew. There was some truth to both accounts, but the episode made an impact on David Dixon, and he considered resigning from the navy and joining the army. He learned later that his brother had distorted the engagement, embarrassed Welles, and been censured.[17]

By now Welles must have felt that he and his navy had been cursed by officers named Porter, but behind the scenes Lincoln and Fox had been hatching a scheme to recall Davis from the Mississippi Squadron. When Farragut was driven back to Baton Rouge by the falling river, Vicksburg became Davis's problem, and nobody in Washington believed the commodore knew how to get the job done. More bothersome was the matter of finding a replacement for Davis, someone who would fight. After a month of debate, Fox convinced Welles that the best man for the job was Commander Porter, a man so far down the seniority list that his appointment would upset a hierarchy sacred to naval tradition. Nonetheless, on September 22, the same day he censured William Porter, Welles wired David Dixon: "You will be assigned to duty West, and on your way report in person to this Department for further orders."[18]

When Porter reached Washington, he had no intimation of why Welles wanted to see him. He expected a cool reception when he entered the Navy Department, but he received sly smiles and hearty handshakes. Welles greeted Porter genially, asked if he felt better, and settled him into a chair. Then he methodically outlined his intention to relieve Davis of the Mississippi Squadron and transfer the command to Porter, thereby elevating the junior commander to the rank of acting rear admiral. The announcement surpassed Porter's wildest expectations. He tried to suppress his joy but finally confessed that if Mr. Welles ever ordered him to go over Niagara Falls in an iron pot, he would do it.[19]

Welles, although promoting Porter and giving him one of the most difficult commands in the navy, confided his misgivings to his diary:

> Porter is but a Commander. He has, however, stirring and positive qualities, is fertile in resources, has great energy, excessive and sometimes not over-scrupulous ambition, is impressed with and boastful of his powers, given to exaggeration of himself,—a Porter infirmity,—is not generous to older and superior living officers, whom he is too ready to traduce, but is kind and patronizing to favorites who are his juniors . . . but [he] is brave and daring like all his family. He has not the conscientious and high moral qualities of Foote to organize the flotilla, and . . . it is a question, with this mixture of good and bad traits, how he will succeed.[20]

It is likely that Welles had been politely urged to promote Porter, for he wrote, "If he does well I shall get no credit; if he fails I shall be blamed. No thanks in any event will be mine." Porter believed the president had interceded on his behalf, but this is not certain, because Welles goes on to say that Lincoln "will sympathize with [Dahlgren], whom he regards with favor, while he had no great admiration or respect for Porter." One can speculate from Porter's past antics with his superiors that while Lincoln must have approved Porter's promotion, Fox must have championed it.[21]

Porter believed his promotion came at Lincoln's urging, and he may have been right. Aside from Farragut, whose esteem in Washington had fallen slightly, no officer in the Gulf or the Mississippi had worked harder, demonstrated more determination in combat, or functioned better with less direction than Porter. He understood the problems of capturing Vicksburg, and he agreed to cooperate with one of the president's pet political generals, Maj. Gen. John A. McClernand, who was raising regiments in Illinois. Porter knew little about McClernand, who ranked every West Point general in the West but Grant. Lincoln held to the mistaken belief that McClernand, a private and comrade in the Black Hawk War, had rescued Grant at Shiloh and would know what to do at Vicksburg. Privately, Porter questioned Lincoln's decision. He had recently met McClernand and sized him up as another "hybrid general" whose presence on the Mississippi would serve as an insult to Grant.[22]

On October 8, Welles met briefly with Porter to "caution him on certain points and encourage him on others." Donning his best grandfatherly demeanor, he on one hand urged Porter to use "great energy, great activity, abundant resources," and on the other attempted to tone down the acting admiral's penchant for recklessness, improvidence, and "presuming and assuming" too much. He reiterated Lincoln's wish that the Mississippi Squadron cooperate with McClernand's command. Grant was suffering the same ebb in popularity as Farragut, and the president hoped that new faces in the West would bring home an important victory.[23]

Porter, now forty-nine years old, still nursed the stigma of his father's 1825 court-martial. Almost everybody in the country had forgotten the incident but David Dixon and his seventy-four-year-old mother. Two days before leaving for his new command, he wrote her, "How proud my old Father would be if he could see me an Admiral. Yet it gives me pain to be hoisted over the heads of those old veterans who have so long considered the Navy as belonging to them. It seems somewhat like the Justice of Providence who takes this method of mortifying them for the treatment of my father."[24]

Porter reached Cairo, Illinois, on October 15, and Davis returned to Washington to resume his scientific studies. For the men in the flotilla, the day marked the beginning of a new and revitalized Mississippi Squadron. For Acting Rear Admiral Porter, it marked the beginning of an opportunity for a glorious career, but many of his enemies waited for him to fall, and some were eager to help. He had climbed the ladder too fast, too undeservedly, and too conspiratorially.[25]

And as long as he carried the probationary rate of "Acting," it was never too late to correct the mistake—and Porter knew it.

TWELVE

Mobilizing
the Mississippi
Squadron

Before Porter departed from Washington on October 9, 1862, to take command of the Mississippi Squadron, Welles suggested he visit the major towns along the Ohio River and assess their capabilities for expanding the freshwater navy. Stopping at Pittsburgh, Porter found the town's industry fully engaged in producing guns, engines, and iron plating, and he urged owners to expand their factories. Because of shoals in the upper Ohio, ironclads projected by the Navy Department could not be built at Pittsburgh, and most of the city's production had to be shipped down the river on barges.

He stopped at Cincinnati to inspect *Chillicothe, Indianola,* and *Tuscumbia,* which were supposed to be ready for service. *Indianola's* immense machinery and sidewheels left no room to quarter the crew. *Chillicothe's* gunports had been improperly cut, patched, and recut, and he found the vessel's steering wheel wedged between two of her forward guns, making it impossible for the helmsman and the gunners to function at the same time. Porter demanded changes to both vessels, but Commodore Hull would not budge without approval from the Navy Department. Writing Fox from Cincinnati, Porter said, "This is a one horse power country. The people are all asleep. You see what I said about the Iron Clad *Indianola*. I was quite wild. . . . If you give me the authority I will have them made comfortable at least." Porter worked out the changes with Lt. Comdr. George Brown and continued his trip down the Ohio.[1]

At St. Louis he inspected the tinclad *Signal,* a unique and lightly armored vessel drawing so little water that its builders, Thomas C. and Andrew J. Sweeney, claimed she "would float on a heavy dew." *Signal* and the tinclads that followed were stern-wheelers, 157 feet long and armed with two 30-pounder Parrott rifles, four 24-pounders, and two 12-pounders. Drawing only four feet, four inches, they were well adapted to scouting, could go almost anywhere, and, with their howitzers and bulletproof armor, provided ample protection from snipers ranging along the banks. Porter liked the concept, and he moved the construction of the next six vessels to Cincinnati so Brown could supervise the work.[2]

At St. Louis Porter also had his first look at *Choctaw* and *Lafayette,* two large and sturdy side-wheelers redesigned and modified by his brother William. These carried more armor on the casemates than other river ironclads, and were fitted with rams. In a strange turnabout, they were the same two vessels whose construction Welles had wanted David Dixon to supervise when the department was in a disciplinary mood. These huge vessels, 280 feet in length, displaced a thousand tons but drew only eight feet. Designed to develop a speed of ten knots, they fell far short of expectations.[3]

On October 15 Porter arrived at the mud-smeared naval center at Cairo dressed in admiral's regalia. Davis fired a salute and lowered his pennant. Porter stepped aboard *Benton* and raised his, a white-starred affair on a field of blue. He found operations stalled and took command of the most curious-looking squadron afloat. At the time, most of the serviceable vessels were below, holding the river above Helena.[4]

Because Porter had been on the opposite side of De Soto Point during the attack on Vicksburg, he had not seen much of Davis's flotilla. The squadron's fighting vessels consisted of seven "Pook Turtles," named after their designer, Samuel M. Pook, and built by James B. Eads. These side-wheelers, all of similar design, were called "city class" and named *Cairo, Carondelet, Cincinnati, Louisville, Mound City, Pittsburg,* and *Baron De Kalb* (formerly *St. Louis*). Round-nosed and

USS *De Kalb,* typical of the Pook turtle designs REPRINTED FROM JOHNSON
AND BUEL, *BATTLES AND LEADERS OF THE CIVIL WAR*

flat-bottomed, each turtle displaced about 512 tons, was 175 feet long,
and had a draft of about six feet. Their slanted casemates were armored
with two and a half inches of iron plate, and each was variously armed
with twelve guns ranging from 8-inch Dahlgrens to 12-pounder howitzers. Plunging shot from the Vicksburg batteries had damaged the turtles, and their casemates needed to be strengthened.

The other ironclads looked nothing like Pook's designs. The 633-ton
Benton was heavier, and when Porter arrived at Cairo and chose her as
his flagship she carried seven 32-pounders, two 9-inch guns, and seven
42-pounder army rifles. The ironclad had been built by Eads and used
by both Foote and Davis as the squadron's flagship. Her construction
was unlike anything afloat, being half again as large as a river steamer.
She had been built on two pontoonlike platforms 75 by 200 feet long,
with a huge paddle wheel rotating aft between twin hulls. The 355-ton
Essex, a name familiar to Porter, looked nothing like his father's sleek
frigate. The ugly center-wheeled ironclad, a converted riverboat, carried an arsenal of three 9-inch Dahlgrens, one 10-inch Dahlgren, and
two 50-pounder rifles. The 700-ton *Eastport,* originally purchased by
Gen. Leonidas Polk and built as a Confederate ironclad, was captured

in the Tennessee River after the fall of Forts Henry and Donelson. The War Department brought her to Cairo, finished the work, and armed her with eight guns.

Porter's wooden gunboats were an odd assortment of river craft modified to carry cannon. Three made excellent scouts—the 575-ton *Tyler,* the 572-ton *Conestoga,* and the 448-ton *Lexington,* all side-wheel steamers transferred from the War Department and modified by Comdr. John Rodgers. *Tyler* carried six 8-inch guns and three 30-pounder Parrott rifles; *Conestoga* carried four 32-pounders; and *Lexington* carried four 8-inch Dahlgrens, a 32-pounder, and a pair of 30s. The 840-ton side-wheeler *General Bragg,* among the lengthiest of the gunboats built by the War Department, mounted three guns. The 151-ton *Little Rebel,* captured at Memphis, and the 86-ton *Alfred Robb,* captured at Florence, Alabama, were the smallest of the squadron, each carrying three or four 12-pounders. *St. Clair,* a 203-ton stern-wheeler, was another riverboat too weak to carry anything heavier than four 12-pounders. When Porter reached Cairo they were all waiting for repairs.[5]

In addition to the gunboats, Porter beheld a spectacular and indescribable assemblage of tugboats, mortar scows, snag boats, supply boats, ammunition boats, dispatch vessels, and barges. There were floating machine shops, blacksmith shops, and old flatboats bearing shanties to house the families of escaped slaves who now labored for government wages. But this was not enough, for Porter had more shoreline to cover than any other squadron in the Union navy. He needed to patrol the Ohio, Cumberland, Tennessee, and central Mississippi watersheds, cooperating with the armies of Grant, William S. Rosecrans, and Ambrose E. Burnside wherever they chose to go. And before Porter could learn the names of all the vessels in his squadron, Welles issued orders to change some of them.[6]

An independent flotilla, Col. Alfred Ellet's Ram Fleet, operated in the Mississippi under the jurisdiction of the War Department. Unlike gunboats, the lightly armed vessels were fast, and the men who served them had been empowered by Secretary of War Stanton to think of themselves as river privateers. Col. Charles Ellet Jr. had modified nine riverboats by fastening heavy timbers to the hulls and cladding the bows with iron, afterward officering them with his friends and family and manning them with a set of daredevils recruited by himself. The fleet cooperated with Davis at Fort Pillow and then at Memphis, where the elder Ellet proved the value of the vessels but met his death. A week later, brother Alfred took over the family fleet and cooperated with Davis at Vicksburg.[7]

When Porter reached Cairo, the Ram Fleet consisted of seven vessels—*Switzerland, Queen of the West, Monarch, Lancaster, Lioness, Horner,* and *Fulton*—and Porter asked for them all, but he was not sure he wanted Ellet and his intemperate volunteers. On November 7, Welles's efforts to change the reporting status of the Ram Fleet culminated in a full cabinet meeting. Fox wrote Porter, "We beat our friend Edwin M. Stanton . . . placing Brigadier-General Ellet under your orders. If Ellet is the right kind of man all will go well, and if it goes wrong, Stanton will say it arose from placing him under a Navy officer. Stanton lost his temper so we beat him. The cool man always wins."[8]

Farragut's return to New Orleans and Davis's withdrawal to Helena had damaged Welles's reputation and injured the Union cause, but the failure taught the government a lesson. Although New Orleans and Baton Rouge had surrendered without a fight, not every river town would capitulate by threat. Lincoln and Welles now understood that no naval force could take cities like Vicksburg without an adequate army, and Stanton finally admitted that Grant needed more than a few gunboats to support his campaigns. Since all strategists agreed on the importance of controlling the Mississippi, Lincoln, Welles, and Stanton finally admitted that the only way to accomplish it was by well-coordinated joint attacks.

When Porter took command of the Mississippi Squadron, military operations in the West had reached a standstill. The river from Helena to Baton Rouge was controlled by the enemy. Across from Helena lay the head of Yazoo Pass and the junglelike Yazoo Delta, which stretched for two hundred miles down the eastern side of the Mississippi to Vicksburg. Grant's Army of the Tennessee, having Vicksburg as its objective but idle since early June, lay east of Memphis, holding the line of the Memphis and Charleston Railroad. General Van Dorn's grayclads, after being whipped at Corinth and Iuka, lay scattered in north-central Mississippi, too weak to take the offensive. Sherman's division of Grant's army waited at Memphis for orders, poised to move south by river or by land. On the opposite side of the great river, the fighting in

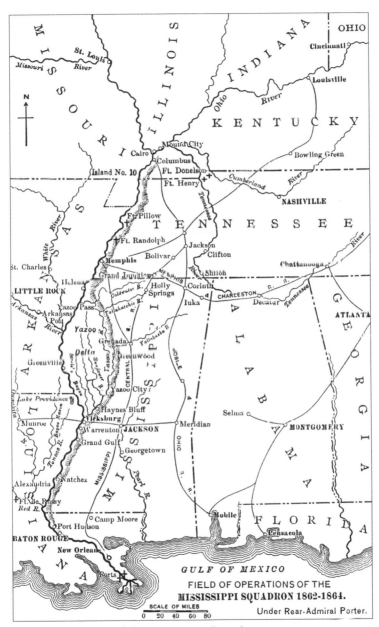

FIELD OF OPERATIONS OF THE
MISSISSIPPI SQUADRON 1862-1864.
Under Rear-Admiral Porter.

Field of operations of the Mississippi Squadron REPRINTED FROM
JAMES R. SOLEY, *ADMIRAL PORTER*

Missouri and Arkansas had withered to small skirmishes with bush-whackers, and General Bragg's Confederate advances into Kentucky had sputtered out during the summer. The whole country, North and South, waited for something to happen.

On October 15 fifty-three-year-old Capt. Henry Walke, a brave and capable officer, came up the river in *Carondelet* to meet Porter. A thin, gaunt-looking officer with wavy brown hair and dark, penetrating eyes, Walke possessed the same nervous energy as Porter and the same fertile mind and fluency for expressing himself. Early in the war, Walke was court-martialed for evacuating Pensacola, but Welles sent him to the upper Mississippi in the summer of 1861. In February 1862, under Flag Officer Foote, he participated in the capture of Forts Henry and Donelson. Two months later he ran the batteries of Island No. 10 in a howling thunderstorm, enabling the army to cross the river and attack the enemy from the rear. During the spring and early summer he participated in the capture of Fort Pillow and the Yazoo expedition under Davis, and by the time Porter reached Cairo, nobody knew conditions on the river better than Walke.[9]

Capt. Alexander M. Pennock, commandant of the Cairo Naval Station, joined the conference. Porter could not have found a man better suited to administrative responsibilities. Pennock demonstrated an intelligent grasp of complex problems and enthusiastically supported the new admiral. Although Porter was seldom at Cairo, he retained it as his depot, his navy yard, and his headquarters. The town was geographically situated at the confluence of the Mississippi and Ohio Rivers and a short distance from the Cumberland and the Tennessee. It was centrally located to all the shipyards, and Pennock, who was already at Cairo, had the station under such superb management that only a fool would move it. Porter wrote Fox, "I have been much pleased with my reception here by . . . Pennock and Walke, who met me with open arms. Pennock is a trump, and is worth his weight in gold."[10]

During the days on the lower Mississippi, Porter had developed a strong affection for Lt. K. Randolph Breese, who commanded one of the mortar flotilla's three divisions. When the admiral reached Cairo, he asked for Breese as his fleet captain. Welles approved the request, but when Breese arrived Porter changed his mind. Pennock possessed superior administrative capabilities. Porter saw it, named Pennock fleet captain, put Breese in command of the flagship *Black Hawk,* and used him as his chief of staff and closest confidant. His relationship with Breese remained unbroken throughout the war.[11]

When the War Department shifted the Ram Fleet to the navy, they also transferred the crews. Porter discovered that the army paid higher wages to men recruited from swamps, hogpens, and pumpkin patches than the navy paid sailors. Easing them down to naval ratings became an awkward and demoralizing process. Sickness had disabled four hundred men, and he gave them discharges. As they dropped out, Porter replaced them with emancipated slaves looking for work. Without a hospital afloat or ashore, he leased a hotel at Mound City, removed the tenants, and filled it with beds. He then imposed sanitary measures on the captains and issued standards of health for the squadron. Having accomplished all he could in his first days at Cairo, Porter asked Fox, "Where is McClernand? Hurry him up, we can't be idle 'till spring."[12]

While waiting for McClernand, Porter worked at his desk from dawn until midnight. With Pennock's assistance, he was determined to put the squadron in fighting trim, no matter what the cost. He demanded and received three hundred guns, purchased and armed fifty-four light-draft vessels, replaced defective ammunition, and printed orders by the hundreds on his own portable printing press. He had no patience for red tape and ignored it, and Fox accused him of circumventing regular channels and currying favor with the president. Welles said nothing, as he had cautioned Porter to do what was necessary and to keep what he did to himself.[13]

Porter gave special attention to marauding guerrilla bands who hounded his supply lines and hampered construction. He reorganized the squadron, detailing specific gunboats to special duty, ordering one group to stop illicit trade and another to disrupt the raids of bushwhackers. Walke took a squadron up the White River to destroy Confederate supplies. Capt. John A. Winslow, commanding *Baron De Kalb,* spotted a party of guerrillas near Memphis and sent a detail of twenty-five volunteers ashore who chased the renegades for nine miles, capturing all of them. When another band of hostiles ambushed the steamer *Gladiator,* Porter sent *Louisville* to Elm Grove with detachments from the 11th and 24th Indiana. They flushed the "scoundrels," chased them, and, when they failed to catch them, returned to the town and burned it. "This is the only way of putting a stop to guerrilla warfare," Porter declared. He established a blockade of the river from St. Louis to Helena with strict orders to levy contributions on offending towns, burn villages, and shell any plantation suspected of supporting the enemy.[14]

Lt. Comdr. Le Roy Fitch commanded the squadron operating in the Ohio, Tennessee, and Cumberland Rivers, and it took a month before Porter decided to keep him there. A new epidemic of guerrilla raids began to disrupt the communications of the various armies dependent upon the Tennessee and Cumberland for supplies. This brought a flurry of appeals for gunboat assistance. To Fitch he said, "You know my views pretty well by this time. Leave no means of crossing the rivers. I look to you to see that quiet is maintained there." Porter hoped for the best from Fitch, but he told Walke, "I find it pretty hard to comply with all the requests of the army. There are so many generals acting independently of each other that the whole American Navy could not comply with their demands."[15]

By November, Porter's reputation for heavy spending extended from Washington to the river towns along the Mississippi watershed. One cartoonist depicted him having the "Treasury of the United States in his foot locker, and was under full sail." Another captioned him as the "Terror of the Mississippi," picturing him as a full-feathered admiral with all the trimmings of an foppish despot.[16]

Porter could not understand why there had been no word from McClernand, who was in Springfield, Illinois, getting married. The general was close enough to Cairo to communicate by rail or telegraph, and while Porter waited another drama unfolded at Grant's headquarters at Jackson, Tennessee. To his surprise and annoyance, Grant learned that McClernand had been instructed by Lincoln to raise an army in Indiana, Iowa, and Illinois and move the troops to Memphis for the purpose of capturing Vicksburg. The orders posed many contradictions, and neither Lincoln nor Stanton knew how to explain them to Halleck or Grant. Grant began asking questions when the first of McClernand's forty-nine regiments trickled into Memphis.[17]

Upset by newspaper accounts and rumors of McClernand's independent command, Grant felt compelled to grasp the initiative. In an abandoned house at Oxford, Mississippi, he met privately with Sherman, who would be assimilated into McClernand's command once the general arrived. In an effort to shelter Sherman, and perhaps to save his own skin, Grant rushed to the offensive. He hurried plans to send Sherman down the river with forty thousand men, who would land on the banks of the Yazoo River and attack Vicksburg from the north. Grant, with his forces in northern Mississippi, would move on Vicksburg from the flank, his actions dependent on the enemy's response. Sherman, who wanted nothing to do with McClernand, rushed back to Memphis with orders from Grant to annex all of McClernand's troops and those of Maj. Gen. Samuel R. Curtis at Helena. Unaware of Grant's offensive, McClernand tarried at Springfield, gathering up the last of his forty-nine regiments.[18]

In mid-November Porter sensed that Grant was planning a campaign, but he puzzled over McClernand's silence. He wrote Fox, "I don't trust the Army. It is evident Grant is going to try to take Vicksburg without us, but he can't do it."[19]

On December 5 Grant wired Halleck, veiling his plans with an idle comment that he thought it "practicable" to send Sherman to the Yazoo River "and thus secure Vicksburg and the State of Mississippi." Halleck was no more enthused about McClernand's involvement than Grant and endorsed the campaign _as long as it was successful._ In replying, Halleck said, "Ask Admiral Porter to co-operate." Neither Grant nor Halleck mentioned the plan to McClernand until December 18, too late for the honeymooning general to rush down from Springfield and take command.[20]

Sherman wasted no time bringing Porter into the scheme, writing, "It will be necessary [for you] to engage the Vicksburg batteries until I have broken all their inland communications. Then Vicksburg must be attacked by land and river. In this I will defer to you."[21]

In Cairo, Porter had been beset with demands from the army and confused by conflicting requests. The time had come to meet with Grant, whom he had never seen before, and to straighten out all the confusion before it became worse.

In early December Grant started up the river to discuss joint operations, but Porter did not know what hour to expect him. Thinking that West Point officers dressed in military finery, he put on his best uniform and attended a supper aboard the quartermaster's ramshackle riverboat. During the meal an officer ushered in a short man with a brown beard who wore a seedy brown coat and dusty gray pants. "Admiral Porter," said the quartermaster, "meet General Grant." The two officers greeted each other warmly, and when Porter explained why he had donned his spotless blues they both had a good laugh. Porter, however, felt uncomfortable attired in military finery and would have preferred a less formal setting for his initial meeting with Grant. He had studied and admired Grant's "bulldog" attack on Forts Henry and Donelson, and from that action he observed a willingness on the part of the general to cooperate with the Navy.[22]

Porter excused himself from the dinner party and seated himself at a small table with Grant. "While I was looking earnestly at Grant, trying to make out how much of a man there was under the plain exterior," Porter wrote, "the General was regarding me to see what amount of work there was under all the gilt buttons and gold lace with which the Department had bedizened my coat."

Grant got right to the point. "When can you move your fleet?" he asked.

"Tomorrow, or whenever you wish to start."

"Then I will get off at once," Grant replied. "Sherman will meet you at Memphis on the 20th with forty thousand men, all embarked on transports. I will leave Holly Springs about the 18th and march on Grenada with all my force. This will draw off the rebel army now at Vicksburg . . . and you and Sherman can get possession of the place, as you will meet inferior numbers. I will be in with the rebels if they fall back on Vicksburg."

Porter asked about McClernand. Grant said the general would only complicate matters and that he preferred to take Vicksburg before McClernand left Springfield. Grant's explanation made sense, and Porter agreed to move down the river, embark Brig. Gen. Andrew J. Steele's division at Helena, escort it to the Yazoo, and make a demonstration along the river. Together, they might capture the great Confederate stronghold. The conference with Grant made a lasting impression on Porter. In their hour together, he decided that some West Point men were not as inflated and pretentious as he had been led to believe.

After Grant departed, Porter recalled an earlier letter to Fox when he wrote, "I don't trust the army. It is evident Grant is going to try and take Vicksburg, but he can't do it." But in Grant, all he saw contradicted that impression. Not only did Grant appear focused on his objective, but he manifested none of the army superiority prevalent in other commands and reached out to Porter as an equal partner.[23]

Maj. Gen. Ulysses S. Grant, the first general
Porter met whom he respected and considered
competent COURTESY U.S. ARMY MILITARY HISTORY
INSTITUTE

The growth of mutual respect and harmony between Porter and Grant began at their first meeting. They shared similar qualities. Both exhibited a directness of character and of expression. There was nothing artificial about their points of view, the way they thought, their speech, or their manners. They shared the same habit of confronting problems head-on and felt the same contempt for sham or pretense. More importantly, each understood his profession and could grasp complex situations in minute detail. But socially, the admiral and the general were exact opposites. Grant was reserved, serious, and often grave; Porter was expansive, and, although stern in matters of discipline and the business of war, he had a natural buoyancy of temper and a quick, often satirical wit. Between them, however, no personal intimacy existed, and as time passed they simply functioned as two colleagues with common objectives.

Two weeks before meeting Grant, Porter had sent Walke's squadron to the mouth of the Yazoo, thinking at the time that Sherman's main thrust would be directed at Grenada. When Porter and Grant met, Walke was in the Yazoo with *Carondelet, Louisville, Cairo,* and six gunboats. After hearing Grant's plan, Porter sent his gunboats down to Helena and authorized Walke to make a reconnaissance up the Yazoo, sound the bars, clear away torpedoes, and secure a safe landing for Brig. Gen. Frederick Steele's troops. Then, on December 14, he moved *Black Hawk* down the river to support Sherman's attack on Vicksburg.[24]

Black Hawk, a huge wooden side-wheeler 260 feet long and 45 feet wide, drew eight feet of water. She had no armor and carried eight small guns. She grounded on the trip downriver, and Porter did not reach Memphis until the 18th.[25]

Porter hastened to Sherman's headquarters at the Gayoso House but learned the general was in the field. Ushered into a reception room, he paced the floor for two hours. Couriers and messengers came and went, no one wore lace and feathers, and the whole atmosphere seemed to be charged with activity. Sherman finally bustled into the room and seemed astonished to find Porter there. He apologized for keeping the admiral waiting—no one had informed him of Porter's arrival. The meeting was another pleasant surprise for the admiral. Forty-two-year-old William Tecumseh Sherman, a tall, raw-boned Westerner with red hair cropped short and a dingy uniform spattered with mud, had the same unassuming demeanor as Grant but the fiery look of a warrior. He had none of the trappings Porter attributed to West Pointers, and in their brief meeting Sherman related in the simplest terms possible all that he had done, all he was doing, and all he intended to do. Never had Porter met another man so open and direct—a man who seemed to have such a complete grasp of the situation. Here was a working general, Porter recalled, "who poked the fire and talked to me as if he had known me all his life." Sherman thought and spoke with the same nervous energy as Porter, and at their first meeting the two officers bonded and would become fast friends, working together in close accord for the rest of their lives. After arranging the final details of the operation, Porter returned to *Black Hawk* to rejoin his squadron.[26]

In Springfield, McClernand sensed a stirring in the new regiments he had sent to Memphis. On December 12 he wired Lincoln, "May I

Maj. Gen. William T. Sherman, who became
Porter's lifelong friend COURTESY U.S. ARMY
MILITARY HISTORY INSTITUTE

not ask therefore to be sent forward immediately?" Five days later he
nervously inquired, "I believe I am superseded. Please advise me." On
the 18th Stanton assigned McClernand to the XXIII Army Corps,
thereby compelling him to wait for orders from Grant. On the 18th
Halleck wired Grant, asking him to divide his force into four army
corps and to include McClernand's as one constituting "part of the river
expedition . . . under your directions." Grant then wired McClernand,
but Confederate cavalry snipped all the telegraph lines along the
Tennessee River and McClernand did not get the order until the 23rd.
Grant wanted nothing to do with McClernand and urged Sherman and
Porter to hurry the attack. McClernand, however, dallied at Springfield
and did not reach Memphis until December 28. By then, Grant's pin-
cer movement and Sherman's attack had become a colossal failure.[27]

But Porter had his own problems, and they had little to do with General McClernand.

THIRTEEN

The Chickasaw Bluffs Fiasco

Grant's threefold plan to capture Vicksburg made tactical sense to Porter. Beginning at the mouth of the Yazoo River, twelve miles north of Vicksburg, Porter would work upstream, sweep it of torpedoes, and cover Sherman's landing. The topography of the area, however, was forbidding, with swampy lowlands along the river and, towering above, Chickasaw Bluffs, which north of Vicksburg bent to the east and met the Yazoo at Drumgould's Bluff, fifteen miles northeast of the fortified city. Porter's role was to secure landing sites for Sherman's army inside the lowlands bounded by the Mississippi River to the west, the Yazoo to the north, and the Chickasaw ridge running between Vicksburg and Drumgould's Bluff. Once Porter secured a lodgment, the army would land and assault the ridge north of Vicksburg. Sherman planned to cross the Chickasaw Bayou lowlands quickly, scale the bluffs, get in the rear of Vicksburg with a superior force, and cut off the city's rail connection with Jackson.

Sherman's and Porter's success, however, depended upon part three of the plan—which was Grant's role. Departing from Oxford, Mississippi, with forty thousand men a few days before Sherman left Memphis, Grant planned to march on Grenada and threaten Jackson.

He would then sweep down the Mississippi Railroad, swing over to the eastern bank of the upper Yazoo River, and force Lt. Gen. John C. Pemberton to meet the attack by drawing off Vicksburg's defenders.

The Confederates, however, were better prepared to meet the back-door assault than either Grant or Sherman realized. On December 20 General Van Dorn destroyed Grant's supply center at Holly Springs, and Maj. Gen. Nathan Bedford Forrest struck Union communications and brought part three of the plan to a standstill. While Van Dorn operated in Grant's rear, Pemberton received word that a large Union flotilla of transports, ironclads, gunboats, and mortars was moving downriver. He grimly read the dispatches and rushed Brig. Gen. John Gregg's brigade to Vicksburg.[1]

What Grant feared most happened. Forced by Van Dorn to withdraw to Grand Junction, Grant left Pemberton free to shift his army to Vicksburg, and Sherman, unaware of Grant's retreat, was left to stumble blindly through the swampy lowlands of Chickasaw Bayou.[2]

A few days before the flotilla departed for Vicksburg, Porter learned of his first casualty. Acting on orders, Walke's squadron entered the Yazoo River on December 12 to secure a landing for Sherman's corps. With the lightdrafts *Marmora* and *Signal* ahead with torpedo-dragging equipment, *Cairo*, *Pittsburg*, and *Queen of the West* followed at a safe distance. As they rounded a bend, *Marmora* stopped to detonate a torpedo. *Cairo*, commanded by twenty-six-year-old Lt. Comdr. Thomas O. Selfridge, stood off the bank when two violent explosions jarred the vessel. *Cairo's* bow lifted, shuddered, and plunged below the water. In two minutes the forecastle filled. Selfridge conned the ironclad against the bank as sailors made a futile effort to man the pumps. *Queen of the West* came alongside and took off the crew. Twelve minutes later *Cairo* lay on the bottom with only the tops of her stacks showing. Miraculously, nobody was injured.[3]

Selfridge met *Black Hawk* coming down the Mississippi, went on board to give his report, and said, "I suppose you will want to hold a court." "Court!" Porter roared. "I have no time to order courts. I can't blame an officer who seeks to put his ship close to the enemy." Then, turning to Breese, he said, "Make out Selfridge's orders to the *Conestoga*." Selfridge departed feeling he could go through "hellfire and water" for a man like the admiral.[4]

*Capt. Thomas O. Selfridge Jr., commander
of USS Cairo* REPRINTED FROM JOHNSON AND
BUEL, *BATTLES AND LEADERS OF THE CIVIL WAR*

The loss of *Cairo* was Porter's first disaster—the worst kind of blow at the outset of a campaign. He blamed the loss on Selfridge's impetuosity, but told Welles, "It was all done in the line of duty," adding that he could lose three or four vessels before the campaign was over. Porter's reaction to *Cairo's* loss was typical of his feelings toward officers who served under him. He never discouraged individuality in his juniors, repressed their zeal, or cooled their ardor.[5]

On the 23rd the Porter-Sherman expedition reached the mouth of the Yazoo. By last accounts, both men expected Grant to be beyond Grenada and driving down the Yalobusha River to the Yazoo. Another force, under Maj. Gen. Nathaniel P. Banks, was supposed to be working up from New Orleans to attack Port Hudson. After leaving their communications behind at Memphis, neither Porter nor Sherman knew that all the telegraph lines had been cut and both attacks had collapsed.

Christmas Day came and went with no celebration and with nothing to eat but rations. Men lolled drearily on the transports, waiting for Sherman's pioneers to hack down trees and corduroy a way through the thicket to the base of the hills. Every day, all day long, snipers hiding in thick brush fired at the work parties, and from upriver the soldiers could hear the navy's guns blasting the woods with grape.

At noon on the 26th the expedition entered the Yazoo, the transports in a long, single line led by *Black Hawk*. Above a levee curled the smoldering wisps of smoke from a large brick home with a sugar refinery, sawmill, cotton gin, and quarters for three hundred slaves, the plantation of Maj. Gen. Albert Sydney Johnston, killed at Shiloh. After passing Steele's Bayou, the transports settled against the bank near Johnson's Farm. Soldiers disembarked and hacked their way through willows and vines choking access to higher ground. As if on cue, after several days of dry, comfortable weather, rain began to fall. With nightfall came confusion. Companies separated, and nobody could find Andrew J. Smith's division.[6]

Johnson's Farm was an island separated from Vicksburg by swamps, lagoons, bayous, and quicksand—not a good place to launch an attack, even in dry weather. The Union right rested on Old River and the left on Chickasaw Bayou, both miserable and muddy wetlands. Sherman's two-day delay in getting his troops ashore gave the Confederates just enough time to bolster their defenses and order up more batteries.

On the eve of Sherman's assault, a slave hailed *Black Hawk* and told Porter that President Davis was in Vicksburg with his wife. Davis was not there but at Jackson, visiting Gov. John J. Pettus at the statehouse, now a dilapidated structure with broken windows and scarred walls. Porter and Davis were old friends, and the admiral must have anticipated with pleasure the prospect of an early reunion.[7]

On December 27 the Mississippi Squadron steamed up the Yazoo to draw Maj. Gen. Martin L. Smith's brigade away from Vicksburg and to clear the river of torpedoes as far as Thompson's Lake. Several gunboats were on the stocks at Yazoo City, and to save them Smith had to stop the Union advance before it passed Haynes' Bluff. Porter intended to destroy the shipyard before the vessels were completed, but his first initiative was to support Sherman's attack.[8]

Taking *Benton*, Lt. Comdr. William Gwin found the enemy laying torpedoes almost as fast as his eight gunboats could haul them up. At noon he arrived below Haynes' Bluff, the point where the ridge running northeast from Vicksburg struck the Yazoo. Gwin observed heavy batteries on the hills, and a huge raft covered with railroad iron blocked the river. He took the point, anchored, and engaged the batteries for two hours. Shots from 64-pounders caromed off *Benton's* pilothouse and side armor but crushed her unprotected deck. Gwin stayed too long on the quarterdeck. A shot ricocheted off *Benton's* casemate and struck him in the chest, ripping out the muscle of his right arm. When *Benton* returned down the river, her deck was a shambles. In the action, seven men had been wounded—two mortally, one being Gwin.[9]

Porter was conferring with Sherman when *Benton* hove in sight, and the enemy's stiff resistance at Haynes' Bluff worried the general. Flanking Vicksburg would not be an easy chore unless Grant arrived on schedule. Reconnaissance parties reported Chickasaw Bayou dismal, desolate, snarled with cypress trees, and tangled with vines, and the bayous brown and stinking with fetid swamp water. The only partially cleared area lay between Thompson's Lake to the east and McNutt Lake to the west, and this mile-and-a-half section was just below Chickasaw Bluffs.

On the wet, dreary morning of the 27th, Sherman's army slogged into position. Steele's division moved to establish a bridgehead on the right bank of Chickasaw Bayou. Brig. Gen. George W. Morgan's division went below to force a crossing of the bayou, gain the river road, and secure a lodgment on Walnut Hills. Brig. Gen. Morgan L. Smith's seven thousand men took position on the right and near the main road from Johnson's Farm to Vicksburg. On the far right, A. J. Smith's division covered Morgan Smith's flank. The division wasted the day getting into position—and then the rain fell in torrents.

On the 28th Sherman skirmished on the left, trying to set up an assault on Chickasaw Bluffs, but the combination of rain, dense fog, and enemy resistance checked the movement. On the 29th he attempted to break through the Confederate center by scaling the heights. All along the line artillery roared, viciously answered by enemy batteries on the heights. At noon the Union army emerged from the woods, only to be knocked apart by a well-entrenched enemy. Brig. Gen. Frank P. Blair's brigade reached the base of the bluffs but stumbled into a withering fire, and when Sherman's all-out attack failed to materialize, Blair's shattered brigade fell back, repulsed with heavy casualties.[10]

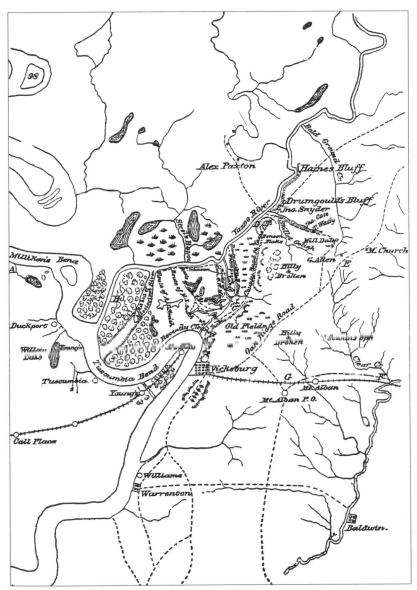

Sketch of Vicksburg's defenses during the Chickasaw Bluffs campaign
REPRINTED FROM *OFFICIAL RECORDS OF THE UNION AND CONFEDERATE
NAVIES*

With the elements, the topography, and the enemy all working against him, Sherman sensed defeat. He had heard nothing from Grant or Banks, and on the night of the 29th he spilled out his problems to Porter, admitting he could not break the enemy's center. In the hope of connecting with Grant's force, Sherman suggested taking ten thousand troops up the Yazoo, assaulting the batteries at Drumgould's Bluff, and flanking the enemy's right while the rest of his force continued to threaten its center.[11]

To complicate matters, General McClernand reached Memphis and found all of his troops gone. He asked where they were. Gone south with Sherman, was his answer. Baffled, the angry general departed in a huff and hastened down the Mississippi to find his command.[12]

Porter, suspecting the upper river had been reseeded with torpedoes, set out on a tug to find his gunboats. He located his commanders, pulled them out of bed, and told them of Sherman's plan. Ellet proposed attaching a giant rake to the bow of the ram *Lioness,* one large enough to tear out the cables holding the devices to their moorings. Ellet said he could keep forty-five feet of water between the rake and his ram, enough to explode the mines without damaging his vessel. Porter told Ellet to do it and be ready to move at dawn.[13]

With this obstacle out of the way, Porter went looking for Sherman. Never had he seen a fog like the one blanketing the Yazoo. Maneuvering in the narrow stream, he collided with Steele's flagship, broke her rudder, and woke the general from a sound sleep. Porter finally located Sherman and promised full support. He cautioned Sherman to select the quietest of his transports, protect their boilers with bales of hay, screen the fireboxes, show no lights, muffle the bells, and camouflage the vessels with mud and brush.[14]

On the night of the 31st Porter embarked Steele's division and Col. Giles A. Smith's brigade, but the maddening fog prevented the expedition from getting under way. At daylight rain poured down so heavily that Sherman suspended the attack and reembarked his army. He had tried to beat both the enemy and McClernand's assumption of command at the same time and failed at each. Porter led the flotilla out of the river and anchored it at Milliken's Bend.[15]

His hurried departure from Memphis now haunted Sherman. In a black, condemning mood, he blamed Grant and Banks for failing him. He tersely summed up the campaign to General in Chief Halleck: "I reached Vicksburg at the time appointed, landed, assaulted, and failed. Re-embarked my command unopposed and turned it over to my successor, General McClernand." The army suffered 1,776 casualties— 208 killed, the others wounded or missing.[16]

Porter, however, did not give up. On January 1 he wrote Sherman, "'Man proposes, God disposes.' It is all right. What next?" But Porter had his own problems. A careless towboat captain rammed a coal scow and sank the admiral's reserve of anthracite. His ironclads could not go far without it, but the lightdrafts burned wood and could go where they pleased. Porter wrote Welles, "While the army leaders are deciding what to do . . . I have no coal and can not move far."[17]

McClernand arrived at Milliken's Bend on the morning of January 2, but before venturing far he stopped at *Black Hawk* to speak with Porter. Instead of finding his personally recruited troops poised for a campaign, he learned they had been defeated at the hands of a "crazy" West Pointer. McClernand departed in a huff and, having no plans of his own, returned late at night with Sherman. Porter met them in his nightshirt. In order to salvage some dignity from a bungled expedition, McClernand wanted to discuss Sherman's proposal for a joint attack on Arkansas Post and asked if Porter would supply gunboat support. During the Chickasaw Bluffs campaign, a rebel steamer had descended from Arkansas Post and captured the steamer *Blue Wing*, loaded with ordnance and towing two coal barges. Porter recalled the theft, so he agreed to support the mission, but he resented McClernand's insolence toward Sherman and told him so, adding, "If General Sherman goes in command of the troops, I will go along with my whole force and make a sure thing of it; otherwise I will have nothing to do with the affair."[18]

Sherman excused himself from the cabin, but when McClernand seated himself at a table to study a map, Porter went in search of the West Pointer and found him on deck. "Admiral," Sherman grumbled reproachfully, "how could you make such a remark to McClernand? He hates me already, and you have made him an enemy for life."

"I don't care," Porter replied, "he shall not be rude to you in my cabin, and I was glad of the opportunity of letting him know my sentiments."

Porter returned to the cabin with Sherman and found McClernand anxious to lead an attack on Arkansas Post. "There is no objection," he asked, "to my going along?"

"None in the world," Porter replied, and, because McClernand had expropriated Sherman's plan, he added, "as long as Sherman commands the army."[19]

After meeting Grant and Sherman, and then listening to the likes of Butler and McClernand, Porter's disdain of political generals grew to outright contempt. With McClernand came scores of news reporters. In exchange for favors they castigated Sherman, who accepted the criticism somberly. Then, after Sherman suggested the expedition to Arkansas Post, McClernand took credit for the idea. Porter observed that McClernand would never drop politics and would never make a good soldier.[20]

On January 4 McClernand assumed command of the military force assembled at Milliken's Bend. To separate it from Sherman's defeated "Mississippi River Expedition," he renamed it the Army of the Mississippi. Then he divided it, placing Sherman in command of the XV Corps and Morgan in charge of the XIII Corps. McClernand would orchestrate the attack on Arkansas Post—not Sherman.[21]

Grant returned to Holly Springs on December 22, but he had heard nothing from Sherman or McClernand. His first indication of trouble arrived by wire from Halleck on January 7: "Richmond papers of the 5th and 6th say Sherman has been defeated. Every possible effort must be made to reinforce him. . . . We must not fail in this if within human power to accomplish it."[22]

The White House expressed great concern. The North had been rocked by reverses. Grant's failure, then Sherman's, only punctuated the Army of the Potomac's bloody repulse at Fredericksburg and Rosecran's stalemate at Stone's River. In the Gulf, a few Texas cottonclads outmaneuvered a small flotilla of Farragut's blockaders and recaptured Galveston. With torrents of invectives reverberating off the halls of the War Department, Stanton and Halleck scrambled for survival while the cabinet resorted to finger-pointing. Referring to the recent disasters, Welles blamed the mess on Halleck, and cries of "We want McClellan!" again appeared in the daily news.[23]

But none of the problems in Washington filtered down the Mississippi to the isolated force at Milliken's Bend. As McClernand advanced his preparations for the assault up the Arkansas River, Grant made an effort to communicate with Sherman, promising to send another fifteen thousand troops to breach Vicksburg's defenses. On the same day, January 8, McClernand made his first attempt to open communications with Grant, advising him of the Arkansas Post expedition. Neither message reached the intended recipient until too late. As Grant started part of his army for Memphis, Porter nosed upstream in *Black Hawk* and headed for the White River cutoff, followed by a string of gunboats and transports.[24]

Grant reached Memphis on January 10 and attempted to communicate with McClernand and Porter. Learning that the expedition had already left Milliken's Bend, he advised Halleck, "General McClernand has fallen back to White River, and gone on a wild goose chase to the Post of Arkansas."[25]

He tried to recall McClernand but was three days late. McClernand's desertion of Vicksburg not only amazed Grant but also stunned Halleck. On the 12th, Halleck wired Grant: "You are hereby authorized to relieve General McClernand from command of the expedition against Vicksburg, giving it to the next in rank or taking it yourself."[26]

This was exactly the order Grant wanted, but to relieve McClernand he had to catch him.

FOURTEEN

McClernand's "Wild Goose Chase"

On January 8, 1863, Porter picked three of his best turtles—*Baron De Kalb, Louisville,* and *Cincinnati*—and, with a squadron of tinclads, headed for the White River cutoff to the Arkansas. With two disgruntled generals following in transports, the expedition manifested all the characteristics of a bad adventure. The flotilla stopped often to cut firewood for the wood-burning steamers towing the admiral's coal-starved ironclads. The invasion caused great consternation among the planters. As the squadron puffed by, farmers frantically drove their hogs and cattle into the woods and emptied their grain into the river.[1]

Rattler took the point and sounded the White River cutoff, followed by the tinclads *Juliet, Forest Rose, Glide,* and *Romeo,* their guns loaded and fuses cut to one second. Then came the steamers towing the turtles, and interspersed among them were *Black Hawk, Signal, Marmora, Springfield, New Era,* and *Lexington.* They entered the Arkansas late on the afternoon of the 9th and began the ascent of the river.[2]

Early in the war, Confederate engineers looking along the Arkansas River for a good site above floodwater to build an earthwork chose a small village called Arkansas Post. Fort Hindman, as it was called, lay 25 miles above the mouth of the Arkansas River and 117 miles below Little

Maj. Gen. John A. McClernand, one of
Lincoln's political generals REPRINTED
FROM JOHNSON AND BUEL, *BATTLES AND
LEADERS OF THE CIVIL WAR*

Rock. It was a square, full-bastioned fort whose exterior scarps between salient angles were each one hundred yards in length with parapets, ditches, and firing steps for infantry. Heavy oak casemates, armored with railroad iron, mounted fourteen guns ranging from 8- and 9-inch Columbiads in the casemates to 6- and 10-pounder Parrotts on carriages. Brig. Gen. Thomas J. Churchill commanded the three thousand– man garrison, which also supported several regiments of Texas cavalry.[3]

On the evening of January 9 the army disembarked four miles below Fort Hindman—well out of range of enemy cannon. Soldiers built campfires, cooked salt pork, boiled coffee, and nibbled on crackers. McClernand, however, had landed the force near a large swamp that had to be crossed to reach the flank of the enemy. Porter met with Sherman to study a map. Neither wanted to fire into the other, which meant that the ironclads would have to anchor about four hundred yards below the fort and angle in their fire. Aware that during the night the enemy might try to board his ironclads, the admiral issued orders to grease the casemates with tallow.[4]

On the morning of the 10th, Porter waited for a signal from McClernand to bring up the ironclads and commence the bombardment, but the Union advance got mired in the swamps. Rather than waste the day, Porter advanced *Black Hawk* and *Rattler* to test the enemy's batteries. Fort Hindman's three Columbiads replied, but the enemy's powder had deteriorated and several shots barely made it over the levee.[5]

After getting the range, Porter pulled back to confer with McClernand and learned that the attack had been delayed until late afternoon. At 5:30 Porter ordered *Baron De Kalb,* under Lt. Comdr. John G. Walker; *Louisville,* Lt. Comdr. Elias K. Owens; and *Cincinnati,* Lt. Comdr. George M. Bache, to move up to the fort and open fire. Each ironclad, anchored en echelon, fired on the three big Columbiads and the four 10-pounder Parrotts in the bastion. Return fire from Col. John W. Dunnington's batteries was steady but ineffective, so Porter brought up *Black Hawk* and *Lexington* to throw in shrapnel and light rifled shell. He saw an opportunity to enfilade the fort and ordered *Rattler* Lt. Comdr. Watson Smith, to pass through the ironclads and get above the fort. Smith ran into heavy fire from the Parrotts and became entangled in submerged piles. The turtles stepped up the fire and silenced the batteries. *Rattler* returned for repairs, and Porter ceased firing. Dusk fell, and McClernand postponed his assault until morning.[6]

At dawn on the 11th, 32,000 bluecoats spent the morning moving into position north of Fort Hindman to attack Churchill's reinforced garrison of 4,900 defenders. McClernand sent word to Porter that as soon as the gunboats opened, he would advance.

At 1:00 P.M. *Baron De Kalb, Louisville, Cincinnati,* and *Lexington* churned upriver and ranged in on their assigned targets—Walker in *De Kalb,* the northeast bastion; Bache in *Cincinnati,* the next casemate; and Owen in *Louisville,* the upper bastion on the riverfront. The fort replied, and in the smoke smothering the valley the tinclads *Rattler* and *Glide* joined the fray.

Porter's signals became obscured by the smoke, so he transferred his flag to the tug *Thistle,* circulated among the squadron, and stepped up the firing. Sharpshooters in the parapets sprayed *Thistle* with musket fire, but Porter stayed on deck, infusing the gunboats with his energy. When fire broke out on *Louisville,* he sent a detail from *Thistle* to put it out. He spared no vessel, forcing the turtles to rely on their armor, and for an hour they took a heavy pounding. Eight times 9-inch shells struck *Cincinnati*'s pilothouse but glanced off "like peas against glass." Porter was curious to see whether smearing tallow on casemates reduced damage and was delighted when the enemy's projectiles caromed off the plates and hurtled into the woods on the opposite shore. Even *Rattler*, slushed down with a heavy coat of tallow, escaped injury after being struck by two 9-inch shells on her flimsy three-quarter-inch plating. *De Kalb*'s forward casemate, however, finally buckled after three hours' hammering by solid shot, and before the contest ended she lost one of her 10-inch Dahlgrens and a 32-pounder.[7]

In the rear of the fort, General Morgan's bluecoated corps, strung out in a line a half-mile long, began its advance. In two hours it moved six hundred yards but was shaken by casualties. The attack bogged down, and Morgan asked Sherman for reinforcements.[8]

On the right, Sherman continued to have problems getting his force through swampy gullies and fallen timber. "Into this," Sherman said, "the attacking columns dashed rapidly, and there encountered the fire of the enemy's artillery and infantry, well direct from their perfect cover, which checked the speed of our advance." He could hear the navy's guns hammering the fort, but "I could not see the gunboats, and had to judge of their progress by the sound of their fire. This was at first slow and steady, but rapidly approached the fort and enveloped it with a complete hailstorm of shot and shell."[9]

Word reached Porter that Morgan's troops had been checked at the rifle pits and were falling back. He hastened to *Black Hawk*, filled her decks with unemployed regiments, and steered for the fort. As he passed through the ironclads the guns of Fort Hindman fell silent. The smashing fire of the turtles at close range had splintered the heavy oaken walls of the bastions, ripped away the iron rails like so many matchsticks, knocked apart the casemates, and crumbled in the roofs. At 4:00 P.M., as *Black Hawk* ran out a line to the levee, white flags popped out along the crumpled parapets.

Porter called up Smith's *Rattler*, along with Ellet's *Monarch* and Lt. Selim E. Woodworth's *Glide*, and ordered them to go above the fort, cut off the enemy's retreat, and clear out enemy shipping. Ten miles above the Post, Smith and Woodworth destroyed a ferry and captured forty prisoners, but the water became too shallow for further operations and all three vessels returned and anchored above the fort.[10]

Outnumbered but game, Churchill's defenders made a valiant stand at the breastworks, repulsing Sherman twice and inflicting heavy casualties. Just when Churchill thought he could hold, he turned and looked down the line. To his horror, he observed white flags fluttering in the parapets and others in the pits. At 4:30 the commander of the fort, Colonel Dunnington, and thirty-six sailors of the marine battery surrendered the bastion to Porter, and Churchill, having no other recourse, surrendered to Sherman. Throughout the fighting, McClernand had remained on *Tigress,* troubled by the fact that the Confederates made no effort to escape. Churchill had been under orders to defend the fort or die in the trenches, which he did with splendid determination until defied by his own command. By the time McClernand reached the field, Churchill's defenders had stacked their rifles and were lounging wearily on the ground.[11]

Porter surveyed the damage, stopping briefly to visit with Colonel Dunnington. "You wouldn't have got us," the colonel growled, "had it not been for your damned gunboats."[12]

During the height of the bombardment, Sherman remembered seeing Porter's flag directly under the fort. Dunnington's surrender, which led to Churchill's defeat, was entirely the work of the navy. Churchill admitted that after three hours of heavy fire, the gunboats "succeeded in silencing every gun we had with the exception of a small 6-pounder Parrott which was on the land side."[13]

At Fort Hindman the work of the navy was through. Every gun opposing Porter's ironclads was either knocked apart or disabled. *Louisville* and *Baron De Kalb,* however, reported six killed and twenty-five wounded, *De Kalb* losing two guns and sustaining severe hull damage, but the other vessels were unhurt.[14]

The capture of Fort Hindman could not have ended any other way. Porter praised the work of his squadron, writing, "We captured every important fort and heavy gun the rebels had in that swampy State. Arkansas is now nothing but some field pieces." McClernand called it a great victory, and from a comfortable seat in Sherman's cabin on *Tigress* he chortled happily, "Glorious! Glorious! I'll make a splendid report." Union casualties, however, exceeded a thousand—most of them in

Sherman's corps. Churchill reported only 60 killed and "75 or 80" wounded, but he lost his entire force, surrendering 4,791 prisoners, 17 pieces of artillery, 3,000 stands of arms, tons of shot, shell, and canister, and 46,000 rounds of small-arms ammunition.[15]

Euphoric over the victory, McClernand sped his report to Memphis and had it telegraphed to Washington. Porter assembled his reports and sent them by gunboat to Cairo. Welles heard the good news from the War Department. He celebrated with his colleagues but urged Porter to speed up his communications. "You will receive the first account of the next battle we have," Porter replied, adding with disgust, "I find that Army officers are not willing to give the Navy credit (even in very small matters) they are entitled to."

Sherman admitted that "McClernand's report of the capture of Fort Hindman almost ignored the action of Porter's fleet altogether. This was unfair, for I know that the admiral led his fleet in person in the river-attack, and that his guns silenced those of Fort Hindman, and drove the gunners into the ditch."[16]

Although the victory was not as great as McClernand claimed, it was a pleasant change from the Chickasaw Bayou fiasco and more than evened the score on losses. Grant thought little of the victory, calling it a waste of time, material, men, and resources. Regardless of what capital it produced in Washington, to the general it was a "wild goose chase."[17]

Grant, however, overlooked a fringe benefit. Lt. Gen. Theophilus Holmes, commanding the Trans-Mississippi with headquarters at Little Rock, had received repeated calls from Pemberton for reinforcements. After Fort Hindman fell, Holmes ignored Pemberton's requests.

Now that McClernand had Fort Hindman, he was not sure what to do with it, and before he could leave it he had to blow it up. And Grant, suspicious that McClernand would stay up the Arkansas as long as possible and keep Porter occupied, decided on January 14 to go there himself and bring the army back to Milliken's Bend.[18]

Grant's instincts served him well, for McClernand was toying with the idea of sending Porter and Sherman to Little Rock. McClernand did not want his force merged with Grant's, and when Porter said he could not reach Little Rock because of low water, McClernand asked him to send a squadron to the White, pick up Brig. Gen. Willis A. Gorman's force, and clean out the enemy's works at St. Charles, De Vall's Bluff, and Des Arc. Grant, who at the time had heard nothing from Porter, sent Col. Josiah W. Bissell of the engineers to Milliken's Bend to confer with the admiral on the practicality of reopening the canal on the peninsula below Vicksburg. Porter was with McClernand and not at Milliken's Bend, thus compelling Grant to find McClernand and, if necessary, drag him back to Vicksburg.[19]

In the meantime, Walker's White River expedition reached St. Charles on the 14th, and the Confederate garrison fled when *Baron De Kalb* and *Cincinnati* hove into sight. *Blue Wing,* a fast steamer recently captured by the Confederates, made off with the fort's guns, and Walker sent the tinclads after her. By the 23rd Walker had destroyed every Confederate outpost for three hundred miles up the White, but he never caught *Blue Wing.* Porter considered the raid useless, writing Welles, "I presume we will now move down the Mississippi to carry out what I conceive to have been the plans for which this army was organized, viz, the capture of Vicksburg. It is rather a waste of time, stopping here and there."[20]

Grant finally caught up with McClernand and ordered him back to Vicksburg. Porter recalled Walker's squadron, posted two timberclads at the mouths of the Arkansas and White, and took his squadron back to Milliken's Bend. When Walker's flotilla rejoined the Mississippi Squadron, Porter was amazed at its broken condition. He praised Walker for cleaning out the White and blamed the damage on McClernand's senseless river raids. The gunboats would be ready, Porter promised Welles, by the time the army arrived.[21]

Fearing assimilation into Grant's command, McClernand howled to Lincoln: "I believe my success here is gall and wormwood to the clique of West Pointers who have been persecuting me for months. . . . Do not let me be clandestinely destroyed, or, what is worse, dishonored without a hearing."[22]

In summing up his feelings to Fox, Porter wrote:

> I think it a great misfortune that McClernand should have superseded Sherman who is every inch a soldier, and has the confidence of his men. McClernand is no soldier, and has the confidence of no one, unless it may be two or three of his staff. Sherman has great difficulty hauling him along. If Sherman was to leave tomorrow (which I think he will do) the whole thing will drop to pieces.

The Army made a poor show at this place,—thirty thousand men could certainly have assaulted the Fort, after we had dismounted every gun, and we waited an hour nearly, after destroying the batteries, to let them try it, but they were severely repulsed by the Rebels, on the first attempt, and we finished the business in ten minutes by a fire that no human beings could withstand.

If we don't succeed in opening the [Mississippi] we lose the whole West, and McClernand won't ever open it.[23]

Grant, however, was not about to leave Sherman with McClernand's command. After lengthy discussions with Porter and his generals, Grant realized that McClernand was the only commander indifferent toward the importance of capturing Vicksburg. He wrote Halleck, "I regard it my duty to state that I found there was not sufficient confidence felt in General McClernand as a commander, either by the Army or Navy, to insure him success. Admiral Porter told me that he had written freely to the Secretary of the Navy, with the request that what he said might be shown to the Secretary of War." Porter, of course, preferred the bristling redheaded West Pointer who damned politics, damned reporters, and believed in hard fighting. Grant attached McClernand's army to his own with the comment, "It was forced upon me [by Porter and Sherman]." Sherman retained command of the XV Corps, and McClernand had to settle for the XIII Corps. A few days later Grant added, "If Sherman had been left in command here, such is my confidence in him that I would not have thought my presence necessary." Lincoln silently agreed.[24]

At Milliken's Bend Porter assessed his squadron. Besides *Black Hawk,* he had seven turtles, nine gunboats, and four of Ellet's rams available for operations at Vicksburg. *New Era* and *Carondelet* were at Island No. 10, *Lexington* was en route to Cairo, *Bragg* and *Conestoga* were at the mouths of the Arkansas and White Rivers, and five boats were up the Tennessee. *Little Rebel, Clara Dolsen,* and *New National* were at Cairo, and five new vessels—*Eastport, Lafayette, Choctaw, Indianola,* and *Tuscumbia*—were fitting out.[25]

On January 24 Porter wrote Senator Grimes: "We are now opposite Vicksburg, with the whole army landed on the neck of land in front of the city. What they are going to do there they only know. I suppose they will swim over when they are ready. . . . My plan is to work up the Yazoo and get in there and for an army to come down the Yazoo, cut off supplies, and attack their rear."[26]

On the 27th the tinclad *Rattler* and the rams *Queen of the West* and *Lioness* ascended the Yazoo to determine whether Confederates had salvaged the sunken *Cairo*. Finding the river much as they had left it in early January, the vessels returned to report their observations. As far as Porter was concerned, the army's opportunities lay up the Yazoo and not in front of Vicksburg.[27]

When Grant reached Milliken's Bend on January 29, he had a pretty good idea of what to expect. The Chickasaw Bayou fiasco had dispelled his notions of a frontal attack. Despite the appeal of getting on Vicksburg's eastern flank, moving transports and supplies above the batteries on Snyder's Bluff and Haynes' Bluff by way of the Yazoo was a recipe for disaster. Grant knew Pemberton was reinforcing his army, and because no Union vessels operated below Vicksburg, he could not get on the town's southern flank—but he was determined to find the key, and Porter would unlock the door.

If the acting rear admiral needed any encouragement, it came by way of a letter from Fox. "You did well at Arkansas Post," he wrote, "and we shall get you a vote of thanks for it. If you open the Father of Waters you will at once be made an Admiral, besides we will try for a ribboned star. Your victory is well timed. . . . [Brig. Gen.] Frank Blair writes very complimentary of your operations and says they are very jealous of it. I trust your people will not show any of it. Let them all see that the public service is your guide."[28]

Fox could not have given Porter a bigger carrot or better advice, and for the second time in his Civil War career, David Dixon received a vote of thanks by Congress. After four months of toil with his freshwater navy, it was just the tonic Porter needed.

FIFTEEN

Convolutions
in the Delta

When Grant arrived at Milliken's Bend on January 29, he brought most of the Army of the Tennessee with him. He divided his force into four corps, assigning the XIII to McClernand, the XV to Sherman, the XVII to Maj. Gen. James B. McPherson, and the XVI to Maj. Gen. Stephen A. Hurlbut, who remained at Grand Junction to hold the line of the railroad while the other three corps concentrated on Vicksburg.

The Confederate army reported to General Pemberton, who commanded the Department of Mississippi with headquarters at Jackson, while Maj. Gen. Carter L. Stevenson commanded the defenders of Vicksburg. To cope with enemy forces threatening his department from three directions, Pemberton had already sent Stevenson more than twenty thousand soldiers to cover the twelve-mile line from Snyder's Bluff to Vicksburg.[1]

Grant hoped to find a way to attack the stronghold from the south by marching eastward to Jackson, cutting off Pemberton's supplies, rolling up his flank, and pressing him into Vicksburg. This meant getting the Union army below Vicksburg with transports and supply vessels, using Porter's squadron for protection. With the valley flooded by unprecedented rains that started during Sherman's Chickasaw Bayou campaign, the inland lakes and bayous were covered with water, and the alluvial bottomlands behind the levees were everywhere overflowed. Sherman's corps camped at Young's Point, located at the base of the peninsula opposite Vicksburg. His men pitched their tents on the levee—the only dry ground to be found—leaving access to his headquarters dependent upon a bridge. The rest of the army stretched for sixty miles upriver. It could only be moved by boat, and it could not be marched down the west bank because such roads as existed were covered by water—so Grant looked for an inland water route west of the river, one deep enough to float the transports below Vicksburg's batteries.[2]

Because of winter conditions—camping on mud that froze each night—Grant could muster only half of his fifty-eight thousand soldiers. Hundreds died, and levees became graveyards where fatigue parties piled the dead in heaps.

Grant, however, intended to keep the men active and put them to work opening Williams' Canal. Once opened, the canal would enable gunboats and army transports to cross the peninsula at Young's Point and reenter the river below Vicksburg's batteries. Sherman detailed more than four thousand soldiers and two thousand blacks to the project, and they spent the winter digging, dredging, and blowing up stumps.[3]

Army engineers hoped the swollen river would cut a new path across De Soto Point and make it an island, but Porter was doubtful. "The canal is simply ridiculous," he declared, "and will never succeed until other steps are taken." Because of an eddy at the point of the cut, he doubted whether the river would cooperate. He warned that before the canal was finished, Vicksburg's batteries would interfere with the work. He suggested the outlet be moved two miles downriver, making the canal three miles long. His prediction matured a few days later. While the army toiled in the ditch, Pemberton mounted guns in the lower town to register on the canal and brought up the gunboat *William H. Webb* to keep watch on the exit.[4]

On March 7 a dam on the upper end of the canal washed out and carried men and weeks of labor with it. Dredgers went to work rebuilding the dams but were driven off by Confederate artillery. Grant kept details working on the canal, but, like Porter, he lost faith in the project.[5]

Grant and Sherman made daily jaunts to *Black Hawk* to meet in Porter's comfortable cabin and discuss other options. From Lake Providence, near the west bank of the Mississippi and seventy-five miles above Vicksburg, lay a network of inland waterways that connected with the tributaries of the Red River. This route, if opened, would bring the fleet halfway down to New Orleans, a distance of four hundred miles. The difficulty, however, lay in opening a ditch six miles long through a cypress swamp standing between Lake Providence and the Tensas River. The bayous were hidden by floodwater and, when located, could be deepened only by dredging and removing trees. Grant wanted his engineers to take a closer look at the project, and on January 30 Porter detailed the tinclad *Linden* with instructions for Acting Master Thomas E. Smith to accompany the expedition, but warned, "Before you attempt to enter or go anywhere have a boat ahead to sound."[6]

Four days later the engineers returned and proposed cutting the levee and letting the river flow through to Lake Providence, thereby inundating the swamps and enabling boats to reach Bayous Baxter and Macon without having to hack a huge swath through the wooded swamps. Grant approved the scheme, as it would keep one of McPherson's divisions employed. Sherman, convinced that work on the canal was "labor lost," seconded the project. The engineers were overly optimistic. The route kept Brig. Gen. John McArthur's division busy until the end of March, but they gleaned no more success for their efforts than Sherman's canal diggers.[7]

As difficulties developed west of the river, Porter suggested cutting the levee at Delta, located six miles below Helena but on the east bank. If gunboats could get into Old Yazoo Pass, a dry river long since forgotten, there was a chance that transports could be floated through the swamps to the Coldwater and Tallahatchie Rivers, and from there down to the Yazoo, coming out above Haynes' Bluff. The route was circuitous and dangerous, but if the scheme worked gunboats could raze the enemy's transports at Yazoo City while Grant's force cut communications and attacked Vicksburg from the flank. Once the batteries on Haynes' and Snyder's Bluffs fell, the army could be supplied from the Yazoo River without going through the Delta. This route had more appeal to Grant than attacking Vicksburg from the south.

In early February the Yazoo Delta was already heavily flooded, but Porter wanted to fill it higher. Acting Master George W. Brown and the men of *Forest Rose* blasted the levee near the town of Delta, and the

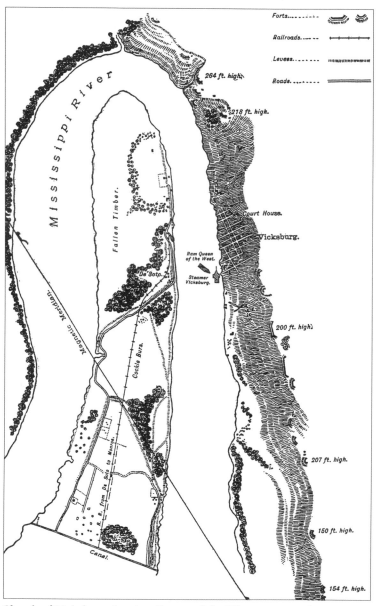

Sketch of Vicksburg showing *Queen of the West* ramming the steamer *Vicksburg* REPRINTED FROM *OFFICIAL RECORDS OF THE UNION AND CONFEDERATE NAVIES*

Mississippi, running nine feet higher than the basin, surged through the cut, sweeping everything before it and carving out a channel eighty yards wide. Brown predicted little trouble in getting to Coldwater, but he said it would take four or five days before boats could go in.[8]

While Brown was cutting the levee at Delta, the steamer *City of Vicksburg* ran the Yazoo blockade and tied to the city landing. Porter spoke with nineteen-year-old Col. Charles Rivers Ellet, who offered to run *Queen of the West* under the town's batteries and ram the enemy vessel. Ellet planned to attack at night, and Porter cautioned him to see that his stokers had a large bed of coals in the firebox to keep down any smoke and sparks. After casting off, he must extinguish all lights, except for three small running lights, and hug the western bank until initiating his ramming run. "Strike the steamer 20 feet forward of the wheel," Porter said, then "fire through her boilers and . . . her machinery as she goes down." Porter told Ellet he would find the steamer *De Soto* standing below the fort, and to look for her if *Queen of the West* became disabled.[9]

Ellet started late, and by the time he rounded the bend dawn streaked the eastern horizon. Vicksburg's batteries opened, but the ram moved so swiftly that only three shots struck her before Ellet spied his target. Coming fast abeam *City of Vicksburg*, the helmsman spun the wheel hard to port, swung across the river, struck an eddy, and glanced off the enemy vessel. Ellet, however, having loaded the starboard gun with turpentine balls, fired them into *Vicksburg's* upper works and set the ship afire. A shell from one of the town's batteries struck a tier of cotton bales protecting *Queen's* starboard wheel and set them ablaze. Ellet feared the loss of his boat if he made another pass at *Vicksburg*. The crew scurried on deck and cut the smoldering bales loose, and Ellet sped downriver, enemy shells splashing in his wake. *De Soto* came to his rescue, but he did not need her, so he tied up to the bank and reported to Porter.

City of Vicksburg stayed afloat by running her pumps and attaching herself to two barges, but she never sailed again. At first neither Ellet nor the admiral realized she had been permanently disabled. But Porter was delighted. The young colonel had passed the formidable hill batteries in daylight without serious damage. He kept Ellet below the forts and urged him to clean out the river.[10]

On February 7 Porter heard from Brown, who had taken *Forest Rose* through Yazoo Pass and snaked his way to Moon Lake. Fallen timber clogged the waterway, and General Gorman sent to Helena for men with axes. While Brown waited, he chatted with three men from the Coldwater region who warned that the rebels were wise to the scheme and felling trees. Brown penetrated seven miles into the pass and found a few trees down but nothing that could not be removed.[11]

The admiral detailed the turtles *Chillicothe* and *Baron De Kalb* and the tinclads *Rattler, Romeo, Forest Rose,* and *Cricket* to the expedition and placed them under the command of Lt. Comdr. Watson Smith. Grant donated six hundred infantry to serve as marines. Porter considered the venture a naval enterprise and was a little upset when Grant detailed twenty-two transports and five thousand men from the XIII Army Corps under division commander Brig. Gen. Leonard F. Ross. Because of conditions in the Delta, the admiral worried that progress would be slowed to a crawl by having so many vessels pressing through the shallow bayous.[12]

On February 24 the expedition chugged through the cut, filed across Moon Lake, and headed for the Coldwater. Moving only by day, the troop carriers—the best Grant could find—frequently broke down. The turtles, each hauling three coal barges, lumbered slowly through the narrow, winding channel. The expedition crept with no evidence of urgency. Instead of moving out at dawn, Smith never got the turtles under way before 7:30 A.M. Four hours later the flotilla stopped for a leisurely lunch. General Ross urged Smith to cast off the coal barges and hasten to the Yazoo, but the commander preferred to crawl along with the transports.[13]

At Yazoo City, Comdr. Isaac N. Brown knew the blueclads were coming in force and asked Pemberton for guns. Brown warned that obstructions would only slow the enemy down—not stop him. He wanted to contain them in the Tallahatchie River and prevent them from reaching the Yazoo.[14]

A week passed before Pemberton considered the threat serious enough to send Maj. Gen. William W. Loring up the Tallahatchie to locate a suitable place to erect a fort. Loring selected a sharp S-curve where the lower bend of the river came within two hundred yards of the Yazoo before curving away to the northeast. Maj. Minor Meriwether of the Confederate engineers rounded up a few hundred men and started to build Fort Pemberton, an earthwork mounting eight guns and bearing up the Tallahatchie. Another detail started work on a raft long enough to swing across the river and block it. None of this work had been started at the time the Union flotilla entered the Delta.[15]

On February 28, after taking four days to go twenty miles, Smith's gunboats rounded into the Coldwater and paused to wait for the transports. Porter had added the gunboat *Petrel* and two of Ellet's rams, *Lioness* and *Fulton,* to the flotilla, and before reaching the Coldwater they had lost their smokestacks and damaged their wheels. Despite a better flow in the Coldwater, Smith still crawled ahead cautiously, keeping the long line of vessels in single file. Rebel cavalry annoyed the transports, and partisans fired at the flotilla as it passed, but for most of the trip down the Coldwater to the Tallahatchie there was little sign of life.

On March 10 the flotilla paused on the Tallahatchie, where Smith learned from slaves of Fort Pemberton, situated about twenty miles downriver. The following day he dropped down with Ross to reconnoiter. *Chillicothe* rounded the bend, eased to within a half mile of the fort, and opened with her heavy guns. Fort Pemberton's batteries replied and in less than thirty minutes riddled *Chillicothe's* casemate, dislodged several plates, and drove in her 9-inch timber backing.

Smith withdrew and patched up *Chillicothe.* The next morning, with *De Kalb* astride and piled high with bales of cotton, he descended once again to blow away Pemberton's batteries. At the narrow bend upriver, both vessels eased their sterns against the bank and, with their beams touching, opened on the fort. A few minutes later solid conical shot struck the face of *Chillicothe* and knocked in her casemate. A second shell came through the gunport and struck an 11-inch shell as it was being loaded. Both shells exploded, killing one gunner and wounding fourteen others. The same explosion tore off the port covers, leaving a huge gap. Smith withdrew to make repairs and urged Ross to take the 30-pounder Parrotts off two of the tinclads, set them up on shore, and shell the rebel earthworks.

On the 13th Smith tried again and at eight hundred yards opened on the fort. *Chillicothe* and *Baron De Kalb* got hammered, but they silenced the Confederate batteries. Smith, after being struck thirty-eight times, had no way of knowing that the enemy had depleted his ammunition, but Smith had drawn heavily upon his own supply. "When about to advance," Smith said, "[I] received information from General Ross of the approach of reinforcements for his command, and a proposal to await their arrival before assaulting the place." Smith waited and by doing so lost his opportunity to take the fort.[16]

Several days passed before Smith renewed the attack, but by then Loring had replenished his ammunition, beefed up his battery with an 8-inch naval gun, and filled his rifle pits with reinforcements. During the interregnum Smith suffered from "softening of the brain," as Porter called it, and turned the squadron over to Lt. Comdr. James P. Foster.[17]

When Brig. Gen. Isaac F. Quinby arrived on March 21 to take command of the Union infantry, Ross and Foster had mutually agreed to abandon the expedition. The pair made the right decision, but Quinby was full of fight and insisted upon finishing the campaign. More men, more guns, and more provisions wound through the swamps to the embattled bluecoats on the Tallahatchie.[18]

Foster led the gunboats back down the river and in a driving rain reopened on Fort Pemberton with no effect. Quinby set up batteries on land and sent reconnaissances in force to find a way to flank the defenders. Without pontoons, they could not cross the Tallahatchie below the fort. The fight settled into a stalemate, and Foster, finding himself with a squadron separated by two hundred miles of unprotected communications, chose to retire.[19]

Long before Quinby gave up the effort, Porter wrote Welles that the "Yazoo Pass expedition does not seem to be doing much beyond exchanging shots with the batteries." He blamed General Ross for failing to take the initiative after *Chillicothe* and *De Kalb* had silenced Pemberton's guns. He also admitted that Smith impeded the expedition with his illness and should have removed himself from command the day the flotilla entered the Delta.[20]

Lt. Col. James H. Wilson, Grant's chief topographical engineer, grumbled, "I'm disgusted with [the turtle's] 7, 9, 10, and 11 inch guns; to let one 6½-inch rifle stop our Navy. Bah! They ought to go up to 200 yards and 'make a spoon or spoil a horn.'" A few days later Wilson discovered what caused the trouble. After inspecting *Chillicothe*'s damage, he declared her a "great cheat and swindle upon the Government [and] is now almost incapable of further service." Instead of the usual twelve-inch backing of timber, the builders had used nine-inch pine, and instead of bolting the plates to the backing they had substituted six-inch spikes. The spikes split the backing going in, and every shot striking the forward casemate jarred the plates loose. "Another 8-inch shot between the ports," Wilson warned, "will bring the whole turret down."[21]

Before the end of March, Porter and Grant mutually agreed to give up on the Yazoo Pass expedition. Back in Washington, Welles and Lincoln were equally anxious to see it end. "The accounts of Porter above Vicksburg," Welles confided to his diary, "are not satisfactory. . . . [He] has capabilities and I am expecting much of him, but," he added with a touch of disdain, "he is by no means an Admiral Foote."[22]

As Welles grumbled to his diary, Porter scrutinized maps and hatched another scheme to get above Haynes' Bluff. The levee cut at Delta had flooded every waterway emptying into the Yazoo River. By going up Steele's Bayou, circling through Black Bayou, Deer Creek, and Rolling Fork, and coming down Big Sunflower River, Porter believed he could bring his squadron into the Yazoo ten miles above Haynes' Bluff. Porter, with Grant on board, led a scouting detail up Steele's Bayou to reconnoiter the feasibility of the expedition. After thirty miles of mushing through the wetlands and sweeping snakes, coons, and rats off the decks of the tinclads, he found five fathoms of water in the bayous but not much room between the banks. Since this route was about half the distance of the Yazoo Pass venture, Porter decided to lead it himself.[23]

On March 14 the squadron passed the old battlefield below Chickasaw Bluffs and filed into the willows overhanging the banks of Steele's Bayou. Porter brought his best turtles—*Louisville, Cincinnati, Carondelet, Mound City,* and *Pittsburg*—followed by four mortar boats and four tugs. Part of Brig. Gen. David Stuart's 2nd Division followed on the transports *Silver Wave* and *Diligent,* and Sherman tagged along to assess the feasibility of bringing Grant's whole army.[24]

Grant had another reason to support Porter's scheme. Ross had just reported the Yazoo Pass expedition checked by the enemy, and Grant advised McPherson, "If we can get our boats in the rear of them in time, it will so confuse the enemy as to save Ross's force. If they do not, I shall feel restless for [Ross's] fate until I know that Quinby has

Map of the Steele's Bayou expedition, March 1863 REPRINTED FROM JAMES
R. SOLEY, *ADMIRAL PORTER*

reached him." A few days later Grant wrote Farragut that the enemy
had detached a large force from Vicksburg to reinforce Fort Pemberton,
and that because of this he had decided to have Porter attempt to get
gunboats in the rear of the enemy.[25]

Grant sanctioned the Steele's Bayou expedition to take pressure off
Ross, and if Porter could open the Yazoo River by coming in from above,
so much the better. Porter, however, was hoping for more than a feint,
and when he started into the bayou on March 14 he planned to carry
his squadron through to the Yazoo and disable the forts on the bluffs.

When the flotilla entered Steele's Bayou, it passed through a forest
shrouded in mist and drenched with a dew that trickled like rainfall
from dangling clumps of Spanish moss. Limbs hanging over the narrow
banks crashed down on the decks of the ironclads as they bulled their
way through wild eglantine, briar, and grapevines. At midday the boats
churned past Muddy Bayou, and thirty river miles later they reached
Black Bayou, the four-mile link to Deer Creek.[26]

Porter entered the narrow bayou, found it rimmed with cypress and willow, and ordered out saws, knives, and cutlasses. Details cut away branches and pulled up trees by their roots. Withes dangling in the narrow bayou jammed the paddle wheels, and when slaves gathered on the banks seeking emancipation, Porter put them to work. The ironclads worked in teams, pushing aside huge trees with their plated bows. While the navy prodded its way through the bayou, foraging parties roamed the interior collecting chickens, hams, eggs, and butter. *Carondelet* led the flotilla. Several times she became wedged between trees and had to be shoved through by *Cincinnati*. "It was terrible work," Porter said, "but in twenty-four hours we succeeded in getting [to] Deer Creek, where we were told there would be no more difficulties." Had this been true, the expedition might have settled the fate of Vicksburg.[27]

At the intersection of Black Bayou and Deer Creek, Sherman waited for his transports to come up while Porter crept forward. Rolling Fork lay ahead—twelve miles by land, thirty two by water—and Sherman planned to take most of his command by land. When no transports appeared, the general became nervous. He commandeered a canoe and paddled down the bayou to find them. Something had gone wrong.[28]

Porter's squadron squeezed into narrow, twisting Deer Creek, wiggling through the willows, making one mile an hour. "We had succeeded in getting into the heart of the country before we were discovered," Porter wrote. "No one would believe that anything the shape of a vessel could get through Black Bayou, or anywhere on the route." Word spread rapidly that Yankees were coming. Confederate agents with firebrands raced to keep ahead of the unexpected invasion. Cotton fires sprang up along Deer Creek, and storehouses filled with corn and pork for Vicksburg's defenders burst into flame. The gunboats fired at the incendiaries to drive them away, and Porter, on the pretense of defraying the cost of the expedition, detached marines with orders to salvage all the cotton they could carry and load it on the lightdrafts.[29]

Standing with Lieutenant Commander Bache on the deck of *Cincinnati*, Porter observed two pillars of cotton stacked on opposite sides of the stream burst suddenly into flame. *Carondelet*, several yards upriver, entered the smoke and disappeared. Porter ordered all ports closed and the decks wetted, then rang two bells to go ahead fast. He and Bache tried to ride through the inferno on the deck, but the heat became insufferable. They jumped inside the iron pilothouse and found the helmsman covered with an old water-soaked flag.[30]

On March 20 word of the Union incursion reached Stevenson's Vicksburg headquarters, and the general ordered Brig. Gen. Winfield S. Featherston's brigade to the junction of Deer Creek and Rolling Fork. Brig. Gen. Stephen D. Lee intercepted the order and reinforced Featherston with a detachment from Col. Samuel W. Ferguson's command. Ferguson pulled his men out of Fort Pemberton and reached Rolling Fork late on the 20th. He set up batteries, chopped down trees, posted sharpshooters, and spread out along the bank to pepper the flotilla as it ranged in sight.[31]

Porter's presence in Deer Creek activated one of Grant's strategies, but nothing happened. When Ferguson pulled part of his brigade out of Fort Pemberton, he weakened the garrison the day before Quinby arrived with five thousand fresh troops. For two or three days Quinby had an opportunity to convert the Yazoo Pass expedition into a success, but he never discovered his advantage.

On the 20th Porter encountered resistance, a single 12-pounder Parrott supported by small-arms fire about seven miles from Rolling Fork. He sent the tug *Thistle,* armed with a boat howitzer, ahead and followed in *Carondelet.* Four miles from Rolling Rock, *Thistle* was stopped by a tree lying across the creek—and farther on there were more. Details worked through the night removing obstructions, and on the 21st the squadron crept ahead, gaining a few yards at a time, but scouts from the flotilla reported the enemy landing in force at Rolling Fork. Porter lamented, "I did not mind the troops so much as the timber they would cut."[32]

Appealing to Sherman for reinforcements, Porter wrote, "We are within 1½ miles of Rolling Fork, having undergone an immensity of labor. . . . I think a large force will be used to block us up here. We must have every soldier to hold this country, or they will do it. Our difficulties increase."[33]

Porter sent Lt. John M. Murphy ahead with two howitzers and three hundred men to hold Rolling Fork until the squadron could batter its way through the last mile and a half of Deer Creek. Once again, men worked all night clearing trees, but willows clogged the waterway and wrapped themselves around the paddle wheels. Ahead lay a pondlike stretch of Deer Creek covered with green scum. Porter sent a tug to reconnoiter. It rushed ahead and abruptly stopped. Porter asked if there was a problem, and the skipper replied that he was stuck fast. Lying beneath the scum were thousands of willow switches. Porter sent *Carondelet* ahead, but the withes caught on the turtle's overhang and brought her to a halt.

Ahead Porter heard firing. Murphy's detachment had struck Featherston's brigade at the junction of Deer Creek and Rolling Fork and began to withdraw. A slave came alongside and shouted that rebels were felling trees front and rear. Porter pulled back about a mile and discovered it was true. If he could not go forward, he might still be able to go backward. *Louisville*, hauling up the rear, now became the point. Porter ordered rudders unshipped and backed the squadron, letting the boats rebound from tree to tree until they came to an obstruction. Snipers drove work parties back to the vessels. Naval guns sprayed the woods with grape, but it did little good. For the time being, Porter's men were safe huddled behind the ship's armor, but the admiral began to doubt if his boats would ever see the Mississippi River again. He could not move very far forward or backward. Escape now depended on Sherman, who was doing his utmost to bring his men through the swamps.[34]

Had Sherman brought his entire force up Steele's Bayou and remained in contact with Porter's squadron, his infantry would have brushed away Featherston's and Ferguson's men, prevented the obstruction of Deer Creek, and been well down the Big Sunflower by now. Some of Sherman's units, however, chose to enter Steele's Bayou by way of Eagle Bend and Muddy Bayou and lost time waiting for a bridge to be built.[35]

On March 19 Sherman found only two of his regiments at Muddy Bayou. The rest of the brigade had gone up the Mississippi to look for a faster way into Steele's Bayou. The only regiment nearby was the 8th Missouri, which had followed Porter as far as Hill's plantation on Black Bayou. From Hill's plantation the flotilla had proceeded slowly upriver without infantry support. On March 21, when Porter realized his squadron was entrapped, he was half a mile from Rolling Fork, the last hurdle. From there he could have moved swiftly into the Big Sunflower and reached Haynes' Bluff in a day—but not without Sherman.[36]

On March 20 Sherman stopped at Hill's plantation with the 6th Missouri and the 116th Illinois and wrote Porter that he had about a thousand men with him and expected another thousand in a day. Porter never received the letter because the messenger was captured. Had Porter seen the note, he might have wondered why Sherman was still at Hill's.[37]

On March 21 Col. Giles Smith arrived with the 8th Missouri. On his way he had counted more than forty trees lying in Deer Creek. Smith did not have enough men to drive off the enemy, so everyone worked through the night to get the squadron back to Steele's Bayou.

The men of *Louisville* now had the chore of slashing through the obstructions and opening a path for the entire squadron. Besides trees, a sunken coal barge barred the way, and the sailors worked late into the night blowing it up. Smith's Missourians, aided by 150 sailors, marched along the bank, exchanging musket fire with the enemy. "Every tree and stump," said Smith, "covered a sharpshooter ready to pick off any luckless marine who showed his head above deck."[38]

On March 22, just as *Louisville* was working around a bend in Deer Creek, slaves reported enemy artillery moving toward the rear of the squadron. Rumors from below estimated from three to five thousand grayclads driving through the woods. The rumor was exaggerated, but Featherston had brought up the 40th Alabama and the 22nd and 33rd Mississippi for one last crack at the flotilla. If they could sink *Louisville,* it would bottle up the Union flotilla indefinitely.[39]

As Featherston's seven fieldpieces raked the gunboats, Porter opened with what guns could be brought to bear. Below the level of the banks, his 11-inch Dahlgrens were powerless. When no word came from Sherman, Porter drafted several hasty messages, one on toilet paper wrapped in a tobacco leaf. Charlie Guild, Porter's secretary and Fox's nephew, carried one of them. The marines unlimbered their howitzers and for a time silenced the enemy's crossfire, but the flotilla remained stationary, stranded in the willows.[40]

Sherman, still far down the creek, did not wait for Porter's messengers. That night, when he heard the distant rumble of naval guns, he urged his men forward. Being on foot himself, he led the men by candlelight down a mud-splattered road running beside Deer Creek. Crossing swamps hip deep, "the smaller drummer boys had to carry their drums on their heads," he wrote, "and most of the men slung their cartridge boxes around their necks." Sherman covered twenty miles and at noon fell in with pickets from the 8th Missouri, who related conditions ahead. Sherman put his mud-caked troops back on the road and slogged on, brushing off detachments of enemy skirmishers. A major in the 8th Missouri offered him a horse. "I got on bareback," Sherman declared, "and rode up the levee, the sailors coming out of their ironclads and cheering most vociferously as I rode by and as our men swept forward across the cotton field in full view. I soon found Admiral Porter, who was on deck of one of his ironclads, with a shield made of the section of a smoke-stack, and I doubt if he was ever more glad to meet a friend than he was to see me."[41]

"Halloo, Porter," hollered the general, "what did you get into such an ugly scrape for? So much for you Navy fellows getting out of your element; better send for the soldiers always. My boys will put you through." The sight of Sherman and his mud-splattered men left a lasting impression on Porter. He affectionately referred to them as "half horse, half alligator, with a touch of snapping turtle."[42]

Sherman was too late to salvage the expedition but just in time to save Porter from disaster. The admiral admitted he had never been "more pleased to see that gallant officer," for without him the squadron may have spent the war resting on the muddy bottom of Deer Creek. Porter had planned to blow up the boats if he could not get out, and the experience taught him an important lesson—he would never get much done in the river without the support of the army.[43]

After Sherman arrived on the 22nd, the fighting ended but for scrapes with enemy patrols watching the departure of the squadron. The retreat, hampered by heavy rain, slowed Sherman's march, but Porter kept the fleet nearby to provide support. When the flotilla steamed out of Steele's Bayou on March 27, the decks were piled high with Confederate cotton and scores of emancipated slaves. Porter found a surprise waiting. As he approached the mouth of the Yazoo, he was hailed by a dispatch boat. Farragut's secretary came on board with a message. *Hartford* was anchored below Vicksburg, and the admiral would like to see him.[44]

During the Civil War, no expedition contributed more to the professional maturity of David Dixon Porter than the failure at Steele's Bayou. Had it happened a year earlier, his letters to Fox and his reports to Welles would probably have condemned Grant and Sherman for initiating foolish expeditions. But Porter leveled with Welles, writing, "The great difficulty seems to have been for want of more promptness in moving troops, or rather, I should say, want of means for moving the troops, for there were never yet any two men who would labor harder than Generals Grant and Sherman to forward an expedition for the overthrow of Vicksburg. . . . I never knew how helpless a thing an ironclad could be when unsupported by troops."[45]

Steele's Bayou was Grant's last effort to turn the enemy's flank by way of the Yazoo Delta. Naval historian James R. Soley considered the effort "brilliantly conceived and boldly and firmly executed," a feat that distinguished Porter's underlying qualities for "daring and original conception . . . of nerve and resourcefulness in situations of overwhelming danger and difficulty." In Soley's opinion, the mission collapsed when the army failed to move two thousand men a distance of forty miles up a perfectly navigable stream on whose banks no enemy could be found. Soley forgets, however, that Porter left Sherman behind at Hill's plantation and cautioned the transports to wait.[46]

Welles, however, was unhappy with the situation despite Grant's praise of Porter's effort. On the heels of the failures in the Delta, two rams had been sunk attempting to pass Vicksburg's batteries during the admiral's absence. The secretary was obviously in a foul mood when he wrote, "It remains for your dispatches to inform the Department whether additional disgrace and disaster is to attach to the Navy from recklessness and disobedience." And perhaps to add more sting to the message, he added, "Rear-Admiral Farragut is below Vicksburg, after a successful and gallant passage of Port Hudson batteries." The occupation of Vicksburg "is of far greater importance than the flanking expeditions. . . . I desire that you consult with Rear-Admiral Farragut and decide how this object can best be obtained."[47]

Instead of brooding, Porter took the scolding manfully. Welles wanted action—but so did Porter.

SIXTEEN

Chaos
on the River

Before Porter started into Steele's Bayou on March 14, he took advantage of Ellet's passage of Vicksburg's batteries and ordered the young officer to take *Queen of the West* down the river to destroy Confederate commerce on the Red River. On February 2 Ellet cast off, and *Queen* sped down the great river at twenty knots, running Warrenton's battery in daylight. News of Ellet's raid preceded him. Pemberton dispatched couriers to warn the authorities at Natchez to clear the river of shipping and send it up the Red River.[1]

Finding nothing of value at Natchez, Ellet steamed past Ellis Cliffs early on the 3rd, and fifteen miles above the mouth of the Red River he boarded the side-wheeler *A. W. Baker*. Her passengers jumped into the river and fled, but the vessel was empty, having deposited her cargo at Port Hudson. When the watch reported another vessel approaching, Ellet put a prize crew on *Baker*, conned the ram toward the approaching steamer, and fired a shot across her bow. *Moro*, crammed to the scuppers with 110,000 pounds of pork and 500 hogs, cut her engines and waited for a boarding party. Ellet put a prize crew on her and headed for the mouth of the Red River—just in time to capture *Berwick Bay* with another load of army provisions. Ellet placed Capt.

Angill Conner in charge of the three prizes and led them back upriver. His trophies, however, could not keep pace with the ram, and with *Queen*'s coal supply dangerously low, Ellet transferred his prisoners to *Queen* and set fire to the steamers.[2]

As Ellet approached Warrenton, he noticed that the enemy had added another battery. Hugging the west bank, *Queen* sped uninjured through shot and shell. Porter was delighted with the mission and wrote Welles, "I hope to be able to get [Ellet] off again as soon as I can get coal . . . to him."[3]

News that a Union gunboat had slipped through Vicksburg's defenses and captured three steamers alarmed Pemberton. He suspected the vessel was still below and alerted the army at Port Hudson. Hearing of the raid from released prisoners, Brig. Gen. Henry H. Sibley detailed a company of cavalry and a section of artillery to the mouth of the Red River. Ellet was no longer there, but he planned to return.[4]

Queen got fuel the easy way. Porter had a barge filled with twenty thousand bushels of coal and set adrift above Vicksburg. It floated by the batteries unnoticed. *De Soto,* waiting below, lashed onto the barge and hauled it into a nearby slough. Ellet added two 30-pounder Parrotts to *De Soto* and promised Porter that he would make her a cottonclad.[5]

With enough coal to keep *Queen of the West* running for a month, Porter cautioned the nineteen-year-old colonel to proceed at night, show no lights, and travel in company with *De Soto* and the barge. When he reached the mouth of the Red River, he was to wait for daylight in some secluded slough and watch for smoke. If he took a prize, he was to demolish the machinery and burn the vessel on the spot. The admiral warned Ellet to look out for CSS *William H. Webb,* the only armed vessel cruising the Red. "If you get the first crack at her," Porter wrote, "you will sink her, and if she gets the first crack at you she will sink you." Just before Ellet sailed, Porter added, "Don't be surprised to see the *Indianola* below. Don't mistake her for a rebel; she looks something like the *Chillicothe*."[6]

The side-wheeler *Indianola,* built at Cincinnati, had a top speed in still water of only six knots. She carried four guns—two 11-inch and two 9-inch Dahlgrens. *Indianola* joined Porter's squadron on February 7, three days before Ellet's second raid down the Mississippi. While Lt.

Comdr. George W. Brown prepped *Indianola* for her first cruise, Ellet cast off Biggs' Landing on the night of February 10 and, with a coal barge lashed to *Queen's* port beam and *De Soto* close behind, steamed by the Warrenton batteries undetected.[7]

On the way down, Ellet made a demonstration at Natchez, destroyed a few flatboats, and created enough havoc to scare away the better prizes. Detaching the coal barge and leaving it behind with *De Soto*, Ellet wasted two days raiding farms along the Atchafalaya and harassing supply wagons belonging to the Valverde Texas Artillery, stationed at Simmesport. Although the Texans lost their rations, patrols tracked *Queen* down the Atchafalaya and wounded First Master James D. Thompson before being chased away by the ram's howitzers. Ellet retaliated and scorched three plantations.[8]

From informants, Ellet learned that several landings on the Red had been fortified Fort Taylor at Gordon's Landing, forty-five miles above the mouth of the Black, and Fort Beauregard at Harrisonburg on the Ouachita River. He also learned that a steamer had passed up the river with guns for *William H. Webb,* which was said to be at Alexandria. On the morning of the 14th Ellet started up the Red, sounding as he went, when *Queen's* lookout reported a smudge of smoke ahead. As *New Era No. 5* rounded a bend in the river and came face to face with the ram, her skipper tried to come about and flee upriver. Ellet's first shot hit the stern of *New Era,* passed through the galley, nicked the cook, and demolished his stove. Ellet boarded the vessel and found *New Era* loaded with corn, passengers, and sixteen men of the 14th Texas Cavalry.

Leaving *New Era* with a prize crew, he continued upriver looking for more steamboats. Forewarned of *Queen's* approach, Capt. John Kelso, commanding Fort Taylor, hastily prepared to give the ram a warm reception when she rounded the bend. Ellet inched cautiously ahead, and the crew manning the bow gun opened fire on three fleeing steamers. Kelso's four 32-pounders answered from the fort, dropping shots a few yards off *Queen's* beam. Ellet shouted to the pilot, Thomas W. Garvey, to reverse engines. Garvey panicked and grounded on the point where Kelso had his guns aimed. Enemy shells crashed through the deck. Steam gushed through broken pipes, driving the men in the engine room topside. Before Ellet could get control of the situation, the crew deserted the guns, tossed bales of cotton over the side, and rafted downriver. Ellet ordered the yawl lowered to take off the wounded, but the crew had gone off with it. He then grabbed a floating bale of cotton and drifted down to *De Soto*. Climbing aboard, he ordered her upriver and sent two officers in a boat to burn *Queen*. The volunteers found the passageways blocked with cotton and returned empty-handed, and no one would strike a match with a wounded man on board. Ellet wanted to try again, but Kelso's men reached her first.

Fog developed as *De Soto* nosed down the river. She got too close to shore and lost her rudder. Without steerage, Ellet let her drift. At 10:00 P.M. he spotted *New Era* and came abeam of her. Ellet transferred his men to the prize, scuttled *De Soto,* and, expecting a visit from the speedy *Webb,* hastened for the Mississippi River.

In a violent thunderstorm, followed by an all-night rain, the crew lightened *New Era* and worked her out of the Red. With fuel running short, Ellet stopped at Union Point and sent a detail ashore to chop wood. With wet, green fuel, the best *New Era* could do against the current was two knots.

Above Ellis Cliffs, Garvey ran the vessel aground on the Louisiana side. Because the vessel drew only two feet, Ellet became suspicious. He arrested Garvey, convinced that the loss of *Queen* had been due to the deliberate treachery of her pilot.

Four hours later the crew worked *New Era* off the bar and got her afloat. By the morning of the 16th she was off Natchez when the lookout reported a gunboat ahead. Believing *Webb* had passed them during the night and was returning to sink them, the crew prepared to surrender, but as the vessel emerged through the fog, cheers of salvation broke out on *New Era*. *Indianola* hailed Ellet, and George Brown invited him on board for coffee. After borrowing supplies from *Indianola*, Ellet and Brown headed downriver to look for *Webb*.[9]

Because of Ellet's rashness in exposing *Queen of the West,* he had allowed the ram to fall into the hands of the enemy. He could not burn her with a wounded man on board, who should have been transferred to *De Soto* before Ellet went into action. He knew *Indianola* was on her way to bolster the navy's presence below Vicksburg, but he could not contain his youthful exuberance, and Porter deserves part of the blame for entrusting an important mission to a brave but foolish nineteen-year-old colonel—and this would prove costly.[10]

When *Indianola* passed Vicksburg's water battery on the misty night of February 13, Porter had great plans for her. He believed that when Brown and Ellet combined forces, the South would lose control of the river between Port Hudson and Vicksburg, and that *Webb* would not try to attack either of them as long as they stayed together. Porter cautioned Brown to "get good pilots" before going up the Red, and "whatever you undertake try and have no failure. When you have not means of certain success, undertake nothing; a failure is equal to defeat."[11]

Brown started downriver on February 14 and encountered nothing unusual until the morning of the 16th, when he was hailed by *New Era*. Instead of adhering to Porter's orders, Brown listened to Ellet and decided to go up the Red, destroy Fort Taylor, and salvage the colonel's reputation by recovering *Queen of the West*. After making hurried repairs to *New Era*'s splintered paddle wheels, Ellet took the point and steamed toward the mouth of the Red. As he approached Ellis Cliffs, the lookout reported a steamer dead ahead. A coating of fog still lay on the river, but Ellet knew she was *Webb* and toggled the steam whistle. Brown heard it and cleared *Indianola* for action. Engineers on board *New Era* made ready a hot-water hose and prepared for a "lively time."[12]

The 656-ton wooden steam ram *William H. Webb* was larger than *Indianola* and capable of generating twenty-two knots, but she carried only one rifled 32-pounder and a pair of brass 6-pounders. Lt. Col. William S. Lovell, an officer on Pemberton's staff, had taken command of the vessel on February 11 and hastily shielded her exposed boilers with bales of cotton. Reaching Fort Taylor and finding *Queen of the West* in Captain Kelso's possession, Lovell questioned nine of Ellet's crew and learned that a "powerful ironclad" was to meet Ellet at the mouth of the Red. Lovell started in chase of *New Era* but had to tie up because of fog. Late on the afternoon of the 16th, *Webb* and *Indianola* met off Ellis Cliffs. Two 11-inch shells fired by *Indianola* splashed near *Webb*. Lovell attempted to return the fire, but his friction primers failed. He turned about and quickly disappeared down the river.[13]

Lovell encountered two cottonclads, *Grand Duke* and *Louis d'Or*, en route to his support, but he turned them back and returned to Fort Taylor. In the meantime, Brown learned that *Queen* had been damaged only slightly and was being repaired. Ellet assured Brown that *Indianola*'s 11-inch guns could subdue both *Webb* and *Queen* if forced to a fight, and after voicing his opinion he bid Brown good-bye and headed back to Biggs' Landing, leaving Brown to fend for himself. Brown, however, sent a message to Porter via Ellet asking for "at least one other serviceable vessel."[14]

When Porter discovered that Ellet had lost *Queen of the West,* he wrote Welles bitterly:

> The best calculations are liable to be upset and mine have been disarranged by the capture of the *Queen of the West,* up Red River. . . . Had the commander of the *Queen of the West* waited patiently, he would, in less than twenty-four hours, have been joined by the *Indianola.* . . . This is a serious disappointment to us all here, as we calculated certainly on starving out the garrison at Port Hudson by merely blockading the mouth of the Red River. My plans were well laid, only badly executed. I can give orders, but I cannot give officers good judgment. The *Indianola* is now there by herself. Whether the commander will have the good sense not to be surprised, remains to be seen.[15]

Ellet, however, returned to Biggs' Landing with $70,000 in cotton, a vessel worth $18,000, and a report claiming the destruction of $100,000 in enemy property. This helped to restore the admiral's faith in the mission, and he began looking for another vessel to send down the river.[16]

Brown, unable to obtain a reliable pilot, remained at the mouth of the Red River for five days. On February 21 he learned that *Queen* had been repaired and that *Webb,* supported by four cottonclads, had started down the river to attack him. To protect his vessel against boarders, Brown stopped at two plantations, secured cotton to barricade his decks, and, with two coal barges in tow, churned up the Mississippi at little more than two knots an hour in the hope of meeting a friendly gunboat. After two days passed, he concluded that either Ellet had been captured or Porter had decided not to risk another vessel. Brown continued his snails-pace journey towing the coal barges.[17]

Webb, now commanded by Maj. Joseph L. Brent, was indeed in pursuit and accompanied by *Grand Era, Dr. Beatty,* and the repaired *Queen.* When *Webb* departed from Fort Taylor on the 22nd, *Indianola* had a ninety-mile head start, but Brent made up half the distance quickly as he steamed down the Red. Once he reached the Mississippi and turned into the current, his pace was slackened by his slower consorts.[18]

Stopping at various points along the river, Brent talked to inhabitants who had observed *Indianola* as she lumbered by. Comparing his speed with hers, he calculated that by nightfall on the 24th *Webb* would overhaul the Union ironclad. Brown, still towing his barges, planned to reach Biggs' Landing by dawn on the 25th. *Indianola* moved so slowly that enemy riflemen posted along the shore tracked her progress and amused themselves by peppering the vessel with musket fire.[19]

Late afternoon on the 24th, Brown observed a trail of smoke far downriver and suspected it came from *Webb*. Night fell, and at 9:30 a lookout in the wheelhouse reported lights about three miles astern. Just above Palmyra Island, Brown cleared for action as men doused the lights and scrambled to their stations. He swung *Indianola* around to protect her vulnerable stern and to meet the enemy with his 11-inch Dahlgrens. With two coal barges still lashed to the beams, Brown attacked.[20]

With Major Brent on board, *Queen* took the lead. *Webb* trailed about five hundred yards astern; *Dr. Beatty* and *Grand Era*, lashed together, were still two miles below. The partially obscured moon provided good light for ramming but not so good for aiming big guns. Brent, peering into the darkness ahead, discovered that *Indianola* had come about and was hugging the east bank. Both vessels withheld their fire, but as *Queen* closed to 150 yards Brent opened with his Parrotts and a 12-pounder howitzer.

Brown replied with two Dahlgrens at point-blank range, but both shots missed. Seeing *Queen* bearing down upon his port wheelhouse, Brown backwatered and swung the ram sideways to let the barge receive the impact. *Queen* crashed into the barge and became entangled. While Brent worked her clear, the 1st Texas Sharpshooter Battalion blazed away at *Indianola*.

Brown's gunners reloaded just in time to observe *Webb*, seventy-five yards off the bow, attacking with a full head of steam. The 11-inch Dahlgrens roared and missed again. At thirty yards *Webb* fired her rifled 32-pounder, smothering the portholes of both vessels with its smoke. Bows on, the two vessels collided with a tremendous crash. Aside from a few plates jarring loose, *Indianola* remained uninjured. *Webb*, however, had eight feet of her bow stoved in. *Indianola*'s gunners scrambled back on their feet to reload the Dahlgrens, but *Webb* slipped to starboard and in doing so ripped away one of *Indianola*'s barges. The impact jarred *Queen* loose and carried away the other barge.

Queen steamed upriver and came about for another run. With both barges gone, *Indianola*'s beams became vulnerable, and nobody in the pilothouse could see what was happening outside. When Brown came to the hurricane deck to get his bearings, musket balls spattered off the casemate. He located *Queen* upstream and ordered the pilot to wheel the ironclad about and take the blow on the bow. *Queen* struck *Indianola* on the forward quarter, glanced off, and in passing took two direct hits from *Indianola*'s aft guns.

Uninjured, *Queen* circled upriver for the kill. Bearing down on *Indianola* for the third time, she struck the ironclad behind the starboard wheelhouse, shattering planks and loosening plates at the point of impact. *Queen* heeled over, bales of cotton tumbled off the deck, and for a few minutes Brent thought she would sink. When she righted herself, he ordered the helm to stand by for another run.

Webb observed *Indianola* pulling away and pursued her. *Indianola*'s injuries, combined with the slowness of her helm, left her stern directly in the path of the onrushing *Webb*. Brown's gunners got one 9-inch Dahlgren in action, but the shot missed. *Webb,* however, was on target and crashed into *Indianola*'s unarmored stern.

The impact started the ram's timbers and crushed the starboard rudder. Water poured into the ironclad, and Brown attempted to scuttle her. With the hold flooding rapidly, he eased the vessel toward the Louisiana shore, knowing that if she was struck again, his crew would drown.

Webb followed as *Indianola* made for the west bank. *Dr. Beatty* came up, her decks loaded with infantry, and as the troops prepared to board *Indianola,* Brown shouted, "I surrender!" *Webb* and *Beatty* attached hawsers to the sinking prize and attempted to tow her downriver, but the ram filled and finally grounded on a bar in ten feet of water. Given time, the Confederates knew they could raise her.

During the ninety-minute fight, the roar of artillery could be heard thirty miles away at Vicksburg. Brown's gunners, however, fired only eleven shots from the two 11-inch Dahlgrens mounted in the bow and six from the 9-inch guns aft. Brown reported one killed, one wounded, and seven missing; Brent reported two killed and four wounded on

Queen and one wounded on *Webb*. Brent collected one hundred prisoners, including Brown.[21]

The loss of *Indianola* crushed Porter's efforts to control the river below Vicksburg and discouraged him from sending down another vessel. The Confederates now had two gunboats from the Union squadron to make Porter's task even harder. On March 2 he informed Welles that *Indianola* had been captured. "The rams *Webb* and *Queen of the West* attacked her twenty-five miles from here, and rammed her until she surrendered. All of which can be traced to a noncompliance of my instructions. . . . If she is not sunk, she may be used against [Farragut's] fleet." Welles wired back: "She is too formidable to be left at large, and must be destroyed."[22]

On February 25 *Queen of the West* proceeded to Warrenton, and Major Brent asked General Stevenson for pumps and workmen to raise *Indianola*. The following day, a hundred-man detail climbed aboard the partially submerged ironclad, set up two 6-pounders on her deck, and started to raise her.[23]

Porter suppressed the temptation to send his cumbersome turtles on a rescue mission. He assumed *Indianola* had been damaged but not sunk, and it became imperative that he do something fast. Porter hit upon a "cheap expedient." He set carpenters to work on an old coal barge, fitting it with a raft of logs three hundred feet long. Workmen added two wheelhouses and an enormous casemate with gaping portholes fitted with five wooden guns. They nailed together two funnels made of hogsheads and set them on two pots filled with a mixture of tar and oakum—flammable ingredients giving off a thick, black smoke. For cosmetics, two old boats hung from broken davits on her beams. The builders coated the apparatus with mud and tar and painted the inscription "DELUDED PEOPLE, CAVE IN" on the wheelhouses. This "fearsome looking monster," Porter declared, cost twelve hours' work and $8.23. With the Stars and Stripes hoisted aft and a banner emblazoned with skull and crossbones forward, tugs took her around De Soto Point after midnight on the 26th and set her adrift.[24]

The unmanned phantom had barely gotten under way when she was observed by the water battery. Drifting uninjured through the barrage, the behemoth intimidated *Queen*, *Webb*, *Dr. Beatty*, and *Grand Era* and drove them downriver. In a panicky effort to get ahead of the "Black Terror," *Queen* rammed *Grand Era,* stove in her port aft, and all but disabled her. From his headquarters in Jackson, Mississippi, Pemberton joined the panic and wired Stevenson: "You must, if possible, blow up the *Indianola.*"[25]

"Black Terror," however, drifted into an eddy below the canal, came about, and lay listless near the west bank. Some of Sherman's men had gone down the river to see the fun, found the raft twirling in the eddy, and pushed her back into the current. With her guns run out and her deck cleared for action, the monster struck the four-knot current and continued her journey down the Mississippi.

Queen and *Webb* stopped briefly at Hurricane Island and took half of the salvage crew off *Indianola.* The remainder volunteered to stay on board, serve the guns, and refloat the ironclad. At nightfall on the 26th they imagined seeing a flotilla of Union gunboats approaching from above. This was more than they could bear. They hurriedly spiked the guns, rolled their two fieldpieces into the river, and lit a fuse to the magazine. About the time they reached the mainland, *Indianola* exploded with a deafening roar. Porter heard the detonation, guessed its source, and wrote Welles that his "only hope is that she has blown up."[26]

Porter waited another week before "Black Terror" struck a mud bank and the *Vicksburg Whig* confirmed *Indianola's* fate:

> The Yankee barge sent down the river last week was reported to be an ironclad gunboat. The authorities, thinking that this monster would retake the *Indianola,* immediately issued an order to blow her up. . . . A few hours later another order was sent down countermanding the first, it being ascertained that the monstrous craft was only a coal boat. But before it reached the *Indianola* she had been blown to atoms; not even a gun was saved. Who is to blame for this folly? This precipitancy? It would seem we had no use for gunboats on the Mississippi, as a coal barge is magnified into a monster, and our authorities immediately order a boat—that would have been worth a small army to us—to be blown up.[27]

The *Richmond Examiner* picked up the story a few days later and suggested that if Porter could build a few more monitors of logs and canvas, the Union navy could do without its ironclads and win the war with dummies.[28]

In the aftermath of the loss of *Indianola,* Porter sent Fox a confidential assessment of George Brown, her commander. "I think him loyal, but he acted like a fool—he never had a prettier chance to capture two vessels—if he had managed his vessels as I told him, he would have knocked daylight through the rebels in short order."[29]

Ellet's prize, *New Era No. 5,* could not be brought above the Vicksburg batteries, and Porter could not spare vessels to protect her, so on February 27 Sherman scuttled her.[30]

So ended Porter's winter campaign to command the great river from Vicksburg to Port Hudson, but his problems did not stop there. With most of his squadron plying the swamps of the Delta, the only ironclad at the mouth of the Yazoo was *Lafayette.* At 1,193 tons she could barely stem the current, and her length of 280 feet made her unfit for service in the bayous. Armed with two 11-inch and four 9-inch Dahlgrens and a pair of 100-pounder Parrots, *Lafayette* made a powerful steam battery but not the kind of vessel to go chasing after *Queen of the West* or *Webb,* so Porter kept her nearby.[31]

Other business kept the admiral occupied. Accidents and attacks by guerrilla bands tormented the fleet. A fire started in an ashpan by a laborer burned through the deck of *Glide* and set her on fire. Through incompetence in the engine room, *Eastport* lost steam on her way to the Yazoo and grounded, knocking in the timbers supporting her boilers. Off Choctaw Island, guerrillas surprised the crew of the ram *Dick Fulton,* disabled the engine, and wounded two men. Another gang of desperadoes jumped on board the tug *Hercules,* killed part of the crew, and burned the vessel.[32]

Upriver, Porter had more to fight than a war. Trade was authorized only in areas occupied by Federal troops, but speculators and Treasury agents, motivated by the prospect of huge profits, circulated through the valley, bartering contraband and Union gold for cotton. Acting Master George W. Brown, commanding *Forest Rose,* became involved in a cotton scheme with General Gorman's son. Porter placed Brown under arrest and wrote Grant, "Can not we stop this cotton mania?" The following day Grant stripped Gorman of command. Ironclads captured a half-dozen unauthorized vessels plying the river for no purpose other than speculation, and in twenty days the navy collected $230,000 in cotton. "If our paymaster at Cairo had the authority to sell the cotton," Porter wrote Welles, "he could easily keep the fleet supplied with funds."[33]

For Porter, nothing seemed to work. His expeditions in the Yazoo Delta had failed and annoyed Welles. The loss of two vessels below Vicksburg had left *Queen of the West* in possession of the enemy. Grant's efforts to flank Vicksburg had failed, and both commanders, knowing they were on probation, felt vulnerable. Now with Farragut waiting for him at Biggs' Landing, Porter was not sure what to expect, and he gathered himself together to learn why his foster brother had come to Vicksburg.

Another Gauntlet to Run

Porter's reunion with Farragut was more cordial than the admiral had anticipated. On the evening of March 14, Farragut had attempted to pass Port Hudson's batteries with seven of his warships; only *Hartford* and the 7 gun *Albatross* succeeded. Grand Gulf's batteries then took their toll, increasing casualties on the flagship to four killed and eight wounded. By the time *Hartford* and *Albatross* limped into Biggs' Landing, they were nearly out of coal.[1]

Farragut explained that after the loss of *Queen of the West* and *Indianola,* the Navy Department had expressed alarm. Instead of waiting for developments, he had decided to come up the river, consult with Porter, and offer his help—but he also asked for an ironclad to help clear the river of Confederate shipping. Porter refused, as he had none to spare, and Farragut did not press the issue because he had contributed to another misfortune during Porter's absence.[2]

While waiting for Porter to return from Steele's Bayou, Farragut had written Grant and mentioned the importance of sending two of Ellet's rams below Vicksburg. He made the same request to Commander Walke, pro tem commander during Porter's absence, who would do nothing until his boss returned. General Ellet, however, learned of the request and agreed to provide Farragut with the rams *Switzerland* and *Lancaster.* He advised Walke that he intended to send the rams below the fort on the night of March 24 and requested that an ironclad accompany them. Walke refused, as he had none to spare.[3]

Ellet placed nephew Charles Rivers Ellet—the same daredevil who had lost *Queen of the West*—in charge of both rams, and Farragut convinced Grant to stage an amphibious attack on Warrenton's batteries. General Ellet agreed to provide a dozen small boats and send them across the river under the protection of the rams, but Colonel Ellet quashed the idea. He would shuttle the troops across himself.[4]

At 4:30 A.M. on March 25, Ellet started late, and as he approached De Soto Point enemy signal lights blinked from Fort Hill to South Fort. *Lancaster,* followed by *Switzerland,* passed the water battery safely, but as she drew abreast of the Marine Hospital battery a shell plunged through her port side, exploded the steam drum, and filled the ram with a cloud of vapor. Men poured from the engine room just as a second shot tore through *Lancaster*'s hull, filling her hold with water. The ram swung about, exposing her vulnerable stern. Without waiting for orders, the crew cut loose the boats and rowed for shore just as the vessel nosed to the bottom. *Switzerland,* following behind, took a shot from the Wyman's Hill battery that penetrated the boiler deck and ruptured the middle boiler. The pilothouse filled with smoke and steam, the engineer cut the engines, and the ram drifted down to the canal. *Albatross* intercepted her and towed her to safety.[5]

Farragut's engineers inspected *Switzerland* and said they could have her running in four days. Grant canceled the assault on Warrenton, and Farragut's men repaired the ram.[6]

At this point Porter emerged from Steele's Bayou and heard the grim news. Vexed to his wits' end by a series of misfortunes, he lashed out at General Ellet: "Will you please inform me by what authority you sent the rams . . . past the batteries at Vicksburg, in open day, and without taking any precautions to guard their hulls?" Ellet acknowledged responsibility for the losses, but added he had acted at the request of Farragut.[7]

When Porter learned the mission had been commanded by Charles Rivers Ellet, he could have predicted the outcome, and when he stepped on board *Hartford* to confront Farragut he found the admiral apologetic. After the loss of *Lancaster* and damage to *Switzerland,*

Farragut dropped his request for an ironclad. He said he would go back to the mouth of the Red River and cooperate with General Banks in an attack on Port Hudson. After hearing the admiral's plans, Porter agreed to leave *Switzerland* with the lower flotilla, but he warned Farragut to keep young Ellet in sight, otherwise "he will go off on a cruise somewhere before you know it, and then get the ship into trouble."[8]

Porter returned to *Black Hawk* and ordered a bargeload of provisions and supplies drifted down to Farragut. On March 31 Farragut departed from Biggs' Landing with *Hartford, Albatross,* and *Switzerland* and headed for the Red River.[9]

By then, all the bad news from the Mississippi had filtered into the Navy Department. In writing Porter, Fox quoted the *New York Tribune* as saying that during the eighty-six years of the navy's existence, never had there been "so many disasters as have taken place within the last year." He asked Porter to take a close look at the competence of his subordinates. "The people," he added in closing, "will have nothing but success, and they are right. The old cry is commencing against Mr. Welles for not giving it to them."[10]

Porter understood the political implications, but one element had turned in his favor. Spring had come. With the land in bloom, it was already like early summer. Dogwood and azalea sprinkled the landscape with color and filled the air with a fragrance rich with promise. The wetlands were filled with spring runoff, but the muddy inland roads were drying in the sunlight. Grant saw marching weather ahead. General in Chief Halleck badgered him to concentrate his forces and coordinate operations with General Banks. If Banks could not get up to Vicksburg, Halleck inquired, "cannot you get troops down to help him at Port Hudson, or, at least, can you not destroy Grand Gulf before it becomes too strong?"[11]

Once again Grant looked for a way to bypass Vicksburg. A new route, laid along the west bank, led through a succession of bayous from Duckport to New Carthage, fifteen miles below the Warrenton batteries. Grand Gulf's fortifications lay another fifteen miles to the south, and Grant wanted to go the extra distance, ferry his troops across the river, and capture the fort. For the plan to work, he needed Porter.

After sending McClernand to blaze a thirty-mile trail to New Carthage, Grant wrote Porter on March 29 that he intended to run the Vicksburg batteries with some of his transports. He asked if one or two gunboats could be sent below to disrupt the enemy's communications and provide protection for the transports. Porter was lukewarm on the proposition, but he agreed to cooperate fully, warning Grant that once the gunboats got below Vicksburg, he had little hope of getting them back up. "If I do send vessels below," Porter said, "[they] will be the best vessels I have," and once there, he warned, they would be dependent upon the army for coal and provisions. Porter approved the idea of capturing Grand Gulf, however, as it would remove another obstacle in opening communications with Farragut.[12]

With the loss of *Indianola* fresh on his mind, Porter's concern for his ironclads was valid because they barely made six knots in still water. With the current running at four knots, the turtles moved at ten knots going downstream, leaving each vessel under Vicksburg's guns for about twenty minutes. Going upstream, however, presented a problem. The speed of the current subtracted from the speed of the vessel left two knots, placing the turtles under fire for more than ninety minutes—and no ironclad could survive that exposure.

Conscious of Porter's predicament, Grant agreed to take one last look at the enemy's Yazoo River defenses before irrevocably committing himself to the New Carthage plan. On April 1 he and Sherman, accompanied by Porter, climbed aboard *Tuscumbia* and steamed up the Yazoo. Stopping at Drumgould's Bluff, Grant scanned the heights. The Confederates withheld fire to conceal their strength and allowed the vessel to pass. The reconnaissance, however, convinced Grant that to attack the bluffs "would be attended with immense sacrifice of life, if not with defeat."[13]

If Porter felt misgivings about running the gauntlet, Welles gave him little choice when he wired a ciphered order, which read, "The Department wishes you to occupy the river below Vicksburg, so that Admiral Farragut can return to his station." Farragut had already departed from the Vicksburg area, but Porter knew that the White House wanted action because Grant had received similar orders.[14]

The general wasted little time mobilizing his campaign and on April 2 sent his engineers to open the wagon road and widen the bayous to New Carthage. He sent orders to St. Louis and Chicago for tugs and barges and cladded six transports with cotton. He intended to move twenty thousand men of McClernand's corps to New Carthage and asked Porter when two gunboats could be provided to support an attack on Grand Gulf.[15]

Two gunboats would not get the job done, and Porter knew it. Grant could not afford another failure, and neither could the acting admiral. Porter split the squadron, leaving *Black Hawk,* the new ironclad *Choctaw,* and the turtles *Cincinnati* and *De Kalb,* together with all the wooden gunboats, tinclads, and auxiliary vessels, above Vicksburg. For the lower squadron he chose *Louisville, Mound City, Pittsburg,* and *Carondelet;* his newest ironclads, *Lafayette* and *Tuscumbia;* and the flagship, *Benton.* As an afterthought, he added the fast, unarmored ram *General Price* to augment the force at the Red River. After committing his finest vessels to the operation, he assumed the added responsibility of preparing and supervising the movement of Grant's transports. Still lukewarm on the expedition, Porter never hesitated to support Grant, but he did not approve of leaving Sherman behind and giving the advance to McClernand.[16]

On the morning of April 16 Porter lined up the flotilla to run the Vicksburg batteries—eight warships and three transports. Each ironclad had a barge with supplies lashed to starboard and a barge with coal lashed to port, but spaced to allow room for the guns to fire. The transports carried no troops, only supplies, and lashed abeam were barges filled with camp equipage, forage, and ammunition. Stacked with logs, wet hay, and bales of cotton to protect the machinery, the flotilla looked like a tawdry assortment of river misfits. Fearing the transports might bolt during the passage, Porter placed *Tuscumbia* in the rear to "whipper in" skippers of failing courage. Boiler fires were lit during the afternoon so they would burn clean and hot by nightfall, thereby reducing telltale plumes of smoke. As darkness approached, sailors labored in an atmosphere of tension, covering ports and extinguishing lights. Porter told his captains to hug the Louisiana shore until doubling De Soto Point, to load their Dahlgrens with canister and grape, and to elevate their guns to a range of nine hundred yards. They were not to fire until engaged by the enemy. After that, it was every ship for herself. The squadron was to weigh anchor at 9:00 P.M. and maintain fifty-yard intervals in the following formation:[17]

Benton, 16 guns, Lt. Comdr. James A. Greer, lashed to the tug *Ivy*
Lafayette, 8 guns, Capt. Henry Walke, lashed to *General Price*
Louisville, 12 guns, Lt. Comdr. Elias K. Owen
Mound City, 14 guns, Lt. Byron Wilson
Pittsburg, 13 guns, Lt. William R. Hoel
Carondelet, 11 guns, Lt. John M. Murphy, followed by the transports
Forest Queen, Silver Wave, and *Henry Clay*
Tuscumbia, 5 guns, Lt. Comdr. James W. Shirk

On the morning Porter prepared his squadron to run the gauntlet,
the *Vicksburg Whig* assured its readers that the concentration of Union
warships above the city threatened "no immediate danger here. We do
not regard the fleet's coming down as at all pointing to an attack here."
The editor admitted an "unusual quietness among the Yankees across
the river," as many soldiers seemed to have disappeared. Neither the
editor nor anyone on Pemberton's staff knew that Grant and Porter had
located, above the mouth of the Yazoo, a secluded anchorage screened
by forests.[18]

Even Pemberton allowed himself to be deceived. Exhaling a sigh of
relief, he wrote General Stevenson: "The enemy is moving up to Memphis." Three days earlier, Pemberton's scouts had reported that the Federals were "preparing two or three boats to pass our batteries, as reinforcements for Farragut," but nobody paid attention to the information
and no measures were taken to alert the town's batteries. Vicksburg
mounted thirty-seven guns and thirteen fieldpieces, an impressive arsenal giving Pemberton great comfort and little fear of attack.[19]

Col. Edward Higgins commanded the city's river batteries, and his
role was to defend the waterfront. A year had passed since Higgins performed the unpleasant task of surrendering Fort Jackson. Now nothing
would give him more satisfaction than to send Porter's flotilla to the
bottom of the Mississippi, but as the sun set on the evening of April 16
no one told him to be ready at dark to even the score.

Waiting for nightfall, Porter wrote Fox:

I am afraid our people are too insatiate; they forget in their desire for
success that the rebels are at the breech of the gun, and we at the muz-
zle. They are like a man inside of a house, windows barricaded, muskets out of a thousand looped holes, "chevaux de frise" all around, and
a wide ditch outside of that—*we* are in the position of boys throwing

Porter's squadron as it started through the gauntlet on the night of April 16,
1863 REPRINTED FROM JOHNSON AND BUEL, *BATTLES AND LEADERS OF THE
CIVIL WAR*

grass at him and expecting him to cave in—yet we win after all—we
don't go backwards, we advance slowly, and by the grace of God I hope
to see us yet with Uncle Abe's foot on Jeff. Davis' neck. I may be used
up in mind and body before that time comes but come it will, as sure
as there is a sun in heaven.[20]

At 9:15 P.M. Porter ordered *Benton* under way, flashing two white
lanterns as a signal for the fleet to follow. The flagship churned slowly
into the current, hugging the shore. As a precaution, a barge carrying
ammunition was cut loose and allowed to drift downstream. The admiral hoped to pass the batteries undetected, and the vessels moved
downstream at a speed barely exceeding the flow of the river. With fireroom doors closed and with steam exhausted through special vents
inside the paddle box, neither a glimmer of light nor a sound escaped
from the darkened flotilla. In the darkness *Benton's* black and yellow
hull blended with the levee, and following behind her for a half mile
crept the rest of the squadron, stealing quietly downriver without a puff
of smoke curling from the funnels.

Fifty thousand soldiers watched from the banks as *Benton* approached the shank of the horseshoe. Grant and his staff hung like spectators at a fireworks display, waiting on the rail of *Henry Von Phul* for the action to open. His wife, Julia, stood next to him on the hurricane deck, with twelve-year-old Frederick wedged between them.[21]

Sherman waited at the lower end of the canal with four yawls manned by soldiers to rescue stricken vessels. He moved nervously about in midstream, peering upriver for the first of Porter's vessels to come in view, but he heard no sound but the creaking of oars and the river slushing by as it lapped against the strakes.[22]

Skirting the dark woods off De Soto Point, *Benton* crept unseen until she rounded the bend. Porter glanced through the pilothouse peephole at the long line of boats, crawling along like "so many phantom vessels" without a light and barely a sound. At the tip of De Soto Point, Porter turned to Greer and said, "The Rebels seem to keep a very poor watch."[23]

The words had barely left his lips when, on the tip of the point, Confederate pickets set fire to an abandoned house. On a hill above the city a calcium flare shot shafts of light across the river. Moments later the entire western shoreline burst into flame as sentinels torched vacant buildings and lit bonfires. Barrels of tar erupted into blazing fires, and heavy black smoke rolled out along the shore, creating a perfect backdrop of light for the gunners below the city to level their pieces on the passing flotilla. "The sight," Grant declared, "was magnificent, but terrible."[24]

Confederate musket fire from shore rattled off *Benton*'s casemate. A single gun roared into action at the water battery, followed by a field-piece on Force Hill. Standing at the helm, Greer wondered if the enemy had gone to bed, but as he led the ironclad down the shank of the peninsula the firing accelerated. *Benton* shuddered as her Dahlgrens on the port quarter replied with 9-inch percussion shells. Broadsides opened with grape and shrapnel. In ten minutes smoke enveloped the length of the horseshoe, and as each vessel swung down the bend it whirled about in eddies directly under the enemy's guns. The smoke from fires blazing on both banks confused the helmsmen, and when they struck the eddies all semblance of order ended as one vessel after another fell out of line. The turtles, notorious for their poor steering qualities and encumbered with barges, twirled about in the firelight and became easy marks. A raking fire plunged down from elevated batteries and crashed through the casemates. Guns from the ironclads roared back, but darkness mixed with a dense smoke reddened by the glare of fires shrouded the enemy's positions, and shells fell helter-skelter all over the landscape.

With the nerves of every officer strained to the utmost, *Benton* forged ahead, laying a course within forty yards of the Vicksburg waterfront. As she passed, her gunners could hear the crash of walls collapsing under the impact of their point-blank broadsides. The Confederates fired back. A shot penetrated the casemate, struck the timbers around her cylinder, and lodged in the stateroom. Another shot tore an opening six feet wide in her side. Four more shots struck the port side, crushing the armor and splintering great gaps in the wooden backing. But *Benton* pressed forward, steadying her course under the batteries. In thirty minutes of fighting she fired eighty-one shots. Fragments of shells struck the Washington Hotel and buildings on Walnut Street. Never before under fire in an ironclad, Porter felt claustrophobic in the "iron pot" of the pilothouse and ventured onto the spar deck where he could see the action. When enemy shots struck the casemate, he went back inside and found five men wounded.[25]

Lafayette, the heaviest of Porter's ironclads, followed *Benton* into the fight and got pounded for her insolence. A shell from the Marine Hospital battery smashed her casemate, another ripped through her wheelhouse. Shots shattered her forward armor, and grape riddled her funnels as she rotated two full turns in the eddy. With *General Price* lashed to one side and a coal barge to the other, the pilot became confused and narrowly escaped running the ironclad onto the bank. The loss would have been devastating for Porter, and his decision to hug the Mississippi shore probably saved her because most of the shells from the hospital battery overshot the vessel. Captain Walke conned *Lafayette* back into the current, but *General Price* took a dozen shots in her upper works, and the coal barge sank when a shell exploded in its hull. *Price* eventually cut herself loose, and *Lafayette*, struck nine times but no longer encumbered, resumed her course under a full head of steam.[26] Later Porter examined *Lafayette*'s damage and wrote Fox in disgust: "[The enemy's] heavy shot walked right through us, as if we were made of putty—as to the *Lafayette*, the shot went in one side and came out the other."[27]

Befuddled by gunfire and glare, *Louisville* rotated into the eddy and collided with *General Price*. Comdr. Selim E. Woodworth, *Price's* skipper, cut himself free and used his superior speed to escape from the chaos. Two shells had cut up *Price* and wounded three men, and by detaching himself from the ironclads Woodworth probably saved all three vessels. Escaping from the eddy, *Louisville* struck the transport *Silver Wave* and lost her coal barge. How *Silver Wave* got so far in advance of the column can only be explained by her skipper's intention to waste no time running the batteries. In passing, *Louisville* fired only six shots, but as she worked by Vicksburg the pilot reported a barge ahead. Lieutenant Commander Owen took it in tow, and when he reached safety he recognized it as his own.[28]

Mound City evaded the eddy, passing *Lafayette* and *Louisville*, but came under heavy fire. Four shots caromed off her armor, but one 10-inch ball plunged through both of her casemates, wounding four men. She was struck again as she passed Warrenton, but the shot bounded harmlessly away.[29]

The pilots of *Pittsburg* and *Carondelet*, watching as *Mound City* evaded the eddy, followed her under the enemy's guns. *Pittsburg* fired forty-three shells, absorbing seven hits herself, but most of them struck her upper works or lodged in the huge timbers lashed to the port side. Had the logs not been there, one of the shells would have penetrated the ship's magazine, and the explosion would have been spectacular. *Carondelet* got pulled into the eddy just as *Louisville* and *Lafayette* cleared it; otherwise a disastrous collision might have occurred. She was hit twice, one shell breaking through the port side and wounding four men.[30]

Confederate gunners now concentrated their fire on the transports. As *Tuscumbia* came up, Lieutenant Commander Shirk noticed that *Forest Queen* and *Henry Clay* had either whirled around in the eddy or were attempting to beat back upriver. Ordered by Porter to "whipper-in" the fleet, and knowing that the success of the campaign depended upon getting the transports below, he made it his business to turn them around.

Shirk backed to stay above the transports, but he made the mistake of withholding fire. By doing so he sacrificed his only chance to buy time and as a consequence gave the enemy uncontested rein to increase their fire and improve their accuracy. The water battery poured shell after shell into the transports. *Henry Clay* burst into flames, edged across the river, and grounded on the western bank. Her crew scrambled ashore and escaped from the wreckage. The wounded vessel, however, drew the enemy's fire and gave Shirk an opportunity to rescue *Forest Queen.* While urging her to come about, *Tuscumbia* ran on the bank and, in reversing engines, collided with the transport. Both vessels drifted helplessly down the river. Shirk could hear cheering from the Vicksburg batteries almost directly over his head. Every gun in the hills opened on the entangled pair, and minutes passed before Shirk worked free. A shot penetrated *Tuscumbia's* port bow below the waterline and started the planks. Water rushed through the seams, and men manned the pumps. *Forest Queen* took a shot through her steam pipe and lost power. Shirk tried to keep behind her but saw that she was sinking. He took her in tow and beached her at a plantation on the Louisiana shore above Warrenton. In the morning a crew pumped fourteen inches of water out of her bilge. Carpenters made repairs, and on the 18th she joined the fleet below.[31]

During the passage, General Sherman waited in a yawl off Biggs' plantation. From his boat in midstream, he peered into the darkness, looking for *Benton.* When the shelling started, he considered it one of the most stirring and awesome sights of the war. Out of the smoke smothering the river, the dark bulk of an ironclad approached. Soldiers bent their backs to the oars and rowed the general within hailing distance. "*Benton* ahoy!" shouted Sherman. Porter was astonished to find his friend, the general, in the middle of the river and invited him on board. Noting that he would soon be under the Warrenton batteries, Sherman pushed off and said good-bye, and in parting added, "You are more at home here than you were in the ditches grounding on willow-trees. Stick to this, old fellow; it suits Jack better." On the way back to Biggs' plantation, he noticed a man riding the current on a piece of timber and hauled him on board. It was *Henry Clay's* pilot, the last man to leave the burning transport.[32]

Above Vicksburg, Grant and his guests followed the fireworks with awe and excitement. Assistant Secretary of War Charles A. Dana, who had been sent by Stanton to keep an eye on Grant, counted 525 shots. As soon as the firing subsided, Grant ordered the captain to take *Henry Von Phul* back to Milliken's Bend. He would have to wait until morning to learn whether Porter had gotten through.[33]

Sherman rowing into the river to meet Porter's flagship below Vicksburg
REPRINTED FROM JOHNSON AND BUEL, *BATTLES AND LEADERS OF THE CIVIL WAR*

Late at night the squadron assembled off Diamond Island, twelve miles above New Carthage, and Porter made a quick tally of his casualties—twelve injured but none seriously, and no irreparable damage to his vessels. He decided to wait for daylight before descending the river. Several years later he wrote, "The danger to the vessels was more apparent than real" and the pyrotechnics "grand in the extreme," but neither as spectacular nor as dangerous as the risks taken by Farragut in passing Forts Jackson and St. Philip.[34]

In the morning McClernand's pickets on the New Carthage levee reported a transport (*Henry Clay*) drifting downriver and still smoldering, and behind it three barges and numerous bales of cotton. The general rescued two of the barges but waited five anxious hours before the first ironclad hove in view. *Pittsburg* pulled up to the levee first and was greeted with a demonstration of cheering and dancing. McClernand went on board and asked Lieutenant Hoel to take her downriver five miles and drive away a rebel encampment near Perkins' plantation. Hoel deferred to Porter, who he said would be along with the rest of the fleet.[35]

At Vicksburg, General Pemberton made his own assessment of the night's work. With few exceptions, he reconstructed the affair with accuracy. He erred in believing *Silver Wave* had been sunk with *Henry Clay*—probably nobody saw her as she sped by undamaged. He learned that the beached *Forest Queen* was at Brown and Johnson's plantation and erroneously declared her wrecked. But with Porter's best vessels below Vicksburg, Pemberton wired Jefferson Davis for more guns and more men. "I regard the navigation of the Mississippi River as shut out from us now," he declared. "No more supplies can be gotten from the trans-Mississippi department."[36]

Encouraged by Porter's success in passing Vicksburg, Grant decided to try it again. On April 20 he ordered twelve barges secured to six transports and made ready to run the batteries on the first dark night. Each vessel, manned mostly by volunteer soldiers, was to carry 100,000 rations and forty days' coal. When a last-minute shortage of cotton "armor" developed, the army filled the gaps with barrels of beef. Grant did not like sending fragile transports by the batteries without gunboat protection, so he tried to improve the odds by burning all the buildings on De Soto Point. The Confederates, however, were prepared, and the big guns of the Wayman's Hill battery beat off a daylight attack. Grant tried again at dark, but the defenders sheltered themselves in buildings and repulsed the Federals with small-arms fire.[37]

The general sent a message to Porter asking that he bring his squadron back upriver to provide support, but the admiral had continued on to Grand Gulf. At two knots per hour against the current, he was not disposed to chugging all the way back to Vicksburg.[38]

Grant assigned the mission to Col. Clark B. Lagow, who on the night of April 22 lined up the transports with *Tigress* first, followed by *Empire City, Moderator, J. W. Cheeseman, Anglo-Saxon,* and *Horizon.* As soon as the moon set, *Tigress* led off, drifting with the flow of the current. Before the flotilla reached the tip of De Soto Point, *Empire City* sped by *Tigress.* Lagow had hoped to pass the batteries undetected, but he was about to receive a shock. The moment *Empire City* nosed around the bend, signal guns on Fort Hill sprang into action. Buildings alongshore and fresh barrels of tar broke into flame and blazed brightly on the waterfront.[39]

Lagow signaled for full speed ahead, and for the next thirty minutes it was every vessel for herself. As each transport rounded the point, it was pounded by the water battery. *Empire City* sustained a shot through her steam pipe and lost all power. *Tigress,* outlined perfectly in the firelight, received a thorough pummeling and drifted toward the Vicksburg shore. When the vessel would not respond to her helm, the skipper cut her loose from the barge and pointed her downstream. She passed the Marine Hospital battery, and just as the crew was about to celebrate *Tigress* shuddered under the impact of a shot that tore a four-foot hole in her stern. Lt. Col. William S. Oliver ordered the pumps started and conned the boat toward the Louisiana shore. He waited a few minutes too long to get her there. The boat filled and sank in shallow water above Brown and Johnson's plantation with her crew clinging to the smokestacks.[40]

Moderator took a battering and lost her engines as she followed *Tigress,* but by careful maneuvering her skipper held to the current and drifted safely by Warrenton. As *J. W. Cheeseman* rounded the Point, a combination of tar smoke and gunsmoke filled the valley and acted as a screen. *Cheeseman* slipped by the batteries uninjured and stopped long enough at the sunken *Tigress* to take off her survivors.[41]

Anglo-Saxon shuddered from a blast from the water battery that cut loose the lashings connected to the barge on her starboard side. She careened out of control and grounded opposite the Wyman's Hill battery. The volunteer crew calmly cut her loose and backed her into the current. A shot disabled her steerage, and another knocked out the starboard engine. As she drifted helplessly by the batteries, thirty shots knocked her to splinters, but she kept afloat.[42]

Last in line, *Horizon* sped by the batteries under a full head of steam, took fifteen shots, and limped down to Biggs' Landing. Lagow ordered her to take *Anglo-Saxon* in tow, and at daylight *Horizon* floated by the Warrenton batteries as sixteen shots whizzed overhead. The seventeenth crashed into the port rudder. Below the batteries, *Horizon* picked up *Anglo-Saxon* and towed her down to New Carthage. With the exception of *Moderator,* the surviving transports were in poor condition, but repairable. Grant had what he wanted—transportation across the river.[43]

Three Confederate strongholds still lay along the Mississippi River— Vicksburg, Grand Gulf, and Port Hudson. Grant and Porter would leave Port Hudson to Banks and Farragut. For the moment, their emphasis shifted to Grand Gulf, the back door to Vicksburg.

On April 22 Porter steamed down the river to size up the fortifications. He did not like what he saw. "If left to themselves, they will make this place impregnable," Porter told to McClernand. "I shall attack the forts in the morning, and I ask that you will send down men to hold them in case I do take them. . . . This is a case where dash will save everything."[44]

EIGHTEEN

A
King's
Reward

Admiral Porter returned his gunboats to fighting trim and on April 20 dispatched *Tuscumbia* and *General Price* to reconnoiter Grand Gulf. Shirk and Woodworth anchored out of range of Fort Cobun, the town's upper battery, which was dug into the side of Point of Rock about seventy-five feet above the river and protected by a parapet forty feet thick. Cobun mounted two rifled 100-pounders, one 68-pounder, and a rifled 30-pounder Parrott. A double line of rifle pits and a covered way passed behind the town for three-quarters of a mile, ending at Fort Wade, which mounted one 100-pounder, one 64-pounder, and two 32-pounders. Five fieldpieces—10- and 20-pounder Parrotts—completed the batteries, all of which were manned by a large force under Brig. Gen. John S. Bowen. Shirk could not see the guns because they were concealed behind deep excavations. Porter wanted action and wrote Grant: "My opinion is that they will move heaven and earth to stop us if we don't go ahead. I could go down and settle the batteries, but if disabled would not be in condition to cover the landing . . . and I think it should be done together. If the troops just leave all their tents behind and take only provisions, we can be in Grand Gulf in four days." Somewhat dolefully, Porter added, "I wish twenty times a day that Sherman was here, or yourself, but I suppose we cannot have all we wish." To Fox he confided, "Grant works like a horse . . . and will wear himself out," and credited Sherman as having "more brains than all put together."[1]

Two days later Porter transferred his flag to *Lafayette* and, with *General Price* and the tug *Ivy*, dropped down to take a closer look at Grand Gulf. He could see Confederates strengthening the earthworks and told Captain Walke to open fire. *Lafayette*'s gunners lobbed shells into Fort Cobun and scattered the work parties. Fort Wade, three-quarters of a mile downriver, replied with its rifled 32-pounders and dropped a few shells off the beam of *Lafayette*. Convinced that the forts were only partly finished, Porter returned to his anchorage at Hard Times, Louisiana, hoping to find Grant.[2]

Grant was still at Milliken's Bend, so Porter contacted McClernand, whose corps had been given the task of capturing Grand Gulf. McClernand reacted with speed and ordered Brig. Gen. Peter J. Osterhaus to embark the 9th Division and follow Porter to Grand Gulf. "If the gunboats succeed in silencing the batteries," he instructed his officers, "take and hold the place."[3]

Osterhaus worked all night rounding up boats and barges to carry three thousand infantry and two batteries, but the morning of April 23 passed with no order to cast off. The delay was caused by a preacher claiming to be a "half Union man" from Grand Gulf who had come on board *Benton* during the night and convinced the admiral that the Yanks were being decoyed. He gave an exaggerated account of the town's defenses, tripling the actual number of defenders to twelve thousand and doubling the number of forts. With this misinformation in his pocket, Porter asked McClernand to send his entire corps.[4]

The general suspected that Porter had been deceived by his informant and decided to make a personal reconnaissance. He borrowed *General Price* from the admiral and on the afternoon of the 23rd dropped down the river with Osterhaus. After scanning the bluffs with field glasses, the generals failed to locate either fort. McClernand returned to Hard Times, told Porter he had seen little activity, and suggested that the admiral send down his fleet to harass the enemy to "keep them from entrenching." Osterhaus disembarked his division to await further developments.[5]

Porter's distrust of McClernand caused him to wait until Grant arrived, and late on the 23rd he found the general at Pointe Clear. Porter advised against a frontal assault, comparing Grand Gulf's topography to Vicksburg's. He suggested the army march down the west bank and cross the river below Grand Gulf. The other option would be to load up transports and barges with infantry and on a dark night float them by the batteries. Either alternative would enable Grant to assault the enemy from the rear. The general listened, but he wanted to take a close look at Grand Gulf first.[6]

On the morning of the 24th, Porter and Grant took *General Price* below to reconnoiter Grand Gulf's earthworks. Grant considered the defenses weak, but he made a serious error when he doubted the presence of heavy artillery at Fort Cobun and predicted that Grand Gulf would fall "within the next two days." The Confederates aided Grant's false impression by withholding fire during the reconnaissance.[7]

In the meantime, Porter confided his worries to Welles because he disagreed with Grant and McClernand. He also felt compelled to explain why he had not made contact with Admiral Farragut as ordered. He used Grand Gulf's defenses as his reason for not wanting to communicate with Farragut until he had "landed the army safely on the other side of the river." Porter explained that if he sent his ironclads below Grand Gulf, he could be stopped from returning to Vicksburg if Grand Gulf remained in possession of the enemy. Sandwiched between two enemy strongholds, the admiral advised Welles that he was "waiting for the army to make a move."[8]

Porter did not intend to waste his vessels on foolish errands. If Grant developed a feasible plan of attack, Porter would support him with every vessel available, but when the general asked for a gunboat to go up the Big Black to prevent "rebels from building scows," the admiral refused to risk an ironclad on such a menial mission.[9]

On April 24 Grant began moving McPherson's corps to Hard Times to cooperate with McClernand in an assault on Grand Gulf. He then met with McClernand on Porter's flagship for the sole purpose of speeding up the Illinois general, who had been giving more attention to his young bride than to his army. Grant wanted McClernand's men back on the transports and ready to assault Grand Gulf as soon as

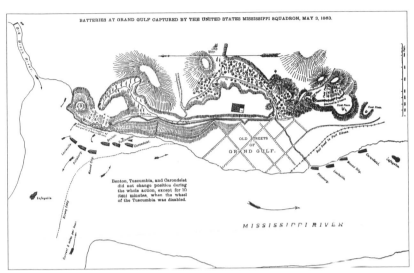

BATTERIES AT GRAND GULF CAPTURED BY THE UNITED STATES MISSISSIPPI SQUADRON, MAY 3, 1863.

OLD STREETS
OF
GRAND GULF.

Benton, Tuscumbia, and Carondelet
did not change position during
the whole action, except for 10
(ten) minutes, when the wheel
of the Tuscumbia was disabled.

MISSISSIPPI RIVER

Sketch of Porter's attack on the batteries of Grand Gulf REPRINTED FROM
OFFICIAL RECORDS OF THE UNION AND CONFEDERATE NAVIES

Porter's gunboats silenced the batteries. McClernand dallied and did not have his corps ready to move until midnight on the 28th. At 3:00 A.M., the steamboats, with barges in tow, cast off to rendezvous with the squadron at Hard Times.[10]

After another reconnaissance Porter believed he knew the location of Grand Gulf's batteries. He outlined the battle plan to his captains, and at 7:00 A.M. on the morning of April 29, *Pittsburg, Carondelet, Mound City, Louisville, Tuscumbia, Benton, Lafayette,* and *General Price* dropped down the river to blow up General Bowen's fortress. McClernand followed in seven transports.[11]

Bowen expected the attack, and he could not understand why Pemberton, at this critical moment, wanted to borrow one of the units at Grand Gulf to counter a Union feint in the Yazoo River. Bowen eventually convinced Pemberton that Grant was at Grand Gulf, not at Snyder's Bluff, and Pemberton finally sprang into action on the 28th and ordered General Stevenson at Vicksburg to hold five thousand troops in readiness to support Bowen "if he called for them."[12]

At 7:50 A.M. on April 29, *Pittsburg, Louisville, Mound City,* and *Carondelet* engaged the batteries at Fort Cobun, but as their primary target was Fort Wade, they passed downriver, leaving *Tuscumbia, Lafayette,* and *Benton* above. All seven gunboats swung about, keeping their bows upstream, their starboard broadsides fully engaged, and their guns charged with shot, shell, grape, and canister. The river formed a bend at Fort Cobun and created eddies, and the gunboats remained under steam and constantly moved about.[13]

Grant observed the bombardment from the tug *Ivy,* and waiting for orders in the rear were the steamers crowded with McClernand's men. Also on board was a special commission led by Assistant Secretary of War Charles A. Dana, who had been sent by Stanton to observe and report on Grant's fitness for command. For six hours the delegation shifted about *Ivy* and restlessly waited as the gunboats pounded the forts.[14]

Porter moved his squadron about to disrupt the aim of the enemy, but many shots hit the plating of the ironclads and caromed off across the river. The admiral signaled *Lafayette* to shift her firing to the lower fort, and for four hours five gunboats concentrated on silencing Fort Wade. They knocked the parapet to pieces, dismounted half of its guns, and killed the battery's commander, Col. William Wade.[15]

After the colonel fell, firing from Fort Wade subsided, and Porter sent two ironclads back upriver to concentrate on Fort Cobun. *Benton* and *Tuscumbia* had taken heavy casualties, and for an hour the flotilla circled off the fort and rotated its fire. The admiral remained on the deck of *Benton* with Greer when a shell exploded, wounding two junior officers and knocking Porter off his feet. This was the only time during the war that the admiral sustained an injury. Another shot passed through *Benton's* pilothouse, disabled the wheel, wounded the pilot, and set the vessel adrift. Fifteen hundred yards downriver she bumped against the bank. Porter fired at Fort Wade while making repairs and eventually worked *Benton* back upriver. A series of shots disabled *Tuscumbia's* port engine, buckled her plates, and jammed her gunports. Unable to stem the current, she dropped below Grand Gulf.[16]

Porter concentrated a savage fire on Fort Cobun, whose gunners were running out of ammunition. After checking on his own depleted magazines, the admiral steamed upriver to confer with Grant. Despite the heavy bombardment, the general considered the batteries strong enough to repulse a frontal attack. Grant told Porter he would take McClernand's corps down the west bank at nightfall if the navy would escort the transports by the forts after dark. Knowing that *Tuscumbia* was already disabled below and vulnerable to attack, Porter agreed. At 1:15 P.M. he broke off the action, leaving *Lafayette* below to continue the shelling and to try to prevent the enemy from making repairs, and returned to Hard Times.[17]

Despite superior firepower, Porter's squadron suffered much damage. *Benton* reported 7 killed and 19 wounded; *Tuscumbia*, 5 killed and 24 wounded; and *Pittsburg*, 6 killed and 13 wounded. *Benton* had been struck 47 times and *Pittsburg* 35 times, but *Tuscumbia* sustained the worst beating, being hit 81 times, with many of the projectiles penetrating her flimsy armor and exploding inside the casemate. "*Tuscumbia*," Porter wrote Welles, "was cut up a great deal and proved herself a poor ship in a hot engagement." Commander Shirk was less kind. He condemned the builder for faulty construction and growled, "Altogether, the *Tuscumbia* is a disgrace."[18]

In contrast to Union casualties, General Bowen reported only three killed and fifteen wounded. He believed as many as three thousand projectiles had been hurled at his forts. As soon as the firing stopped, fatigue parties turned out and by nightfall they had the parapets repaired and the guns remounted.[19]

At 7:45 P.M. Porter cast off at Hard Times and led the squadron back down the river. Trailing behind the gunboats came the transports and the barges. At dark the ironclads arrayed themselves off Grand Gulf and renewed the bombardment. Like so many shadows cast upon the river, the transports slithered by the town, hugging the Louisiana shore. Smoke from Porter's guns screened their passing, and an hour later they tied up uninjured on the west bank four miles below Grand Gulf. After six long months of struggle on the river, Grant finally had his troops where he wanted them.[20]

That night Porter made Stanton's nosy commissioners comfortable on *Benton*. Since nobody had tents, he offered Halleck's elderly adjutant general, Lorenzo Thomas, his stateroom. He helped unpack the general's carpetbag, located his nightshirt, and then mixed him a good, stiff toddy. The whiskey gave Thomas a glow, and he confessed that he and his fellow commissioners had been sent by Lincoln because "great complaints" had come to the president "from someone in the army before Vicksburg in regards to Grant's manner of conducting operations." Porter suspected McClernand of backstabbing and loosened Thomas's tongue with another toddy.

After bolting it down, Thomas swore Porter to secrecy and said, "I carry in my bag full authority to remove General Grant and place whomever I please in command of the army." Leaning forward, he added, "What do you think of that?"

Porter reflected a moment and then asked Thomas who he had in mind to replace Grant.

"Well," the general grunted. "That depends; McClernand is prominent."

"Let an old salt give you a piece of advice," Porter replied. "Don't let your plans get out, for if the army and navy should find out what you three gentlemen came for, they would tar and feather you, and neither General Grant nor myself could prevent it." Porter failed to mention whether Thomas slept well that night.[21]

In the morning Grant began his march. McClernand's corps, having bivouacked a few miles below, boarded the transports. Escorted by *Benton,* they headed downriver. Grant and Porter stood together on deck, searching for a landing site. Near Bruinsburg, Lieutenant Commander Greer conned the vessel against the east bank and gave the signal to land, and the first wave of Union troops flooded ashore. With his beachhead established, Grant sent for Sherman's corps.[22]

On May 1, as soon as McClernand had his corps organized, Grant struck inland toward Port Gibson and, in a battle that consumed the better part of the day, shoved General Bowen's grayclads to the banks of the Big Black River.[23]

The audacity of Grant's tactics impressed Porter. With three days' rations in their pockets and no supply train, the army pushed into enemy territory, determined to live off the land. In four days thirty-two thousand blueclads passed inland, wedging their way between the armies of Pemberton at Vicksburg and Johnston at Jackson, some forty thousand men.[24]

Around midnight on May 3, Porter heard three tremendous explosions from upriver. He assembled his squadron at daylight and steamed up to Grand Gulf to investigate. Smoke streaked the sky, and when he reached the town it lay smoldering and gutted without a soul to defend it. While sailors poked through the rubble, Porter scratched a report to Welles. Then, with Grant marching inland, the admiral moved with promptness. Leaving *Louisville, Carondelet,* and *Mound City* behind to look after the damaged *Tuscumbia,* he divided his force. Departing from Grand Gulf at 11:00 A.M. with *Benton, Lafayette, General Price, Pittsburg,* and the tug *Ivy,* he set a course for the Red River, two hundred miles below. *Switzerland* had come up the river on May 2 with dispatches from Farragut for Grant, and when Porter stopped briefly at Bruinsburg he picked her up and took her with him.[25]

Porter believed he could relieve Farragut and return to Vicksburg before Grant's army arrived. *Webb* and *Queen of the West* were still somewhere on the Red, and he hoped to capture them. He found Farragut toiling at the mouth of the river with the gunboats *Arizona* and *Estrella.* The admiral agreed to leave every vessel on the Mississippi above Port Hudson with Porter, including *Hartford,* and then he bid his foster brother good-bye. Porter hastened up the Red, prowled through deserted Fort De Russy, ripped through a raft that obstructed the river, and took possession of Alexandria, Louisiana. Twenty-four hours later General Banks brought a force up from Opelousas and occupied a noisy town full of professed Union sympathizers. Porter considered going to Shreveport, but the river above Alexandria was falling rapidly.[26]

With Alexandria in his possession, Banks had three options —pursue the enemy to Shreveport, join Grant at Vicksburg, or assault Port Hudson. Banks chose the latter. On May 14 his command marched out of Alexandria, crossed the Atchafalaya at Simmesport, and trekked down the west bank of the Mississippi to Bayou Sara. Ferried across the river on the night of the 23rd, Banks's army struck the rear of Port Hudson the following morning.[27]

After placing Walke in command of the vessels below Grand Gulf and leaving *Lafayette, Switzerland, Pittsburg,* and Farragut's four gunboats to cooperate with Banks and patrol the Red River, Porter set a course for Vicksburg.[28] At Grand Gulf he learned that Lieutenant Commander Owen had sent a work detail of blacks to clean the mud out of the sunken *Indianola.* The vessel was nearly high and dry above Diamond Island, her engines undamaged, and her bunkers filled with about a thousand bushels of coal. Porter made a mental note to try to raise her.[29]

Passing Warrenton on May 15, he discovered that sailors and marines from *Mound City* had destroyed the water battery and burned the town. He praised Lieutenant Wilson, writing, "Thus ended a fort in the space of an hour which had taken the rebels five months to build."[30]

The admiral expected to soon hear the sound of Grant's artillery booming in the rear of Vicksburg. He disembarked at Biggs' Landing, walked to Young's Point, and climbed aboard *Black Hawk*. Breese greeted him with a huge stack of reports. On occasion the daily mail contained as many as three hundred communications, and Porter had been gone for three weeks. A letter from *Indianola*'s commander, George Brown, piqued his interest. Before being exchanged, Brown had been in eleven different prisons. He recalled Porter's threat to hang guerrillas and wrote, "General Pemberton was quite anxious for you to hang someone so he could retaliate on me."[31]

Porter set clerks to work on the pile of correspondence because he needed time to organize his squadron for Grant's final thrust. His vessels were scattered all over the Mississippi watershed, from the Ohio, Tennessee, Cumberland, and Arkansas to the Red River and beyond. Grant had started his circuitous march to Vicksburg with no base of operations and without a wagon train, and the admiral knew the army would need rations, ammunition, and medical supplies.

But Porter had his own problems. Vessels at St. Louis and Cincinnati shipyards were nearly finished, and he needed to man them. He scribbled a message to Admiral Foote, now in charge of the Bureau of Equipment and Recruiting: "I have written you about men; do all you can for us. They send us all the rubbish here. . . . This squadron will soon number 80 vessels, and we want every one of them. The rebels are not going to give up this river without a struggle." Conscious of Welles's impatience, Porter grumbled: "If anybody else can do better, and keep this big squadron going on . . . better than I have, let him come." Porter had not quite broken his habit of criticizing others. Perhaps his whiskey-induced conversation with General Thomas had not worn off. Porter had the deepest respect and admiration for Grant and Sherman, yet he told Foote, "Had I been general and admiral at the same time I could have entered Vicksburg three months ago."[32]

While waiting for Grant, Porter learned why the army's landing at Bruinsburg had been unopposed. In late April the admiral had left a squadron at the mouth of the Yazoo under Fleet Captain Breese with instructions for him to support Sherman. On the 27th Grant sent Sherman a message suggesting a demonstration against Fort Haynes, hoping it would confuse Pemberton and delay reinforcements at Grand Gulf. Sherman complied and on the 28th asked Breese for naval support. The red-haired general had more in mind than a feint and hoped Breese could clear a way to the bluffs.[33]

At 9:00 A.M. on April 30, Breese took all the gunboats but the tinclad *Petrel* up the Yazoo to shell the heights. An hour later, led by the ironclads *Choctaw* and *Baron De Kalb*, the flotilla leveled their heavy guns on the scarred slopes of Drumgould's Bluff and opened fire. Because of high water in the Yazoo, Breese could not anchor and was forced to engage the battery with his broadsides, thereby exposing the vessels' thinly protected stern. He knew the risks but considered Sherman's feint of great tactical importance.

A few minutes later *Black Hawk* and *Tyler* opened on the enemy's artillery emplacements, and three mortar schooners joined the bombardment, lofting two hundred–pound shells into the earthworks. Three tinclads anchored abaft *Tyler* trained their guns on the shore and watched for Confederate infantry. Army transports tied up to the left bank of the Yazoo in plain sight of Confederate observers, and soldiers disembarked.[34]

The sudden appearance of gunboats and troopships alarmed Brig. Gen. Louis Hébert, who rushed his men to the earthworks and had them concentrate fire on *Choctaw,* the only ironclad within range. He became excited when some of Sherman's men attempted to climb the cliffs, but he felt quite proud when the flotilla withdrew on the night of May 2. The feint, however, was well timed. General Stevenson, commanding Vicksburg, went on record as opposed to sending troops to Grand Gulf.[35]

Choctaw, at 1,004 tons, was the heaviest ironclad in Porter's fleet and manifested all the defects of *Lafayette.* After four hours of firing, Breese withdrew to inspect damage. *Choctaw* had been struck forty-seven times, and her casemate and wheelhouse were badly cut up.[36]

Breese renewed the attack on May 1 while Sherman's corps reconnoitered the approaches to Drumgould's Bluff. Having accomplished nothing in the morning, he was meeting with Sherman to discuss the afternoon's operations when an urgent message arrived from Grant. Porter's squadron had passed Grand Gulf, and Grant ordered Sherman to join the main army as quickly as possible. The gunboats remained engaged until the transports departed, and at dark Breese withdrew to the mouth of the Yazoo. Two weeks later, the admiral returned.[37]

On May 18 Porter heard the distant thunder of artillery in the rear of Vicksburg. Moments later, guns roared beyond the reaches of Chickasaw Bayou. Grant had made good time. With *Baron De Kalb, Choctaw,* and four lightdrafts, Porter moved up the river, conscious that the firing was becoming heavier. Studying the heights, he witnessed the welcome sight of Sherman's artillery moving into position between Haynes' Bluff and the city. The squadron's expectations soared. Men cheered. Vicksburg would be sealed from all sides.

Porter communicated with Grant and Sherman and sent back orders for waiting supply vessels to hustle up the Yazoo. He also violated a canon of military protocol when he dispatched a message to General Hurlbut at Memphis urging him to send every available soldier to Grant. "He will have the hardest fight ever seen during this war," Porter wrote. "The attention of the nation should now be devoted to Vicksburg."[38]

On the 20th Porter sent Walker up the Yazoo to clear away obstacles. *Baron De Kalb* and *Choctaw* pushed up to Fort Haynes, found it abandoned, and in a hour reduced it to rubble. Walker continued up to Snyder's Bluff and blew up the works. By the end of the day, fourteen Confederate forts from Haynes' Bluff to Vicksburg lay in ruins. Porter admitted having never seen such a network of defenses.

On May 21, as the squadron came in sight at Yazoo City, the Confederates torched their unfinished ironclads and skedaddled. Walker stopped long enough to demolish the navy yard, sawmills, machine shops, and all public buildings. Upriver the flotilla overhauled seven steamers and burned them. Porter estimated the damage at two million dollars.[39]

While Walker operated in the Yazoo, Porter called up the squadron from Grand Gulf and ordered it to bombard the hill batteries below Vicksburg. At midnight on the 18th, the ironclads moved up to the city and shelled it for an hour.

On the evening of the 21st Porter received word from Grant that he intended to assault the enemy's works at 10:00 A.M., with Sherman on the right, McPherson in the center, and McClernand on the left. Porter placed six mortar boats above the city with orders to fire night and day. The ironclads joined the bombardment, rotating around the clock. *Benton, Mound City,* and *Carondelet* moved upriver and shelled the water batteries. Enemy projectiles clanged off the ironclads' armored bows. *Benton* received thirteen hits, four at the waterline. In the morning *Tuscumbia* lumbered up from below and joined in the barrage, but in less than an hour she withdrew, her turret disabled. Because the attack occurred during daylight, the ironclads took a battering. So furious was the bombardment that Porter could not hear Grant's attack. In reporting the action to Welles, Porter admitted it was the hottest fire the gunboats had ever been under.[40]

When Grant's attack stalled, McClernand erroneously reported a lodgment in the enemy's works. Encouraged by McClernand's unexpected success, Grant ordered a second assault, but it was repulsed with heavy loss. McClernand's flawed judgment and the distorted account he aired in the press eventually led to his dismissal. The Union army gained a little ground and squeezed the defenders closer around the city. On the 22nd Grant advised Porter he would be compelled to besiege the town unless Sherman could roll up the enemy's flank. He asked if the gunboats could silence the upper water battery and clear the rifle pits along the second range of hills above Yazoo Bottom, thereby opening the way for Sherman's corps. Grant believed the enemy had begun to shift guns from their water batteries to the land approaches, and he wanted the effort stopped. Porter did not think the enemy had weakened their upper water battery, which contained some of the heaviest guns at Vicksburg, but he agreed to support Sherman and on the 26th dispatched *Cincinnati*, the only ironclad not engaged elsewhere.[41]

George Bache, commanding *Cincinnati*, attempted to run downriver and enfilade the enemy's left flank. He worried that if the vessel became disabled she would drift downriver and be pummeled by the town's batteries. On the hill, General Sherman, protecting Grant's right flank, prepared to take advantage of the ironclad's shellfire. *Cincinnati,* weakly armored with logs and hay, nosed into the current and steamed toward the upper water battery. Every gun on the hill opened on her. The water batteries were as strong as ever and poured in shot and shell—two shots hit her shell room and one of them bounded up her wheel and splintered her paddles. A third shot penetrated her magazine, flooded it, and carried away the starboard tiller. A fourth shot went through the deck and disabled her broadside guns. With the ship sinking and the helmsman killed, Bache took the helm, came about, and limped back upriver. He conned her close to the bank, ran out a plank, and removed the wounded. Before the crew could tie her to a tree, she sank in three fathoms of water.[42]

Porter, after hearing the firing, started down in a tug to check on her movements. As he approached the bend, he observed *Cincinnati* coming upstream under heavy fire. Not seeing any shots strike her, he did not believe she had been damaged. The ironclad disappeared around a point, and Porter assumed she was taking the shortcut to the Yazoo through Old River. He later discovered she had sunk with her colors still flying. After explaining the loss of another vessel to Welles, Porter added, "She can be raised when the water falls." In the attack, Bache lost forty men, and Porter chalked up another disaster.[43]

Sherman witnessed the sinking of *Cincinnati* from the bluffs and felt dreadful, but Porter took the loss philosophically and while riding a horse behind the lines told Sherman that he was "willing to lose all the boats if he could do any good." During this meeting, he offered to send up Captain Selfridge with a pair of 8-inch howitzers. Sherman accepted the offer and provided a detail to help haul the guns up the hill. Porter dipped deeper into his arsenal, and by the 5th Sherman had fifteen 8- and 9-inch naval guns bearing upon the enemy, with bluejackets to serve them.[44]

Porter sent Walker back up the Yazoo River with *De Kalb, Forest Rose, Linden, Signal,* and *Petrel* to destroy everything afloat in the Delta and to prevent supplies from reaching Vicksburg. The expedition departed on the 24th and was gone for a week. Stopping below Fort Pemberton, Walker burned four steamers blocking the passage. He continued up the Yazoo, entered the Big Sunflower, and sent boat expeditions deep into Rolling Fork and Deer Creek, the same swampy waterways where Porter's expedition had bogged down in March. After navigating two hundred miles of the Delta and destroying nine vessels and tons of supplies, Walker returned to the mouth of the Yazoo with only two casualties.[45]

By June 1 siege operations were in full swing, with Grant's army pressing Vicksburg from the plateau and the Mississippi Squadron completing the investment on the river. Grant, conscious that General Johnston was building his forces at Jackson, kept pressure on Pemberton's army. West of the river the trans-Mississippi armies had little to occupy their attention, and they made repeated attempts to force a crossing at places like Milliken's Bend, Goodrich's Landing, and Helena. But Johnston never moved to relieve Vicksburg.

Porter, weary of merely lofting shells into Vicksburg, looked for innovative ways to support the army. He sent the cavalry of Ellet's undisciplined Marine Brigade up the Yazoo with orders to clean out guerrilla activity in Sherman's rear and across the river in Louisiana. The admiral doubted if Ellet's force would obey orders, but he knew the free-wheeling assignment would appeal to them. He also put Ellet to work emplacing Parrotts on De Soto Point to range in on the water battery. To Porter's surprise, Ellet's men performed both missions in fine style.[46]

At 3:00 A.M. on June 7 two Confederate brigades attacked Grant's supply bases at Young's Point and Milliken's Bend. Both were manned by lightly armed black soldiers, many of whom did not know how to fire a musket. At Milliken's Bend the Confederates attacked their former slaves with ferocity, driving them back to the river. Those they captured they shot in the head. A massive slaughter was about to commence when *Lafayette* and *Choctaw* hove into sight, obtained a crossfire, and drove the raiders back to the woods.[47]

June continued hot and humid. Insects swarmed everywhere, bloated carcasses of dead cattle floated down the river, and conditions became steadily worse. A year had passed since Porter first brought his bummers to Vicksburg, and the fortress still stood defiantly on the hill with every flag flying. On the 8th the admiral celebrated his fiftieth birthday by ignoring his correspondence. He paid a visit to Sherman, who, he said, "is so close [to the enemy] that he cannot get nearer without going in." Sherman took the admiral over to McPherson's and McClernand's parallels, where two more batteries of 8- and 9-inch naval guns had been dragged up the bluffs. Grant already had Vicksburg caged in with 220 cannon, mostly light fieldpieces.

Porter returned to *Black Hawk* and on the 9th shared his concerns with Welles: "Not a soul is to be seen moving in the city, the soldiers lying in their trenches . . . the inhabitants being stowed in caves." He linked the city's stubborn resistance to the likelihood that General Johnston was building a force in Grant's rear. "If the city is relieved, and our army have to retire, we will lose everything we have. . . . If we do not get Vicksburg now, we never will."[48]

To escape the continuous bombardment, many of the city's four thousand inhabitants obtained planks and floated down the river until they were picked up by the gunboats. Porter questioned them, and rumors persisted that Johnston, with ten thousand men, had crossed into Louisiana to attack De Soto Point. Informants said that Pemberton was waiting with five hundred skiffs, ten yawls, and two barges to evacuate his force by crossing the river. There was barely a house in Vicksburg that had not been pierced by shellfire, and those badly damaged had been ripped apart and the lumber used to build flatboats. Porter looked each morning across at the city and saw fewer homes standing. He ordered the gunboats to be vigilant and, if a crossing was attempted, to "go right in and give them grape and canister right and left, fore and aft." Johnston, however, had no such plans, but Pemberton was looking for a way to save his army, and as each day passed the admiral girded for trouble. So certain was Porter of an imminent attack that he alerted the entire fleet and posted Ellet's Marine Brigade on De Soto Point with orders to hold the canal at all costs.[49]

When Grant ordered a general bombardment on June 20, Porter retrieved three heavy guns from the sunken *Cincinnati*, mounted them on floats, and anchored them opposite the town. Lieutenant Ramsey of *Choctaw* brought the makeshift battery to bear on the enemy's left and enfiladed the heavy works and rifle pits in front of Sherman's corps. The bombardment silenced the enemy's guns but not their determination.[50]

On June 25 General McPherson exploded a mine under the enemy's main fort but, in a furious attack, failed to secure a lodgment. By then the defenders were eating "Confederate beef," otherwise known as mule meat. Living on quarter rations, two hungry deserters slipped down to the river and told Porter that if not relieved by the 4th of July, Pemberton would surrender. Grant had heard the same himself, but the admiral went an extra step. He believed Pemberton might capitulate sooner if his soldiers knew his intentions. Porter gathered up the captured Confederate correspondence, handed it to Commander Woodworth, and told him to put it in an empty shell and shoot it into Vicksburg. Woodworth had a better idea. He built kites and flew the letters into town.[51]

A letter found among Pemberton's papers after the war appeared to be a petition signed by "Many Soldiers" and directed to the general as an appeal to surrender before everyone starved. Porter never mentioned the letter as one of the documents floated into Vicksburg by kite, but it is possible he wrote it because it was characteristic of his wit and looked like his scribbling. Speaking for some tattered soul dressed in butternut, the letter read, "Everybody admits that we have all covered ourselves in glory, but, alas! alas! general, a crisis has arrived in the midst of our siege. . . . You had better heed a warning voice, though it is a voice of a private soldier. This army is ripe for mutiny, unless it can be fed." The prose is classic Porter.[52]

On July 3, with the deep-throated naval guns roaring a few miles downriver, a signal officer on board *Black Hawk* handed Porter a message from Grant: "The enemy has asked armistice to arrange terms of capitulation. Will you please cease firing until notified, or hear our batteries open. I shall fire a national salute into the city at daylight if they do not surrender."[53]

Porter silenced the fleet but maintained a vigil at De Soto Point. For the first time in forty days, the sounds of evening could be heard off Vicksburg. Porter waited all night for further word. From time to time he heard musket firing above the city. At 5:30 A.M. Grant's wire came—"The enemy has accepted in the main my terms of capitulation, and will surrender the city, works, and garrison at 10 a.m."[54]

Remembering his promise to Welles, Porter drafted a telegram—"Sir: I have the honor to inform you that Vicksburg has surrendered to the U.S. forces on this 4th of July"—and as soon as Grant confirmed the articles had been signed, the admiral sent it by dispatch boat to the telegraph at Cairo. With it went his secretary, Charlie Guild, bearing a stack of reports for Washington.[55]

With the squadron following, Porter eased *Black Hawk* downriver and waited off Vicksburg for the official surrender. At 11:30 the Confederate flag flying over the courthouse came down and the Stars and Stripes unfurled in a sultry breeze. Steam whistles hooted, and each vessel fired a national salute that seemed, Porter said, "like a renewed attack." The admiral spied Grant and his officers riding toward the levee and eased the flagship over to the landing. He met Grant on the gangway, and the two commanders greeted each other warmly. Porter looked about for Sherman, but he was off to Jackson, Grant explained, in pursuit of General Johnston. Porter opened his wine locker, poured a toast, and enjoyed watching it disappear "down the parched throats which had tasted nothing for some time but bad water." Grant, however, contented himself with a cigar and manifested the same calm demeanor he always bore, whether in adversity or in victory. Porter joined the general in a tour of the town, observing an hour after the surrender that soldiers of both armies bonded together "as if they belonged to the same party." That night, 29,491 Confederate parolees watched a fireworks display celebrating the Fourth.[56]

Porter's message informing Welles of Vicksburg's surrender reached Washington at 12:40 P.M. on July 7. The secretary excused himself from a meeting with a delegation of disgruntled Maine fishermen and hurried over to the Executive Mansion. Welles found Lincoln discussing Grant's situation with Secretary of the Treasury Salmon Chase. Gettysburg had just been fought to a standstill, and the president was anxious for Maj. Gen. George G. Meade to take the initiative and catch Lee before he withdrew to Virginia. When Welles announced the fall of Vicksburg, Lincoln leaped to his feet and said, "I myself will telegraph this news to General Meade." He seized his hat, but suddenly stopped, his face beaming with joy. He caught Welles's hand and gave him a hug, saying, "What can we do for the Secretary of the Navy for this glorious intelligence? He is always giving us good news. I cannot, in words, tell you my joy over this result. It is great, Mr. Welles, it is great!"[57]

In summing up the admiral's contribution, Grant wrote: "The Navy under Porter was all it could be during the entire campaign. Without its assistance the campaign could not have been successfully made with twice the number of men engaged. The most perfect harmony reigned between the two arms of the service. There never was a request made, that I am aware of, either of the Flag-officer or any of his subordinates, that was not promptly complied with."[58]

Porter, in summing up the campaign, credited the capture of Vicksburg to the army and to Grant's good planning: "The conception of the idea originated solely with General Grant, who adopted a course in which great labor was performed, great battles were fought, and great risks were run; a single mistake would have involved us in difficulty, but so well were all the plans matured [and] the movements timed . . . that not a mistake occurred. . . . So confident was I of the ability of General Grant to carry out his plans when he explained them to me, that I never hesitated to change my position from above to below Vicksburg."[59]

More than a year had elapsed since Porter had confided to Fox, "I don't believe in our generals anymore than I do in our old fogies of the Navy." Porter's exposure to generals of Grant's and Sherman's caliber transformed his opinion of West Point officers but confirmed his doubts about Lincoln's political generals. Of the latter, he hoped he had seen the last.[60]

Lincoln had become one of Porter's staunchest supporters. He wasted no time striking the word "acting" from Porter's temporary commission and jumped him three grades to the permanent rank of rear admiral, retroactive to July 4, at the head of which was Farragut, followed by Goldsborough, Du Pont, Davis, and Dahlgren. Porter learned of his advancement from the newspapers, but he did not receive it until Charlie Guild returned from Washington with a note from Fox, saying, "You have nobly earned it, though it is a king's reward."[61]

Porter now found himself side by side with the most victorious squadron commanders of the war. If that were not enough, he received by name the thanks of Congress in a joint resolution "for the eminent skill, endurance, and gallantry by him and his squadron in cooperation with the army in opening the Mississippi River."[62]

On July 9 Port Hudson fell to the combined forces of Farragut and Banks, and, in Lincoln's jubilant words, the mighty Mississippi now flowed "unvexed to the sea." Farragut, on orders from the Navy Department, turned the control of the river above New Orleans over to Porter.[63]

On July 29 Welles rewarded the admiral with a leave of absence, reminding him that relaxation was "absolutely necessary" to his health. Take "a month or six weeks," Welles suggested. "The squadron can be left in charge of the senior commanding officer."[64]

But Porter declined. Despite the miserably hot summer months, he felt good, and there was still much to do.

Campaigning
with Banks

Rear Admiral Porter had several reasons for not taking leave. His command was spread all over the Mississippi watershed, and on the very day Vicksburg surrendered, Lt. Gen. Theophilus H. Holmes, with two divisions of Confederate troops from Arkansas and Missouri, struck the Helena garrison at daybreak. Maj. Gen. Sterling Price, leading his own division of butternuts, predicted, "As sure as the sun rises, the fort . . . will be ours." Price, however, forgot about the presence of the Union navy.[1]

Porter learned from deserters that a strong Confederate column planned a raid, and he suspected their target was Helena. The only gunboat there was a small tinclad, *Hastings,* so on June 29 he detached the battle-tested *Tyler,* under Lt. Comdr. James M. Prichett, and *General Bragg,* under Lt. Joshua Bishop, and sent them to Helena with orders to watch for a surprise attack. Maj. Gen. Benjamin M. Prentiss, commanding the Helena garrison, placed little credence in rumors of an attack until Porter's gunboats anchored off the town.[2]

At daybreak on July 4, Holmes struck with his entire force. As soon as the action opened, Prichett weighed anchor and ranged back and forth opposite the line of advancing Confederates. *Tyler*'s 8-inch shells stopped the attack before it could gather steam. Marksmanship from the timberclad was extraordinary. The attack stalled and at noon Holmes withdrew, losing more than sixteen hundred men—20 percent of his force. During the fight, Prichett cut his fuses to explode in ten to fifteen seconds. He fired 413 rounds, mostly 8-inch shells, and accounted for about six hundred of the enemy's casualties. Prentiss was effusive in his praise of Prichett, but he failed to follow up on the advantage given him by the navy. Although Holmes's force sustained a bad beating, attacks like this convinced Porter that he should not go home.[3]

By the summer of 1863, the Mississippi Squadron had grown to seventy-three gunboats, twelve tugs, and seven rams of Ellet's Marine Brigade—enough to keep any admiral busy. The axiom of safety in numbers, however, did not always apply to Porter's vessels. When General Johnston began to fortify Yazoo City in mid-July, Porter and Grant decided to send up five thousand troops to dislodge the rebel garrison. Walker took four turtles, led by *Baron De Kalb,* to protect the transports and drive off the work details. Ranging up to Yazoo City, he threw in a few shells to draw fire and then backed off to give the army time to land their troops. When he observed the rebels withdrawing, he hastened back upriver to prevent the enemy from removing their guns. At the lower end of town *De Kalb* struck two torpedoes and sank in fifteen feet of water. Once again Porter took the loss philosophically, claiming nineteen steamers scuttled and six guns and three thousand bales of cotton captured, altogether worth more than $1,350,000—enough, he said, "to pay for the [sunken] gunboat."[4]

In mid-August, with his expanded area of control, Porter divided his command into eight districts: the first from New Orleans to Donaldsville; and working northward, the second from Donaldsville to the Red River; the third to Natchez; the fourth to Vicksburg; the fifth to the White River; the sixth to Cairo; the seventh to the head of the Tennessee; and the eighth to the upper Ohio and the source of the Cumberland. He placed a reliable officer in charge of each district, but he had less than fifty regular navy officers in the command, and this deficiency gave him another reason to postpone his furlough.[5]

Eight district commanders could not keep the volunteer officers from getting into trouble. On September 13 Acting Master Walter E. H. Fentress, commanding *Rattler,* disobeyed standing orders and took sixteen men ashore to attend divine worship at Rodney, Mississippi. With *Rattler* nearby, Fentress felt perfectly safe when he entered the church. Moments later fifty rebel riders surrounded the building and captured the churchgoers. After Porter learned of the incident, he commented dourly, "I feel no sympathy whatever for Mr. Fentress, but regret the loss of those with him." To Greer, commanding the 4th District, he said, "I will omit nothing to have [Fentress] dismissed from the service."[6]

At the time, Porter was on a scout up the Red River to determine whether he could get his ironclads above the falls at Alexandria. General Banks had been considering an invasion of northern Louisiana, but Porter found the river too dry in places. The campaign would have to wait for the spring runoff. The scout, however, returned dividends. The Marine Brigade captured a Confederate payroll—$2,200,000 for the soldiers at Little Rock—and Porter recovered the gunboat *Paw,* which had snagged in early August and sunk in shallow water.[7]

But Banks had more on his mind than the occupation of northern Louisiana. With the Mississippi open from its source to its mouth, speculators flocked to Washington to obtain permits allowing them to trade within the enemy's lines. Banks favored a policy giving senior army officers authority to negotiate privately with friends in the Confederacy for the release of cotton. He already knew where much of it could be found because he had sent spies into enemy country to make maps marking the plantations where cotton was stored. It came as no surprise to Banks to learn that most of it lay up the tributaries of the Red River. Unlike Butler, Banks showed more interest in lining the pockets of his New England friends than lining his own, but by enabling any person with political influence to obtain a permit, he opened Mississippi and Louisiana to a new form of invasion.[8]

Against the wishes of Secretary of the Treasury Salmon P. Chase, Lincoln bent to political pressure and began to issue permits on his own stationery. The Treasury also issued permits and opened offices from Memphis to New Orleans. They attempted to be selective in deciding who among the hundreds of applicants could be trusted to turn their cotton over to the government in exchange for the authorized commission. Chase's effort to deny permits to less-than-credible traders failed because any applicant denied a permit forged one. Some simply harangued Lincoln until they got one, and a permit issued by the president ordered that "all Military and Naval commanders will give to the [bearer] protection and safe conduct from Cairo to Red River, and up said river, and its tributaries, till he shall pass beyond our Military lines, and also give him such protection and safe conduct, on his return to our lines, back to Cairo with any cargoes he may bring."[9]

The order, if interpreted narrowly, put the army and the navy at the disposal of speculators, but especially the navy because of the imposed shuttle service. The admiral could find nothing good to say about the agents and in late October wrote Sherman, "A greater pack of knaves never went unhung. . . . It is very much like setting a rat to watch the cheese to see that the mice don't get at it." Porter's concern extended beyond the authorized traffic because he caught speculators exchanging war materials and other contraband for cotton. Vessels of every description set up shop along the Red River and openly traded with guerrillas. Agents threw drinking parties on their vessels to ingratiate themselves with the partisans and to solicit their help in gathering plunder. The scheme backfired when a band of guerrillas came aboard the steamer *Mist*, took what they wanted, and burned the vessel.

Speculators feared interference from the navy, and the longer they could keep gunboats out of the Red River, the bigger their haul of cotton. Samuel L. Casey, a politician who had secured a permit from Lincoln, enjoyed presidential immunity as he rambled through northern Louisiana gathering twenty thousand bales of cotton. Banks condoned the enterprise, but Porter condemned it because Casey paid for the cotton with sterling. When word got back to Casey, he wired Lincoln, "Do not let Admiral Porter send an expedition up Red River until you hear from me again. If he should he will defeat all my plans." Porter could not get up the Red, and in his letter to Sherman he added, "You don't know how I miss my old occupation. It has been very dry work since Vicksburg fell."[10]

Porter asked that Ellet's Marine Brigade be transferred to Grant, who agreed that the brigade should be broken up, the vessels used as transports, and the officers and men discharged. Porter disliked the Ellets, and the feeling was mutual. The brigade's "robberies and house burning are shameful," he declared, and as for the Ellets, they "have been guilty of some very dirty, underhand[ed] work toward myself . . . were guilty of gross falsehoods in making malicious statements, and lied deliberately after making them." Porter's skin had not thickened much since prewar days.[11]

Halleck, however, could not locate the Marine Brigade. On November 3 Fox wrote Porter, "Stanton will transfer them if you will only tell us where they are." Porter promised to find them, adding that the unit "has been the most expensive affair, for the little done, ever got up in the country. If it should be permitted to operate independently, the Navy would bear all the odium of its doings."[12]

In late November Porter learned that Grant had reached Chattanooga, but Sherman was still at Eastport. Grant wanted Sherman's army to be transported across the Tennessee River and brought to Nashville. Sherman had been unable to cross and brooded for two weeks waiting for the river to fall. Both armies were short supplies, so Porter assembled a squadron of his best lightdrafts, loaded twenty barges with provisions, put Phelps in command, and sent it up to Eastport. According to Porter, Phelps's boats "could run on a heavy dew." The vessels had been fitted with long spars on their bows so they could jump like grasshoppers over the shoals. When a boat reached a shoal, the spars would be planted on the riverbed and the vessel pressed forward, vaulting over the rocks. Sherman was waiting on his horse when Phelps rounded the bend and steamed into sight. "Sherman was so glad to see Phelps," Porter recalled, "that he almost shook his arm off."[13]

December blew in manifesting all the signs of winter, and with Grant and Sherman ensconced in Tennessee, Porter took *Black Hawk* to Cincinnati to inspect a pair of new ironclads. The temperature dropped to zero, and he caught a severe cold. Seventeen-year-old David Y. Porter, a distant relative who had joined the squadron in November as master's mate, died of double pneumonia. Evelina Cora, Porter's sister, died unexpectedly, and her husband, Gwynn Harris Heap of the Navy Department, asked for duty in the West. Fox understood the request and sent him to Cairo.[14]

For Porter, the bitter winter of 1864 could not end soon enough. *Black Hawk,* roomy and comfortable in the summer, dripped with icicles and creaked with agony as frigid blasts of air whistled through the thin bulkheads. While nursing his cold through the dark days of

USS *Black Hawk,* Porter's spacious flagship, with tug REPRINTED FROM
JOHNSON AND DUEL, *BATTLES AND LEADERS OF THE CIVIL WAR*

January, he missed the company of Grant and Sherman. Reflecting on
his army friends, Porter believed that whatever was lacking in Grant,
Sherman supplied, and that the two of them together made a very good
general.[15]

Porter's contact on the Mississippi became Banks, who, like Butler,
had no military training. Promoted to major general from the Speaker-
ship of the House, the forty-seven-year-old politician was the second-
highest-ranking general in the army and a man most at comfort in social
settings. In New Orleans the townsfolk mirthfully called him "Dancing
Master" Banks because of his frequent banquets. In the spring of 1862
Banks's division had been driven out of the Shenandoah Valley by Brig.
Gen. Thomas J. "Stonewall" Jackson. Three months later Banks was
defeated at Cedar Mountain. In 1863 his ineptitude at Port Hudson
caused heavy Union losses. Late in the summer he launched an expedition into Texas that was so poorly planned that the Confederates
repulsed the attack and captured two Union vessels at the mouth of

the Sabine River. Now, as the ice in the Ohio began to pass down the river, Porter steeled himself to the prospect of a spring campaign with an army commanded by another political general.[16]

Early in January Sherman stopped at Cairo to confer with Porter. The admiral wanted his trusted friend—not Banks—to command the expedition to Shreveport, but Grant advised against it. Banks ranked every major general in the army but Butler. Sherman confided to his wife, "I wanted to go up the Red River but as Banks was to command in person I thought it best not to go."[17]

Instead, Grant ordered Maj. Gen. Frederick Steele's VII Army Corps to cooperate with Banks, and Sherman detached the XVI Army Corps, ten thousand men under Brig. Gen. Andrew J. Smith, with the condition that Banks return the corps to Tennessee by April 15 to participate in the Atlanta campaign. Sherman promised to have Smith's corps at Alexandria by March 17 if Porter agreed to the plan. The admiral had no choice. He had already committed "every ironclad vessel in the fleet" to the campaign.[18]

Before the war Sherman had taught at the Louisiana State Seminary at Alexandria, and he assured Porter that as soon as the snow melted there would be plenty of water in the river until June. On March 2 Porter reached the mouth of the Red and found it unseasonably low. Having brought with him the squadron's best vessels, he apprehensively waited for further word from Sherman, who had gone to New Orleans to confer with Banks. Shreveport lay five hundred miles up the narrow, crooked river, where high banks and hidden shoals gave the enemy numerous advantages. But the most serious danger came from the low stage of the river. He worried that if he made the ascent, he might not get out before the river fell. If the squadron became stranded, he might have to destroy it, and he wondered if Banks could be depended upon to defend it. Aware of Grant's timetable in Georgia, Porter expressed his doubts to Welles: "I much fear that the movement cannot come off, without interfering with the plans formed by General Grant." If the admiral hoped for saner minds to postpone the expedition, the time for changing directions had passed.[19]

Porter anticipated no problems in reaching Alexandria, but he had seen the rapids above the town where two falls formed an obstruction to navigation. The usual depth between the falls was about four feet, but the spring runoff took it as high as twenty. For his ironclads Porter needed about eight feet of water at the falls. This year's rise had been slight. The low level of the river, combined with Grant's timetable for the return of Smith's corps, demanded a swift campaign.

In early march Sherman stopped at the mouth of the Red and told Porter that Banks's command, under Maj. Gen. William B. Franklin, was at Opelousas and ready to go to Alexandria. Banks, however, had no time to devote to military affairs until after the inauguration of the new Union governor of Louisiana. The general had prepared a great banquet for March 4 and was totally absorbed by social matters. Sherman considered such ceremonies out of place at a time when the war demanded "every hour and every minute" of Banks's time.[20]

General Steele was also operating to a political agenda—the election of Union officials in Arkansas—and he wrote Banks asking to be excused from the campaign but promised to make a demonstration. Sherman saw the letter and, instead of waiting for Banks to reply, told Steele to "push straight for Shreveport with all he has." When Grant learned of the letter, he ordered Steele not to demonstrate but to cooperate in the capture of Shreveport. Of the five commanders involved in the expedition, only Porter and A. J. Smith remained committed to a timetable.[21]

Banks's force, including Smith's corps, contained about thirty-six thousand men. Lt. Gen. Edmund Kirby Smith, commanding the Confederacy's Trans-Mississippi Department with headquarters at Shreveport, could put his hands on about thirty thousand men, but they were broadly dispersed through a country with few roads. He attempted to bring General Price's five thousand infantry over from Arkansas, but the troops he collected to oppose Banks added up to about sixteen thousand infantry and cavalry under the command of Maj. Gen. Richard Taylor.[22]

On March 10 A. J. Smith's ten thousand men from Sherman's army embarked on twenty-one transports and departed from Vicksburg. Among the transports were the rams of Ellet's Marine Brigade, now under the management of Grant. By nightfall, March 11, Smith's corps joined Porter's gunboats in Old River, and on the 12th they disembarked at Simmesport.[23]

Below Alexandria the Confederates had rebuilt Fort De Russy, and it had to be destroyed. Smith started his corps up the Atchafalaya, marched cross-country, and brushed away weak Confederate resistance.

On the afternoon of the 14th, Porter opened on the fort from the river and Smith attacked from the rear. De Russy, manned by about 350 men, surrendered after a sharp exchange of artillery. Porter came ashore, walked through the earthwork with Smith, and was impressed by its strength. "Colonel De Russy," Porter noted, "is a most excellent engineer to build forts, but does not seem to know what to do with them after they are constructed. The efforts of these people to keep up this war remind one of the antics of Chinamen, who build canvas forts, paint hideous dragons on their shields, turn somersets, and yell in the faces of their enemies to frighten them, and then run away at the first sign of an engagement."[24]

Porter remained behind with Smith to blow up the fort, but he detached Phelps and sent him to Alexandria to cut off the Confederate retreat. Phelps arrived on the afternoon of the 15th and found the town evacuated by General Taylor, who had loaded six steamers with public property and sent them to Shreveport. Phelps pushed *Eastport* to the falls just as the last of Taylor's paddleboats steamed out of sight, but there he stopped, as the channel was jutted with rocks and precariously low. Porter and Smith arrived on the 16th with the transports and the Marine Brigade. Taylor, who had gathered up his grayclads and marched to Bayou Boeuf, issued orders for his columns to meet at Natchitoches.[25]

Smith and Porter had heard nothing from Banks, who instead of traveling light had assembled a train of a thousand wagons, and Franklin's march from Opelousas bogged down on poor roads covered with wheel-deep mud. Sherman had told Porter that Banks promised to have his force at Alexandria before Smith arrived, but the last infantry units did not slog into the town until March 26—eight days late.[26]

On the 24th Banks arrived by boat, accompanied by dozens of cotton buyers who could not disguise their horror when they observed cotton piled high on Porter's gunboats. The admiral had kept the squadron busy while waiting for the overdue general, and the tars used great imagination in confiscating over six thousand bales of cotton. They commandeered wagons and teams, painted mules with the letters "USN" to designate them as the property of the navy, and penetrated as deep as ten miles into the country in search of booty. Porter approved, admitting

Maj. Gen. Nathaniel P. Banks, another of
Lincoln's political generals disliked by Porter
COURTESY U.S. ARMY MILITARY HISTORY INSTITUTE

that "Jack made very good cotton bales." Unlike the army, the navy still operated under an old prize law. Fifty percent of the value of captured property went to the captors, and 5 percent of that went to Porter.

Selfridge admitted cutting stencils for the letters "CSA" and marking the captured cotton. With a second set of stencils, his men marked each bale with the letters "USN," thereby identifying the navy as the new owner. At supper one evening Col. James G. Wilson asked Porter if the letters stood for "Cotton Stealing Association of the United States Navy." No doubt Porter enjoyed the joke and blamed the whole affair on Banks's tardiness. By the time the general arrived, Porter had his loot stacked, under guard, and ready for shipment to Cairo.[27]

Porter's confiscation of cotton spoiled the plans of Banks's boatload of buyers. What the tars failed to capture, the enemy burned. Banks appealed to Porter, claiming heavy losses to the national treasury if the navy's indiscriminate confiscation continued. Porter doubted if the treasury would see much cotton money because many of the agents wandered the hinterland with permits from the president. For a few days competition raged between soldiers and seamen to see who could acquire the most booty. One group stole from the other. The admiral was all for bringing the contest to an end by getting up the river before it fell. Banks, however, was beset by angry and disillusioned agents, and delays caused by the cotton imbroglio benefited General Taylor, who collected reinforcements and waited for Banks to advance.[28]

On March 26, in the midst of Banks's cotton problems, an order arrived from Grant, who for two weeks had been general in chief of the armies. He reminded Banks of the importance of capturing Shreveport and of the necessity of returning A. J. Smith's corps to Memphis by April 15—even if doing so meant abandoning the campaign. Grant scotched any hope Banks may have nurtured of retaining Smith's corps for a lengthier campaign by reaffirming the fixed deadline. Banks's reputation could scarcely absorb another military disaster, so he turned to Porter.[29]

On March 29, after three days of labor, Phelps finally succeeded in getting the ironclad *Eastport* over the falls. *Woodford,* the hospital ship of the Marine Brigade, struck the lower falls and sank. With *Eastport* above, Porter sent up twelve more vessels, but he kept those drawing more than six feet below. While tars sweated and grunted to get the vessels over the falls, Banks lost time organizing an election in Alexandria to choose delegates to a forthcoming convention of the newly fledged state administration. On April 1, with flags flying and guns booming, three hundred Unionist voters tramped to the polls to exercise their right of franchise. Porter waited impatiently above the falls. On April 2 he transferred his flag to the tinclad *Cricket* and ordered the flotilla to Grand Encore, followed by A. J. Smith's thirty transports.[30]

Banks left a garrison of thirty-six hundred troops at Alexandria—troops he would later need—and in the evening followed Porter's squadron upriver. He planned to join his army in the morning, writing Halleck that he would be in Shreveport by the 10th of April and would "pursue the enemy into the interior of Texas." Banks added that he feared Taylor would not fight him. Lincoln read the message reflectively and said, "I am sorry to see this tone of confidence; the next news we shall hear from there will be of a defeat."[31]

At noon on April 3 Porter landed at Grand Encore and made a quick inspection of the squadron. *Eastport* had grounded, *Chillicothe* reported late, and the four turtles—*Carondelet, Louisville, Pittsburg,* and *Mound City*—lay off the bank. Three new river monitors—*Osage, Ozark,* and *Neosho*—had gone above with the gunboats *Fort Hindman, Juliet, Cricket,* and *Lexington.* Two of A. J. Smith's transports lay aground, and Porter sent tugs to pull them off. The river rose slightly, and the tars spent the next three days collecting cotton while waiting for word from Banks.[32]

On April 1 Franklin's corps camped in an area between Natchitoches and Grand Encore and waited for marching orders. Banks arrived on the 4th, and because he had poor maps he sent his chief of staff, Brig. Gen. Charles P. Stone, to speak with one of Porter's pilots, an Ohioan who had settled in Louisiana and claimed to know the area. The pilot outlined an inland road to Pleasant Hill and Mansfield, one that would keep Banks separated from Porter. The admiral never understood why Banks chose that route, because another road followed the river all the way to Shreveport with "good wide fields on all sides" and plenty of provisions. Reflecting on Banks's retreat a few days later, Porter wrote, "Why General Banks went through a desert where he could not even find water . . . instead of a prolific country, I can not say."[33] The answer, however, lay with Banks, who refused to make a reconnaissance, arguing that it would require time he could not spare, and in ignorance took the inland route.

By an agreement with Banks, Porter started *Chillicothe, Fort Hindman, Lexington, Osage, Neosho,* and *Cricket* for Loggy Bayou, a point on the Red 110 miles farther upriver and 40 miles below Shreveport. Twenty transports followed with a division of Smith's corps. Because they frequently grounded, Porter shuttled back and forth on *Cricket* to keep the vessels moving. The river wound erratically around sharp bends where partisans emptied their muskets on the passing convoy. Lt. Joseph P. Couthouy, commanding *Chillicothe,* came on deck to direct his guns on a bothersome squad of enemy cavalry. A ball tore through his chest, and he died in the morning.[34]

Farther up, deep-draft vessels struggled over shoals, but most of them arrived at Loggy Bayou the morning of the 10th, an hour ahead of the army's scheduled march to Shreveport. Banks, however, was not there. Porter discovered a huge steamer, *New Falls City,* stretched end to end across the river. A detail had begun to dismantle the vessel when a courier on a sweat-lathered horse rode into Loggy Bayou and informed Porter that Banks had been repulsed at Mansfield and was falling back to Pleasant Hill. Moments later orders came for A. J. Smith's division, under Brig. Gen. Thomas Kilby Smith, to reboard the transports and return to Grand Encore.[35]

The order amazed Porter. "We had disembarked the troops," he declared, "none dreaming of anything but victory to one of the best appointed armies I ever saw in the field, and after getting in our pickets and getting the troops on board, I reversed the order of steaming and with a heavy heart started downward, anticipating that the rebels, flushed with victory, with our army in full retreat before them, would come in on our flank and cut us to pieces."[36]

As the admiral joined the retrograde movement, details of the army's retreat filtered into his cabin. Banks's line of march from Grand Encore had manifested all the symptoms of a long, straggling column, and every noncommissioned officer now had a servant and every servant a mule. The countryside was barren of provender and forested with pine. General Taylor, determined to keep Banks separated from Porter, held a strong position at Sabine Crossroads, about two miles southeast of Mansfield. On April 8 Taylor surprised Banks and attacked in force. The bluecoats recoiled in confusion, and the battle was saved from becoming a rout by a gallant stand made by Brig. Gen. William H. Emory's division of the XXIX Corps.[37]

On the 9th Banks withdrew to Pleasant Hill, where his force was again assaulted by Taylor. As the rebels advanced, A. J. Smith's corps struck Taylor's flank and shattered the attack. With the grayclads brushed from the field, Banks rode up to A. J. Smith, shook his hand, and declared, "God bless you, general; you have saved the day." Smith wanted to finish the work and go on to Shreveport, but Banks nervously ordered the army back to Grand Encore and dispatched a courier to Porter advising him to fall back.[38]

On the morning of the 10th Taylor sent Banks a flag of truce, asking permission to bury his dead. "They were, doubtless, much astonished to find no one there to receive it," Porter noted. "This is one of those instances when two armies ran away from each other."[39]

The Red River campaign was over for Banks, but not for Porter. With the river falling, the admiral had a new enemy, and it waited for his flotilla at the falls of Alexandria. As Porter soon discovered, Banks's hasty retreat may have saved his squadron.

TWENTY

Escaping
Disaster

On the afternoon of April 10, Porter prepared for the treacherous return to Grand Encore. Turning the squadron around in the narrow channel took the entire day. *Chillicothe* struck a snag and had to be pulled off by a transport. With the banks of the river higher than the pilothouses, partisans sniped at the vessels, and sailors worked all night emplacing howitzers on the hurricane decks. The flotilla did not get under way until the morning of the 11th, and then it barely moved because the transports had to back until they found enough room to turn around. Inch by inch, the water that floated the flotilla as far as Loggy Bayou began to seep out of the river—and the trouble was only beginning.[1]

At no time during the Civil War did Porter face more obstacles than those that lay ahead, and no battle ever taxed his tenacity and energy more than extricating the fleet from the falling river. Banks deserted him and forgot him. Porter had no reports of the enemy's strength, and he could not get tinclads below to scout the river because army transports jammed the descent and constantly went aground. He did not know that most of Taylor's army had been withdrawn to Arkansas to meet the approach of General Steele. His one salvation was the presence of Kilby Smith's division. "The rebels were soon aware of our turning back," Porter noted, "and were after us like a pack of wolves." Smith lined the transports with captured cotton, brought soldiers top-side, and sprayed the woods with musket fire. Porter noted that enemy cavalry galloped along the river roads and fired from both banks, but, he said, we always "foiled them."[2]

Banks reached Grand Encore on the 11th, the same day Porter started down from Loggy Bayou. He had no interest in the admiral's problems. Porter wrote Sherman confidentially, "Had Banks been victorious, as any ordinary general . . . we would have had no trouble at all, but he has led all hands into an ugly scrape. I did all I could to avoid going up this river with him, but he would have thrown all the blame of failure on me had I failed to go. I have risked a great deal and only hope for a rise of water."[3]

The flotilla snaked down the Red, crawling at the speed of a giant caterpillar, and accidents began to occur. Late on the 11th Confederate cavalry opened on the gunboats. The tars replied with shrapnel, comparing the gunplay to hunting partridges with 11-inch Dahlgrens. Just before sunset the transport *Emerald* ran aground, stopping the squadron. On the 12th *Lexington* collided with the transport *Rob Roy,* staving in her wheelhouse and forcing her to lay to for repairs. At dark *Chillicothe* ran aground and could not get off, and her crew could hear heavy gunfire from somewhere downriver.[4]

Knowing that Porter would follow Banks's retreat, Taylor sent two brigades of cavalry across Bayou Pierre to capture the flotilla. Late afternoon on the 12th, Brig. Gen. Thomas Green's infantry reached the south bank of the Red just below Blair's Landing and opened on the Union transports with a four-gun field battery. Green could not have timed his attack better. The transport *Hastings* was tied to the landing for repairs. *Alice Vivian,* carrying four hundred cavalry horses, had grounded midstream, blocking the channel, and *Emerald* and *Clara Bell,* with hawsers attached to her, were occupied in pulling her free. Below lay the grounded monitor *Osage,* assisted by the transport *Black Hawk.* Porter's flotilla was in a bad situation, but the admiral was still upriver in *Cricket* and looking for Banks.[5]

Lexington dropped down from above and opened on Green's battery. *Rob Roy, Emerald,* and *Black Hawk* fired guns mounted on their hurricane decks and sprayed the woods with grape and shrapnel. Infantry huddled behind bales of hay fired into the cottonwoods. *Hastings* cut loose from the landing and eased back into the channel. *Neosho* and *Fort Hindman* worked down the river, pouring canister into the enemy's positions along a two-mile stretch of river. *Osage* floated free, came to the rescue of *Alice Vivian,* and opened on Green's guns. Canister struck the rebel general and killed him instantly. After that, the fight went out of the Confederates. Selfridge, commanding *Osage,* called the two-hour battle "the heaviest and most concentrated fire of musketry I have ever witnessed."[6]

The firing stopped almost as quickly as it started. *Fort Hindman* returned upriver and at 2:00 A.M. pulled *Chillicothe* off the shoal. The other boats headed down and tied up until daylight. In the morning the transport *John Warner* went aground and caused another delay, giving Brig. Gen. St. John R. Liddell's Confederate artillery time to post themselves on the north bank and open on the stalled flotilla. Selfridge steamed up in *Osage* and with his pair of 11-inch Dahlgrens drove Liddell away. *Rob Roy* broke its rudder trying to float *John Warner* and had to be taken in tow by *Clara Bell.* T. Kilby Smith had seen enough and sent every transport downriver that could make the trip on its own, leaving *John Warner* above, protected by *Fort Hindman.*[7]

Hearing firing on the afternoon of the 12th, Porter came down the river to investigate. By the time he reached Blair's Landing, the fight had ended. In the morning he wound through the vessels aground at Campti and went down to Grand Encore to ask for infantry support. Banks was more interested in the safety of his army than in Porter's problems. Ignoring Banks, A. J. Smith organized a relief brigade to protect the fleet from further attacks. Porter was not satisfied, and Banks finally detached a second brigade. Smith met the boats coming down with *John Warner,* and by the 15th the entire flotilla lay off Grand Encore.[8]

Banks dallied at Grand Encore, his army of twenty-five thousand hemmed in by less than five thousand Confederates. In an effort to retain the command of A. J. Smith, whose time to rejoin Sherman had come, he informed Grant that he intended to renew the march to Shreveport. On April 17 Banks changed his mind, and while he deliberated Porter held his squadron in readiness and nervously watched the river drop. Fearing for the safety of his ironclads, he started them downriver. *Eastport* struck a torpedo and sank in the channel. Porter went to Alexandria to order up pump boats and was shocked by the low level of water at the falls. From there he sent a message to Sherman, asking for authority to keep A. J. Smith's corps because "my whole fleet depends on his staying here. His is the only part of the army not demoralized. You know my opinion of political generals. It is a crying sin to put the lives of thousands in the hands of such men, and the time has come when there should be a stop put to it." Porter suspected Banks would go off on some new venture and strand the navy above the falls. Grant then agreed to leave Smith's corps with Banks until the end of April—but only if Shreveport could be taken.[9]

While waiting for Banks to decide what to do, Porter crafted a searching letter to Welles, knowing it would be read by Lincoln: "I don't see why a fleet should not have the protection of the army as well as an army have the protection of a fleet. If we are left here aground, our communications will be cut off and we will have to destroy the vessels. I do not intend to destroy a rowboat if it can be helped, and if the proper course is pursued, we will lose nothing. . . . I wish the Department would give me its views without delay. . . . I must confess I feel a little uncertain how to act."[10]

Banks had no intention of marching to Shreveport, and on the 22nd he started back to Alexandria, using as his reason Porter's "unequivocally expressed" opinion that no advance should be made until the river rose.[11]

For three days Porter labored at raising *Eastport*, and on the 21st he got her afloat. Phelps could not find the leak and built a bulkhead to contain the water. Taken in tow by pump boat *Champion No. 3*, Porter followed, towing *Eastport's* guns on a flatboat. On the 22nd the ironclad lodged on a bed of sunken logs, and Phelps worked the crew through the night to get her off. She grounded again on the 23rd, and after two more days of winching and wrenching *Eastport* down three miles of the Red, she finally stuck fast. Pilots took soundings below and found insufficient water to float her to Alexandria. Phelps worked on her another day, but enemy snipers appeared in droves. Porter soon learned the reason why. Banks had deserted Grand Encore and left both sides of the river in the undisputed control of the enemy. Cavalry began to appear in force, and on the morning of the 26th *Cricket's* crew had to fight off a boarding party. *Fort Hindman* made a final, furtive attempt to float *Eastport* but only succeeded in lodging her tighter. With enemy musket fire harassing the tars from both banks, Porter ordered *Eastport* scuttled, and at 2:10 P.M. on the 26th Phelps blew her up.[12]

With three tinclads and two pump boats, Porter left the remains of *Eastport* behind and headed downriver. As he approached the mouth of the Cane River, a battery of six guns opened on *Cricket*. Porter replied with the vessel's 24-pounders. Moments later, bullets fired by two hundred horsemen rattled against the tinclad, driving the blue-jackets to cover.

Cricket's skipper, Lt. Henry H. Gorringe, stopped in midstream to fight his guns and cover the boats astern. "I corrected this mistake," Porter declared, "and got headway on the vessel again, but not soon enough to avoid the pelting shower of shot and shell which the enemy poured into us—every shot going through and through us, clearing all our decks in a moment." As he stepped on deck to direct the fire of the gunners, an enemy shell struck the after gun, killing or wounding every man. Another shell swept away the forward gun crew, crashed into the fireroom, exploded, and wounded all the firemen but one. Porter replaced the gun crews with blacks and turned the engine room over to the assistant engineer. Returning to the pilothouse, he found the pilot wounded and took the helm himself. Flames erupted on *Cricket*. Porter worked the vessel around the lower bend, and while one detail hosed down the fire the gun crew shelled the enemy from the rear with the only two guns still operable.[13]

Champion No. 3 followed *Cricket* and carried about 175 blacks from upriver plantations. An enemy shell shattered her boiler, and scalding steam killed more than a hundred of the refugees. Hulled and sinking, the transport grounded near the enemy's battery.

Next in line came the tinclad *Juliet*, lashed to *Champion No. 5*. A shell cut *Juliet's* tiller ropes and steam pipe, filling her with steam. After the vapor cleared, *Juliet's* captain discovered that both vessels had come about and were faced upstream, and that the crew of the pump boat was trying to cut it loose from the tinclad. Under heavy fire, William Maitland, *Juliet's* pilot, jumped aboard *Champion No. 5* and made his way to the pilothouse. He took the wheel and had a line passed to *Juliet*. Covered by *Fort Hindman*, *Juliet* towed the pump boat back upstream, leaving *Cricket* below the battery while taking the others above it.

Porter headed downriver for help, but *Cricket* grounded below Cane River and the admiral spent four frantic hours getting her afloat. At nightfall he heard artillery fire below and found *Osage* engaged with another enemy battery. *Lexington* had passed those same guns earlier in the day and had retired to patch eighteen shots that went "into and through" her. Porter decided against sending *Osage* to the assistance of the others and ordered her to Alexandria.[14]

With Porter below, Phelps took command of *Juliet*, *Fort Hindman*, and *Champion No. 5*. He worked the crew feverishly through the night making repairs, and by daylight *Juliet* and *Champion* were patched and ready to make the run. Phelps chose not to wait until dark, and at 9:00 A.M. on the 27th he started downriver—*Fort Hindman* in the lead towing *Juliet*, *Champion No. 5* following. A half mile above the rebel battery, *Juliet* hit a snag and punctured her hull. Phelps towed her back upriver, made repairs, and started down, shelling the woods as he passed. At five hundred yards the enemy opened with heavy fire. A shell passed through *Fort Hindman*'s pilothouse and carried away her tiller ropes. Shots tore through *Juliet*'s upper works and disabled her machinery. Both vessels lost power. Bouncing from bank to bank, they barely missed the sunken wreck of *Champion No. 3*, and by good fortune they drifted through the barrage to safety below. The enemy concentrated their fire on *Champion No. 5*, knocked apart her steerage, and forced her onto the opposite bank. The crew escaped in the woods, but for Porter the action was costly. He lost two pump boats and *Eastport*, the finest ironclad in the fleet. *Cricket* carried the scars of thirty-eight shots, losing twenty-five in killed and wounded—half her crew. *Juliet* and *Fort Hindman* were picked up by *Neosho* later in the day and taken down to the falls. Both vessels were disabled. Together they added eighteen more men to the casualty list.[15]

In retrospect, Porter admitted he should have blown up *Eastport* and not risked five boats in an effort to save her, but that was before he discovered "we were a secondary consideration to the army." The admiral lamented the loss, but it paled in comparison to the problems awaiting his return to Alexandria.[16]

Porter arrived at the upper falls late on the 27th and found *Carondelet* and *Mound City* aground and the other vessels scraping bottom. He needed seven feet of water to get the squadron over the rapids, but in places only three feet, four inches covered the jagged rock piles. There was barely a channel, and the situation was complicated by a second set of rapids flowing more than a mile below the first and ending at the falls above the town. During Porter's absence, no effort had been made to get the fleet below. The situation baffled Porter. He could not lighten the boats enough to float them over the falls, and blasting a channel down the mile-long rapids—a suggestion made by Acting Ensign Thomas A. Quin—would take all summer. With *Mound City, Louisville, Pittsburg, Carondelet, Neosho, Chillicothe, Osage, Ozark, Lexington,* and *Fort Hindman*—among the best vessels of the Mississippi Squadron—stranded above the falls, Porter warned Welles, "Unless instructed by the Government, I do not think General Banks will make the least effort to save the navy."[17]

At first Banks displayed absolute indifference to the navy's difficulties. He offered no infantry support to drive off guerrilla attacks and forced Porter to deploy skirmishers to protect his vessels. On the 29th he asked the admiral for an armed convoy to take the army downriver, thereby drawing off the few gunboats below the falls. Porter had visions of the army abandoning Alexandria and forcing him to destroy the squadron—a catastrophe certain to end his professional career and shatter the prestige of the Navy Department.[18]

Since April 27 Banks had been preoccupied by the unexpected arrival of Maj. Gen. David Hunter, who carried orders from Grant urging an attack on Mobile and asking how soon it could be done. With the sad state of affairs on the Red River, Banks envisioned sparks flying at the War Department as Stanton sharpened his official axe.[19]

While Banks fretted, the precarious condition of the fleet came to the attention of General Franklin, who knew an officer in the 4th Wisconsin who had a proposition. Lt. Col. Joseph Bailey came from the logging country and was perhaps the only engineer in the army who had enough talent and practical experience to elevate the level of the river with a temporary dam. Franklin sent him to Porter with a letter of introduction. The admiral listened to the plan and grumbled laconically that, "if damning would get the fleet off, he would have been afloat long before."[20]

Bailey had studied civil engineering and gained years of experience floating log booms down shallow rivers. Using simple logging technology, he suggested erecting a dam at the lower falls, leaving a narrow

opening in the middle, and floating the vessels through the spillway.
Porter was getting desperate and welcomed the plan, and on April 29
Bailey took the scheme to Hunter and Banks. Hunter thought the plan
should be tried because Franklin, who was a competent engineer, endorsed it. With Hunter peering over his shoulder, Banks agreed to the
proposal and on the evening of the 29th issued the necessary orders.[21]

On the morning of April 30, pioneers from Wisconsin, Iowa, and
Illinois, two regiments of black troops, and lumbermen from Maine
assembled above the falls with a train of wagons and draft animals. At
the site of the proposed dam the river was 758 feet wide, with the
depth varying between four and six feet. The current in the threadlike
channel ran at ten miles an hour, but both sides of the rocky riverbed
were now bare. Because there were two falls a mile and a quarter apart,
Bailey needed to raise the level of the water about seven feet at the
upper falls. Between the upper and the lower falls the river fell thirteen
feet, and at the lower falls the river dropped another six feet before
deepening off Alexandria. Bailey hoped to raise the water enough to
float the gunboats over the upper falls, down the rapids, and through
the chute at the lower falls.[22]

During the first days of May, Bailey's dam became the center of
interest at Alexandria. At first men scoffed at the project, calling it a
hopeless waste of time, and the dam became the butt of many jokes. So
great did the skepticism become that Bailey had trouble recruiting volunteers. As the work progressed, however, three thousand men bent
their backs in an effort to liberate the squadron from the upper falls.
"Every man in the fleet was engaged in the . . . construction of the
dam," Porter declared, "conveying stone in boats to weight the big cob-
frames forming the dam, moving the frames into position—a tedious
and dangerous duty—and floating down the logs which were cut and
hauled by the soldiers to the river banks."[23]

Bailey started work at the lower falls, building a wing dam from the
north bank, where plenty of large trees grew. Crews layered the logs, the
tops toward the current and tied by cross-logs, with everything weighted
down by stone and brick. From the cultivated south bank, where trees
were scarce, Bailey built a crib of logs and filled it with stone and with
machinery taken from sugarhouses and cotton gins. The old military
academy where Sherman once taught was demolished to provide lumber for the cribs, and when more was needed, other buildings came

down. Details opened quarries near the river, and a steady parade of flatboats hauled tons of stone to the cribs. Suspense mounted daily as the two ends approached each other, each about 300 feet long and with a gap of 150 feet between. Four coal barges, loaded with brick from the town, were towed to the gap and sunk.[24]

One night before the gap was closed, word spread that a rise had been detected. An officer from the 15th Maine sat on his horse long after dark watching men—mostly colored troops standing neck-deep in water—work on the dam by the light of bonfires. A solitary figure rode up on a horse and asked, "Do you notice the slightest indication of a rise?" The officer turned and recognized the rider as Banks. Porter admitted that Banks, for whom he had little respect, gave the dam his "whole attention night and day, scarcely sleeping while the work was going on . . . to see that all the requirements of Colonel Bailey were complied with on the instant. I do not believe there was ever a case where such difficulties were overcome in such a short space of time."[25]

With three thousand men and more than two hundred wagons at work on the project, Confederate scouts watched Bailey's progress with growing frustration. Gen. E. Kirby Smith had pulled most of Taylor's force into Arkansas to fight Steele, leaving a weak detachment of about six hundred men under General Liddell to harass the dam builders. Liddell, having no artillery, could do little more than watch the work and send messages back to headquarters requesting reinforcements—which never came.[26]

As the dam neared completion, the tars lightened the gunboats, barging stores, guns, cables, and anchors ashore and carting them to Alexandria. Porter destroyed eleven old 32-pounders and put crews to work stripping plates from the sides of the turtles and sinking them in pools of quicksand. Men coated the bows with tar to conceal the bare casemates. Later, Porter discovered that the turtles ran two and a half knots faster without the iron, and he never replaced it.[27]

By May 8 the crib extending from the south bank reached the nearest barge, and the only gaps remaining were three twenty-foot openings between the four sunken barges at the dam, through which the banked-up water flowed. Porter watched the rise at the upper rapids and sent *Neosho, Osage,* and *Fort Hindman* over the falls and into the pool above the lower dam. Bailey said he would break the dam on the 9th, and

USS *Lexington* passing over the falls at the lower dam of the Red River
REPRINTED FROM JOHNSON AND BUEL, *BATTLES AND LEADERS OF THE CIVIL WAR*

Porter lined up the rest of the squadron, six gunboats and two tugs, at the upper falls to run the chute in the morning.

Below, the water at the dam rose through the evening, exerting enormous pressure on the barges. At midnight Banks rode down to the river to inspect the dam. Worried that it would give way, he galloped upriver and urged Porter to be ready to move at dawn. At 5:00 A.M., before anything could be done, the river shoved two barges aside, and water spilled through the breach. Porter was riding to the dam when it broke. He swung about and galloped back to the upper falls, shouting for Bache to get *Lexington* under way and—if he got through the rapids—to go straight on through the chute. Bache ordered steam, and, with the water falling rapidly, *Lexington* scraped over the upper falls and sprinted down the channel. "She entered the gap with a full head of steam," Porter wrote, "pitched down the roaring current, made two or three spasmodic rolls, hung for a moment on the rocks below, and then was swept into deep water by the current and rounded to, safely into the bank." Without waiting for an invitation, *Neosho, Fort Hindman,* and *Osage* followed. In shooting the rapids, *Neosho*'s pilot panicked as the vessel entered the chute, and he shut down the engines. She dove nose first under the water, and everyone watching thought she was lost. Rising slowly, she righted herself. Swept along over the rocks by the current, she twirled into deep water with no more than a small puncture in her hull. The spectacle was witnessed by thousands, who cheered as the vessels coasted toward the wharf.[28]

Porter's inability to get the other half of his fleet below the falls came as a blow to Banks, who had cut marching orders to withdraw the army from Alexandria on the 9th. Bailey, however, did not wait while Banks deliberated. After studying the problem at the lower falls, he found that the barges had left a sixty-foot opening that would make a perfect exit for the passage of the rest of the fleet. He started building two wing dams at the upper falls: a stone crib on the south bank and a tree dam on the opposite bank. He expected the upper dam, when finished, to add fourteen inches to the rise and bring the flow between the two dams to six feet, six and one-half inches.[29]

Banks rescinded his marching orders and sent a staff officer upriver to impress upon the admiral the importance of getting the fleet over the falls. Porter did not need to be impressed upon and replied, "Don't suppose because the vessels seem quiet that nothing is being done; everything is being done that can be. I hope you will look this matter patiently in the face." Porter assured Banks that Bailey's new dams were almost complete and with "8 inches more" the boats would get down. The Northern press had been critical of Banks's generalship, and Porter attempted to assuage the nervous commander by adding, "Now, general, I see nothing that should make us despond. You have a fine army, and I shall have a strong fleet of gunboats to drive away an inferior force in your front. . . . I hope, sir, you will not let anything divert you from the attempt to get these vessels all through safely, even if we have to stay here and eat mule meat." In the meantime, Banks learned that A. J. Smith had promised to stay with the fleet even if the rest of the army withdrew. Sensing a troublesome political imbroglio, Banks agreed to not depart until the vessels were safe.

In writing Porter, Banks can be accused of listening to the grumbles of his dam builders, who complained that the navy had not been doing its share. To the contrary, the tars had been working around the clock prying the vessels over the upper falls. *Carondelet* became wedged in an S-shaped section of the channel. *Mound City* grounded beside her, and while Bailey built wing dams the tars arduously winched the gunboats over the rocks a foot at a time and lined them up for the final plunge down the rapids.[30]

On the 10th the predicted rise fell inches short. Bailey conferred with Lt. Col. Uri B. Pearsall, who suggested adding a bracket dam below the wing dam on the north bank. Pioneers from the XIII Army Corps started work that night, setting trestles for the dam near the stern of the two ironclads. At 11:00 A.M. on the 11th, another foot of water swirled around *Carondelet* and *Mound City,* lifted them off the rocks, and pushed them into the channel. By midnight, all the boats were in position to make a pass at the lower dam.[31]

On the 12th, aided by a slight natural rise of the river, *Mound City, Carondelet,* and *Pittsburg* battened down their hatches to run the rapids. Soldiers turned out in force to cheer the passage. To the blare of bands playing along the levee, all three vessels shot through the chute and settled into the quiet water below. *Louisville, Chillicothe, Ozark,* and the squadron's two tugs followed on the morning of the 13th. In the wild ride through the chute, one man fell off the deck of a tug and drowned. As soon as the vessels eased to a stop, Banks issued marching orders. By 3:00 P.M. Porter had his squadron coaled and ready to move. "All steamed down the river," Porter wrote Welles, "with the convoy of transports in company." In a letter to his mother on the 16th he wrote, "I am clear of my troubles, and my fleet is safe out in the broad Mississippi. I have had a hard and anxious time of it."[32]

For several days the admiral felt poorly. The constant toil to refloat his squadron, coupled with sleepless nights and swollen legs, had sapped his energy. Back in his airy cabin on *Black Hawk,* Porter finally relaxed. On the 16th he felt better, and with the ordeal at the falls now history, he found a few words of praise for Banks, who had also endured sleepless nights attending to the needs of the dam builders. But Porter could not say enough in praise of Bailey:

> This is without a doubt the best engineering feat ever performed. Under the best circumstances a private company would not have completed the work under one year, and to the ordinary mind the whole thing would have appeared as an utter impossibility. . . . [Bailey] has saved the Union a valuable fleet worth $2,000,000; more, he has deprived the enemy of a triumph which would have emboldened them to carry on this war a year or two longer, for the intended departure of the army was a fixed fact, and there was nothing to do in case that event occurred but destroy every . . . vessel. The highest honors the Government can bestow on Colonel Bailey can never repay him for the service he has rendered the country.[33]

In the aftermath of the Red River fiasco, a bitter crop of quarrels emerged from the bungled campaign. Franklin quit the department in disgust, A. J. Smith departed more in anger than in sorrow, and Porter and Banks exchanged recriminations in language testing the limits of "parliamentary privilege." Porter, however, had reason to be angry. When Banks repulsed Taylor at Pleasant Hill on April 9, a general with good military training would have pressed his advantage and advanced on Shreveport. Instead, Banks withdrew, thereby deserting Porter and exposing the squadron to capture or destruction. When Porter reached Grand Encore, Banks again abandoned the fleet, and this resulted in the fight at Cane River, the loss of two transports, and more than two hundred casualties.[34]

Bailey refuted accusations made by Banks regarding a lack of energy on behalf of the navy when he wrote, "Admiral Porter furnished a detail from his ship's crews under command of an excellent officer, Captain Langthorne of the *Mound City.* All his officers and men were constantly present, and to their extraordinary exertions and to the well-known energy and ability of the admiral, much of the success of the undertaking is due."[35]

In wartime, matters like this tend to work themselves out. On June 7 Bailey was breveted brigadier general. Four days later he received the thanks of Congress. Nobody could have been happier than Porter. Banks, however, fared poorly. Although some of the admiral's remarks about Banks were unwarranted, his opinion of the commander's generalship was justified. James R. Soley, Porter's early biographer, wrote, "As a result of the campaign, Banks was virtually deprived of his command, while the whole country learned to recognize in Porter a leader as great in defeat as in victory."[36]

In December hearings began on the Red River fiasco, and Porter was called to testify. By then, rumors pegged the entire campaign as a ruse concocted by politicians to raise enough money by trading in cotton to enable Banks to beat Lincoln in the forthcoming Republican convention. When Porter was questioned on the matter, he admitted the affair had the makings of a big cotton raid. As to his own acquisitions, the admiral simply stated that wherever his men found cotton, they seized it as a prize of war. In his opinion, "Cotton killed that expedition."[37]

Welles never blamed his admiral for contributing to the disaster on the Red River, and Porter's testimony finished Banks's military career. The general resigned from the army and returned to Massachusetts to resume his political life.

While resting on *Black Hawk* in late May, Porter wrote Fox. Referring to the Red River debacle, he said, "If the Court knows herself, it is the last one of the kind I will get mixed up in. I shall be sure of my man before I cooperate with any soldier." The words were wasted. Porter had not seen the last of political generals. Ben Butler was still muddling about in the battlefields of Virginia—and the war would soon unite them again.[38]

TWENTY-ONE

A Huge Puff of Smoke

For the first time in more than two months, Porter found time to catch up on the war in the East. Without A. J. Smith's corps, Sherman had advanced into Georgia, driving General Johnston's grayclads back upon Atlanta. Grant had moved his headquarters to the Army of the Potomac and, having the advantage of numbers, was bullying his way through the wilderness of Virginia and to the outskirts of Richmond and Petersburg. With the Mississippi River in the possession of Porter's gunboats, the lifeline of the Confederacy had been trimmed to three ports—Mobile, Charleston, and Wilmington.

Acting on orders from Welles, Farragut had consolidated the Gulf Squadron for the long-postponed attack on Mobile Bay, and Maj. Gen. Edward R. S. Canby, who superseded Banks, was marshaling his command to cooperate with the admiral in assaulting the bay's two bastions, Forts Morgan and Gaines.

By June 1864 Charleston Harbor had become invested to the extent that blockade runners shied away from the port. Operating mainly out of Nassau or Bermuda, they preferred using two inlets to the Cape Fear River, where ten forts situated near the river's mouth provided protection for their entry and exit. The port city also provided the only haven on the southern coast for Confederate cruisers, which on occasion stole to sea and raided Union commerce.

The inlets of the Cape Fear River were the most difficult to blockade on the Southern seacoast. At New Inlet loomed Fort Fisher, the most massive and heavily fortified earthwork in North America, and at Old Inlet stood Fort Caswell, flanked by three smaller forts. Between the inlets lay Smith's Island and Frying Pan Shoals, the latter a natural hazard jutting far offshore. Forty miles separated the inlets, and because of shoals and the forts on the beaches the North Atlantic Blockading Squadron could not approach the inlets without risk of grounding. Channels into the river were narrow and unpredictable. Bars constantly shifted, making it dangerous for ironclads to enter the river. To reach Wilmington one had to pass Fort Fisher, and this required a cooperating land force. And now, with the flow of supplies from the trans-Mississippi stifled by Porter's gunboats, Lee's Army of Northern Virginia became increasingly dependent on Wilmington for imported ammunition and provisions.

Halleck, who now served as Grant's chief of staff, had lost much of his power but little of his influence. He considered an attack on Wilmington an injudicious waste of infantry and convinced Grant to reject any application from the navy for troops. When Grant came east as commander in chief, Halleck persuaded him to take personal command of the Army of the Potomac and then advised him to keep his army concentrated and move frontally en masse upon Richmond. Months passed before Grant would listen to a proposal for a joint operation to capture Wilmington, and during those months, two divisions of the huge North Atlantic Blockading Squadron under Rear Adm. Samuel P. Lee rocked off the Cape Fear River, and blockade runners continued to slip through the cordon to deliver tons of supplies to the Confederate army.[1]

When Fox wrote Porter on May 25 suggesting he come East for a visit, the capture of Wilmington had not risen to the top of the Navy Department's priorities. Admiral Du Pont had been repulsed in April 1863 when he attempted to capture Charleston, and the navy was not prepared to risk another disaster, especially after Porter's recent escape from the Red River. For his failure, Du Pont lost his command, and the

Union army and navy turned to other—though equally unsuccessful—means to capture the city.[2]

After hearing from Fox, Porter received another note, this one from Welles: "When you feel that you have made such arrangement of your squadron as will admit of your absence . . . for a short period, I will be pleased to have you proceed to Washington and report in person."[3]

Porter had not been home for eighteen months, but he read the invitation with mixed emotions. With more than three thousand miles of river to patrol, he had just reorganized his command into ten new naval districts and issued orders for the fleet to interdict all smugglers—including Treasury agents found exchanging military supplies for cotton. He sent Welles a comprehensive report on the commercial imbroglio in the West and backed it up with sheaves of conflicting regulations issued by the Treasury, War, and Navy Departments.[4]

Porter had grown fond of the Mississippi Squadron, the most diversified in the navy and so isolated that most of the secretary's duties devolved upon himself. Because his Civil War career had started rashly, Porter never completely trusted any demonstration of solicitude from Welles. He had made mistakes during the Red River campaign and worried that his own cotton raids had upset the Navy Department. From Cairo, however, the admiral could not read Welles's mind, and no warning of recriminations had come from Fox.

For more than a month Porter found excuses to remain in the West, unaware that the secretary's personal feelings toward him had mellowed since the fall of Vicksburg. Welles admired Porter's miraculous escape from the Red River, and, despite heated disputes with the Treasury over trade on the Western rivers, Welles supported Porter's views. He believed war on the Mississippi was over, and he urged Fox to inquire whether the admiral would consider a command in the East.[5]

One matter kept Porter occupied in the river. Farragut had requested two new double-turreted river monitors, *Winnebago* and *Chickasaw*, to bolster his squadron off Mobile Bay. Porter worried that the vessels would founder in Gulf storms, but Welles ordered them down. After seeing them off on June 30, Porter spent the next two days scribbling orders to his command, covering such mundane matters as the procedure to follow in celebrating Independence Day.[6]

The admiral reached Washington on the 6th and went directly to the Navy Department. Welles received him cordially, and after a lengthy discussion of affairs on western waters, he granted the admiral a leave of absence so he could join his family at Perth Amboy. At the close of the interview, Porter thanked the secretary for his expression of confidence and departed with a high regard for the man now known affectionately in naval circles as "Father Neptune."[7]

At Perth Amboy the admiral divided his time between his family and the telegraph office, and after a month of romping with his children and luxuriating in the affections of his family, Porter realized how much he enjoyed being home. On August 15 he sought an extension to his leave. Welles replied, "Extend thirty days, unless sooner required."[8]

While Porter enjoyed the midsummer sun at Perth Amboy, Farragut captured Mobile Bay and Sherman entered Atlanta. In Washington Welles held one of his frequent meetings with Fox. "Something must be done," he declared, "to close the entrance to Cape Fear River and port of Wilmington." Fox agreed, but nobody in the War Department, including Grant, showed any interest. Lincoln, now certain of reelection, agreed to the plan but deferred to Grant. Welles poked around the War Department and found Maj. Gen. Quincy A. Gillmore, who was recovering from a fall from his horse and waiting for orders. Stanton sent for Gillmore to learn his views. If Gillmore could be made available and given a few thousand men, Welles would have to name a naval commander.

The secretary had several options. His first choice was Farragut, but the admiral felt poorly and demurred. Being in no hurry, Welles decided to wait for Farragut's answer. Command of the South Atlantic Blockading Squadron, however, had weakened Admiral Dahlgren's constitution, and he asked to be relieved. Fox suggested switching Dahlgren and Porter. When Welles said the change would gratify neither admiral, Fox suggested giving Porter a flying squadron for the defense of the coast. Welles sent for Porter and suggested it. The admiral said he preferred to stay with his present command but would go wherever Welles wished.[9]

Porter returned to Cairo, but the situation on the Atlantic Coast continued to develop. On September 6 Gillmore submitted two plans to Halleck and Grant for a joint operation against Wilmington. The first plan required five thousand infantry to occupy Smith's Island, thereby enabling Union vessels to enter the Cape Fear River and blockade the port from inside New Inlet. The second plan called for ten thousand troops supported by a large fleet, whose combined role would be to reduce Fort Fisher by bombardment and capture it by siege. In January, when he was still general in chief, Halleck had turned down a proposal to attack the port. He felt no differently now and, because the plan originated in the Navy Department, advised Grant to reject it.[10]

The navy preferred the second plan, but Fox made the mistake of allowing Gillmore to present the scheme to Butler, in whose geographical department the expedition would take place. In the opening phase of the Richmond campaign, Gillmore's corps, largely through the general's incompetence, had lost an opportunity to capture Petersburg while its defenses were weak, and Butler had demanded his dismissal. Gillmore's involvement in the proposal gave Grant a valid reason to hesitate, and he remained noncommittal.[11]

Welles, however, proceeded on the assumption that Grant would agree to the expedition. On September 5 he relieved Admiral Lee, put Farragut in charge of the North Atlantic Squadron, and asked him to prepare for a joint attack on Wilmington by October 1. The message did not reach the admiral for two weeks, and, to the secretary's dismay, Farragut complained of vertigo, saying, "I must have rest." He offered several reasons why the expedition should not be attempted, and closed by adding, "I do not feel equal to such a task."[12]

Farragut's reply stunned Welles. Reading between the lines, it became apparent to the secretary that the admiral considered the expedition foolish and certain to fail. Fox, however, had a solution. If the expedition ended in disaster, no admiral could shift the blame to the army more skillfully than Porter. Besides being the youngest admiral, Porter's ability as an organizer and innovator surpassed that of every other senior officer, and if the mission turned out to be as difficult as Farragut predicted, only Porter could make it successful. Fox had another motive for recommending Porter—the admiral's close relationship with Grant. Welles agreed with his assistant and on September 22 transferred Lee to the Mississippi Squadron and ordered Porter to Washington.[13]

The assignment appealed to Porter and he hastened east, hoping to be on hand to finalize naval preparations. Instead, he found turmoil. Welles considered the closing of Wilmington "paramount to all other questions"—more important than the capture of Richmond. Grant considered the expedition a distraction, but to placate Porter and Fox he agreed to cooperate if Fort Fisher could be taken by a small force.[14]

Porter thought it could and made a fast trip to Cairo to bid his squadron farewell and pave the way for Admiral Lee. On September 28, in a final message to the men of the squadron, he praised them for their accomplishments, and no tar could have read the tribute without knowing how difficult it was for their admiral to leave—so difficult, in fact, that he stayed at Cairo for a week. Telegrams urging him to Washington piled up on his desk. "When may we expect you?" Fox inquired. "Southern concern is going under. Time flies."[15]

On October 6 Porter stopped briefly at the Navy Department on his way to Hampton Roads. Welles wished him success, but after Porter departed the secretary reflected, "It is with reluctance that he comes into this transfer, but yet he breathes not an objection. . . . He will have a difficult task to perform and not the thanks he will deserve . . . if successful, but curses if he fails."[16]

If Porter manifested doubts in Washington, they vanished by the time he reached Hampton Roads. He expected to be met by Lee, who was still at sea. Rather than wait, he steamed up the James River to General Butler's canal at Dutch Gap. There he found gunboats lying idle within range of enemy batteries, and he asked why no orders had been given to destroy them. Not satisfied with the response, he returned to Hampton Roads. Lee was still not there, so Porter wired Welles, "Shall I assume command before Admiral Lee comes? There is much to be done, and it is necessary." Before Welles could reply, Lee steamed into Hampton Roads and agreed to transfer the squadron in the morning.[17]

As soon as the ceremony ended, Porter took command of the North Atlantic Blockading Squadron and divided its eighty-seven vessels into five divisions. He had not been at sea since his days with Farragut off the Mississippi delta, but the ships of the squadron brought back memories. Among the twenty-five vessels of the first division, under Commodore Henry K. Thatcher, rocked the rickety *Powhatan,* his first command, and the huge *Colorado.* The second division, under Commodore Joseph Lanman, contained *Brooklyn* and the aging steam frigate *Minnesota,* vessels with which he once shared blockade duty in the

Gulf of Mexico. In the third division, commanded by Commodore Sylvanus W. Godon, he found the *R. R. Cuyler,* and in the fourth division, now commanded by Capt. Melancton Smith, he caught sight of *Miami,* a gunboat from his own mortar flotilla. No vessel in the Mississippi Squadron, however, compared to the five ironclads under Commodore William Radford. The armor-belted *New Ironsides,* looking more like a new-age cruiser than the turreted monitors, carried some of the heaviest broadside guns in the world. *Saugus, Mahopac,* and *Canonicus,* each with one turret, and *Monadnock,* with two, made up the balance of the division. Porter transferred his pennant to *Malvern,* a captured blockade runner of moderate size but great speed, which enabled the admiral to move about rapidly.[18]

For the next three weeks, vessels detached from other squadrons steamed into Hampton Roads and reported to Porter. He sent many of them to Norfolk for repairs, taxing the navy yard beyond its capacity. Most of the vessels were shorthanded, and on October 14 Porter wired Welles for "500 seamen and 300 ordinary seamen." By the end of October the admiral had the largest and most powerful naval force ever assembled under one command—150 vessels—and more on the way.[19]

Porter also used the time to become better acquainted with his five division commanders, all of whom held from four to ten years more seniority. To buffer any animosity within Admiral Lee's corps of officers, Porter brought from the Mississippi Squadron six of his most trusted officers: K. Randolph Breese as fleet captain, and five commanders— Francis M. Ramsay, John G. Walker, Thomas O. Selfridge, George M. Bache, and James M. Pritchett. To Porter's relief, he found no bitterness among his division commanders, and the only change he made was to transfer Melancton Smith to the command of the USS *Wabash* and elevate Commodore James F. Schenck to command of the third division.

Porter soon discovered the vastness and importance of his new command. Managing it was a full-time job without the added worry of mobilizing an expedition to Fort Fisher. The department spanned the eastern Atlantic seaboard, ending at the northern border of South Carolina. It contained seven distinct centers of operation, with two being at the mouth of Cape Fear River—one at New Inlet, the other at Old Inlet.

Another center operated in the sounds of North Carolina, where in April 1864 the Confederate ironclad *Albemarle* sank the USS *Southfield*, damaged *Miami* and *Sassacus*, limped back up the Roanoke River, and boomed herself in off Plymouth. *Albemarle* posed a constant threat, and when daredevil Lt. William B. Cushing applied to Porter for permission to attack her with a spar torpedo slung from the bow of a steam launch, the admiral approved the mission. Cushing, who at Annapolis had graduated at the bottom of his class, was already more famous than all of his classmates. He was thin, energetic, and only twenty-one years old. Later, when Cushing explained his plan to Porter, the admiral could not mistake in the young man all the traits he once possessed himself. On the night of October 27, Cushing slipped up the Roanoke River, surprised the sentinel on *Albemarle*, detonated the torpedo under the ironclad's hull, and sank her. To save himself, he dove into the river, swam downstream, stole a skiff, and made his way back to the fleet. Cushing at once received promotion to lieutenant commander, along with the thanks of Congress, the president, and the naval secretary. Porter was so pleased with Cushing that he rewarded him with command of the flagship.[20]

The most important center, however, was at Hampton Roads, which encompassed the naval station at Norfolk and protected the army's entire line of communications on the James River, specifically, Butler's Army of the James and Grant's enormous supply depot and fleet of transports at City Point. Just above Trent's Reach and a few miles below Richmond, Flag Officer John K. Mitchell commanded several gunboats and three Confederate ironclads—*Richmond, Virginia,* and *Fredericksburg*. Porter remembered Mitchell from the surrender of Fort Jackson and considered him a timid man, but he could not ignore the threat of a surprise attack on Grant's supply line.[21]

A month earlier, when Fox warned Porter that "Southern concern is going under," the admiral did not understand Fox's message until he spoke with Grant at City Point. The general did not want to deplete his army and as a consequence waited until December to commit a land force. Rather than detach the splendid troops of the Army of the Potomac, he tapped Butler's Army of the James for sixty-five hundred infantry and placed them under the command of Brig. Gen. Godfrey Weitzel, whom he trusted better than Gillmore. Grant provided the expedition with some of his weakest regiments, little artillery, no siege guns, and no reinforcements. His instructions to Butler lacked the tone and thoroughness of a commander absolutely committed to a campaign and ended by ordering the units back to the James if "the troops under General Weitzel fail to effect a landing at or near Fort Fisher." Grant added, however, that if the landing succeeded, the troops should entrench themselves, cooperate with the navy, and capture the fort.[22]

Whatever indifference Grant felt toward the enterprise was not shared by Porter, or for that matter by Butler, who later decided to accompany the expedition. Once again Porter found himself paired with a political general—one who revived old animosities bred on the lower Mississippi. While walking with Grant at City Point, Porter noticed the general approaching and said, "Please don't introduce me to Butler. We had a little difficulty at New Orleans, and although I attach no importance to the matter, perhaps he does." Grant chuckled and replied, "You will find Butler quite willing to forget old feuds, and as the troops who are to accompany you will be taken from his command, it will be necessary for you to communicate with him from time to time."[23]

If bitterness existed between the general and the admiral, they put their differences aside and worked—for a while—in perfect harmony. Porter knew the expedition would be the last naval campaign of the war, and he wanted it to succeed. Here was a fort worth taking, perhaps the strongest in the world. Knowing that Farragut had advised against the enterprise motivated Porter even more, and as Fox had often said, good things happen to naval officers who capture forts. For Butler, however, it was his last opportunity to redeem himself as a military commander—a credential he coveted, and one that could revitalize his political career. Both men were anxious for success, and to set the campaign on the best footing, the admiral and his wife called upon Mrs. Butler one afternoon in early November. The gesture led to a round of dinner parties on *Malvern* where the general and the admiral displayed a mutual regard for each other.[24]

In some respects, Porter and Butler were alike. Both men were intellectually gifted and independent thinkers whose talent for innovation ranged from the brilliant to the absurd. Socially they got along admirably, and on military matters each enjoyed contriving new contraptions to discomfit the enemy. Porter was especially interested in finding a way to disable the fort without risking the loss of his vessels, and Butler needed to capture the fort quickly because Grant opposed a protracted siege. Impressed by the impregnability of Fort Fisher, Butler recalled hearing of great destruction for miles around Erith, England, when a large quantity of gunpowder exploded accidentally. In early November Butler went to Washington to convince Lincoln and Fox that the accident in England demonstrated the feasibility of disabling Fort Fisher by packing a barge with powder and exploding it near shore. Fox was skeptical, but Porter, who had faith in gimmicks, declared, "I was not opposed, myself, to the experiment (for I think everything worth trying)."[25]

Porter wasted no time putting the plan in motion. He ordered Lt. Comdr. Pendleton G. Watmough at New Inlet to take soundings off Fort Fisher and find the best spot for running close to shore "a vessel drawing 8½ feet and carrying 350 tons of powder. . . . My calculations are that the explosion will wind up Fort Fisher and the works along the beach, and that we can open fire with the vessels without damage. . . . Have all the information ready by the time I [get] down."[26]

Fort Fisher, guarding New Inlet, was regarded by both sides as the strongest earthwork ever built, and its sole purpose was to protect the trade of Wilmington, located eighteen miles up the Cape Fear River. The leg on the fort's northern face angled 680 yards across a slender, sandy peninsula bounded by the ocean on the east and the Cape Fear River on the west. Known as the landward side, this section contained twenty-two heavy barbette guns and rifles mounted in pairs and separated by massive bombproof traverses. As an extra precaution against a land attack, the beach in front of the landward face had been seeded with an electrically detonated minefield. Behind this was a heavy palisade of sharpened logs nine feet high and pierced for musketry. A strong redoubt on the northeastern angle provided an enfilading fire. The most vulnerable spot in the fort was the left flank along the river where the Wilmington Road, screened for more than five miles by a high hill known as Sugar Loaf, entered the rear of the work and was weakly guarded by only a section of light fieldpieces.

On the sea face the fort stretched north to south along the beach for nineteen hundred yards and contained ten batteries mounting twenty-four heavy guns, some in embrasure connected by heavy curtains. Huge traverses rose fifteen feet above the parapets, shielding the batteries

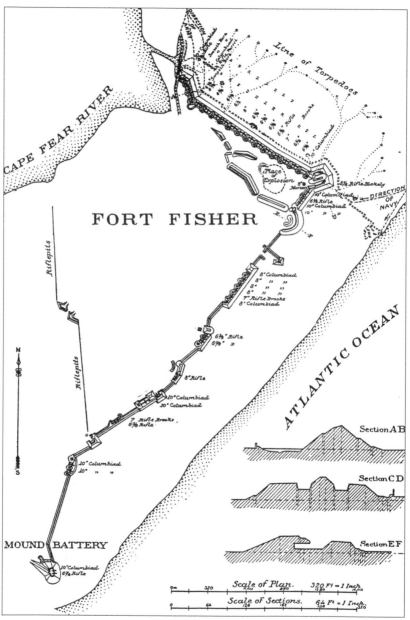

Sketch of the works and defenses of Fort Fisher REPRINTED FROM JOHNSON AND BUEL, *BATTLES AND LEADERS OF THE CIVIL WAR*

from enfilading fire. At Confederate Point (once known as Federal Point) on the southern end of the fort, and bearing directly on the shoals off New Inlet, rose The Mound, a forty-three-foot earthwork armed with a 10-inch Columbiad and a 6.5-inch rifle. A mile south of The Mound lay Fort Buchanan, with four guns bearing on New Inlet's channel and emplaced to cross fire with a battery on Zeek's Island. Except for a line of rifle pits running on an angle from The Mound to the river, Fort Fisher was exposed from the rear.[27]

Twenty-nine-year-old Col. William Lamb commanded Fort Fisher. He had built it and armed it, and he understood its strengths and weaknesses better than any other officer in the South. Lamb had absolute confidence in his ability to repulse an attempt by the enemy to reach Wilmington by way of the river. This confidence, however, began to ebb in December 1864, when the War Department stripped his garrison and left him with about eight hundred troops of the 36th North Carolina to man more than a mile and a half of fortifications. Aside from firing their pieces on occasion, the garrison had seen little action during the war.[28]

Neither Porter nor Butler was aware of Lamb's weakness, but both were absorbed in a scheme to blow Fort Fisher off the face of the earth without firing a gun. The plan involved filling an old steamer with gunpowder, laying her close to the beach near the fort's northeastern angle, and detonating it. Butler originally suggested exploding 150 tons of powder in a barge, but the project grew to 300 tons, the balance to be supplied by the navy and packed into the 295-ton *Louisiana,* a dilapidated iron steamer. There is evidence that Welles accepted the scheme because Grant, in October, refused to allocate the ten thousand troops requested by Fox, and if the fort could be flattened by the powder boat, General Weitzel would not need so many troops to take the fort.

Porter had good reason to support the experiment. If it worked, half the credit would go to the navy, with no loss of vessels; if it failed, it would be Butler's fault. The Navy Department, however, endorsed the idea exclusively as Butler's in order to obtain Grant's commitment of infantry.[29]

Porter's ability to shift the blame for failures to the army was a reason Fox used when he encouraged Welles to put the admiral in charge of the North Atlantic Squadron. Porter, however, had more to gain from a successful mission than from a failure, especially after his stumble on the Red River, and he turned his energies to getting the expedition under way before the storms of winter made the coast unapproachable.

In mid-November the plan encountered obstacles before Butler donated his first ounce of powder. Stanton asked Brig. Gen. Richard Delafield of the engineers to comment on the effect of large atmospheric explosions. Delafield replied that "a vessel load of gunpowder at the nearest point it can approach . . . Fort Fisher (about 950 yards), can produce no useful result toward the reduction of these works." He said the powder boat would be destroyed by the fort before it could be deployed and recommended the idea be dropped. Stanton agreed and refused to give Butler the powder.[30]

With the scheme unraveling late in November, Fox convened a meeting in Washington of seven ordnance experts—four from the navy, three from the army, but none from the army engineers. With the exception of Brig. Gen. Alexander Dyer of the Army Ordnance Bureau, all agreed that Fort Fisher would be seriously injured if three hundred tons of powder were detonated within 450 yards of the earthwork, or roughly 250 yards from the beach. All agreed, however, that the purpose of the explosion was to silence the shore batteries long enough for the flotilla to pass up the Cape Fear River and assault Fort Fisher from the rear. Nobody conferred with Porter or Butler, however, to make certain that this was their plan.[31]

Confronted by differing opinions, Grant consented to the Wilmington expedition on December 2 but committed only sixty-five hundred troops. In Porter's view this made the powder boat, which was then at Norfolk for modifications, absolutely essential. *Louisiana* languished in the navy yard until the 10th, and Grant urged Butler to either get the expedition rolling or drop it. Butler, however, had already delivered his half of the powder to the navy and had General Weitzel's troops waiting on transports. Porter, who had left the matter of the navy's powder in the hands of Fox, discovered that the "good" powder had been sequestered by the Ordnance Bureau and substituted with "second-class" powder, which could not be delivered for a week.[32]

The onus of delay now rested with the navy—or, from Butler's point of view, with Porter. Grant, whose concern for Sherman's march to the sea had mounted, now found merit in the enterprise and urged that the expedition get under way without the powder boat. To placate the army, Porter sailed on the 13th. *Sassacus* towed the half-empty *Louisiana* to Beaufort, where Porter had ninety tons of powder stored.[33]

As the fleet moved south from Hampton Roads, Porter was surprised to see Weitzel's transports scattered among his squadron. They were supposed to have waited thirty-six hours before sailing to give the slower ironclads time to reach North Carolina. Among them was Butler's flagship, *Ben De Ford*. The general had joined the expedition, and Grant could not stop him. A New York soldier expressed the feeling of the army when he wrote, "Old Butler is here and will perhaps command the expedition—in order to assure its failure."[34]

Sassacus steamed into Beaufort with *Louisiana,* and after loading her with eighty-five tons of powder she lay so low in the water that Porter feared she would sink at the dock. So with only 235 tons of powder instead of 300, he took *Louisiana* in tow and on December 17 set a course for Fort Fisher. He advised Butler to be there the morning of the 18th, as he planned to blow her up. He cautioned the general to keep the transports twenty-five miles to sea until after the explosion.[35]

In the original plan, the powder boat was to be disguised as a blockade runner forced ashore, but Porter worried that the old tub would bilge or get so close to the fort she could be boarded. He told Comdr. Alexander C. Rhind, a New Yorker and an experienced skipper, to anchor her in the surf. The Naval Ordnance Bureau had supplied Porter with three methods for triggering the explosion, as fuses had been woven through the packed powder and arranged to explode simultaneously. Porter, however, feared they might fail and ordered Rhind to build a fire in the stern before leaving the vessel. He also told Rhind that he did not believe the explosion would be the "dreadful earthquake" anticipated by Butler, but severe enough to stun men a few hundred yards away, demoralize them, and reduce their resolve to withstand a bombardment. He predicted the collapse of The Mound, guns buried beneath the ruins, and houses in Wilmington jolted off their foundations. "I think," he added, "if the Rebels fight after the explosion they have more in them than I gave them credit for."[36]

Rhind arrived off Fort Fisher on the 18th and at dark edged toward the fort. The breeze freshened out of the east. Breakers piled up on the shore. At 9:30 P.M. Rhind reported he was ready to take her in, but visibility worsened and he dallied offshore. In the meantime Butler decided his men could not land in the surf and postponed the attack.[37]

On the 19th, with heavy weather hammering the coast and his men running short of rations, Butler took his transports to Beaufort to reprovision and recoal. Porter expected them back in three days, certainly no later than four, and with the sea calming on the 23rd and a favorable tide at midnight, he gave Rhind permission to blow up *Louisiana* at 2:00 A.M.—regardless of whether Butler was back. He reminded Rhind to build a fire aft because "there may be something yet unthought of that will affect the clocks and fuses, but there will be no mistake in a fire."[38]

Porter dispatched an aide early on the evening of the 23rd to inform the general that the powder boat would be exploded late that night and followed by a bombardment in the morning. He urged Butler to hasten back and be prepared to land. Porter expected to see the transports by midday, but his messenger did not locate the general until daylight on the 24th—ninety miles away and still at Beaufort.[39]

At 8:00 P.M. Rhind advanced toward his target, towed by the USS *Wilderness,* but with no moon to guide him he could not see the fort. With Porter's stirring words promising that "the names of those connected with the expedition will be famous for all time to come," Rhind must have felt a heavy burden. When he heard the sound of breakers crashing ahead, he cut loose from *Wilderness* and steamed closer to shore. Estimating his distance from the beach at three hundred yards, he dropped the stern anchor. Unaware that he was more than eight hundred yards north of the fort, he set the devices to detonate at 1:18 A.M. and kindled a fire aft. He discovered the anchor dragging and the vessel drifting out to sea, so he dropped the bow anchor. Satisfied he could do no more, he hurriedly departed and rejoined Porter's fleet twelve miles at sea.[40]

Most of the squadron turned out to watch the fireworks. From the tops some of the men claimed they could see the fire burning in *Louisiana*'s stern. One o'clock ticked by, and the observers steadied themselves for the expected eruption. The countdown started, minute by minute, and when 1:18 passed Rhind mentally praised Porter for having the foresight to ask for a fire. Finally at 1:40 A.M. the sky blossomed with a great fire, followed by another and then another, exactly at the point where they had been watching. Twenty seconds passed before four dull thuds, followed by a slight if not imaginary concussion, swept over the fleet. The tars glumly returned to their hammocks. Nobody had been knocked off his feet. So feeble was the explosion that the defenders of Fort Fisher thought a Union gunboat had grounded and been blown up by her crew. Colonel Lamb considered the disturbance curious because there was no trace of the mysterious cause at daylight.[41]

The reason for the puny thuds soon came to light. Because the fire kindled astern reached the powder first, it exploded piecemeal, compartment by compartment, rather than simultaneously, and because there was no packing on top of the powder stored below, the blast went straight up in the air like a huge puff of smoke. The admiral later learned that 80 percent of the powder never exploded.[42]

At daybreak on the 24th Porter scanned the shore. He saw no sign of *Louisiana*, but Fort Fisher looked the same as ever. He then turned his glass on the horizon, searching for Butler's transports, but none were there. Nevertheless, he deployed his vessels to attack whatever remained of Fort Fisher.

At 11:00 A.M. the ironclads, led by *New Ironsides*, ranged within three-quarters of a mile of the land face, anchored, and opened with their heavy guns. At noon the first division, composed of steam frigates, anchored a mile off the sea face and attempted to enfilade the land face. The second division, containing wooden gunboats, engaged The Mound and the lower batteries on the sea face. Each division had reserve vessels waiting a half mile in the rear. Porter's instructions were quite thorough, but they assumed the fort would be disabled and that Butler's men would be standing by in surfboats.[43]

An hour and a half into the bombardment, Fort Fisher's guns fell silent. By then a cloud of heavy smoke had settled between the fort and the flotilla, but the tars kept to their guns, firing blindly. Porter edged toward shore, and from the deck of *Malvern* he could see smoke rising above the fort. Witnessing two explosions, he believed Fisher's magazines had been hit. Seeing no sign of Butler, he continued to pound the fort at the rate of 115 shells a minute throughout the afternoon. He hoped the general would hear the shelling, as the sea was calm and ideal for landing. Butler, however, arrived on his flagship at sunset, but most of his transports were still on their way from Beaufort.[44]

Fort Fisher's guns had not been silenced by Porter's squadron but by Colonel Lamb's orders. His smoothbores could not reach the fleet, so the men settled into their bombproofs and crunched crackers as every projectile known to the Union navy thudded into the grounds. Aside from the quarters catching fire, Lamb reported one killed, twenty-two wounded, two guns disabled, and four damaged but still serviceable. He had little shot and shell and decided to save it for the expected land attack. Lamb reported that most of the enemy's shells fell on the grounds, in the river, or in the sea.[45]

Porter, however, lost guns and men, but not because of Lamb's artillery. Five 100-pounder Parrotts burst, killing twenty-two men and wounding twenty-four others. One of the vessels fell out of line, and Porter, steaming through the squadron, stopped it and asked, "What's the trouble?" The deck officer replied, "My 100-pounder exploded." Porter ordered him back in line, shouting, "Then why the hell don't you go back and use your other guns?" Once word spread, however, gunners no longer trusted the piece. The navy carried 627 guns into the fight, so it was not surprising to have accidents, especially with the notoriously troublesome 100-pounder Parrotts.[46]

Annoyed by Butler's absence, Porter sent a brief message to Welles reporting that Fort Fisher had been silenced at 2:00 P.M. "There being no troops here to take possession," he declared, "I am merely firing at it now to keep up practice . . . and all that is wanted now is the troops to land."[47]

When Butler arrived, Porter believed the fort had been severely disabled—"blown up" and "demolished" were the words he used to describe the damage. He was satisfied with the day's work but rankled by the general's tardiness. He did not know that his message to Butler failed to reach him until morning, and that the general was unaware of the naval attack until after it started. Butler and Weitzel departed from Beaufort with half of the transports and arrived just as the fleet withdrew. What started as a congenial joint operation began to deteriorate as the final hours approached.[48]

As the fleet withdrew, *Ben De Ford* pulled abeam *Malvern,* and Butler sent a staff officer to tell Porter that General Weitzel and Col. Cyrus B. Comstock would come aboard later to discuss the landing of troops in the morning. Butler was angry that Porter had exploded the powder boat and engaged the enemy without the army present. Porter was nettled that Butler had dallied at Beaufort and let the navy deplete its ammunition. Butler suspected the navy of bungling *his* experiment by trying to snatch a victory while the army was away. He made no effort to see Porter in person, which suited the admiral, who had taken a bad fall the previous day and felt poorly. Weitzel and Comstock, however, came aboard later in the evening to discuss the tactics for Christmas Day.[49]

Porter assured Weitzel that his bombardment, combined with the explosion of the powder boat, had rendered the fort defenseless. Weitzel doubted it. He had been a critic of Porter's bombardment of Fort Jackson, and since then he had commanded bloody assaults against entrenched positions in Virginia that had supposedly been softened up by shelling. He expected strong resistance, but Porter assured him that once the army established a beachhead, they could walk into the fort and take it. Weitzel disagreed, arguing that the garrison had probably taken refuge in bombproofs and were quite capable of offering resistance. Instead, he suggested that Porter take his gunboats into the river and enfilade the fort from its undefended rear. Once they were inside the river, Weitzel argued, Wilmington, like New Orleans, would become vulnerable and Fort Fisher would become useless. If the fort was as defenseless as Porter claimed, the navy should be able to get inside the river with no trouble. The admiral refused, claiming the channel was too shallow for his ironclads, contained torpedoes, and was imbedded with obstructions. He agreed to provide a covering bombardment—as long as his ammunition lasted—and deploy a squadron of gunboats to support the landing.[50]

After a two-hour discussion with Porter, Weitzel returned to *Ben De Ford* convinced that Fort Fisher was strong enough to repulse a landing. Butler agreed because he believed Porter's precipitant detonation of the powder boat destroyed any chance for success. He even suggested that Porter never intended "that the attack of the army should succeed"—as if some grand conspiracy to humiliate him existed between Grant and the admiral. Butler favored returning to Fort Monroe and quitting the mission, denouncing Porter for spoiling the expedition by seeking to grab all the glory for the navy. Colonel Comstock urged patience and suggested they put a reconnaissance ashore at daylight, assess the resistance, and then decide what to do. Butler finally agreed, and late that evening he advised Porter of his decision, leaving the details to be finalized in the morning between the admiral and General Weitzel.[51]

On Christmas Eve, thousands of men went to sleep with no notion of their duties in the morning. Butler proposed the navy engage the fort at 6:30 A.M. so the landing could take place at 8:00. The suggestion made no sense to Porter. He would not know Weitzel's plan of attack until morning, and at 6:30 it would be too dark to open with a bombardment. The admiral had no ammunition to waste, and he did not know the scope of Weitzel's planned attack.

Porter went to bed thinking. He did not rule out Weitzel's suggestion of taking a squadron through New Inlet and attacking Fort Fisher from the rear. He had considered the tactic before, always rejecting it as too dangerous, and with his ammunition running low, the notion was riskier now—but perhaps worth a try.

General Butler, however, went to bed in a rage. For a week he had stood off Fort Fisher in fair weather waiting for Porter to bring up the powder boat, and the moment the transports departed for supplies, up came the navy—and without so much as a warning, the admiral blew up the boat, bombarded the fort, and destroyed the element of surprise. Whatever modicum of cooperation existed between the two commanders at the beginning of the expedition vanished on Christmas Eve. Neither man fully understood how deeply he had provoked the resentment of the other until later—and later was soon to come.

TWENTY-TWO

Fort Fisher Falls

On Sunday, Christmas Day, Porter met with Weitzel at 6:30 and learned that the army's surfboats had not arrived from Beaufort. He offered to lend him the navy's boats, and the general replied that he would assault the beach at noon. Weitzel asked for a ninety-minute bombardment prior to landing and said he would take the troops ashore near Flag Pond Hill, four miles north of Fort Fisher. Porter agreed to support the landing party with a detachment of gunboats. He expected Weitzel to attack in force and did not know Butler had restricted the assault to a reconnaissance in force.[1]

At 7:00 A.M. Porter signaled his squadron to commence firing at 10:30, and the vessels moved up as they had on the 24th. He detached twelve gunboats under Capt. Oliver S. Glisson to cover the landing and sent him to Butler's flagship to coordinate with Weitzel. Glisson was stunned when Butler said he intended to land only five hundred men. He reminded the general of the weather and urged him to land in force. Butler waved him off, replying that he preferred not to land at all.[2]

At 10:30 the squadron opened with a slow, deliberate fire, and the fort replied down the length of the earthwork. A half hour later Glisson's gunboats fired on the Flag Pond Hill battery. Porter noticed a double-ender edging out of line and steamed over to investigate. "Where are you going now?" he shouted. "To repair a damage in my side," the commander replied. "Go back to your place," Porter hollered, "or I will send you and your boat to the bottom."[3]

Noon came and went, and Porter could not understand why the army did not launch its attack. At 2:00 P.M. he observed the first boats push off from the transports and make for shore. Some were filled with bluejackets. Porter thought the battery had been deserted and was surprised to see a white flag pop up minutes after the landing. Among the first to reach the beach were sailors from the gunboat *Britannia*. They outraced Weitzel's soldiers, rushed to Flag Pond Hill, and captured about seventy prisoners—boys from the North Carolina Junior Reserve.[4]

With so weak a response from the enemy, Porter believed the army could march directly into the fort and take it. He moderated the bombardment along the sea face and stepped up the fire on The Mound. Believing the fort was disabled, Porter considered working up the river, getting in the rear of the earthwork, and supporting Weitzel's right flank.[5]

Acting under the admiral's orders, Comdr. John Guest led ten double-enders to New Inlet to engage The Mound while a boat detail under Lieutenant Cushing dragged the channel for torpedoes and set markers. Cushing found the channel cluttered with hulks, and when Battery Buchanan opened on the detail he withdrew after one boat was struck and split in two, spilling its crew into the water. Running the river looked risky, so at 2:30 P.M. Porter recalled Guest's squadron and sent it back up the beach to assist with landing the army.[6]

With ammunition running dangerously low, Porter signaled the fleet to slacken fire. All down the line guns fell silent. Moments later, Fort Fisher opened for the first time with its 150-pounder Arm-strong. The accuracy of the gun seemed uncanny. Shot and shell crashed through the decks of *Colorado* and *Minnesota*. Below the waterline, 10-inch bolts punched holes in their hulls. For self-preservation, both vessels reopened on the fort and continued to fire until retiring at sunset.[7]

At the landing site, the first wave of five hundred troops, under Brig. Gen. N. Martin Curtis, moved up to within seventy-five yards of Fort Fisher and filed into abandoned rifle pits. There they stayed, annoyed by enemy snipers posted in the palisades. Another two thousand troops came ashore but huddled on the beach and waited for orders. Four thousand more lounged on transports and watched. At 3:00 P.M. Weitzel and Comstock went ashore and found Curtis's brigade pinned down in the pits. Curtis urged that reinforcements be brought up and an assault made on the western flank of the works. Weitzel took a quick look at the batteries on the ramparts and returned to the landing site. He rowed out to advise Butler that an attack was simply hopeless. The news was exactly what Butler expected to hear, and, without notifying Porter or bothering to confirm Weitzel's observations, he ordered a withdrawal.[8]

Since midafternoon, when *Ben De Ford* signaled that Weitzel was on the beach with a heavy force, Porter had paced the deck and waited with confidence for more good news. Growing impatient, he came abeam *Ben De Ford* and shouted through his speaking trumpet, "How do you do, General?" Butler replied, "Very well, thank you." Porter looked at the operation on the beach and asked, "How many troops are you going to land?" "All I can," replied the general. Butler asked for no help, so Porter returned to his squadron to await the outcome of Weitzel's assault.[9]

An hour later, signals flashed indicating that Weitzel's troops were reembarking. Porter could not believe it. He steamed toward the landing site but was met by a dispatch boat with a letter from Butler claiming that the fort could not be carried because the land face was materially uninjured and supported by fifteen heavy guns. The general claimed, however, that some of Curtis's troops had entered the fort through a sally port and captured a flag from the parapet, but he did not explain why others did not follow and assault the batteries. Another company killed a courier and captured his horse. Prisoners had informed Weitzel that two brigades from Maj. Gen. Robert F. Hoke's division had been detached from Richmond and were en route from Wilmington. Rather than verify the rumor, Butler withdrew, because, he declared, "a regular siege . . . did not come within my instructions. In view of the threatening aspect of the weather. . . . I shall therefore sail for Hampton Roads as soon as the transport fleet can be got in order." Butler, however, was wrong. He failed to follow Grant's instructions, which specifically ordered him to entrench if he secured a beachhead.[10]

The weather remained calm until late afternoon. Butler withdrew part of his force, but he stranded Curtis's command on the beach— leaving them under fire in foxholes dug by hand in a drenching rain. The soldiers were furious, not just because they had been deserted, but because they believed the fort could have been taken had Weitzel sent reinforcements.[11]

When Porter learned men were still on the beach, he ordered Captain Alden to retrieve them. "We must get those poor devils of soldiers off today," he wrote, "or we will lose them."[12]

Porter fumed through the night at Butler's incredulous withdrawal. In the morning he sent a message to the general asking somewhat sarcastically why more of his "gallant fellows" did not follow the officer who took the flag from the parapet. "I think they would have found [the fort] an easier conquest than supposed." He advised Butler that some of the gunboats had gone to Beaufort to replenish ammunition, and he promised they would be back in time to renew the attack. He also predicted that by 3:00 P.M. the beach would be calm enough to resume the attack. Butler did not reply, however, except to deny that his men had entered the fort after claiming they did.[13]

Disgusted with Butler's lack of enterprise, Porter wrote Welles, "Until further orders I shall go on and hammer away at the forts, hoping that in time the people in them will get tired and hand them over to us. It is a one-sided business altogether. . . . The government may also think it of sufficient importance to undertake more serious operations against these works. An army of a few thousand men investing it would soon get into it with the aid of the Navy."[14]

On December 27 the USS *Nereus* removed the last of Colonel Curtis's brigade from the beach. Officers and soldiers alike complained of being deserted by Butler. All agreed that had they been reinforced on the afternoon of the 25th the fort would have fallen. They may have been correct, because Lamb's North Carolinians had no experience fighting infantry. Porter collected the soldiers' comments and sent them to Welles.[15]

As the last days of 1864 approached, a stiff wind blew off the Atlantic and dumped cold rain on the deck of *Malvern*. Butler departed without so much as a good-bye, and Porter marked time in his cabin while the squadron shuttled back and forth from Beaufort replenishing provisions and ammunition. By the 29th he learned more about what had happened ashore and was convinced that Curtis could have taken the fort with his brigade if Butler had let him. In a confidential message to Welles, he wrote:

> I feel ashamed that men calling themselves soldiers should have left this place so ingloriously; it was, however, nothing more than I expected when General Butler mixed himself up in this expedition, starting his troops out from Hampton Roads with only a few days' provisions, and without water . . . the result was when the time arrived for action the troops were all in Beaufort.
>
> General Butler only came here to reap the credit of this affair, supposing that the explosion would sweep the works off the face of the earth. Had he supposed in the first instance that there would have been difficulties he would never have joined the expedition.
>
> If this temporary failure succeeds in sending General Butler into private life, it is not to be regretted, for it cost only a certain amount of shells, which I would have expended in a month's target practice anyhow. . . . I ask that you not break up the present squadron of attack until I say that I can't get into Fort Fisher.[16]

Porter dispatched Breese with a letter for Sherman, who had just captured Savannah. "[Fort Fisher] is merely on your way to Richmond," he wrote. "Take this place and you take the *creme de la creme* of the rebellion." After condemning Butler's withdrawal, he added, "I do hope, my dear general, that you will second me here, and let our people see the folly of employing such generals as Butler and Banks. I have tried them both, and God save me from further connection with such generals."[17]

God did not save Porter from "connections with such generals," but Grant did. Writing from City Point on the 30th, he asked Porter to "hold on where you are for a few days and I will endeavor to be back again with an increased force and without the former commander. It is desirable that the enemy should be lulled into all the security possible, in the hopes he will send back here or against Sherman the reinforcements sent to defend Wilmington."[18]

The bulk of Hoke's division had reached Wilmington late on December 26th, and General Bragg dispatched two brigades to reinforce Fort

Fisher. By then, however, the crisis seemed over, and Grant wanted it to appear that way. Porter, relieved to know Grant intended to try again, kept the blockading squadron on station off the Cape Fear River but sent the battle fleet back to Beaufort to prepare for the next assault. This time there would be no powder boat.[19]

For the failure of the first attack, however, Porter deserved a portion of the blame. Although the powder boat was Butler's idea, Porter endorsed it. His correspondence suggests that he depended upon it, but he tampered with the fusing—which may have failed anyway—and then initiated the attack without Butler present. Porter maintained a legitimate concern for the weather, but the attack had been postponed once and could have been postponed again. Butler, however, performed poorly throughout the affair, but both the admiral and the general deserve criticism for placing a wall between their communications at the critical stage of the landing. Porter's overtures of friendship to Butler meant little because the early relationship between the admiral and the general seethed with mutual distrust. Grant, who held the highest regard for Porter, worried when he learned Butler had joined the expedition. He was disappointed by the outcome—but not surprised.

What changed Grant's mind had little to do with Butler but everything to do with Sherman and Halleck. After Savannah fell on December 21, Grant had planned to transfer Sherman's sixty thousand men by sea to reinforce the Army of the Potomac. Sherman, however, argued that by marching through the Carolinas he would drive Lee out of Petersburg, thereby enabling the Union army to fall on him from the rear. When Halleck endorsed the plan, Grant conceded, holding to the axiom that a supreme commander, unfamiliar with distant conditions, should never impose a plan not recommended by the general who must carry it out.[20]

Grant felt uneasy about Sherman's army living off the land during the months of winter, especially if every rebel unit in the deep South converged on the Carolinas to stop him. Foraging for supplies in North Carolina would be no easy task, as the harvest had been shipped to Lee's army. By the end of December, Grant considered the capture of Wilmington crucial to the safety of Sherman's army, and when Butler's assault failed he wasted no time selecting a seasoned fighter, Maj. Gen. Alfred H. Terry, to command the next expedition.[21]

Maj. Gen. Alfred H. Terry, who led the
second attack on Fort Fisher REPRINTED
FROM JOHNSON AND BUEL, *BATTLES AND*
LEADERS OF THE CIVIL WAR

Terry, a thirty-seven-year-old lawyer turned soldier, had led the 2nd
Connecticut at First Bull Run and the 7th Connecticut in the capture
of Port Royal. In the autumn of 1863 he assumed command of the X
Corps in Butler's Army of the James and witnessed the first Fort Fisher
assault. Terry was one of the few generals in Butler's command to have
Grant's confidence. This time, however, Grant took no chances. He added a siege train, a division from Maj. Gen. Philip H. Sheridan's command, and extra ammunition and supplies, and instructed Terry to
work closely with the navy. Porter did not see Grant's orders to Terry
until after the war. Grant did not want any of Butler's or Weitzel's preju-
dices to rub off on Terry and wrote, "I have served with Admiral Porter,
and know that you can rely on his judgment and his nerve to undertake
what he proposes. I would, therefore, defer to him as much as is con-
sistent with your own responsibilities."[22]

The admiral preferred Sherman to Terry, but his friend was busy in Georgia. "I hold it to be a good rule never to send a boy on a man's errand," Porter cautioned Grant, but added, "There is no use fretting over the past; we must endeavor to avoid mistakes in the future, and if any expedition fails now to take the works, the sagacity of the leaders of the late expedition will be applauded." Porter was aware that some Northern newspapers upheld Butler's version of the fiasco. He did not want to vindicate Butler by being associated with another failure and urged Grant to give Terry additional troops.[23]

Porter's preparations were also more thorough. This time there would be no shortage of ammunition, coal, or provisions once the attack began, nor any recriminations against the navy if the expedition failed.[24]

Terry's command reached Beaufort on January 8, and for two days a winter storm forced the vessels to shelter in the harbor. The delay had its advantages and enabled Porter and Terry to resolve tactical issues. They agreed to disembark five miles north of Fort Fisher, where supplies could be landed with comparative ease. On the morning of the 12th, with skies fair and wind moderate, the flotilla sailed from Beaufort for the landing site. The wind changed, huge waves crashed upon the beach, and night fell. Reluctantly, the fleet anchored off Half Moon Battery and waited for daylight, the element of surprise doused by the weather.[25]

Porter arranged his fifty-eight-ship squadron into three attack columns and four reserve units, with the heaviest guns bearing on the fort's land-face batteries. Terry planned to assault the western salient, marching along the partially screened Wilmington Road and entering the fort at its weakest point, thereby enabling the navy to shell the sea face during the attack. Porter organized his own assaulting force, which would move down the beach and attack the redoubt at the eastern angle of the land face. He posted the ironclads inshore to cripple the redoubt, thereby opening the way for the sailors. Both wings of the attack would strike the flanks of the land face without crossing the enemy's electrically activated minefield—which, unknown to Porter, had been disabled by the bombardment. The attack, however, would be delayed until all eight thousand men were ashore with their artillery, siege guns, and twelve days' rations.[26]

During the past three weeks, Colonel Lamb had restored Fort Fisher to its former strength, remounted disabled guns, and strengthened the palisades. For more than two weeks, General Hoke's brigades had been camped a few miles away at Sugar Loaf and within striking distance of Terry's flank. What Lamb did not know until too late was that General Bragg on the 12th had recalled a brigade from Sugar Loaf and was hurrying it back to Wilmington.[27]

At 4:00 A.M. on January 13, Porter's first column, which included the ironclads, moved into position to cover the attack. The first wave of Terry's infantry dropped into surfboats and landed unopposed. At 8:00 A.M. the second wave hit the beach. With no enemy to contest the landing, the monitors *New Ironsides, Monadnock, Mahopac, Canonicus,* and *Saugus* steamed up to the fort and at a thousand yards opened on the land face. Thirteen gunboats, led by *Brooklyn,* fell in behind the monitors and concentrated fire on the parapets.

After the December attack on the fort, Porter learned from his mistakes. These were different men, not those who had fought with the Mississippi Squadron and knew his ways. In the first bombardment he had seen shells wasted, so this time he ordered the squadron to lengthen fuses "to lodge the shell in the parapets, and tear away the traverses under which the bombproofs are located." He wanted the bastion at the angle demolished before the sailors landed and ordered the first column to fire deliberately, dismount the guns, and knock away the casemates. He established new signals to improve the fleet's marksmanship and to coordinate the firing with Terry's assault. He took special interest in landing the bluejackets safely. They had the most dangerous route to take—straight up the beach, over the earthwork, and into the bastion. He wanted the angle pounded until the gunners saw the tars approaching the parapets. As an afterthought he added, "Don't waste shells on the flagstaff, they are placed at a point to entice us to shoot at them."[28]

The ironclads *Mahopac, Canonicus, Saugus,* and *Monadnock,* because of their closeness to shore, drew the heaviest fire. Comdr. Enoch G. Parrott, commanding *Monadnock,* observed that the fire from the fort was more accurate and intensive than in December. This suited the gunners on the ironclads because it pinpointed the location of the enemy's batteries. "We aimed almost wholly at their guns," Parrott declared, "watching the effect of each shot, and waiting for the smoke to clear away before firing another." Lt. Comdr. George E. Belknap, commanding *Canonicus*, considered the fire from the fort more accurate and spirited than before. He counted thirty-six hits on the armor and reported "everything about the deck not shotproof . . . badly cut up."[29]

On the night of the 12th, when mounted enemy pickets observed the first vessels of the Union armada, Colonel Lamb had about eight hundred men of the 36th North Carolina present for duty. He telegraphed Maj. Gen. William H. C. Whiting for reinforcements, and during the 13th and 14th about seven hundred men arrived—North Carolina companies of light and heavy artillery—bringing Lamb's force to about fifteen hundred men. During the bombardment on the 13th, Whiting came up with his staff. Lamb offered to step aside, but Whiting declined, replying that he had come to counsel, not to command.[30]

During the December attack, Lamb had fired 1,272 rounds, depleting about a third of his projectiles. In the interval between the first and second attacks, he asked for ammunition but received none. On January 13, when the second attack commenced, the fort's inventory of shot and shell had been reduced to 2,328 rounds. To conserve ammunition, he issued orders that each of the forty-four guns be fired only once every thirty minutes. He noted, however, that Porter's squadron fired about two projectiles a second.[31]

For two days and nights the Union navy hammered the fort, and traverses began to collapse on the eastern angle. The bombardment on the 14th was especially heavy, and Porter reported that "by sunset the fort was reduced to a pulp; every gun was silenced by being injured or covered up with earth." This was not quite true, but by viewing the damage from a mile offshore, it looked that way.[32]

With a stiff wind blowing sand in their faces, Terry's men spent most of the 14th lugging artillery ashore and moving it across the beach to the Wilmington Road. Brig. Gen. Adelbert Ames posted the 2nd Division of the XXIV Army Corps along the road to prepare the attack for the morning of the 15th. The 3rd Division, under Brig. Gen. Charles J. Paine, took a supporting position behind Ames. Terry made a careful reconnaissance of the fort in the afternoon, and because of the unpredictability of the weather, he decided to attack on the 15th if Porter reported the traverses disabled. That evening Terry met with the admiral, who reaffirmed his plan to send a detachment of sailors and marines up the beach to assault the angle. The two men parted, setting the time for the attack at 3:00 P.M.[33]

The bombardment on the 14th had been especially fierce, with 11- and 15-inch shells slamming into the parapets all day long and showering the palisades with shrapnel. After meeting with Terry, Porter called for volunteers to support the land attack. Everybody knew this would be the squadron's last big fight. More men stepped forward than the admiral could spare. He tried to confine the detail to 1,400 men but settled for 1,600 sailors and 400 marines. Then, to give the enemy no rest, he ordered the monitors to bombard the fort throughout the night.[34]

If Porter could have looked inside the fort, he would have seen few men on the palisades. "We could barely gather and bury our dead without fresh casualties," Lamb admitted. "At least two hundred had been killed or wounded . . . [and] only three or four of my land guns were of any service."

At sunrise on the 15th, Lamb scanned the fleet shelling the parapets. The sea was calm, the enemy's fire annoyingly accurate. His instincts told him that today he would be attacked. He counted his men—twelve hundred effectives to defend two miles of fortifications. He watched as Terry's troops dug rifle pits near the minefield and as another column massed along the river road. By noon every gun on the land face had been dismounted but one old piece on the angle. He shuttled three Napoleons from the sea face and moved them into position to check Terry's attack. Then he noticed another force—Union sailors and marines—moving down the beach and throwing up shallow trenches as they advanced. Then, thirty minutes before the attack, he welcomed 350 men from the 21st and 25th South Carolina who landed below the fort and ran into a bombproof, winded and demoralized by the constant explosion of shells. But Porter's gunboats never let up, and Lamb could do little more than watch and steady his men for the attack.[35]

Early on the 15th Terry and Porter held a final meeting before initiating the assault. It was a fine winter day, perfect for what the two commanders had in mind, and at 10:00 A.M. Porter signaled the fleet— "Arm and away all boats." Two boats from *Susquehanna* dropped into the water with fifty bluejackets and eighteen marines. One hundred seamen and marines from *Powhatan,* commanded by Porter's brother-in-law, Lt. George Bache, waited on the off side of the vessel for the signal to go ashore. Fifty-five men from *Tuscarora* joined the fray, including landsmen and coal heavers who had never had a crack at the enemy. Cushing took forty men off *Monticello* and a detail from *Malvern,* including Lt. Benjamin H. Porter and Fleet Captain Breese. Hundreds more from almost every vessel in the fleet clambered into surfboats and waited for the admiral's signal.[36]

Every sailor had a revolver and a well-sharpened cutlass but those in the special detail under Lt. Samuel W. Preston. They carried shovels and had the task of getting within range of the redoubt on the angle and throwing up rifle pits. When the ditch reached a depth of about three feet, the marines were to come up, followed by sappers who would extend and deepen the pits. Porter cautioned his men to wait for the signal confirming Terry's assault before moving forward.

He divided the bluejackets into four columns and placed them under the command of Fleet Captain Breese. Capt. Lucien L. Dawson led the marines, who were armed with rifles. Their objective was to cover the assault of the sailors—whose cutlasses and revolvers would be useless outside the fort—and then gain the parapets and pick off the enemy in the works. The other three columns were led by Charles H. Cushman of *Wabash,* James Parker of *Minnesota,* and Thomas O. Selfridge of *Huron.* Their task was to breach the works and capture the fieldpieces emplaced inside. If The Mound turned its guns on the sailors breaching the parapets, Porter told the men to grab a prisoner, pitch him over the walls, and then get behind the fort for protection.[37]

At 10:00 A.M. the entire squadron opened with a heavy fire directed at the parapets. Thirty minutes later the sea swarmed with surfboats pulling for shore. Preston's detail dashed up the beach and started digging rifle pits. The marines followed, and by 2:00 P.M. the sappers had advanced the pits to within two hundred yards of the fort. The sailors formed along the beach and drew up to within about a mile and a half of the fort. They crouched on the sand and waited for the army to initiate the assault. Word came from Terry that the attack would commence at 3:00 P.M. sharp, and Breese advanced the sailors to within a half mile of the fort. Lt. John R. Bartlett commanded the second company of the first division and was to lead the attack. He lay at the head of his company and listened to friendly shells whoosh overhead and crash into the palisades. Occasionally one fell among the men, hurling

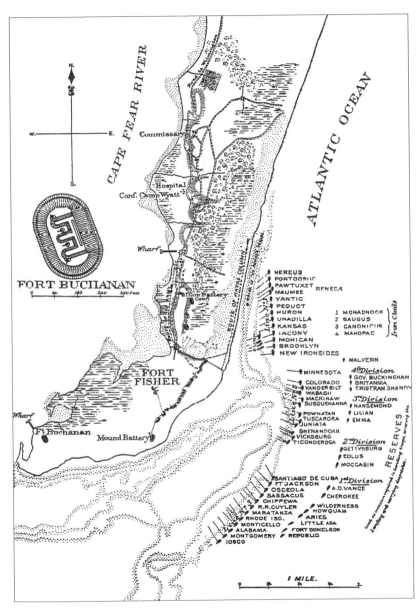

Sketch of the bombardment of Fort Fisher on January 15, 1865
REPRINTED FROM JOHNSON AND BUEL, *BATTLES AND LEADERS OF
THE CIVIL WAR*

Array of Porter's squadron bombarding Fort Fisher REPRINTED FROM
JOHNSON AND BUEL, *BATTLES AND LEADERS OF THE CIVIL WAR*

bodies in the air. Bartlett tried to look ahead. "We were getting very hungry," he re-called, "as we had taken our breakfast at daybreak. I was anxious to get into the fort to try some rebel provisions."[38]

Lamb spent the early part of the afternoon watching Terry's brigades form along the river road on the left. Whiting wired Bragg that Fort Fisher was about to be attacked and renewed his request for reinforcements. Lamb left Whiting on the land face, passed through the galleries, and ordered up sharpshooters to pick off the officers in Terry's columns. At 3:00 P.M. firing from the gunboats stopped, and seconds later the screech of every whistle in the fleet howled a signal to friend and foe alike that the crucial moment had come. Lamb hurriedly shifted the South Carolinians to the far left, and then he jogged down to the eastern salient.[39]

When Lamb reached the sea face, he looked out across the beach and was stunned by the size of Porter's force. He now believed the main assault was coming from the beach and shifted three hundred men to the ramparts above the bastion and two hundred more along the sea face, thereby weakening the left, Terry's point of attack. Hundreds of grayclads took cover along the sea face and poured a murderous fire into the sailors. Moments later both guns in The Mound opened, plowing up the sand with grape and canister.[40]

The beach became untenable. Officers shouted orders, marines broke formation to snipe at the enemy, and sailors surged forward with a cheer. They paused behind three sand hills to catch their breath and then double-quicked up the palisades. Their legs cramped from too little exercise, but they rushed forward, breaking into small groups all running at the same speed. Armed with revolvers and cutlasses, they could not fight until they entered the fort, and dozens began to hesitate. "Oh, such a fire as we were under," Lieutenant Bartlett recalled. "Sailors and officers were dropping all around me." He started through the stockade with a dozen officers and twenty sailors. When he turned around to see how many men had followed, there were no more, and those with him tumbled back down to the beach and gouged out shallow pits. "Every time I threw up a handful of sand," he recalled, "a dozen bullets would skip over my head. It was rather unpleasant, as it knocked the sand all down on me."[41]

Ensign Robley D. Evans of *Powhatan* spoke with seaman James Flan-nigan on the evening before the attack. Flannigan insisted upon joining the assault, but late that night he brought a box of trinkets to Evans and asked that they be given to his sister. Evans told Flannigan to give them to her himself, but the seaman answered, "I'm going ashore, and will be killed." Evans asked, "Do you know how many bullets it takes to kill a man?" Flannigan ignored the reply and walked away. When the attack began, Evans noticed a man reel to one side and drop in the sand. He rushed to the man's side and asked if he was hurt, but Flannigan—like so many others that afternoon—was dead.[42]

Porter watched the attack from the deck of *Malvern*, saw the bluejackets scatter, and noticed the forms of many men lying prostrate on the beach. He could not see who was down. Lt. Sam Preston, who led the shovel detail, lay dying in a pool of blood, his femoral artery severed by a minié ball. A bullet struck Lt. Roswell H. Lamson of *Gettysburg* in the shoulder, whirled him around, and dropped him just below the parapet. He slid back down the slope, tied off his wound, and noticed Preston lying a few paces below him. He crawled toward the lieutenant but found him dead. Lt. Cushman of *Wabash*, who led one of the four attack columns, took a ball in his leg. A few feet away lay the body of Lt. Benjamin Porter of *Malvern*, one of the admiral's favorites—a huge hole in his chest.[43]

Porter could not see the advance of Terry's force, but he knew the bluejackets were in trouble. His young son, Carlisle, had gone ashore with Cushing. This amplified his worry. Cushing, after seeing Ben Porter and Preston fall, tried to rally the sailors sheltering under the palisade. He looked for Breese but could not find him. With Carlisle Porter at his side, Cushing dashed across the beach, now covered with the dead and wounded, and gathered a detail to move to higher ground those who would be drowned by the incoming tide. He had collected all the able-bodied sailors for another assault when he received a message from Terry asking him to hold the line of rifle pits in the rear against a surprise attack by Confederate reinforcements. No attack materialized, but Cushing and Carlisle Porter spent the night shivering with the men in the trenches. The admiral was much relieved to see his son in the morning.[44]

Before occupying the rifle pits, Cushing could not find Breese because the fleet captain was with Selfridge further up the palisades. At the moment Selfridge's men passed through the stockade and into the work, the tars in the rear inexplicably panicked and ran for cover. Bache, commanding the right wing of Selfridge's column, was hit by a ball and helped off the field during the rout. Breese stood in their midst, waving his sword and shouting at them to go back up, but the bluejackets streamed by him as fast as their sea legs would carry them. Parker, who led the second column, noticed a hail of bullets splattering around Breese. That night he declared, "How [Breese] escaped death is a marvel to me."[45]

Breese had maintained good control of the sailors up to the moment of the attack. The marines, instead of lying in their pits and sniping at enemy sharpshooters, joined in the attack. Without any fire to pester them, the rebel defenders ranged along the palisades and picked off the sailors with ease.[46]

As the bluejackets fled from the palisades, Lamb glanced down the land face, and what he saw gave him a jolt. "I turned to look at the western salient," he said, "and saw, to my astonishment, three Federal battle-flags upon our ramparts. General Whiting saw them at the same moment and [called] on the men to pull down those flags and drive the enemy from the work." Whiting recovered a gun chamber but was wounded twice during the ensuing hand-to-hand combat. Lamb

The attack on Fort Fisher by Porter's bluejackets REPRINTED FROM JOHNSON AND BUEL, *BATTLES AND LEADERS OF THE CIVIL WAR*

stepped through a sally port to look down the land face and observed a wave of Union infantry streaming into the galleries.[47]

When Porter realized that his force on the beach had withdrawn, he ordered the monitors to open on the traverses still occupied by the enemy. With the tide rising, Commodore Radford worked the ironclads close to shore and opened with deadly precision, frustrating Lamb's efforts to organize a defense. Fifteen-inch shells crashed through the traverses, and when Battery Buchanan opened on the rear of the land face occupied by the Union, chaos took command of the battle, disorienting friend and foe alike.[48]

As night fell the firing slowly subsided as more of Terry's men poured into the fort. The ironclads ceased fire. Lamb and Whiting left the field on stretchers, hoping to find a friendly steamer at Battery Buchanan, but the battery's occupants had spiked their guns and deserted. A column from the garrison trailed behind the wounded officers, mainly to get away from the fort and seek safety at The Mound. At 9:00 P.M. fighting in the fort stopped, and Bvt. Brig. Gen. Albert M. Blackman's 27th U.S. Colored Regiment, accompanied by a detachment of artillery, trudged down to Battery Buchanan and found Lamb, Whiting, and remnants of the garrison waiting to be rescued. There were no boats to carry off the wounded generals, and at 10:00 P.M. they surrendered to Blackman.[49]

Signals from the fort flashed to the ships at sea. Where the celebration first started, nobody knew, but Bartlett recalled returning to *Susquehanna* with a boatload of wounded when suddenly at 10:30 "the whole fleet gave three rousing cheers, threw up rockets, and blew their whistles."[50]

In keeping with his promise to Welles, Porter dispatched the speedy USS *Vanderbilt* to Hampton Roads ten minutes after he learned of Fort Fisher's surrender. He went to bed confident that the navy would have the honor of breaking the good news to Washington. When he went on deck at daybreak, he was shocked to see *Vanderbilt* anchored off Fort Fisher. Muttering invectives, he signaled the ship's commander, Capt. Charles W. Pickering, "Proceed without delay. Wait for nothing." The vessel finally got under way, but it never caught up with Terry's dispatch boat. Welles piled public praise on Porter, but he never understand why the admiral, with so many fast steamers, lost the race to the army. For his tardiness, Pickering was detached and sent to the New York Navy Yard, grumbling that this was "the first time in forty-three years . . . in the service that I have been thus censured."[51]

There was little sleep that night—none in Fort Fisher and little on Porter's flagship. In the fort, looting and revelry continued through the night. Armed with torches, sailors, marines, and soldiers moved from one bombproof to another, rifling through the Confederate commissary for its supply of spirits. On *Malvern,* Porter prepared to ascend the river at daylight to confer with Terry about going on to Wilmington.

At 7:30 A.M. on the 16th Porter sent boats to sound New Inlet when an explosion inside the fort shook the ground and sent tons of earth into the air. He learned the reason later. Soldiers snooping through the chambers of the fort stumbled upon the main magazine. Not knowing its contents, they took torches inside to investigate. Moments later, thirteen thousand pounds of powder exploded, killing or wounding two hundred men, some of them asleep on the sod covering the magazine.[52]

After the explosion, the army's butcher's bill increased to 664 killed, wounded, and missing. To this the navy added 393 more, with 7 killed by the eruption of the magazine. The enemy's losses are clouded by poor records. General Bragg estimated 500 killed, wounded, and missing, and General Terry reported 112 officers and 1,971 men captured, bringing the enemy's total engaged to 2,583. If Terry's report is correct, and it probably is, then Bragg's estimate of casualties is probably high, because Lamb never claimed to have more than about 2,200 men present.[53]

Porter never completed his count of ammunition expended by the gunboats. This he left to official compilers thirty-five years later. In the first attack, the squadron fired 20,271 projectiles weighing 1,275,299 pounds. In the second attack the fleet consumed 19,682 projectiles weighing 1,652,638 pounds—together nearly three million pounds. Although the number of projectiles fired in each attack was about equal, those fired in the second attack found their mark and disabled almost every gun in the fort.[54]

The admiral did not fully appreciate the strength of Fort Fisher until he walked through it with General Terry. He found it more formidable than the great fortress of Malakhov, which he had visited with English friends in 1855. In sending the fort's flag to Welles by express, he gave high praise to Terry in words usually conserved for only Sherman. Having criticized Grant for saddling him with Butler on the first expedition, he now praised him for choosing a soldier who knew how to fight. "A timid man," Porter said, "would have hesitated to attack these works by assault." In keeping with his biases, the admiral added a few references disdaining Butler's lack of military skill.[55]

By sheer coincidence, Secretary of War Stanton stopped at Fort Fisher on his way back to Washington. He had been to Savannah to speak with Sherman and did not know the fort had fallen. He rejoiced at the victory, calling it a "great achievement." Terry took the flag from The Mound and presented it to the secretary, who bid the admiral and the general good-bye and resumed his journey to Washington.[56]

On January 4, 1865, Grant asked Stanton for permission to remove Butler from the Army of the James, warning that if something happened to him, Butler, as senior officer, would have command of the Army of the Potomac. The president agreed and issued Executive Order No. 1, deposing the general and sending him back to Massachusetts. On January 8 Butler said good-bye to his army. Unable to accept his own ineptness as a commander, Butler blamed his expulsion on his enemies, and no one had criticized Butler's performance more than Porter.[57]

The admiral did not hear the good news until later. He grieved over the loss of his men at Fort Fisher but privately celebrated the dismissal of Butler.

TWENTY-THREE

Mr. Lincoln and Admiral Porter

On January 16 Porter brought three gunboats over the bar and stationed them above Fort Caswell, isolating all the batteries below Confederate Point from Wilmington. At 1:30 A.M. the garrison at Fort Caswell abandoned the work and blew up the magazine. Three lesser explosions followed—Fort Holmes, Fort Campbell, and Fort Johnston. Porter came on deck to witness the fireworks just as two enemy steamers burst into flame. When he went to bed that night, he knew that Wilmington, the supply line of the Confederacy, would no longer feed Lee's tattered army.[1]

At daylight Lieutenant Cushing guided *Monticello* through New Inlet and hoisted the Stars and Stripes over the remains of Fort Caswell and the town of Smithville. With the lower river in control of the navy, Porter relit the blockade runners' light at The Mound. On the night of January 19, *Stag* and *Charlotte,* two inbound runners from Bermuda loaded with arms, blankets, and shoes, fell into the trap and anchored beside *Malvern.* The decoy worked well until word got back to Nassau and Bermuda, where three dozen British runners lay ready to deliver guns, ammunition, and two and a half million pounds of bacon to Wilmington.[2]

During a hard campaign the admiral's health always suffered, and for three days he took life easy and tried to get some sleep. On January 21 he admitted to Fox, "The excitement over the last month has quite broken me down, my mind was on a stretch for a long time, and when the work was over I collapsed. I am all right again today and have not smoked more than twelve cigars."[3]

In a letter to Welles, Porter gave high praise to Terry: "I don't know that I ever met an officer who so completely gained my esteem and admiration." After bad experiences with Banks and Butler, Porter had finally found a volunteer general he could respect. The admiral was not alone in his praise. Terry later became one of the few non–West Point major generals who remained in the regular army and retained his rank.[4]

On January 24 Congress passed resolutions thanking the men serving in the expedition for "the unsurpassed gallantry and skill exhibited" in the attack upon Fort Fisher. Porter received his fourth resolution of thanks, attached to a personal note from Lincoln. At the time, he did not know he had become one of the president's favorite warriors.[5]

In many respects, Porter served his personal interests better when fighting a war than when he had time to reflect. He still commiserated over the Christmas fiasco and held Grant responsible for having sent Butler. He wrote a confidential letter to Welles on January 24 expressing his disdain of Grant's management of the first expedition. He never intended the letter to be seen by anybody but Welles, but it was stuffed into the department's files and remained there unnoticed for several years. Welles, however, knew that Grant never intended for Butler to lead the expedition. He also knew Grant needed the admiral in the James, and, like a good mediator, he suggested that the general pay Porter a visit, although he never explained why.[6]

On January 28 Grant came down from City Point to visit with Porter and to determine what force was required to capture Wilmington. During their three-and-a-half-hour meeting on *Malvern,* Grant explained that he never intended for Butler to accompany Weitzel on the first expedition. Porter discarded his doubts about Grant, and the two commanders quickly renewed the friendship and the mutual trust they had shared on the Mississippi. When Grant returned to City Point, he detached Maj. Gen. John M. Schofield's corps to cooperate with Porter in capturing Wilmington.[7]

By the time Schofield arrived, Porter had sent most of his squadron elsewhere, retaining as his only ironclad the monitor *Montauk.* To support Schofield's advance up the river, Porter needed to get five miles above Fort Fisher to disable Fort Anderson and a battery at Sugar Loaf, where torpedoes and obstructions blocked the ascent of the army's transports. Being lean on firepower, he resorted to an old trick and constructed a huge dummy out of a worthless scow, some barrel staves, and a few bolts of canvas. On February 18, Cushing piloted the bogus ironclad upriver with the flood tide and at midnight sent it past Fort Anderson. "Johnny Reb let off his torpedoes without effect on it," wrote Comdr. William G. Temple, "and the old thing sailed across the river and grounded in flank and rear of the enemy's lines on the eastern bank, whereupon they fell back in the night. She now occupies the most advanced position of the line, and Battery Lee has been banging away at her, and probably wondering why she does not answer."[8]

On the 19th Porter's lightdrafts, joined by Schofield's transports, started for Wilmington. Hundreds of torpedoes floated downriver, keeping the admiral's picket boats busy with nets. One struck the wheel of *Osceola* and destroyed her wheelhouse. Two men in a cutter were killed when a sailor shot at a torpedo and blew it up too close to the boat.

On the 20th and 21st the squadron engaged the last four batteries and cleared the way to Wilmington. Confederate forces, pressed by Schofield from both sides of the river, evacuated the town on the 22nd. *Malvern* tied up at Wilmington and was welcomed by hundreds of blacks who sang, danced, and rollicked on the wharf. To celebrate the victory, Porter ordered a Washington's Birthday salute. As guns roared, the blacks scattered in all directions. Sherman now had his base for operations against General Johnston's army, but Porter learned of a new problem—this one on the James River.[9]

Flag Officer John K. Mitchell, commanding the remnants of the Confederate navy on the James and Roanoke Rivers, had been viewing Grant's supplies at City Point, and on January 24th he started three rams and eight gunboats downriver to destroy them. At Trent's Reach, two rams, *Virginia* and *Richmond,* and two gunboats, *Drewry* and *Scorpion,* grounded on the ebb tide and remained there until they were refloated by the morning flood. Mitchell hurried the rest of his squadron back upriver but could do nothing to help the others.

Porter had placed Comdr. William A. Parker in charge of the James River Division, consisting of several gunboats and the huge *Onondaga,* a double-turreted monitor armed with two 15-inch Dahlgrens and two 150-pounders. When Mitchell's rams grounded, Parker had a marvelous opportunity to smash the Confederate fleet, but he stood off and let light Federal batteries posted along the shore bang away at the enemy. Mitchell lost both gunboats but neither of the rams.

When Grant learned of the episode, he criticized Parker. Welles removed Parker, replaced him with Comdr. Edward T. Nichols, and tried to bring Farragut to the rescue. By then the opportunity to destroy the rams had been lost. Parker, reaching for an excuse to explain his inaction, blamed Porter for ordering him to keep *Onondaga* out of range of the enemy's batteries. The admiral rejected the excuse as nonsense and wrote, "No man ever had a better chance than you . . . to make yourself known to the world"—and one, Porter admitted, that for some time he had wanted for himself.[10]

With the Union army in possession of Wilmington, and Mitchell's rams anchored below Richmond, Commodore Radford took command of the James River Division, and Porter hastened back to Washington to testify before the Joint Committee on the Conduct of the War. Arriving March 4, the day after Lincoln's inauguration, he found the city congested with officials speculating on what the president meant by offering "malice toward none and charity for all." When the admiral entered the Navy Department, he found Welles quite critical of the new vice president, Andrew Johnson, who had just taken the oath of office "either drunk or crazy."[11]

On March 7 Porter testified before the Joint Committee investigating the Red River campaign and the first Fort Fisher expedition. He said exactly what he thought, as did Banks and Butler, leaving it to the committee to sort out the facts. Both generals had been discredited, but the war with the South was winding down and future battles would be fought at the polls. "Congress did not get at the truth, nor did it desire to do so," Porter wrote. "Wherever it stuck down a spade, it struck a politician." After completing his testimony, Porter spent the evening with Welles and on March 16 departed for the James River with Fox.[12]

Porter spoke with Grant on the morning of March 20, and they both agreed that the navy should not take the offensive. Grant had just invited the Lincolns to City Point, so Porter went upriver and shuttled between Trent's Point and Aiken's Landing, guarding against a surprise attack.[13]

He remained at Aiken's Landing until the 25th, when he dropped down to Jones' Landing to cover the crossing of Maj. Gen. Philip Sheridan's army, which was returning from a campaign of destruction on Lee's flanks. Sheridan was still crossing on the afternoon of the 26th when *River Queen* arrived from City Point with Generals Grant and Ord, Mr. and Mrs. Lincoln, and their son Tad. Porter had a barge prepared for his visitors and towed them up to the ironclads stationed below Trent's Reach. Lincoln said he wanted to be near the front when the army began its final campaign. He was visibly nervous and anxious for the war to end.[14]

On the 27th Porter received a telegram from Grant advising him that General Sherman would arrive at City Point that evening. "Can you not come down and see him?" Grant asked. "He will probably return tonight, and I know will be disappointed if he does not meet you."[15]

The admiral accepted the invitation and early in the evening landed at City Point. He went ashore to find his old companion in arms, whom he had not seen for more than a year. Grant and Sherman were waiting for him, and after an exchange of greetings they went on board *River Queen* for a conference with the president. The session lasted late into the night and was followed by another in the morning.

It was here that Porter participated in two of the most famous conferences of the Civil War. Sherman had General Johnston's force bottled up in North Carolina, and Grant had Lee's army on the verge of collapse. The only question was whether Grant could prevent Lee from joining forces with Johnston. Grant thought he could—but not without one more bloody battle. Lincoln wanted the war to end without further loss of life, but he accepted Grant's prediction as inevitable. Porter quotes the president as saying, "Let them surrender and go home. They will not take up arms again. Let them all go, officers and all, let them have their horses to plow with, and, if you like, their guns to shoot crows with. I want no one punished. Treat them liberally all around." Twelve days later, April 9, General Grant presented those terms to General Lee at Appomattox.[16]

On the morning of the 29th Grant bid the president good-bye and returned to the front to begin a flanking movement that would drive Lee's army out of the Petersburg trenches. On April 1 Lincoln sent his wife back to Washington, but he and Tad stayed with Porter. The admiral had little to do but look after the needs of the president, who for two days squeezed himself into a small cabin on *Malvern*. "Uncle Abe is having a good time down here," Porter wrote Fox, "and would have had a better one had he come alone. Mrs. Lincoln got jealous of a lady down here, and rather pulled his wig for him. We put him through the Navy and did all we could to make him forget the cares of office."[17]

Lincoln refused to take the admiral's cabin and spent the first night cramped for legroom. Porter had carpenters lengthen the cabin, and the following morning the president came to breakfast smiling and said, "A greater miracle than ever happened last night; I shrank six inches in length and about a foot sideways."[18]

The president needed rest, and for ten days he stayed with Porter. They spent time discussing telegrams as news arrived from the front. The fighting moved to Five Forks, and there was little the admiral and the president could do but to trace the army's progress on maps. The vice president, the secretary of war, and members of Congress came down to City Point. Lincoln denied himself to all of them, and it became the admiral's duty to prevent any intrusion upon the president's privacy. They rode horseback and took pleasure in each other's company, for Lincoln had finally found a man who could spin as many yarns as himself.[19]

When the president reflected on his generals, he sometimes omitted their names. One evening, referring to Butler's powder boat, he said, "I don't think, Admiral, your friend the General was very much of an engineer." Porter quietly agreed. "I don't think," Lincoln added, "that your friend the General was much of a general either."[20]

At nightfall on April 1, two days before the evacuation of Richmond, Lincoln lounged on *Malvern*'s upper deck. He turned to Porter and asked, "Can't the Navy do something at this particular moment to make history?" Porter replied that by being in the James, the navy was holding Richmond's fleet in check. "But can't we make a noise?" Lincoln asked.[21]

Porter complied and sent Comdr. William Ronckendorff up the James with orders for the monitors to open fire on the enemy's works above Howlett's Battery. His instructions carried all the trimmings of a fireworks display, with rockets, coston signals, blue lights, and a brisk cannonade of 10-inch shells. "The object," Porter said, "is merely to make the rebels think that we are about to make an attack. They are prepared to sink their gunboats at the first sign of one. . . . The only object is to make a noise."[22]

The demonstration in the early morning hours of April 2 preceded the evacuation of Richmond and the scuttling of the Richmond flotilla, now commanded by Admiral Semmes, by a day. At 7:30 A.M. Capt. Henry A. Adams Jr. came on board *Malvern* to report Richmond evacuated. Two hours later an explosion from upriver rocked the flagship. "I hope to Heaven one of our vessels has not blown up," Lincoln declared. Porter assured him the explosion was farther up the river and no doubt a Confederate ironclad.[23]

An hour later Lincoln received a message from Grant announcing the capture of Petersburg, and he asked Porter to take him there. At 9:00 A.M. they left City Point and rode by train to Patrick Station, where Grant had an escort waiting. Capt. Robert Lincoln met them at the station with horses for his father and Tad but none for Porter, who wore an old naval cap and looked like a railroad conductor. One of the troopers lent Porter a horse—"a hard trotter, and a terrible stumbler"—which the admiral offered to buy after reaching Petersburg. Lincoln advised against it, warning, "He's fourteen years old if he's a day. . . . He's spavined, and has only one eye. What do you want with him? You sailors don't know anything about a horse." Porter replied, "I want to buy it and shoot it, so no one else will ever ride it again." Lincoln chuckled, admitting "it was the best reason he had ever heard for buying a horse."[24]

At Petersburg Lincoln received an urgent message from Secretary of War Stanton, who had learned of the president's wanderings and reminded him that "commanding generals are in the line of their duty in running such risks; but is the political head of a nation in the same condition?" Lincoln laughed off the advice, and upon returning to City Point late in the afternoon he replied, "Thanks for your caution, but I have already been to Petersburg. Staid with General Grant an hour and a half and returned here. It is certain now that Richmond is in our hands, and I think I will go there tomorrow. I will take care of myself."[25]

Lincoln had already decided to visit the Confederate capital, and Porter had his crews busy clearing torpedoes and obstructions from the river. At 10:35 A.M. on the 4th, *River Queen,* bearing the president, came alongside *Malvern,* and both vessels headed for Richmond, followed by *Bat,* the transport *Columbus,* and a tug. *Malvern* grounded below Richmond, forcing Porter to transfer the president to a barge towed by the tug. Twenty-four marines accompanied the party, and as they neared the city, smoke still curled from the ashes of dozens of warehouses, and fires still burned throughout the city. A mile below the landing a Confederate flag-of-truce boat had gone aground, and its occupants asked Porter for assistance. Lincoln wanted to help them, so Porter detached the tug and told her skipper to give them a hand. Leaving most of the marine guard on the tug, the president's escort diminished to the admiral, three officers, and ten sailors from the barge. "Here we were," Porter recalled, "in a solitary boat, after having set out with a number of vessels flying flags at the mast-head, hoping to enter the conquered capital in a manner befitting the rank of the President with a further intention of firing a national salute in honor of the happy result." Lincoln, however, was amused by the affair, reflecting, "But it is well to be humble."[26]

The streets of Richmond were comparatively empty until an old slave by the wharf recognized Lincoln's conspicuous figure. He fell at the president's feet, wailing "Bless the Lord" and "Hallelujah! . . . Here is the great Messiah!" Lincoln was embarrassed and said kindly, "Don't kneel to me, that is not right. You must kneel to God only and thank him for the liberty you will hereafter enjoy." Porter remembered the president's face, which seemed to say "I suffer for you all, but will do all I can to help you." The words left a lasting impression on the admiral, who many years later recalled "his face lit up with a divine look as he uttered these words. Though not a handsome man and ungainly in his person, yet in his enthusiasm he seemed the personification of manly beauty, and that sad face of his looked down in kindness upon these ignorant blacks with a grace that could not be excelled. He really seemed of another world."[27]

Dozens of liberated slaves converged on the small party walking to General Weitzel's headquarters at the Confederate White House, Jefferson Davis's former residence. It was all Porter could do with his handful of sailors to keep the crowd away from the president. A cavalry patrol trotted over to the procession to investigate the commotion, and Porter sent them off to ask Weitzel for an escort. A few minutes later a troop of cavalry arrived and cleared the street. Porter and Lincoln toured the city with Weitzel. They visited public offices that had escaped the fire, but the admiral did not rest until he had the president back on *Malvern*. "It was a gala day," Porter recalled, "and no man was ever accorded a warmer welcome. The heat of the weather was suffocating; the president towered a head and shoulders above the crowd, fanning himself with his hat, and looking as if he would give the Presidency for a glass of water."[28]

On April 5 Weitzel came down the river and joined the president on board *Malvern*. They talked of reconstruction until late in the morning, after which the admiral and the president took the barge to Dutch Gap, where marines rowed them through the canal to the waiting *River Queen*. Lincoln was anxious to get back to the telegraph and reached City Point late in the afternoon.

There he waited for word from Grant, the admiral at his side, as dignitaries and Washington officials borrowed *River Queen* for daily tours to the Confederate capital. On the 8th Lincoln decided to go back to Washington, and the admiral took leave of his friend, the president. They had a pleasant parting conversation—but madness gripped the mind of John Wilkes Booth, and this was to be their last meeting.

The admiral stayed with the fleet until word came of Lee's surrender at Appomattox. He rejoiced, but the war that had made him an admiral was now all but over. He dallied off City Point until the 14th, when he transferred his flag to *Tristram Shandy* and steamed down to Fort Monroe. The president had been much on his mind, and he hastened up the Chesapeake, intending to catch a train at Baltimore and ride to Washington. When he touched at the Baltimore wharf, his worst apprehensions stunned him at the shocking news of Lincoln's assassination.

To Porter, the loss was dreadful. He took the first train to Washington to pay his last respects to the man he had come to admire more than any other. "To me," Porter recalled, "he was one of the most interesting men I ever met. He had originality about him which was peculiarly his own, and one felt when with him as if he could confide his dearest secret to him with absolute security against its betrayal. There, it might be said, was 'God's noblest work—an honest man,' and such he was all through. I have not a particle of the bump of veneration on my head, but I saw more to admire in this man, more to reverence, than I had believed possible. . . . He was as guileless in some respects as a child. How could one avoid liking such a man?"

Porter paid his respects to the family and cast one long, last look at the man lying peacefully in his casket.

"There," Porter said to a friend beside him, "lies the best man I ever knew or ever expect to know."[29]

David Dixon Porter had finally found a mortal who was greater than his father.

TWENTY-FOUR

The Postwar Years

With the war entering its final days, Welles detached Porter from the North Atlantic Blockading Squadron on April 28, 1865, and brought to an end the admiral's four years of active service. From April 1, 1861, when he colluded with the president to divert *Powhatan* and save Fort Pickens, until May 1, 1865, when he pulled up to the wharf at the Washington Navy Yard, Porter had taken but two leaves of absence— the first in the summer of 1862 to recover from malaria, and the second shortly before he took command of the North Atlantic Squadron. From the Mississippi to the James River, no senior naval officer had seen more war or participated in more campaigns than Porter—not even Farragut, who was now the navy's sole vice admiral.[1]

The war, which in the beginning almost ended Porter's career, in the end enhanced it. His early friends, men like Farragut and Fox, and his later friends, soldiers like Grant and Sherman and civilians like Lincoln and Welles, gave Porter time to politically mature and to realize there was more to be gained by cooperation than by exercising a pent-up hostility to vindicate his father—who needed no vindication—and, to a lesser degree, his brother William, who David Dixon admitted cast additional shame upon the family name.[2]

Porter never overcame his loathing of political generals, and the ineptitude of McClernand, Butler, and Banks left the admiral with a stigmatized impression of all political generals. Terry, whom he came to admire almost as much as Grant and Sherman, did not fit Porter's definition of a political general because Terry earned his stars as a volunteer. Although the admiral moderated many of the strong opinions he held at the beginning of the war, his personal view of the world still collided with the opinions of others. No other officer in the navy, however, advanced from the rank of lieutenant to rear admiral or worked harder to earn promotion.

On May 3 Welles assigned Porter to the Board of Visitors at the Naval Academy and asked him to witness examinations and report on the general management of the institution, which had been transferred to Newport, Rhode Island, early in the war. Odd things had happened under the elderly guidance of Commodore George S. Blake, and the numerous civilian teachers failed to break from the prewar scholastic regimen. The secretary's son had been tossed overboard from the school ship *Constitution,* and Porter's second son, Carlisle, had been forced to resign. Many of the academy's graduates who had fought under the admiral during the war were delighted when on August 28 he was appointed the school's superintendent. Porter was also delighted, perhaps remembering an old letter to Fox in which he wrote, "I would ask nothing better after this war is over than to have command of the Naval Academy, and get the right set of officers into the Navy. A new era should be instituted."[3]

During the war, the army occupied the Naval Academy at Annapolis, and the once elegantly manicured grounds had been scored by sheds and booths for sutlers and camp followers. The buildings had been used as hospitals and temporary barracks for thousands of transient soldiers. To restore the institution to its prewar eminence required more than a coat of paint and a little landscaping—it required a total renovation of its academic program as well. Porter understood the needs of the navy, and Welles tossed him into the project of rebuilding the school because he knew the admiral would devote his energy and experience in revamping the organization and changing the curricula to meet the needs of a modern navy.

Throughout the war, Welles often complained that Porter spent too much money, and when the admiral rebuilt the Naval Academy he showed no respect for budgetary restraints. He had more in mind than renovation and revival. Porter wanted to create a military school equal in every way to West Point for developing professional naval officers of high character and superior ability. He expanded the grounds and added new buildings—a gymnasium, a new chapel, cadets' quarters, and a mess hall—and he converted the old colonial mansion of the governors of Maryland into a well-stocked library. Porter discarded antiquated technologies preserved by Blake, added mechanical and marine engineering, and erected a building to house a steam engine for training midshipmen. Twenty-two years later he discovered the old engine was still there and demanded its replacement.[4]

Unlike Blake, Porter believed in physical fitness and established new standards for smartness and precision in drill and exercise. He revived outdoor sports—baseball, competitive sailing, and sculling—and, mindful of his own pranks as a midshipman, allowed all rational sorts of amusements as long as they remained harmless frolics. At the age of fifty-two, Porter still retained a spirited sense of humor, and he was greatly amused by cadet shenanigans—as long as they violated no standards of professional decorum.

When Welles appointed Porter to the academy, he feared the admiral would seed the institution with too many of his wartime cronies. Porter did so, but carefully. Superintendent Blake's comportment toward the cadets had been one of aloofness and suspicion—often adversarial. Porter brought instructors and administrators to the academy who, like himself, were buoyant and socially gracious—men who would spend time with the cadets and offer them the hospitality of their homes. During the war Porter had developed skills in building team spirit—not so much with superiors, perhaps, as with those who served under him. He understood what needed to be done to revamp the academy and chose the men who could do it. He built his entire staff from veterans, men like Breese, Walker, Dewey, Ramsay, Selfridge, and Greer—all young in age but hardened by four years of war.

Porter also imposed his personal standards on the cadets and instigated a code of honor. They were just boys, but he took them on trust. He believed in them, and from the first contact to his last he imbued

them with a sense of honor and then relied upon it. He encouraged
them to see that honor was not the forced result of discipline and cor-
rection but the natural outcome of their training as cadets being edu-
cated by their country for an elite service. When Welles visited the
academy with Farragut in June 1867, he admitted that Porter was "a
hard officer to control . . . his demands and requisitions are great," but
the institution looked marvelous and the midshipmen were "a credit to
the country."[5]

During Porter's first year at the academy, he rose in rank. A bill introduced in Congress on December 22, 1864, had created the grade of
vice admiral. When it passed, Lincoln signed it and nominated Farragut to the post. A year and a half later Congress created the grade of
admiral, and on July 25, 1866, Farragut was again promoted. Porter,
who had received no advancement since the Vicksburg campaign, became vice admiral. Grant, by the same act, was elevated to full general,
and two years later he became the eighteenth president of the United
States.[6]

Welles served as secretary of the navy to the end of Andrew Johnson's administration, leaving office on March 4, 1869, after paring
down the navy list to 203 vessels and establishing a record for tenure
that has never been broken. Grant cast about to replace Welles, and his
personal choice was Vice Admiral Porter—a trusted comrade-in-arms
with intimate knowledge of the navy. Since the appointment would be
contrary to the tradition of civilian authority, Grant deviously appointed
Adolph E. Borie, a friendly Philadelphian who had never held public
office, knew nothing about the navy, and had no interest in the department. He then empowered Porter to act as Borie's advisor and to run
the department. Three days after occupying his new office, Borie issued an order that "all matters relating to the Navy coming under the
cognizance of the different bureaus will be transmitted to Vice Admiral
Porter before being transmitted to the Secretary of the Navy." Porter
now had two jobs, running the navy and running the Naval Academy.[7]

Porter passed most of his time in Washington functioning as naval
secretary, and Borie collected his pay and felt increasingly useless. The
admiral attempted to run the department as he would a squadron of
warships, and he soon learned that civilian employees resented change.
They silently conspired to bring the Borie-Porter regime to an end.

Borie accelerated the process by stumbling and falling to the floor—with Grant and his cabinet present—during a "June Week" ball held at Annapolis. Borie withdrew from office on June 25, 1869, and returned to Philadelphia. On the 26th, George M. Robeson succeeded him. Robeson did not want help from Porter, who had accumulated too many critics, and he elbowed the admiral out of the department.[8]

During Porter's brief tenure in the Navy Department, he avoided the details of administration and concentrated only on matters directly affecting the standing navy. For too many years he had been an absolute autocrat with no patience for bureaucracy. Throughout the war he had managed his own affairs, solved his own problems, worked with imperfect equipment, and, through a combination of brute force and energy, overcome one problem after another. Then there was no structure to follow—only the one he created for himself. Most successful naval commanders dealt with problems the same way. The vice admiral was too good a sailor to make a good landsman, so when he came into the Navy Department he attempted to induce change by issuing general orders, a method that worked quite well during wartime but failed in 1869. During his last two years in office, Welles had issued only five general orders. In less than four months, Borie issued forty-five—written, of course, by Porter. James R. Soley, an admirer of Porter, studied all of Borie's ghostwritten directives and admitted that some were "rather fanciful, some . . . were ill-timed, and some were distinctly harmful."[9]

Porter made enemies among civilian employees in the Navy Department, and one incident threatened his friendship with Grant. In August 1870 Farragut died, and Porter became the pro tem admiral of the navy. While his nomination was pending, some scurrilous employee remembered a "private" letter Porter had sent to Welles after the first Fort Fisher expedition and found it in the files. Porter could not believe it when he saw the letter published in a newspaper just as his confirmation to admiral was being discussed in Congress. The letter accused Grant of incompetence for taking so little interest in the expedition as to give command of it to General Butler. A few days after writing the letter Porter had learned directly from Grant that Butler had imposed himself upon the operation, whereupon the admiral laid all his criticism aside, neither mentioning the letter nor expecting to see it again. Embarrassed, Porter went to Grant, explained the letter, and apologized for its emergence. Grant graciously laid aside his annoyance, and Porter's advancement to admiral was confirmed.

On November 16, 1870, Secretary of the Navy Robeson sent Porter a letter defining the fifty-seven-year-old admiral's responsibilities. Porter had already withdrawn from the affairs of the Navy Department, and he spent the rest of his life as the ceremonial admiral of the fleet and president of the Board of Inspection. He remained in close touch with all branches of the service, and in his annual reports to the secretary he fearlessly pointed to the lamentable state of the American fleet, using as his basis the technological advancements of the navies of Europe.[10]

Twice during Grant's first administration war with Spain threatened to erupt. On December 8, 1873, Robeson ordered "every available iron and wooden ship" to Key West and placed the fleet under the command of Porter. To confront the threat, Porter had only thirty-nine wooden ships of war and six monitors. He warned that a 2-gun Spanish "clipper" armed with 10-inch rifles could blow a 50-gun frigate out of the water. "It would be much better to have no navy at all than one like the present," Porter stated. "One such ship as the British ironclad *Invincible* ought to go through a fleet like ours and put our vessels *hors de combat* in a short time, for she could either run them down or destroy them at long range with her heavy rifled guns. We have no ordnance that would make any impression on such a ship at a distance of six hundred yards, and no vessel of equal speed in our navy would be placed under her fire by a prudent commander."[11]

Porter found it frustrating to watch the decline of the American navy and not be able to do much about it. Between March 1869 and January 1881 the number of vessels on the navy list dropped from 203 to 139—a result both of losses at sea and of obsolescence. By then the admiral had only fifty vessels in commission, and the number continued to decline. His principal concern was to protect the American coast from invasion or blockade, and, having little money with which to experiment, he devoted resources to improving torpedoes. Authorized $600,000 in March 1871, Porter spent three years building two torpedo boats, *Intrepid* and *Alarm,* each 173 feet long, iron plated, and equipped with a thirty-foot ram. *Alarm,* designed by Porter, was considered well adapted for the service. The science of torpedoes and torpedo boats, however, was still in its infancy—but growing rapidly in Europe.[12]

With deep concern, Porter recognized the enormous advances in naval ordnance abroad. Rifles had replaced smoothbores, breechloaders had replaced muzzleloaders, and wrought-iron guns had replaced cast-iron ones. Robeson allowed the navy to work on breech-loading small arms, and in 1879 Hotchkiss rifles were issued to some of the ships, but little else had been done beyond rifling some of the navy's old smoothbores. In 1880, Secretary of the Navy Richard W. Thompson reported, "We have less than 250 guns afloat in our entire navy, and of these less than 40 are rifles . . . all the rest are antiquated smoothbores." Porter felt helpless against a bureaucracy that refused the money he needed to revamp the navy.[13]

If withholding funds was not enough, Congress reduced the number of ratings for naval officers and in 1873 passed a law discontinuing the grades of admiral and vice admiral on the deaths of Porter and Stephen Rowan. Congress also reduced the number of officers on the rolls, and morale declined to the point where most seamen serving on American warships were of foreign extraction.[14]

Porter spent his last years in dignified ease in the historic house at 1718 H Street, formerly the British legation, which he purchased before leaving the Naval Academy. If he could do little to bring life to a new navy, there was nothing to stop him from giving color to the old. Always a prolific writer, he produced several books—none of them of marked importance, for Porter was not a man of letters but a man of action. Despite his reputation for having a photographic memory, his *Naval History of the Civil War,* published in 1886, contained errors that could have been avoided had he spent more time reading his own wartime correspondence. It unveiled many of the admiral's biases that made up his character, but it also provided narratives of his personal experiences. He sometimes referred to his *Incidents and Anecdotes of the Civil War,* published in 1885, as his "Joke Book," as many of the stories came from his unpublished wartime journal. Although the book had slight credibility as a work of history because of the highly flavored dialogue, it reflected the admiral's feelings, affections, and disaffections for the historic figures with whom he fought. For Porter, 1885 was also a year of sadness, for it marked the death of an old comrade-in-arms— President Grant, who died of cancer.

On March 10, 1889, Porter and his wife, Georgy, celebrated their golden wedding anniversary, but it would be his last social reception. His heart had grown weak, and although he ate and drank sparingly, as he had most of his life, he suffered an acute attack in the summer of 1890 while vacationing in Rhode Island. He rallied enough to return to Washington, but he never again stepped outside of his home. During the autumn he lingered, slowly weakening, and by winter he lapsed into a state of semiconsciousness. At eight o'clock on February 13, 1891, seventy-eight-year-old David Dixon Porter died on his sofa, in the upright, seated position of a naval officer, and the great office of admiral died with him—but only for eight years.[15]

Three weeks before the admiral's death, General Sherman, who had retired in 1884, came to Washington and, on hearing of his friend's condition, stopped to pay his respects. Porter was asleep, and Sherman refused to wake him up. To Georgy he said, "I would rather not see Porter unless I could see him as he always was when I knew him." To the admiral's daughter he added jokingly, "I shall be the next one, and perhaps I may go before Porter." Sherman, whom some called the "fighting prophet," survived Porter by a single day. Two old veterans, whose friendship began along the muddy banks of the Mississippi and flourished ever after, left an indelible mark on the history and the future of this country. Both were great commanders and great storytellers. Perhaps their destinies were locked together from the beginning. Two warriors, much alike, whose time came and went, their last battles fought—forever.[16]

Notes

ONE
The Legacy

1. Richard S. West Jr., *The Second Admiral: A Life of David Dixon Porter* (New York: Coward-McCann, 1937), 3–4.
2. For the cruise of *Essex,* see David Porter, *Journal of a Cruise Made to the Pacific Ocean in the U.S. Frigate Essex, 1812–1814,* 2 vols. (New York: Wiley & Halstead, 1822).
3. Archibald D. Turnbull, *Commodore David Porter, 1780–1843* (New York: Century, 1929), 240–42.
4. West, *Second Admiral,* 6–7.
5. Paul Lewis, *Yankee Admiral* (New York: McKay, 1968), 5–6, 8–9; James R. Soley, *Admiral Porter* (New York: Appleton, 1903), 18.
6. Turnbull, *Commodore Porter,* 255–58.
7. Lewis, *Yankee Admiral,* 10; West, *Second Admiral,* 12–13.
8. Lewis, *Yankee Admiral,* 11.
9. James Fenimore Cooper, *History of the Navy of the United States of America,* 3 vols. in 1 (New York: Putnam, 1856), 3:28–30.
10. Turnbull, *Commodore Porter,* 264–82; David F. Long, *Nothing Too Daring: A Biography of Commodore David Porter, 1780–1843* (Annapolis, Md.: Naval Institute Press, 1970), 250–53.

11. Long, *Nothing Too Daring*, 260–62; David D. Porter, *Memoir of Commodore David Porter of the United States Navy* (Albany, N.Y.: Munsell, 1875), 349–52; Turnbull, *Commodore Porter*, 283–85.

12. Porter, *Memoir of Commodore Porter*, 252–53; West, *Second Admiral*, 18.

13. Turnbull, *Commodore Porter*, 286.

14. Long, *Nothing Too Daring*, 262; Lewis, *Yankee Admiral*, 17.

15. Porter, *Memoir of Commodore Porter*, 252–53; West, *Second Admiral*, 20–21.

16. Porter Collection, "Letter Book U.S.N.A.," 879–81, Library of Congress (hereafter abbreviated LC).

17. Ibid., 881–86; Porter, *Memoir of Commodore Porter*, 364–65, 369–74.

18. Porter, *Memoir of Commodore Porter*, 365; Lewis, *Yankee Admiral*, 20.

19. "Letter Book U.S.N.A.," 886–95, Porter Collection, LC.

20. Lewis, *Yankee Admiral*, 21–22; Long, *Nothing Too Daring*, 276.

21. Soley, *Admiral Porter*, 29–30; West, *Second Admiral*, 27.

TWO

A Matter of Money

1. West, *Second Admiral*, 28–29; Soley, *Admiral Porter*, 32–34.

2. Soley, *Admiral Porter*, 33–34; Lewis, *Yankee Admiral*, 32–34.

3. Turnbull, *Commodore Porter*, 306–8.

4. Lewis, *Yankee Admiral*, 36–37.

5. Soley, *Admiral Porter*, 35–36; West, *Second Admiral*, 31.

6. Quoted in the *Philadelphia Press*, Mar. 12, 1889.

7. Soley, *Admiral Porter*, 36, 43; Lewis, *Yankee Admiral*, 41. Passed midshipman is equivalent to the rank of ensign.

8. West, *Second Admiral*, 34; Soley, *Admiral Porter*, 43.

9. Lewis, *Yankee Admiral*, 43.

10. Soley, *Admiral Porter*, 48–49; West, *Second Admiral*, 34–35.

11. Soley, *Admiral Porter*, 48–49; West, *Second Admiral*, 35.

12. Porter, *Memoir of Commodore Porter*, 425–26; Long, *Nothing Too Daring*, 302–5; Lewis, *Yankee Admiral*, 49–51. Soley, *Admiral Porter*, 77–79, gives an account of the early service records of the Porter family.

13. Benjamin F. Sands, *From Reefer to Rear Admiral* (New York: Stokes, 1899), 121–23; Soley, *Admiral Porter*, 50–51.

14. Porter, *Memoir of Commodore Porter*, 416–21; Turnbull, *Commodore Porter*, 312; West, *Second Admiral*, 38.

15. D. D. Porter to Evalina Porter, Oct. 28, [1843], Porter Papers, Naval History Section, New York Historical Society.

16. D. D. Porter to Evalina Porter, Oct. 18, 1845, ibid.

17. D. D. Porter to Evalina Porter, Oct. 16, [1845], ibid.; Senate to Evalina Porter, June 15, 1844, Porter Family Papers, LC; D. D. Porter to Evalina Porter, Apr. 5, 1860, ibid.; Long, *Nothing Too Daring*, 318.

THREE
Twenty Years of Indecision

1. Soley, *Admiral Porter*, 45; Lewis, *Yankee Admiral*, 57–60.
2. David D. Porter, "Secret Missions to Santo Domingo," *North American Review* 128 (July 1879): 616–17.
3. Paolo E. Coletta, *American Secretaries of the Navy*, 2 vols. (Annapolis, Md.: Naval Institute Press, 1980), 1:218–19; Soley, *Admiral Porter*, 46.
4. Porter, "Secret Missions," 618–30.
5. West, *Second Admiral*, 43.
6. Quoted in Soley, *Admiral Porter*, 59–60.
7. Ibid., 62–63; West, *Second Admiral*, 44.
8. Winfield Scott, *Memoirs of Lieut.-General Winfield Scott, LL.D., Written by Himself* (New York: Sheldon, 1864), 423–24.
9. West, *Second Admiral*, 46.
10. Soley, *Admiral Porter*, 65 70; Lewis, *Yankee Admiral*, 69–71.
11. For an account of the Veracruz campaign, see K. Jack Bauer, *The Mexican War, 1846–1848* (New York: Macmillan, 1974), 232–58.
12. Ibid., 337.
13. Porter Papers, 1842–1864, in his Mexican War Journal for June 11–20, 1847, LC.
14. Quoted in Lewis, *Yankee Admiral*, 74.
15. West, *Second Admiral*, 51–52.
16. Soley, *Admiral Porter*, 80; Coletta, *American Secretaries of the Navy*, 1:231, 233. Porter later commanded *Powhatan*, one of the four steamers built by Mason.
17. Lewis, *Yankee Admiral*, 81.
18. West, *Second Admiral*, 54.
19. F. Colburn Adams, *High Old Salts* (Washington, D.C.: Government Printing Office, 1876), 73.
20. Lewis, *Yankee Admiral*, 82–84.
21. The *New Orleans Daily Picayune* gives a full account of the "Crescent City Affair" in editions dated between Sept. 7 and Oct. 27, 1852.
22. Lewis, *Yankee Admiral*, 85–86.
23. Soley, *Admiral Porter*, 80–81; West, *Second Admiral*, 59–62.
24. Lewis, *Yankee Admiral*, 88.
25. Soley, *Admiral Porter*, 81–83; West, *Second Admiral*, 64–68; Porter's letters and reports on the camel expedition are published in *Senate Executive Document No. 62, 34th Congress, 3rd Session, 1856–57* (Washington, D.C.: Government Printing Office, 1857).
26. Porter to Heap, Apr. 15, 1858, Porter Papers (Memorial Collection), LC.
27. Soley, *Admiral Porter*, 84–86; Lewis, *Yankee Admiral*, 88–90.
28. Gideon Welles, *The Diary of Gideon Welles, Secretary of the Navy under Lincoln and Johnson*, 3 vols. (Boston: Houghton Mifflin, 1909–11), 2.255–56; David D. Porter, *Incidents and Anecdotes of the Civil War* (New York: Appleton, 1885), 7–10.

FOUR
Intrigue at the White House

1. Coletta, *American Secretaries of the Navy,* 1:315; Toucey to Walker, Jan. 7, 1861, and Walker to Toucey, Jan. 15, 1861, *Official Records of the Union and Confederate Navies in the War of the Rebellion,* 30 vols. (Washington, D.C.: Government Printing Office, 1894–1922), ser. 1, vol. 4:220, 221 (hereafter cited as *ORN,* with series 1 implied unless otherwise stated).

2. Allan Nevins, *The Emergence of Lincoln,* 2 vols. (New York: Scribner, 1950), 2:100–112.

3. Coletta, *American Secretaries of the Navy,* 1:321–23; See also John Niven, *Gideon Welles: Lincoln's Secretary of the Navy* (New York: Oxford University Press, 1973), chapters 12–13, 16–18.

4. Porter, *Incidents,* 13–14.

5. Fox to Scott, Feb. 8, 1861, *ORN,* 4:223; Welles, *Diary,* 1:14.

6. Porter, *Incidents,* 14–15; Welles to Mercer, Mar. 28, 1861, *ORN,* 4:227.

7. Lincoln to Seward, Porter, Mercer, and Breese, Apr. 1, 1861, *ORN,* 4:108–9.

8. Porter, *Incidents,* 16.

9. Welles to Breese, Apr. 1, 1861, *ORN,* 4:229.

10. Welles, *Diary,* 1:19, 35–36.

11. Lincoln to Welles, Apr. 1, 1862, ibid., 1:16–18, 36.

12. West, *Second Admiral,* 82.

13. Lincoln's Order, Apr. 1, 1861, *ORN,* 4:108.

14. Welles to Mercer, Mar. 28, and Welles to Breese, Apr. 2, 1861, ibid., 4:227, 230.

15. Porter, *Incidents,* 18.

16. Foote to Welles, Apr. 4, 1861, *ORN,* 4:234.

17. Welles to Foote and Mercer, and Foote to Welles, Apr. 5, 1861, ibid., 4:234, 235, 236, 237.

18. Welles to Foote, and Porter to Foote, Apr. 5, 1861 (8:00 P.M.), ibid., 4:111, 237.

19. Welles, *Diary,* 1:23–25.

20. Foote to Welles, Apr. 6, 1861, *ORN,* 4:238–39.

21. Seward to Porter, Foote to Welles, and Roe to Foote, Apr. 6, 1861, ibid., 4:112, 239.

22. Porter to Seward, Apr. 6, 1861, ibid., 4:112.

23. Porter to Foote, Apr. 6, 1861, ibid., 4:112.

24. Porter, *Incidents,* 22.

25. *War of the Rebellion: A Compilation of the Official Records of the Union and Confederate Armies,* 130 vols. (Washington, D.C.: Government Printing Office, 1880–1901) (hereafter cited as *ORA,* with series 1 implied unless otherwise stated). See Powell to Maynadier, Jan. 6, 1861, *ORA,* 6:332.

26. Armstrong to Toucey, Jan. 25, 1861, *ORN,* 4:16–17; Slemmer's Report, Feb. 5, 1861, *ORA,* 1:334–41.

27. Toucey to Adams, Jan. 21, and Holt and Toucey to Adams and Slemmer, Jan. 29, 1861, *ORN,* 4:67, 74.

28. Welles to Adams, Apr. 6, 1861, and Worden to Fox, Sept. 20, 1865, ibid., 4:110, 111; Vogdes to Adams, Apr. 13, 1861, ibid., 4:116; J. H. Gilman, "With Slemmer in Pensacola Harbor," in *Battles and Leaders of the Civil War*, ed. Robert U. Johnson and Clarence C. Buel, 4 vols. (hereafter cited as *B&L*) (New York: Century, 1887–88), 1:26–32.
29. Brown to Bragg, Apr. 17, 1861, *ORA*, 1:380; Porter to Seward, Apr. 21, and Brown to Meigs, Apr. 17, 1861, *ORN*, 4:122–23.
30. Porter, *Incidents*, 23; Meigs to Porter, Apr. 17, 1861, *ORN*, 4:123.
31. Porter, *Incidents*, 24; Porter to Brown, and Brown to Porter, Apr. 18, 1861, *ORN*, 4:124.
32. Porter, *Incidents*, 27.
33. Porter to Brown, Apr. 28, and Brown to Townsend, May 2, 1861, *ORA*, 1:401–3.
34. Porter, *Incidents*, 28.
35. Welles to Porter, May 13, *ORN*, 4:166; Lincoln's Proclamation, Apr. 19, 1861, ibid., 4:156. On Apr. 27 Lincoln extended the blockade to include Virginia and North Carolina.
36. Adams to Bragg, May 13, and Bragg to Adams, May 14, 1861, ibid., 4:168
37. Niven, *Gideon Welles*, 356–57; *New York Times*, Apr. 21, 1861.
38. James R. Soley, *The Blockade and the Cruisers* (New York: Scribner, 1890), appendix A; McCauley to Welles, Apr. 25, 1861, *ORN*, 4:288; List and Stations of Vessel in Commission, *ORN*, 1:xv–xvi.
39. Robert M. Thompson and Richard Wainwright, eds., *Confidential Correspondence of Gustavus Vasa Fox, Assistant Secretary of the Navy, 1861–1865*, 2 vols. (Freeport, N.Y.: Books for Libraries, 1972), 2:79 (hereafter cited as *Fox Correspondence*).
40. Patricia L. Faust, ed. *Historical Times Illustrated: Encyclopedia of the Civil War* (New York: Harper & Row, 1986), 462.
41. Log of *Powhatan*, *ORN*, 4:208.

FIVE

The Chase

1. Log of *Powhatan*, *ORN*, 4:208; Poor to McKean, and Porter to Welles, May 30, 1861, ibid., 4:188–89, 191.
2. Moore to Andrews et al., May 28, 1861, ibid., 4:218.
3. Porter to Welles, June [?], 1861, ibid., 16:533–34.
4. J. Thomas Scharf, *History of the Confederate States Navy* (New York: Rogers & Sherwood, 1887), 88–90; Porter to Welles, June [?], 1861, *ORN*, 16:534.
5. Charles Grayson Summersell, *The Cruise of the C.S.S.* Sumter (Tuscaloosa: University of Alabama Press, 1965), 55–56. David Dixon Porter, *The Naval History of the Civil War* (New York: Sherman, 1886), 602.
6. Porter to Welles, June [?] and 19, 1861, *ORN*, 16:534, 563.

7. Poor to Welles, June 7, and Porter to Mervine, June 19, 1861, ibid., 16:528, 563.

8. Welles to Mervine, May 7, 14, 17, 1861, ibid., 16:519–20, 522, 523.

9. Mervine to Welles, May 23, June 27, 1861, ibid., 16:525, 561; Faust, *Historical Times Illustrated,* 489.

10. Raphael Semmes, *Memoirs of Service Afloat during the War between the States* (Baltimore: Kelly, Piet, 1869), 95–107; Summersell, *Cruise of the C.S.S. Sumter,* 43–45.

11. Porter to Mervine, July 4, 1861, *ORN,* 16:571–72.

12. Semmes, *Memoirs of Service Afloat,* 112–13; Poor to Mervine, June 30, 1861, *ORN,* 1:34; Journal of *Sumter,* June 30, 1861, ibid., 1:694.

13. Porter, *Naval History,* 605–6.

14. Porter to Mervine, July 4, 1861, *ORN,* 16:572.

15. Ibid., 16:571.

16. Journal of *Sumter, ORN,* 1:744; See Welles, Mervine, and McKean correspondence in *ORN,* 16:578, 579, 590, 597–602.

17. Journal of *Sumter,* July 25–28, Semmes to Ruhl, July 26, 1861, ibid., 1:624, 698–99.

18. *Fox Correspondence,* 2:73–79.

19. Welles to Mervine, July 8, 1861, *ORN,* 16:575.

20. Porter to Mervine, July 19, 1861, ibid., 16:601–2.

21. Porter to Mervine, Aug. 6, 1861, ibid., 16:614.

22. Porter to Welles, Aug. 13, 1861, ibid., 1:65.

23. Semmes to Mallory, July 26, 1861, ibid., 1:622–23.

24. Porter to Welles, no date, ibid., 1:83.

25. Porter, *Incidents,* 36.

26. Porter to Welles, Aug. 19, 1861, *ORN,* 1:68–69.

27. Porter to Welles, Aug. 23, and Welles to McLane, Aug. 27, 1861, ibid., 1:71–72, 73.

28. Semmes to Crol, July 17, and Log of *Sumter,* July 16–24, 1861, ibid., 1:621–22, 697–98; Semmes, *Memoirs of Service Afloat,* 148–50.

29. Porter to Welles, Aug. 30, and Porter to Crol, Aug. 30, 31, Sept. 1, 1861, *ORN,* 1:78–82.

30. Porter to Mervine, Oct. [?], 1861, ibid., 1:105.

31. Semmes to Mallory, Nov. 9, 1861, ibid., 1:633–34; Porter to Welles, Sept. 24, and Porter to Mervine, Oct. [?], 1861, ibid., 1:91–92, 105.

32. Porter to Mervine, Oct. [?], 1861, ibid., 1:106.

33. Porter, *Naval History,* 616; Semmes, *Memoirs of Service Afloat,* 207–16; Porter to Welles, Sept. 14, 1861, *ORN,* 1:91–92; Journal of *Sumter,* ibid., 1:710; Porter to Mervine, Oct. [?], 1861, ibid., 1:107.

34. Semmes to Mallory, Nov. 9, 1861, *ORN,* 1:635.

35. Porter to governor of Maranhão, Sept. 23, and Porter to Mervine, Oct. [?], 1861, ibid., 1:92–95, 107.

36. Porter to Mervine, Oct. [?], 1861, ibid., 1:108–9.

37. Journal of *Sumter,* Sept. 25–26, 1861, ibid., 1:711–12.

38. Journal of *Sumter,* Sept. 30, 1861, ibid., 1:712.

39. Porter, *Naval History,* 617.
40. Reference to Porter's promotion is in Pope's Report, Aug. 22, 1861, *ORN,* 16:643.
41. Fox to Mervine and McKean, Sept. 6, and Pope to McKean, Oct. 3, 13, 1861, ibid., 16:660, 696–97, 703–5; for a complete account of Pope's Run, see Chester G. Hearn, *The Capture of New Orleans, 1862* (Baton Rouge: Louisiana State University Press, 1995), 81–95.
42. Porter to McKean, Oct. 25, and McKean to Porter, Oct. 28, 1861, *ORN,* 16:750–51.
43. Pope to McKean, Oct. 13, ibid., 16:703–5; *New Orleans Daily Delta,* Oct. 13, 15, 1861.

SIX
Porter Picks a Flag Officer

1. Du Pont to Welles, Nov. 8, 11, 1861, *ORN,* 12:262–66; Daniel Ammen, "Du Pont and the Port Royal Expedition," *B&L,* 1:671–91.
2. Barnard to Welles, Jan. 28, 1862, *ORN,* 18:15–23.
3. *Fox Correspondence,* 2:80; Porter, *Incidents,* 63; West, *Second Admiral,* 113.
4. Gideon Welles, "Admiral Farragut and New Orleans," *The Galaxy: An Illustrated Magazine of Entertaining Reading* 12 (November 1871): 677.
5. Porter, *Incidents,* 64.
6. Ibid., 64–66; Soley, *Admiral Porter,* 138–39; West, *Second Admiral,* 114–15.
7. Welles, "Admiral Farragut," 677.
8. Montgomery Blair, "Opening the Mississippi," *The United Service: A Monthly Review of Military and Naval Affairs* 4 (January 1881): 38.
9. Fox to Welles, Aug. 12, 1871, Fox Papers, Henry E. Huntington Library and Art Gallery.
10. Porter to Fox, July 5, 14, 1861, *Fox Correspondence,* 2:73–80; Porter, *Incidents,* 65.
11. Welles, "Admiral Farragut," 677–78. After Welles and Fox died, Porter wrote: "In reference to Mr. Welles's narrative in the *Galaxy,* it would be charitable to suppose that age had impaired his memory, although his mind was vigorous to the last. I know his friends were disappointed when the above-mentioned article appeared. The ex-Secretary evidently wrote under a wrong impression, and was disingenuous, to use the mildest expression." Quoted in *Incidents,* 65; see Soley, *Admiral Porter,* 139–40.
12. Welles, "Admiral Farragut," 679.
13. Welles to Porter, Nov. 18, 1861, *ORN,* 18:3.
14. Welles, *Diary,* 2:116–17; Welles, "Admiral Farragut," 679–81; Blair, "Opening the Mississippi," 38; Soley, *Admiral Porter,* 140.
15. Welles, *Diary,* 2:117.
16. Blair, "Opening the Mississippi," 38; Porter, *Incidents,* 66; Soley, *Admiral Porter,* 141–46, gives a balanced account of Farragut's selection.

17. Welles, "Admiral Farragut," 682.

18. David D. Porter, "Private Journal of Occurrences during the Great War of the Rebellion, 1860–1865," 81, Porter Papers, LC (hereafter cited as "Journal"; all references are to volume 1).

19. Ibid.; David D. Porter, "The Opening of the Lower Mississippi," *B&L,* 2:26; Charles Lee Lewis, *David Glasgow Farragut: Our First Admiral* (Annapolis, Md.: Naval Institute Press, 1943), 12.

20. Welles to Farragut, Dec. 15, and Farragut to Welles, Dec. 17, 1861, *ORN,* 18:4; Blair, "Opening the Mississippi," 39.

21. Welles, "Admiral Farragut," 683.

22. Blair, "Opening the Mississippi," 38; Welles, "Admiral Farragut," 678.

23. Lewis, *Farragut,* 12; Welles to Farragut, Jan. 9, 1862, *ORN,* 18:5; also in Loyall Farragut, *The Life of David Glasgow Farragut, First Admiral of the U.S. Navy* (New York: Appleton, 1879), 208.

24. Faust, *Historical Times Illustrated,* 283.

25. Blair, "Opening the Mississippi," 39; *Fox Correspondence,* 2:82–100.

26. West, *Second Admiral,* 118–19.

27. Welles to Porter, Dec. 2, 1861, *ORN,* 18:3–4; Welles, *Diary,* 1:167.

28. Welles to Porter, Feb. 10, 1862, *ORN,* 18:25.

29. Porter, *Incidents,* 109–10.

30. Ibid., 110–12; Porter to Fox, Feb. 17, 1862, *Fox Correspondence,* 2:83.

31. Welles to Wainwright, Feb. 11, and Wainwright to Welles, Feb. 24, 1862, *ORN,* 18:26–27, 38; Porter to Welles, Feb. 28, Mar. 2, 1862, ibid., 18:42, 43; The mortar flotilla is listed in ibid., 18:25.

32. Porter to Welles, June 3, 1862, ibid., 18:376–77.

33. Farragut to Welles, Feb. 12, 15, 21, 1862, ibid., 18:28, 29, 33–34.

34. Porter to Welles, Mar. 13, 18, 1862, ibid., 18:64, 71–72; Fox to Porter, Mar. 11, 1862, *Fox Correspondence,* 2:84–89.

SEVEN

Porter's Bummers

1. *Fox Correspondence,* 2:84; Porter to Welles, Mar. 13, 1862, *ORN,* 18:64; Duncan to Devereaux, Sept. 17, 1861, *ORA,* 53:740–41; Smith to McKean, Sept. 20, 1861, *ORN,* 16:677–78.

2. Farragut to Welles, Feb. 21, 1862, *ORN,* 18:33–34.

3. Farragut to Craven, Feb. 22, Farragut to Welles, Mar. 14, and Farragut to Fox, Mar. 16, 1862, ibid., 18:35, 65, 67.

4. Bell to Farragut, Mar. 13, 1862, ibid., 18:62–63.

5. Farragut's General Order, Mar. [5], 1862, ibid., 18:48–49.

6. Farragut to Welles, Mar. 3, 6, 1862, ibid., 18:43–44, 49–50.

7. Farragut to Porter, Mar. 4, and Farragut to Fox, Mar. 5, 1862, ibid., 18:46, 47.

8. Farragut to Fox, Mar. 16, 1862, ibid., 18:67, 68; Log of *Hartford,* ibid., 18:717; Farragut to Welles, Mar. 18, 1862, ibid., 18:71.

9. Welles to Farragut, Mar. 12, 1862, ibid., 18:59.
10. Farragut to Fox, Mar. 5, 1862, ibid., 18:47.
11. *New Orleans Daily Delta*, Mar. 6, 1862.
12. Porter to Welles, Mar. 18, 1862, *ORN*, 18:71–72.
13. General Order No. 1, *ORA*, 6:704; Farragut, *Life of David Glasgow Farragut*, 212; Benjamin F. Butler, *Autobiography and Personal Reminiscences of Major-General Benj. F. Butler: Butler's Book* (Boston: Thayer, 1892), 355 (hereafter cited as *Butler's Book*).
14. Log of *Richmond*, *ORN*, 18:732.
15. Lovell's testimony, *ORA*, 6:556–59.
16. Farragut to Bailey, Mar. 28, 1862, *ORN*, 18:88.
17. *Fox Correspondence*, 2:90–91.
18. Ibid., 2:89 91.
19. Ibid., 1:310.
20. Ibid., 2:97–98; Porter, "Journal."
21. Farragut to Welles, Apr. 8, 1862, *ORN*, 18:109.
22. Duncan's Report, Apr. 30, 1862, *ORA*, 6:522–23.
23. Barnard's Memoir, Jan. 28, 1862, *ORN*, 18:15–23.
24. Porter's Report, Apr. 30, 1862, ibid., 18:362; Gerdes's Journal, Apr. 13–17, 1862, ibid., 18:423–24.
25. Porter's Report, Apr. 30, 1862, ibid., 18:362.
26. George W. Brown, "The Mortar Flotilla," in *Personal Recollections of the War of the Rebellion* (New York: New York Commandery, 1891), 175–76.
27. Porter's Report, Apr. 30, 1862, *ORN*, 18:362–63.
28. *Fox Correspondence*, 2:93; B. S. Osbon, ed., "The Cruise of the U.S. Flag-Ship *Hartford*, 1862–1863, From the Private Journal of William C. Holton," *Magazine of American History* 22, no. 3, extra no. 87 (1922): 19.
29. Porter's Report, Apr. 30, 1862, *ORN*, 18:363.
30. Bell's Diary, ibid., 18:693; Logs of *C. P. Williams* and *Seafoam*, ibid., 18:402, 421.
31. Duncan's Report, Apr. 30, 1862, *ORA*, 6:525.
32. Bell's Diary, *ORN*, 18:694.
33. Queen to Porter, May 3, 1862, ibid., 18:406–7.
34. Log of *Owasco*, ibid., 18:381.
35. Queen to Porter, May 3, 1862, and Log of *Arletta*, ibid., 18:407, 404.
36. Duncan's Report, Apr. 30, 1862, *ORA*, 6:525.
37. Porter's Report, Apr. 30, 1862, *ORN*, 18:364; David D. Porter, "Opening of the Lower Mississippi," *B&L*, 2:35.

EIGHT

Farragut Scores a Victory

1. *New Orleans Bee*, Apr. 19, 1862; *New Orleans Daily Delta*, Apr. 19, 1862.
2. *New Orleans True Delta*, Feb. 7, 1862; Lovell's Court of Inquiry, *ORA*, 6:578.
3. Kroehl to Welles, June 2, 1862, *ORN*, 18:428.

4. Bell's Diary, ibid., 18:694; Log of *Oneida*, ibid., 18:775–76.

5. Logs of *Maria J. Carlton* and *Norfolk Packet*, ibid., 18:410, 399.

6. Porter to Welles, Apr. 30, 1862, ibid., 18:365.

7. Smith to Porter, May 3, ibid., 18:398; Duncan's Report, Apr. 30, 1862, *ORA*, 6:525.

8. Benjamin F. Butler, *Private and Official Correspondence of General Benjamin F. Butler during the Period of the Civil War*, ed. Jesse A. Marshall, 5 vols. (Norwood, Mass.: privately published), 1:416.

9. *New Orleans True Delta*, Apr. 20, 1862.

10. Breese to Porter, Apr. 30, 1862, *ORN*, 18:413–14.

11. Logs of *Norfolk Packet* and *Hartford*, ibid., 18:399, 720; Porter to Welles, Apr. 30, 1862, ibid., 18:367.

12. Farragut's Report (Unfinished), Apr. 20, 1862, ibid., 18:136.

13. Porter's Proposition, ibid., 18:145–46.

14. Bell's Diary, ibid., 18:695.

15. Farragut's General Order, Apr. 20, 1862, ibid., 18:160.

16. Bell's Diary, ibid., 18:695–96; George B. Bacon, "One Night's Work, Apr. 20, 1862: Breaking the Chain for Farragut's Fleet at the Forts below New Orleans," *Magazine of American History* 15 (1886): 305–7.

17. Logs of *Hartford, Richmond, Sciota*, and *Iroquois, ORN*, 18:720, 738, 756, 800.

18. Investigation of the Navy, *ORN*, ser. 2, 1:519–21; Hearn, *Capture of New Orleans*, 204.

19. Duncan's Report, *ORA*, 6:526; See also Duncan-Mitchell correspondence in *ORN*, 18:329.

20. Porter to Welles, Apr. 30, 1862, *ORN*, 18:366.

21. Duncan to Pickett, Apr. 30, 1862, *ORA*, 6:526–27.

22. Albert Bigelow Paine, *A Sailor of Fortune: Personal Memories of Captain B. S. Osbon* (New York: Doubleday, 1906), 182.

23. Paine, *Sailor of Fortune*, 183–84.

24. Porter to Welles, Apr. 30, 1862, *ORN*, 18:367.

25. Farragut to Welles, May 6, 1862, and diagram of attack formation, ibid., 18:156, 166.

26. Farragut to Welles, May 6, and Porter to Welles, Apr. 30, 1862, ibid., 18:156, 367.

27. Farragut's prize cases, May 1, 1872, ibid., 18:252; Duncan to Pickett, Apr. 30, 1862, *ORA*, 6:527.

28. Paine, *Sailor of Fortune*, 190–91.

29. William B. Robertson, "The Water-Battery at Fort Jackson," *B&L*, 2:99–100; Porter, "Opening of the Lower Mississippi," *B&L*, 2:41–42.

30. George E. Belknap, ed., *Letters of Capt. Geo. Hamilton Perkins* (Concord, N.H.: Evans, 1886), 67–68.

31. Paine, *Sailor of Fortune*, 191.

32. Log of *Brooklyn, ORN*, 8:759; John Russell Bartlett, "The *Brooklyn* at the Passage of the Forts," *B&L*, 2:62–63.

33. Morris to Farragut, Apr. 28, and Craven to Mrs. Craven, May 16, 1862, *ORN,* 18:201, 197; Porter, "Opening of the Lower Mississippi," *B&L,* 2:43. Bartlett, "*Brooklyn* at the Passage," *B&L,* 2:62–65.

34. Russell to Farragut, Apr. 29, 1862, *ORN,* 18:24–25.

35. Caldwell to Farragut, Apr. 24, and Nichols to Farragut, Apr. 30, 1862, ibid., 18:225–27.

36. Boggs to Farragut, Apr. 29, 1862, ibid., 18:210–22; Beverley Kennon, "Fighting Farragut below New Orleans," *B&L,* 2:76–89.

37. Porter to Welles, Apr. 30, 1862, *ORN,* 18:368.

NINE

Surrender of the Lower Mississippi

1. A. F. Warley, "The Ram *Manassas* at the Passage of the New Orleans Forts," *B&L,* 2:91; Porter to Welles, Apr. 25, 1862, *ORN,* 18:357–58.

2. Guest to Porter, Apr. 28, 1862, *ORN,* 18:379.

3. Log of *Owasco,* ibid., 18:383; Smith to Porter, May 3, and Porter to Farragut, Apr. 25, 1862, ibid., 18:398, 143.

4. Farragut to Welles, May 6, and Farragut to Porter, Apr. 24, 1862, ibid., 18:158, 142.

5. Porter to Farragut, Apr. 25, 1862, ibid., 18:143.

6. Duncan's Report, Apr. 30, 1862, *ORA,* 6:529–30; movement of *Louisiana,* ibid., 6:546.

7. Duncan's Report, Apr. 30, ibid., 6:530; Porter to Higgins, Apr. 26, 1862, ibid., 6:543.

8. Albert Kautz, "Incidents of the Occupation of New Orleans," *B&L,* 2:91–94; Marion A. Baker, "Farragut's Demands for the Surrender of New Orleans," *B&L,* 2:95–99.

9. Higgins to Porter, Apr. 27, 1862, *ORA,* 6:543–44.

10. Duncan's Report, Apr. 30, 1862, ibid., 6:531.

11. Ibid., 6:531, 544.

12. Ibid., 6:531–32.

13. Mitchell to Mallory, Aug. 19, 1862, *ORN,* 18:298–99.

14. Porter, "Opening of the Lower Mississippi," *B&L,* 2:51. Mitchell's statement in *B&L,* 2:102, refers to Porter's account as exaggerated.

15. Porter to Welles, Apr. 30, 1862, *ORN,* 18:370–71.

16. Ibid., 18:371; Articles of Capitulation, ibid., 18:438.

17. Porter, "Opening of the Lower Mississippi," *B&L,* 2:52–53.

18. Mitchell to Mallory, Aug. 19, 1862, *ORN,* 18:300.

19. Barron's opinion, ibid., 319–20; also *ORN,* ser. 2, 1:431.

20. Butler, *Private and Official Correspondence,* 1:428; Butler to Stanton, Apr. 29, May 8, 1862, *ORA,* 6:504–5, 506; Phelps's Report, Apr. 30, 1862, ibid., 6:508–9.

21. Porter to Welles, Apr. 30, 1862, *ORN,* 18:372.

22. Ibid.; *B&L*, 2:75.
23. Butler to Stanton, Apr. 29, 1862, *ORA*, 6:505; Phelps's Report, Apr. 30, 1862, ibid., 6:509–10.
24. Porter to Welles, Apr. 30, 1862, *ORN*, 18:372–73; Gerdes's Report, n.d., ibid., 18:426–27.
25. See carpenters' reports and others, ibid., 18:169–227; Porter, "Opening of the Lower Mississippi," *B&L*, 2:54.
26. Fox to Porter, May 13, and Porter to Fox, June 2, 1862, *Fox Correspondence*, 2:101, 113.
27. Porter to Fox, May 10, 1862, ibid., 2:100.
28. Gideon Welles, "Admiral Farragut and New Orleans," *The Galaxy: An Illustrated Magazine of Entertaining Reading* 12 (December 1871): 827–28.
29. Welles to Porter, May 10, 1862, *ORN*, 18:374a.
30. Lincoln to Congress, May 14, and Welles to Farragut, July 31, 1862, ibid., 18:247–48.

TEN

On to Vicksburg

1. Roe's Diary, *ORN*, 18:772.
2. Butler to Stanton, May 8, 1862, *ORA*, 6:506.
3. Journal of *Richmond*, *ORN*, 18:743.
4. Welles to Farragut, Jan. 20, 25, 1862, ibid., 18:8, 9.
5. Farragut, *Life of Farragut*, 262.
6. Farragut to Porter, May 1, 2, 1862, *ORN*, 18:462–63, 464.
7. Porter, *Incidents*, 96.
8. Craven to his wife, June 3, 1862, *ORN*, 18:528–32; Logs of *Oneida* and *Iroquois*, ibid., 18:782, 801.
9. Craven to his wife, June 3, 1862, ibid., 18:534; Bell's Diary, ibid., 18:705–7.
10. Porter to Welles, May 10, ibid., 18:478–79; Arnold's Reports, May 10, 15, 1862, ibid., 18:479–80.
11. Fox to Porter, May 17, 1862, *Fox Correspondence*, 2:101–2; Fox to Farragut, May 16, 17, 1862, *ORN*, 18:498–99.
12. Porter to Fox, Apr. 8, May 10, 1862, *Fox Correspondence*, 2:97–98, 100.
13. Porter to Welles, May 10, 1862, *ORN*, 18:478–79.
14. Farragut to Welles, May 30, 1862, ibid., 18:521; Brown to Ruggles, May 29, June 4, 1862, ibid., 18:647–48; Farragut to Porter, May 31, June 3, 1862, ibid., 18:576, 580.
15. Lewis, *Farragut*, 92.
16. Porter to Farragut, June 3, 1862, *ORN*, 18:577.
17. Farragut to Welles, June 3, 5, 1862, ibid., 18:580–81.
18. Porter to Fox, June 17, 1862, *Fox Correspondence*, 2:117.
19. Porter to Farragut, June 16, 1862, *ORN*, 18:558–59.
20. Porter to Butler, June 9, 1862, *ORA*, 15:464.

21. Porter to Fox, June 12, 1862, *Fox Correspondence*, 2:121; Porter to Farragut, July 3, 1862, *ORN*, 18:638–39.
22. Craven to Farragut, June 22, 1862, *ORN*, 18:557; Bell's Diary, ibid., 18:710–11.
23. Lovell to Jones, Apr. 24, 27, 1862, ibid., 18:330, 331; Lovell to Pettus, Apr. 28, 1862, *ORA*, 6:653; Porter's sketch, July 26, 1862, *ORN*, 18:646.
24. Porter to Fox, June 21, 1862, Porter Papers, LC.
25. Porter to Craven, June 24, 1862, *ORN*, 18:571, 572.
26. Bell's Diary, ibid., 18:709; Farragut to Fox, June 12, 1862, *Fox Correspondence*, 1:316.
27. Samuel H. Lockett, "The Defense of Vicksburg," *B&L*, 3:484–85.
28. Porter to Farragut, July 3, and Farragut to Welles, July 2, 1862, *ORN*, 18:639, 609.
29. Log of *Brooklyn*, ibid., 18:762.
30. Bell's Diary, ibid., 18:711; Farragut's General Order, June 25, 1862, ibid., 18:586.
31. Journal of *Richmond*, ibid., 18:751; Bell's Diary, ibid., 18:713.
32. Richard S. West Jr., *Mr. Lincoln's Navy* (New York: Longmans Green, 1957), 189.
33. Porter to Farragut, July 3, 1862, *ORN*, 18:640.
34. Farragut to Craven, and Craven to Farragut, June 28, 1862, ibid., 18:595–97.
35. Farragut to Craven, Russell, and Preble, June 29, 1862, ibid., 18:599.
36. Craven's, Russell's, and Preble's Reports, June 30, 1862, ibid., 18:599–602.
37. Farragut to Craven, June 30, July 1, Craven to Farragut, July 1, and Farragut to Bell, July 1, 1862, ibid., 18:602–3, 605–6.
38. Bell's Diary, ibid., 18:714.
39. Porter to Farragut, July 3, 1862, ibid., 18:641–43.
40. Ibid., 18:642–43.
41. Farragut to Welles, July 7, 1862, ibid., 18:638.
42. Porter to Farragut, July 3, 1862, ibid., 18:641–42.
43. Porter to Fox, June 30, 1862, *Fox Correspondence*, 2:122–24.
44. Lockett, "Defense of Vicksburg," *B&L*, 3:483.

ELEVEN

An Unexpected Surprise

1. Faust, *Historical Times Illustrated*, 238–39; Warren D. Crandall and Isaac D. Newall, *History of the Ram Fleet and the Mississippi Marine Brigade* (St. Louis: Buschart Bros., 1907), 47–84.
2. Farragut to Davis, June 28, 1862, *ORN*, 18:589; Bell's Diary, ibid., 18:714; Farragut to Halleck, and Farragut to Welles, June 28, 1862, ibid., 18:590, 588.
3. Log of *Hartford*, ibid., 18:728; Journal of *Richmond*, ibid., 18:751; Farragut, *Life of David Glasgow Farragut*, 282–83.
4. Faust, *Historical Times Illustrated*, 206.
5. Halleck to Farragut, July 3, 1862, *ORN*, 17:593; Welles, *Diary*, 1:218.

6. Journal of *Richmond, ORN,* 18:751–52.

7. Welles to Farragut, July 5, and Farragut to Welles, July 6, 1862, ibid., 18:629, 630; Farragut to Porter, July 8, 1862, Porter Papers, LC; Farragut to Bell, July 9, 1862, *ORN,* 18:632.

8. Porter to Farragut, July 13, and Porter to Welles, July 26, 1862, *ORN,* 18:678–81, 644–45.

9. Porter to Fox, July 26, 1862, *Fox Correspondence,* 2:124–25.

10. Ibid.; for a description of the fight see *B&L,* 3:572–80, and for Davis's reluctance to engage *Arkansas* see the Farragut-Davis correspondence in *ORN,* 19:4–17.

11. West, *Second Admiral,* 163.

12. Ibid., 164–65; Welles to Porter, July 25, 1862, *ORN,* 19:90.

13. Fox to Porter, Aug. 4, 1862, *Fox Correspondence,* 2:126; Porter to Fox, Aug. 5, 1862, ibid., 2:127.

14. Soley, *Admiral Porter,* 231–32; Porter to Fox, Sept. 10, 1862, *Fox Correspondence,* 2:135–37.

15. Porter, *Incidents,* 199–200.

16. Fox to Porter, Sept. 6, and Porter to Fox, Sept. 10, 1862, *Fox Correspondence,* 2:135, 136.

17. William Porter to Welles, Aug. 1, 6, 11, 1862, *ORN,* 19:60–62, 117, 121–22; *New Orleans Picayune,* Aug. 9, 1862; Butler to Stanton, Aug. 10, 1862, *ORN,* 19:121; for a full account, see *B&L,* 3:572–80; Welles to William Porter, Sept. 22, 1862, *ORN,* 19:122–23.

18. Welles to Porter, Sept. 22, 1862, *ORN,* 23:373.

19. Porter, *Incidents,* 121–22; Welles to Porter, Oct. 1, 1862, *ORN,* 23:388.

20. Welles, *Diary,* 1:157–58.

21. Ibid., 1:158.

22. Porter, *Incidents,* 122–23; Porter, "Journal," 415.

23. Welles, *Diary,* 1:167; Secretary's Office Records, *ORN,* 23:396.

24. Porter to Evelina Porter, Oct. 7, 1862, Porter Papers, LC.

25. Davis to Welles, Oct. 15, 1862, *ORN,* 23:395.

TWELVE

Mobilizing the Mississippi Squadron

1. Porter to Fox, Oct. 12, 1862, *Fox Correspondence,* 2:137–38.

2. Statistical Data of *Signal, ORN,* ser. 2, 1:208–9; Soley, *Admiral Porter,* 239.

3. Statistical Data of *Choctaw* and *Lafayette, ORN,* ser. 2, 1:57–58, 124.

4. Davis to Welles, Oct. 15, 1862, *ORN,* 23:395.

5. Complete descriptions of each vessel are in Statistical Data of U.S. Ships, *ORN,* ser. 2, 1:32–228 passim; Davis's Report, Sept. 30, 1862, *ORN,* 23:386.

6. Secretary's Office Records, *ORN,* 23:396; Welles to Porter, Oct. 15, 1862, ibid., 23:417.

7. Ellet to Stanton, Apr. 19, 1862, ibid., 23:65; Faust, *Historical Times Illustrated,* 238–39.

8. Ellet to Porter, Dec. 4, Porter to Welles, Oct. 16, and Fox to Porter, Nov. 8, 1862, *ORN*, 23:532, 418, 469; Order transferring Ram Fleet, Oct. 1, 1862, ibid., 23:388–89.
9. Faust, *Historical Times Illustrated*, 796.
10. Porter to Fox, Oct. 17, 1862, *Fox Correspondence*, 2:140.
11. Soley, *Admiral Porter*, 247.
12. General Order No. 9, Oct. 20, 1862, *ORN*, 23:424–25, Porter to Fox, Oct. 21, 1862, *Fox Correspondence*, 2:142–43.
13. Secretary's Office Records, *ORN*, 23:396; Fox to Welles, Nov. 11, 1862, Welles Papers, LC.
14. Porter to Walke, Oct. 18, Winslow to Porter, Oct. 25, Meade to Porter, Oct. 21, and Porter to Welles, Oct. 27, 1862, *ORN*, 23:423, 447, 431, 451–52.
15. Porter to Fitch, Nov. 27, and Porter to Walke, Nov. 28, 1862, ibid., 23:508, 512.
16. West, *Second Admiral*, 179.
17. Stanton to McClernand, Oct. 21, 29, 1862, *ORA*, 17, pt. 2:282, 302.
18. William T. Sherman, *Memoirs of General W. T. Sherman*, 2 vols. (New York: Appleton, 1875), 1:309–10.
19. Porter to Fox, Nov. 12, 1862, *Fox Correspondence*, 2:150.
20. Grant to Halleck, Dec. 5, 1862, *ORA*, 17, pt. 1:472; Halleck to Grant, Dec. 7, and Grant to McClernand, Dec. 18, 1862, ibid., 17, pt. 2:473, 425.
21. Sherman to Porter, Dec. 8, 1862, ibid., 17, pt. 2:392.
22. Porter, "Journal," 429–30.
23. Ibid., 414, 424–26; Porter to Fox, Nov. 12, 1862, *Fox Correspondence*, 2:150.
24. Secretary's Office Records, *ORN*, 23:397, Porter to Walke, Nov. 21, and Porter to Sherman, Nov. 24, 1862, ibid., 23:495–96, 500–502.
25. Statistical Data, *ORN*, ser. 2, 1:46; Porter to Welles, Dec. 12, 1862, *ORN*, 23:542–43.
26. Porter, "Journal," 435–38, 467.
27. McClernand to Lincoln, Dec. 12, 17, 1862, *ORA*, 17, pt. 2:401, 420; General Order No. 210, Dec. 18, 1862, ibid., 17, pt. 2:432 33; Halleck to Grant, Dec. 18, and McClernand to Grant, Dec. 28, 1862, ibid., 17, pt. 2:461, 501–3.

THIRTEEN

The Chickasaw Bluffs Fiasco

1. Van Dorn to Pemberton, Dec. 20, 1862, *ORA*, 17, pt. 1:503; Pemberton's Report, Feb. [?], 1863, *ORN*, 23:611. Forty-eight-year-old John C. Pemberton, a West Pointer from Philadelphia who adopted the South, was a slender, austere, stern, and tough-minded individual who had seen service in twenty different military posts. Faust, *Historical Times Illustrated*, 569.
2. Forrest to Bragg, Dec. 24, 1862, Faust, *Historical Times Illustrated*, 593–95; Samuel Carter III, *The Final Fortress: The Campaign for Vicksburg, 1862–1863* (New York: St. Martin's, 1980), 94–95.
3. Selfridge to Walke, Dec. 13, 1862, *ORN*, 23:548–50.

4. Thomas O. Selfridge Jr., *Memoirs of Thomas O. Selfridge, Jr., Rear Admiral, U.S.N.* (New York: Putnam, 1924), 116–17; Porter to Selfridge, Dec. 17, 1862, *ORN,* 23:556.

5. Porter to Welles, Dec. 17, 1862, *ORN,* 23:544.

6. Frank Moore, ed., *The Rebellion Record: A Diary of American Events,* 12 vols. (New York: D. Van Nostrand, 1862–69), 6:310; *New York Times,* Jan. 19, 1863, 1.

7. Moore, *Rebellion Record,* 6:297; William Howard Russell, *My Diary North and South* (London: Bradley & Evans, 1863), 299.

8. Brown to Pemberton, Dec. 8, 1862, *ORA,* 17, pt. 2:788; Walke to Porter, Dec. 1, 1862, *ORN,* 23:522.

9. Porter to Welles, Dec. 27, 1862, *ORN,* 23:572–74.

10. Sherman, *Memoirs,* 1:319; Sherman's Report, *ORA,* 18, pt. 1:608; Blair's Report, Dec. 30, 1862, ibid., 18, pt. 1:655–66.

11. Sherman's Report, Jan. 3, 1863, *ORA,* 17, pt. 1:606–9.

12. Earl Schenck Miers, *The Web of Victory* (New York: Knopf, 1955), 62, 67.

13. Ellet's Report, Jan. 3, 1863, *ORA,* 17, pt. 1:662–63.

14. Porter to Sherman, Dec. 30, 1862, *ORN,* 23:588.

15. Porter to Welles, Jan. 3, 1863, ibid., 23:604–5.

16. Sherman to Halleck, Jan. 5, 1863, *ORA,* 17, pt. 1:613; Return of casualties, ibid., 17, pt. 1:625.

17. Porter to Sherman, Jan. 1, and Porter to Welles, Jan. 3, 1863, *ORN,* 23:597, 605.

18. Sherman to Rawlins, Jan. 3, 1863, *ORA,* 17, pt. 1:610; Curtis to Meigs, Jan. 3, 1863, ibid., 22, pt. 2:11; Sherman to Porter, Jan. 3, 1863, ibid., 23:606.

19. Sherman, *Memoirs,* 1:324–25; Porter, *Incidents,* 130–31.

20. Soley, *Admiral Porter,* 262–63.

21. General Order No. 1, Jan. 4, 1863, *ORA,* 17, pt. 2:534.

22. Halleck to Grant, Jan. 7, 1863, ibid., 17, pt. 2:542.

23. Welles, *Diary,* 1:218; *Cincinnati Daily Commercial,* Jan. 15, 1863.

24. Grant to Sherman, and McClernand to Grant, Jan. 8, 1863, *ORA,* 17, pt. 2:548, 546–47.

25. Grant to Halleck, Jan. 11, 1863, ibid., 17, pt. 2:553.

26. Grant to McClernand, Jan. 11, and Halleck to Grant, Jan. 12, 1863, ibid., 17, pt. 2:553–54, 555.

FOURTEEN

McClernand's "Wild Goose Chase"

1. Porter to Welles, Jan. 11, 1863, *ORN,* 24:107; Moore, *Rebellion Record,* 6:370.

2. Porter's Order, Jan. 7, 1863, *ORN,* 24:100.

3. McClernand's Report, Jan. 20, 1863, *ORA,* 17, pt. 1:705; see also 760–62.

4. Porter's Orders, Jan. 10, 1863, *ORN,* 24:104; Walker to Porter, Jan. 12, 1863, ibid., 24:109.
5. Porter to Welles, Jan. 11, 1863, ibid., 24:107; Churchill's Report, May 6, 1863, *ORA,* 17, pt. 1:780.
6. Porter to Welles, Jan. 11, 1863, *ORN,* 24:107–8.
7. Ibid.; Porter to Welles, Jan. 12, 1863, ibid., 24:116.
8. Morgan's Report, Jan. 17, 1863, *ORA,* 17, pt. 1:723.
9. Sherman's Report, Jan. 13, 1863, ibid., 17, pt. 1:756.
10. Porter to Welles, Jan. 13, 1863, *ORN,* 24:119.
11. Porter to Welles, Jan. 11, 1863, ibid., 24:107–8.
12. Porter, "Journal," 482.
13. Sherman's Report, Jan. 13, and Churchill's Report, May 6, 1863, *ORA,* 17, pt. 1:756, 781.
14. Reports to Porter, Jan. 22, 1863, *ORN,* 24:109–17.
15. Porter to Grimes, Jan. 24, 1863, ibid., 24:194; Sherman, *Memoirs,* 1:329; Union returns, *ORA,* 17, pt. 1:716–19; Churchill's Report, Jan. 12, and McClernand's Report, Jan. 20, 1863, ibid., 17, pt. 1:782, 708.
16. Porter to Welles, Jan. 28, 1863, *ORN,* 24:127; Sherman, *Memoirs,* 1:302–3.
17. Grant to Halleck, Jan. 11, 1863, *ORN,* 24:106.
18. Grant to Halleck, Jan. 14, 1863, ibid., 24:165–66.
19. Porter to McClernand, Porter to Walker, and Grant to Porter, Jan. 12, 1863, ibid., 24:151–52, 153, 149.
20. Porter to Welles, Jan. 16, and Pennock to Welles, Jan. 23, 1863, ibid., 24:154, 155–56.
21. Porter to Walker, Jan. 19, and Porter to Welles, Jan. 26, 1863, ibid., 24:158, 159.
22. McClernand to Lincoln, Jan. 16, 1863, *ORA,* 17, pt. 2:566–67.
23. Porter to Fox, Jan. 16, 1863, *Fox Correspondence,* 2:154–55.
24. Grant to Halleck, Jan. 20, and Grant to Kelton, Feb. 1, 1863, *ORA,* 24, pt. 1:8–9, 11.
25. Porter's Report, Jan. 16, 1863, *ORN,* 24:172–73.
26. Porter to Grimes, Jan. 24, 1863, ibid., 24:195.
27. Porter to Smith, and Smith to Porter, Jan. 27, 1863, ibid., 24:203–4.
28. Fox to Porter, Feb. 6, 1863, *Fox Correspondence,* 2:157.

FIFTEEN

Convolutions in the Delta

1. Stevenson to Lovell, Jan. 25, 1863, *ORA,* 24, pt. 3:604.
2. Sherman, *Memoirs,* 1:304–5.
3. Ulysses S. Grant, *Personal Memoirs of U. S. Grant,* 2 vols. (New York: Webster, 1885–86), 1:445–46. Williams' Canal has been variously called Butler's Ditch, De Soto Canal, and Young's Point Canal.

4. Porter to Welles, Jan. 28, 1863, *ORN,* 24:204–5; Pemberton to Moore, Jan. 25, 1863, *ORA,* 24, pt. 3:608.

5. Grant to Halleck, Mar. 7, 1863, *ORA,* 24, pt. 1:19–20.

6. Grant to Porter, and Porter to Smith, Jan. 30, 1863, *ORN,* 24:211–12.

7. Duff to Rawlins, Feb. 3, 1863, *ORA,* 24, pt. 1:15–16; Grant to McPherson, Feb. 5, and Sherman to Grant, Feb. 4, 1863, ibid., 24, pt. 3:33, 32.

8. Brown to Porter, Feb. 3, and Porter to Welles, Feb. 7, 1863, *ORN,* 24:228, 321.

9. Alfred T. Mahan, *The Gulf and Inland Waters* (New York: Scribner, 1901), 124; Porter to Ellet, Feb. 1–2, 1863, *ORN,* 19:217–18.

10. Porter to Welles, Feb. 2, 8, Ellet to Porter, Feb. 2, 1863, *ORN,* 19:220–22, 219–20.

11. Brown to Porter, Feb. 7, 1863, ibid., 19:251.

12. Porter to Smith, Feb. 6, 1863, ibid., 19:244; Wilson to Totten, Apr. 9, 1863, *ORA,* 24, pt. 1:388.

13. Wilson to Grant, June 18, 1863, *ORA,* 24, pt. 1:390; Smith to Porter, Nov. 2, 1863, *ORN,* 24:245.

14. Brown to Pemberton, Feb. 9, 17, 1863, *ORN,* 24:294, 295.

15. Loring to Pemberton, Feb. 21, 1863, ibid., 24:296; Loring to Memminger, Mar. 22, 1863, *ORA,* 24, pt. 1:415. Fort Pemberton was also called Greenwood or Fort Greenwood, for a nearby village.

16. Smith to Porter, Mar. 2, Nov. 2, 1863, *ORN,* 24:247, 273–74.

17. Pemberton to Fuller, Apr. 7, 1863, *ORA,* 24, pt. 3:721–22; Smith to Porter, Mar. 22, 1863, *ORN,* 24:285; Porter, "Journal," 532.

18. Foster to Porter, Mar. 18, 1863, *ORN,* 24:284; Quinby to McPherson, Mar. 21, 1863, *ORA,* 24, pt. 1:407.

19. Foster to Porter, Apr. 13, 1863, *ORN,* 24:283.

20. Porter to Welles, Mar. 26, Apr. 13, 1863, ibid., 24:281–82.

21. Wilson to Rawlins, Mar. 13, and Wilson to Grant, Mar. 16, 1863, *ORA,* 24, pt. 1:379, 383.

22. Welles, *Diary,* 1:247.

23. The Steele's Bayou route was about 130 miles.

24. Porter to Welles, Mar. 26, and Grant to Sherman, Mar. 16, 1863, *ORN,* 24:474, 481.

25. Grant to McPherson, Mar. 16, and Grant to Porter, Mar. 21, 1863, *ORA,* 24, pt. 3:112, 123.

26. Private Journal of an officer on *Cincinnati, ORN,* 24:493.

27. Ibid., 24:493–94; Porter to Welles, Mar. 26, 1863, ibid., 24:474.

28. Sherman, *Memoirs,* 1:308.

29. Porter to Welles, Mar. 26, 1863, *ORN,* 24:475.

30. Porter, *Incidents,* 149–50.

31. Stevenson to Maury, Mar. 29, 1863, *ORA,* 24, pt. 1:455; Lee's Report, Mar. 30, 1863, ibid., 24, pt. 1:461.

32. Porter to Welles, Mar. 26, 1863, *ORN,* 24:476; Private Journal of an officer on *Cincinnati,* ibid., 24:494.

33. Porter to Sherman, Mar. 19, 1863, ibid., 24:486–87.

34. Porter to Welles, Mar. 26, 1863, ibid., 24:476–77.
35. Stuart's Report, Mar. 29, 1863, *ORA*, 24, pt. 1:437–38.
36. Sherman's Report, Mar. 21, 1863, ibid., 24, pt. 1:432–33.
37. Sherman to Porter, Mar. 20, 1863, ibid., 24, pt. 1:457.
38. Log of *Louisville*, *ORN*, 24:698; Smith's Report, Mar. 28, 1863, *ORA*, 24, pt. 1:439.
39. Featherston's Report, Apr. 3, 1863, *ORA*, 24, pt. 1:459.
40. Log of *Louisville*, *ORN*, 24:698.
41. Sherman, *Memoirs*, 1:309–10.
42. Porter, *Incidents*, 168; Porter, "Journal," 562–63.
43. Porter to Welles, Mar. 26, 1863, *ORN*, 24:477; Porter's General Order, Mar. 21, 1863, ibid., 24:488–89.
44. Pennock to Welles, Mar. 24, 1863, ibid., 24:512.
45. Porter to Welles, Mar. 26, 1863, ibid., 24:478–79.
46. Soley, *Admiral Porter*, 311.
47. Welles to Porter, Apr. 2, 1863, *ORN*, 24:522.

SIXTEEN

Chaos on the River

1. Porter to Ellet, Feb. 2, 1863, *ORN*, 24:217–18, 221–22; Ellet's Report, Feb. 5, 1863, *ORA*, 24, pt. 1:337–38; Ferguson to Pemberton, Feb. 3, 1863, ibid., 24, pt. 3:615.
2. Ellet's Report, Feb. 5, 1863, *ORA*, 24, pt. 1:338.
3. Ibid.; Porter to Welles, Feb. 6, 1863, *ORN*, 24:223.
4. Gardner to Waddy, Feb. 5, and Sibley to Gardner, Feb. 4, 1863, *ORA*, 24, pt. 1:339.
5. Ellet to Porter, Feb. 6, 7, 8, 1863, *ORN*, 24:372–74.
6. Porter to Ellet, Feb. 8, 10, 1863, ibid., 24:374, 370.
7. Statistical Data, *ORN*, ser. 2, 1:107; Ellet to Porter, Feb. 21, 1863, *ORN*, 1:383–84.
8. Ellet to Porter, Feb. 21, 1863, *ORN*, 1:384.
9. Ibid., 1:384–86; see also H. Allen Gosnell, *Guns on the Western Waters: The Story of River Gunboats in the Civil War* (Baton Rouge: Louisiana State University Press, 1949), 183–88.
10. Mahan, *Gulf and Inland Waters*, 128.
11. Brown to Porter, Feb. 18, and Porter to Brown, Feb. 12, 1863, *ORN*, 24:377–78, 376–77.
12. Brown to Porter, Feb. 18, 1863, ibid., 24:378; Gosnell, *Guns on the Western Waters*, 190.
13. Statistical Data, *ORN*, ser. 2, 1:271; Lovell to Pemberton, Feb. 28, 1863, *ORA*, 24, pt. 1:345–46.
14. Brown to Porter, Feb. 18, 1863, *ORN*, 24:378–79.
15. Porter to Welles, Feb. 22, 1863, ibid., 24:382–83.

16. Ibid.; Porter to Welles, Feb. 23, 1863, ibid., 24:383.

17. Brown to Welles, May 28, 1863, ibid., 24:379–80.

18. Brand to Gardner, Feb. 26, 1863, *ORA*, 24, pt. 1:363.

19. Brent's Report, Feb. 25, 1863, ibid., 24, pt. 1:364.

20. Brown to Welles, May 28, 1863, *ORN*, 24:380.

21. Brent's Report, Feb. 25, 1863, *ORA*, 24, pt. 1:365–68; Brand to Gardner, Feb. 26, 1863, ibid., 24, pt. 1:363–64; Brown to Welles, May 28, 1863, *ORN*, 24:380–81.

22. Porter to Welles, Feb. 27, and Welles to Porter, Mar. 2, 1863, *ORN*, 24:388.

23. Adams to Reeve, Mar. 1, 1863, ibid., 24:411.

24. Porter to Welles, Mar. 7, 1863, ibid., 24:389; Porter, *Incidents,* 134; Gosnell, *Guns on the Western Waters,* 199–200.

25. Porter to Welles, Mar. 12, 1863, Porter Papers, LC; Brand to Gardner, Feb. 26, 1863, and Pemberton to Stevenson, Feb. 27, 1863, *ORN*, 24:409.

26. Adams to Reeve, Mar. 1, 1863, and Porter to Welles, Feb. 27, 1863, ibid., 24:411, 391.

27. Porter to Welles, Mar. 10, 1863, ibid., 24:397.

28. *Richmond Examiner,* Mar. 12, 1863.

29. Porter to Fox, Apr. 16, 1863, *Fox Correspondence,* 2:166.

30. Sherman to Woods, Feb. 27, 1863, *ORA*, 24, pt. 3:70.

31. Walke to Porter, Mar. 6, 1863, ibid., 24, pt. 3:460; Statistical Data, *ORN*, ser. 2, 1:124.

32. Pennock to Welles, Feb. 9, Phelps to Porter, Feb. 5, Smith to Porter, Feb. 10, and Simonds to Porter, Feb. 18, 1863, *ORN*, 24:308, 312, 337, 423.

33. Porter to Grant, Feb. 14, Porter to Gorman, Feb. 15, Grant to Porter, Feb. 15, and Porter to Welles, Mar. 7, 1863, ibid., 24:341–42, 344, 342, 462.

SEVENTEEN
Another Gauntlet to Run

1. Farragut to Welles, Mar. 19, 1863, *ORN*, 20:3–4.

2. Porter, "Journal," 551.

3. Farragut to Grant, Mar. 22, and Ellet to Walke, Mar. 24, 1863, *ORN*, 20:9, 16.

4. Farragut to Grant, and Grant to Steele, Mar, 23, 1863, *ORA*, 24, pt. 3:132, 133; Ellet to C. R. Ellet, Mar, 24, 1863, *ORN*, 20:17.

5. Ellet's Report, Mar. 25, 1863, *ORN*, 20:18–22.

6. Farragut to Grant, Mar. 25, 1863, *ORA*, 24, pt. 3:143.

7. Porter to Ellet, and Ellet to Porter, Mar. 25, 1863, *ORN*, 20:23.

8. Farragut to Porter, Mar. 25, and Porter to Farragut, Mar. 26, 1863, ibid., 20:24–25, 29.

9. Farragut to Porter, Mar. 30, 1863, ibid., 20:39.

10. Fox to Porter, Apr. 6, 1863, ibid., 24:533.

11. Halleck to Grant, Apr. 2, 1863, *ORA*, 24, pt. 1:25.

12. Grant to Porter, and Porter to Grant, Mar. 29, 1863, ibid., 24, pt. 3:151–52.

13. Grant to Porter, Apr. 1, ibid., 24, pt. 3:168; Porter to Welles, Apr. 6, 1863, *ORN,* 24:520.

14. Welles to Porter, Apr. 15, 1863, *ORN,* 24:552.

15. Grant to Porter, Apr. 2, 1863, ibid., 24:521.

16. Porter to Welles, Apr. 6, 19, 1863, ibid., 24:532, 553; Porter to Fox, Apr. 25, 1863, *Fox Correspondence,* 2:172–73.

17. Porter's General Order, Apr. 10, 1863, *ORN,* 24:554–55.

18. *Vicksburg Whig,* Apr. 16, 1863; Pemberton to Stevenson, Apr. 11, 1863, *ORA,* 24, pt. 3:73; Grant, *Memoirs,* 1:461.

19. Stevenson to Pemberton, Apr. 13, 1863, *ORA,* 24, pt. 3:740.

20. Porter to Fox, Apr. 16, 1863, *Fox Correspondence,* 2:168.

21. James H. Wilson, *Under the Old Flag,* 2 vols. (New York: Appleton, 1912), 1:163–64.

22. Sherman, *Memoirs,* 1:317.

23. Porter, *Incidents,* 175–76; Log of *Benton, ORN,* 24:682.

24. Robert S. Henry, *The Story of the Confederacy* (New York: Garden City, 1931), 253; Grant, *Memoirs,* 1:463–64.

25. Greer to Porter, Apr. 17, 1863, *ORN,* 24:555–56; Porter, "Journal," 569.

26. Walke to Porter, Apr. 17, 1863, *ORN,* 24:557–58; Henry Walke, *Naval Scenes and Reminiscences of the Civil War in the United States* (New York: Reed, 1877), 354.

27. Porter to Fox, Apr. 17, 1863, *Fox Correspondence,* 2:169.

28. Owen to Porter, Apr. 17, 1863, *ORN,* 24:558; Log of *Louisville,* ibid., 24:698.

29. Wilson to Porter, Apr. 17, 1863, ibid., 24:559; Log of *Mound City,* ibid., 24:701.

30. Hoel to Porter, and Murphy to Porter, Apr. 17, 1863, ibid., 24:560, 561.

31. Shirk to Porter, Apr. 17, 1863, ibid., 24:562–64; Log of *Tuscumbia,* ibid., 24.704.

32. Sherman, *Memoirs,* 1:318; Sherman to Rawlins, Apr. 19, 1863, *ORA,* 24, pt. 3.207–8; Porter, *Incidents,* 177.

33. Charles A. Dana, *Recollections of the Civil War* (New York: Appleton, 1898), 36–37.

34. Porter to Welles, Apr. 19, 1863, *ORN,* 24:554; Porter, *Naval History,* 311.

35. McClernand to Grant, Apr. 17, 1863, *ORA,* 24, pt. 3:200.

36. Pemberton to Cooper, Apr. 17, and Pemberton to Davis and Chalmers, Apr. 18, 1863, *ORN,* 24:566–67, 717.

37. Grant to McClernand, Apr. 20, and Sherman to Grant, Apr. 21, 1863, *ORA,* 24, pt. 3:212, 216; Dana to Stanton, Apr. 20, 22, ibid., 24, pt. 1:77–79.

38. Grant to Porter, Apr. 21, 1863, ibid., 24, pt. 3:215.

39. Oliver to Lagow, and Fisk to Lagow, Apr. 24, 1863, ibid., 24, pt. 1:565–66, 567–68.

40. Oliver to Lagow, Apr. 24, 1863, ibid., 24, pt. 1:565–66.

41. Ibid.; Thomas to Stanton, Apr. 23, 1863, ibid., 24, pt. 1:564–65.

42. Fisk to Lagow, n.d., ibid., 24, pt. 1:567–68.

43. Kennard to Lagow, Apr. 23, 1863, ibid., 24, pt. 1:568–69.

44. Porter to McClernand, Apr. 22, 1863, ibid., 24, pt. 3: 222.

EIGHTEEN

A King's Reward

1. Porter to Grant, Apr. 20, 1863, _ORA,_ 24, pt. 3:211; Porter to Welles, May 3, 1863, _ORN,_ 24:627; Porter to Fox, Apr. 25, 1863, _Fox Correspondence,_ 2:176.

2. Log of _Lafayette, ORN,_ 24:682–83; Walke, _Naval Scenes and Reminiscences,_ 366.

3. McClernand to Osterhaus, Apr. 22, 1863, _ORA,_ 24, pt. 3:221.

4. Porter to McClernand, Apr. 23, 1863, ibid., 24, pt. 3:225–26.

5. McClernand to Grant, Apr. 24, 1863, ibid., 24, pt. 3:228.

6. Dana to Stanton, Apr. 24, 1863, ibid., 24, pt. 1:79.

7. Dana to Stanton, Apr. 25, 1863, ibid., 24, pt. 1:80; Grant to Sherman, Apr. 24, 1863, ibid., 24, pt. 3:231.

8. Porter to Welles, Apr. 24, 1863, _ORN,_ 24:606–7.

9. Dana to Stanton, Apr. 27, 1863, _ORA,_ 24, pt. 1:81.

10. Dana to Stanton, Apr. 25, 27, 28, 1863, ibid., 24, pt. 1:80–82; Grant to McClernand, Apr. 27, 1863, ibid., 24, pt. 3:237–38.

11. Porter's General Order, Apr. 27, 1863, _ORN,_ 24:607–9.

12. Bowen to Memminger, Apr. 27, Bowen to Pemberton, Apr. 28, and Pemberton to Bowen, Apr. 28, 1863, _ORA,_ 24, pt. 3:792–93, 797, 800.

13. Porter's General Order, Apr. 27, 1863, _ORN,_ 24:607–9.

14. Grant, _Memoirs,_ 1:475–76; Dana, _Recollections,_ 30–34.

15. Bowen to Pemberton, Apr. 29, 1863, _ORA,_ 24, pt. 1:575.

16. Porter, "Journal," 591; Porter's Report, Apr. 29, and Shirk's Report, Apr. 30, 1863, _ORN,_ 24:610–11, 620; Walke, _Naval Scenes and Reminiscences,_ 375.

17. Grant, _Memoirs,_ 1:476; Porter's Report, Apr. 29, 1863, _ORN,_ 24:611.

18. See various captains' reports in _ORN,_ 24:611–28; Shirk to Porter, May 2, 1863, ibid., 24:659.

19. Bowen to Pemberton, Apr. 29, 1863, ibid., 24:632.

20. Porter to Welles, Apr. 29, 1863, ibid., 24:611; Mahan, _Gulf and Inland Waters,_ 161–62.

21. Porter, _Incidents,_ 181–82.

22. Grant, _Memoirs,_ 1:458; Dana to Stanton, Apr. 30, 1863, _ORA,_ 24, pt. 1:83; Log of _Benton, ORN,_ 24:682.

23. McClernand's Report, June 17, 1863, _ORA,_ 24, pt. 1:143–46.

24. Porter, _Naval History,_ 316.

25. Porter to Welles, May 3, 7, 1863, _ORN,_ 24:626–27, 645.

26. Porter to Welles, May 7, 1863, ibid., 24:645.

27. Banks's Report, Apr. 6, 1865, _ORA,_ 26, pt. 1:11–12.

28. Porter to Welles, May 13, Porter to Walke, May 12, 1863, _ORN,_ 24:647, 651.

29. Owen to Porter, May 10, 1863, ibid., 24:665.

30. Porter to Welles, May 15, 1863, ibid., 24:664.

31. Brown to Porter, May 31, 1863, Officers' Letters, Mississippi Squadron, Naval Records and Library.

32. Porter to Foote, May 16, 1863, *ORN*, 24:677–78.

33. Grant to Sherman, Apr. 27, 1863, ibid., 24:591.

34. Breese to Porter, May 2, 1863, ibid., 24:589–91; Breese's General Orders, Apr. 30, May 1, 1863, ibid., 24:595.

35. Hebert's Report, May 4, 1863, *ORA*, 24, pt. 1:577–78.

36. Ramsey to Breese, May 3, 1863, *ORN*, 24:593; Log of *Choctaw*, ibid., 24:695–96.

37. Grant to Sherman, Apr. 29, 1863, *ORA*, 24, pt. 3:246; Breese to Porter, May 2, 1863, *ORN*, 24:590.

38. Porter to Hurlbut, May 18, 1863, *ORA*, 24, pt. 3:325.

39. Porter to Welles, May 20, 24, and Walker to Porter, June 1, 1863, *ORN*, 25:5–6, 7–8, 133–34.

40. Porter to Welles, May 23, 1863, ibid., 25:22.

41. Grant to Porter, May 22, and Porter to Sherman, May 25, 1863, ibid., 25:31, 39.

42. Bache to Porter, May 29, 1863, ibid., 25:42–43.

43. Porter to Welles, May 27, 1863, ibid., 25:38; Dana to Stanton, June 5, 1863, *ORA*, 24, pt. 1:93.

44. Sherman to Grant, June 2, 1863, *ORN*, 25:56; see also *ORA*, 24, pt. 3:372.

45. Walker to Porter, June 1, 1863, ibid., 25:133–34.

46. Ellet to Porter, June 24, July 9, and Porter to Welles, June 18, 1863, ibid., 25:77–80, 175.

47. Porter to Grant, June 7, 1863, ibid., 25:164–65.

48. Porter to Welles, June 9, 1863, ibid., 25:66.

49. Porter to Greer, and Porter to Woodworth, June 16, 21, 1863, ibid., 25:72, 86–87; Porter's General Order, June 23, 1863, ibid., 25:91–92.

50. Porter to Welles, June 20, 1863, ibid., 25:83.

51. Porter to Grant, June 28, 1863, *ORA*, 24, pt. 3:447; Woodworth to Porter, June 29, 1863, *ORN*, 25:99.

52. Many Soldiers to Pemberton, June 28, 1863, ibid., 25:188–89.

53. Grant to Porter, July 3, 1863, ibid., 25:102.

54. Grant to Porter, July 4, 1863, ibid., 25:103.

55. Porter to Welles, July 4, 1863, ibid., 25:103.

56. Porter, *Naval History*, 327; Porter, *Incidents*, 200.

57. Welles, *Diary*, 1:364.

58. Ulysses S. Grant, "The Vicksburg Campaign," *B&L*, 3:538; Grant, *Memoirs*, 1:574.

59. Porter to Welles, July 13, 1863, *ORN*, 25:279–80.

60. Fox to Porter, July 16, 1863, ibid., 25:307; Porter's Commission, Officers' Letters, Mississippi Squadron, March–August, 1863, Naval Records and Library.

61. Porter to Fox, Mar. 28, 1862, *Fox Correspondence*, 2:94.

62. Soley, *Admiral Porter*, 349.

63. Porter to Welles, Aug. 1, 1863, *ORN*, 25:335.

64. Welles to Porter, July 29, 1863, ibid., 25:332.

NINETEEN
Campaigning with Banks

1. Edwin Cole Bearss, *The Vicksburg Campaign,* 3 vols. (Dayton, Ohio: Morningside, 1986), 3:1217.
2. Prentiss to Hurlbut, June 27, 1863, *ORA,* 22, pt. 2:339; Porter to Welles, July 9, 1863, *ORN,* 15:227.
3. Porter to Welles, July 5, 1863, *ORN,* 25:227–28; Smith's Report, July 5, 1863, ibid., 25:229; Prentiss to Porter, July 9, 1863, ibid., 25:231.
4. Porter to Welles, July 1, 14, 22, 23, 1863, ibid., 25:219–20, 282–84, 285–86.
5. General Order No. 80, Aug. 19, 1863, ibid., 25:378.
6. Fentress to Porter, Nov. 15, Porter to Welles, Sept. 25, and Porter to Greer, Sept. 25, 1863, ibid., 25:409, 404, 408.
7. Porter to Welles, Sept. 15, 1863, ibid., 25:413–14.
8. Ludwell H. Johnson, *Red River Campaign: Politics and Cotton in the Civil War* (Gaithersburg, Md.: Butternut, 1986), 49–78.
9. Roy P. Basler, ed., *The Collected Works of Abraham Lincoln,* 9 vols. (New Brunswick, N.J.: Rutgers University Press, 1953), 7:62–63, 114–16; Lincoln to Casey, Dec. 14, 1863, *ORN,* 25:633.
10. Casey to Lincoln, Dec. 19, 1863, Lincoln Papers, LC.
11. Porter to Sherman, Oct. 29, 1863, *ORN,* 25:521–24.
12. Fox to Porter, Nov. 3, and Porter to Fox, Nov. 14, 1863, ibid., 25:529, 558.
13. Grant to Porter, Nov. 21, 1863, ibid., 25:489; Porter, *Incidents,* 209.
14. Porter to Fox, Dec. 6, 1863, *Fox Correspondence,* 2:197–98.
15. West, *Second Admiral,* 242–43.
16. Faust, *Historical Times Illustrated,* 38; Halleck to Banks, Aug. 10, 1863, *ORA,* 34, pt. 1:673; Franklin's Report, Sept. 7, 1863, ibid., 34, pt. 1:294–97.
17. M. A. De Wolfe Howe, ed., *Home Letters of General Sherman* (New York: Scribner, 1909), 286–87.
18. Sherman to Banks, Mar. 4, and Grant to Steele, Mar. 15, 1864, *ORA,* 34, pt. 2:494, 616; Porter to Greer, Feb. 13, 1864, *ORN,* 25:747–48.
19. Sherman to Porter, Jan. 26, 1864, *ORN,* 25:716, and Porter to Welles, Mar. 2, 1864, ibid., 26:7.
20. Sherman, *Memoirs,* 1:396–97.
21. Steele to Banks, Feb. 28, and Grant to Steele, Mar. 15, 1864, *ORA,* 34, pt. 2:448–49, 616.
22. Banks's Returns, ibid., 34, pt. 1:167–68; Smith to Cooper, Apr. 12, 1864, ibid., 34, pt. 1:476.
23. Walter G. Smith, ed., *Life and Letters of Thomas Kilby Smith* (New York: Putnam, 1898), 356.
24. Smith to Sherman, Sept. 26, 1864, *ORA,* 34, pt. 1:305; Porter to Welles, Mar. 16, 1864, *ORN,* 26:29.
25. Phelps to Porter, Mar. 16, 1864, *ORN,* 26:30–31; Richard Taylor, *Destruction and Reconstruction: Personal Experiences of the Late War* (New York: Appleton, 1879), 156; Taylor to Boggs, Mar. 20, 1864, *ORA,* 44, pt. 1:500.

26. Sherman to Porter, Apr. 3, 1864, *ORN,* 26:41.
27. Johnson, *Red River Campaign,* 101–3; Thomas O. Selfridge, *Memoirs,* 96–97.
28. Johnson, *Red River Campaign,* 103–5.
29. Grant to Banks, Mar. 18, 1864, *ORA,* 34, pt. 2:610–11.
30. Porter to Welles, Mar. 29, 1864, *ORN,* 26:39; Log of *Cricket,* ibid., 26:781.
31. Banks to Halleck, Apr. 2, 1864, *ORA,* 34, pt. 1:179–80; John G. Nicolay and John Hay, *Abraham Lincoln: A History,* 10 vols. (New York: Century, 1909), 8:291.
32. Porter to Welles, Apr. 14, 1864, *ORN,* 26:50–51.
33. Porter to Sherman, Apr. 16, 1864, ibid., 26:60.
34. Log of *Chillicothe,* ibid., 26:777; Bache to Porter, Apr. 4, 1863, ibid., 26:42.
35. Porter to Sherman, Apr. 16, 1864, ibid., 26:60; Stone to Porter, Apr. 9, 1864, *ORA,* 34, pt. 3:99.
36. Porter to Sherman, Apr. 16, 1864, *ORN,* 26:60–61.
37. Emory's Report, Apr. 12, 1864, *ORA,* 34, pt. 1:389–93.
38. A. J. Smith's Report, Sept. 26, 1864, ibid., 34, pt. 1:308–9.
39. Porter to Welles, Apr. 14, 1864, *ORN,* 26:46.

TWENTY
Escaping Disaster

1. Logs of *Chillicothe* and *Cricket, ORN,* 26:778, 781.
2. Porter to Sherman, Apr. 16, 1864, ibid., 26:61; Smith's Report, Apr. 16, 1864, *ORA,* 34, pt. 1:381.
3. Porter to Sherman, Apr. 16, 1864, *ORN,* 26:62.
4. Logs of *Chillicothe, Cricket,* and *Lexington,* ibid., 26:778, 81, 789.
5. Taylor's Report, Apr. 18, and Smith's Report, April 16, 1864, *ORA,* 34, pt. 1:570–71, 381.
6. Ibid., 34, pt. 1:382; Selfridge to Porter, Apr. 16, 1864, *ORN,* 26:49.
7. Smith's Report, Apr. 16, 1864, *ORA,* 34, pt. 1:382.
8. Ibid.; Porter's Report, Apr. 15, 1864, *ORN,* 26:52.
9. Banks to Grant, Apr. 13, 17, 1864, *ORA,* 34, pt. 1:185, 188; Banks to Sherman, Apr. 14, 1864, ibid., 34, pt. 3:266; Porter to Sherman, Apr. 14, 16, 1864, *ORN,* 26:56, 62.
10. Porter to Welles, Apr. 16, 1864, *ORN,* 26:47.
11. Banks to Grant, Apr. 30, 1864, *ORA,* 34, pt. 1:190.
12. Log of *Cricket, ORN,* 26:781–82; Phelps to Porter, Apr. 28, 1864, ibid., 26:78–79.
13. Taylor's Order, Apr. 26, 1864, ibid., 26:167; Log of *Cricket,* ibid., 26:781–82; Porter to Welles, Apr. 28, 1864, ibid., 26:74–75.
14. Ibid., 26:75; Log of *Lexington,* ibid., 26:790–91.
15. Phelps to Porter, Apr. 28, and Watson to Porter, May 1, 1864, ibid., 26:82–83, 83–84.
16. Porter to Welles, Apr. 28, 1864, ibid., 26:76.

17. Porter to Welles, Apr. 28, and Mitchell to Porter, Apr. 29, 1864, ibid., 26:94, 95–96.
18. Smith's Order, Apr. 29, 1864, ibid., 26:96; Banks to Porter Apr. 29, 1864, ibid., 26:96–97.
19. Grant to Hunter, and Grant to Banks, Apr. 17, 1864, *ORA,* 34, pt. 3:190–92.
20. Porter, *Naval History,* 526.
21. Porter to Welles, May 16, 1864, *ORA,* 34, pt. 1, 219–20; Bailey's Report, May 17, 1864, ibid., 34, pt. 1:402–3.
22. Ibid., 34, pt. 1:403; Richard B. Irwin, "The Red River Campaign," *B&L,* 4:358–59.
23. Porter, *Naval History,* 526.
24. Irwin, "Red River Campaign," *B&L,* 4:359. Porter to Welles, May 16, 1864, *ORA,* 34, pt. 1:219–20.
25. *ORA,* 34, pt. 1:221; Johnson, *Red River Campaign,* 261.
26. Liddell's Report, July 2, 1864, *ORA,* 34, pt. 1:635–36.
27. Porter to Welles, May 19, 1864, *ORN,* 26:156.
28. Log of *Lexington,* ibid., 26:791; Porter to Welles, May 16, 1864, ibid., 26:264.
29. Irwin, "Red River Campaign," *B&L,* 4:359.
30. Porter to Banks, and Banks to Porter, May 11, 1864, *ORN,* 26:140–42; Porter, *Naval History,* 527.
31. Pearsall to Drake, Aug. 1, 1864, *ORA,* 34, pt. 1:255.
32. Porter to Welles, May 16, 1864, *ORN,* 26:132–33; Porter to Mrs. Porter, May 18, 1864, Porter Papers, LC.
33. Porter to Welles, May 16, 1864, *ORN,* 26:132–33.
34. Irwin, "Red River Campaign," *B&L,* 4:361.
35. Bailey's Report, May 17, 1864, *ORA,* 34, pt. 1:404.
36. Congressional Resolution No. 34, ibid., 34, pt. 1:406; Soley, *Admiral Porter,* 405.
37. Johnson, *Red River Campaign,* 287–88.
38. Porter to Fox, May 27, 1864, Porter Papers, LC.

TWENTY-ONE
A Huge Puff of Smoke

1. Stephen E. Ambrose, *Halleck: Lincoln's Chief of Staff* (Baton Rouge: Louisiana State University Press, 1962), 160–61.
2. Fox to Porter, May 25, 1864, *ORN,* 26:324–25; Faust, *Historical Times Illustrated,* 131.
3. Welles to Porter, May 27, 1864, *ORN,* 26:329.
4. General Order No. 199, May 27, 1864, ibid., 26:329–30; Porter to Welles, May 31, 1864, ibid., 26:340–51.
5. Welles, *Diary,* 2:37, 129.
6. Welles to Porter, June 25, Porter to Canby, and General Order No. 230, July 1, 1864, *ORN,* 26:438, 453, 454.

7. Ibid., 26:67; Porter to Pennock, July 3, 1864, ibid., 26:459–60.

8. Porter to Welles (with Welles's endorsement), Aug. 15, 1864, ibid., 26:508.

9. Welles, *Diary*, 2:127–29.

10. Halleck to Stanton, Jan. 6, 1864, *ORN*, 9:386–87; Halleck to Grant, Sept. 1, and Gillmore to Halleck, Sept. 6, 1864, *ORA*, 42, pt. 2:624, 731–34.

11. Rowena Reed, *Combined Operations in the Civil War* (Lincoln: University of Nebraska Press, 1978), 332.

12. Welles to Farragut, Sept. 5, 1864, *ORN*, 10:430; Farragut to Welles, Sept. 22, 1864, ibid., 21:655–56.

13. Welles to Porter, Sept. 22, 1864, ibid., 21:657; Welles, *Diary*, 2:145–47.

14. Welles, *Diary*, 146; James M. Merrill, "The Fort Fisher and Wilmington Campaign: Letters from Rear Admiral David D. Porter," *North Carolina Historical Review* 35 (October 1958): 464–65.

15. Porter to Squadron, Sept. 28, and Fox to Porter, Sept. 30, 1864, *ORN*, 26:570–72, 574.

16. Welles, *Diary*, 2:172.

17. Porter to Welles, Oct. 11, and Lee to Welles, Oct. 11, 12, 1864, *ORN*, 10:552, 554.

18. General Order No. 2, Oct. 12, 1864, ibid., 10:558; Soley, *Admiral Porter*, 411.

19. Porter to Welles, Oct. 14, 1864, *ORN*, 10:566; List of Vessels, Dec. 15, 1864, ibid., 11:192–94.

20. Chester G. Hearn, "The Brief But Illustrious Career of the Ram *Albemarle*," *Blue and Gray Magazine* 2 (July 1985): 25–33; Cushing's Report, Oct. 30, 1864, *ORN*, 10:611–13.

21. Soley, *Admiral Porter*, 409–10; Mitchell's Report, Oct. 3, 1864, *ORN*, 10:768.

22. Grant to Butler, and Turner to Weitzel, Dec. 6, 1864, *ORA*, 42, pt. 1:971–73.

23. Porter, *Incidents*, 262.

24. West, *Second Admiral*, 271.

25. *Butler's Book*, 775; Porter to Welles, Jan. 22, 1865, *ORN*, 11:268.

26. Porter to Watmough, Dec. 8, 1864, *ORN*, 11:217.

27. William Lamb, "The Defense of Fort Fisher," *B&L*, 4:643–45.

28. Rod Gragg, *Confederate Goliath: The Battle of Fort Fisher* (Baton Rouge: Louisiana State University Press, 1994), 14–21. Lamb's Report, Dec. 27, 1864, *ORN*, 11:369.

29. *Butler's Book*, 775–76; Porter, *Naval History*, 684, 692–93.

30. Delafield to Dana, Nov. 18, 1864, *ORA*, 24, pt. 3:639–41.

31. Memorandum of discussion, Nov. 23, 1864, *Report of the Joint Committee on the Conduct of the War, 38th Congress, 2nd Session* (Washington, D.C.: Government Printing Office, 1865), 2:30 (hereafter cited as *JCR*).

32. Porter to Fox, Dec. 2, and Butler to Porter, Dec. 4, 1864, *ORN*, 11:119; Grant to Butler, Dec. 4, 6, 1864, Butler, *Private and Official Correspondence*, 5:379, 382.

33. Porter to Chase, Dec. 12, 1864, *ORN*, 11:219.

34. Quoted in Gragg, *Confederate Goliath*, 44.

35. Porter to Butler, Dec. 13, 16, 18, 1864, *ORN,* 11:191, 196, 223–24.
36. Porter to Rhind, Dec. 17, 1864, ibid., 11:222–23; Casey's Report, Dec. 29, 1864, *ORA,* 42, pt. 1:988–99.
37. Log of *Wilderness, ORN,* 11:241–43; Breese to Porter, Jan. 11, 1865, ibid., 11:224; Butler's Report, Dec. 20, 1864, *ORA,* 42, pt. 1:964–65.
38. Porter to Rhind, Dec. 17, 19, 23, and Porter to Watmough, Dec. 23, 1864, *ORN,* 11:223, 224, 225; Porter to Welles, Jan. 11, 1865, ibid., 11:227–28.
39. Porter's testimony, Mar. 7, 1865, *JCR,* 2:87–104.
40. Rhind's Report, Dec. 26, 1864, *ORN,* 11:226–27; Log of *Wilderness,* ibid., 11:243–44.
41. Daniel Ammen, *The Old Navy and the New* (Philadelphia: Lippincott, 1891), 403; Lamb's Diary, ibid., 371; Whiting's letter, *JCR,* 2:106–7.
42. Jeffers to Porter, Feb. 14, 1865, *JCR,* 2:255.
43. General Order No. 70, Dec. 10, 1864, *ORN,* 11:245–47.
44. Porter to Welles, Dec. 26, 1864, ibid., 11:255–56.
45. Lamb's Report, Dec. 27, 1864, ibid., 11:366–67.
46. Porter to Welles, Dec. 26, 1864, ibid., 11:256; *New York Times,* Dec. 31, 1864.
47. Porter to Welles, Dec. 24, 1864, *ORN,* 11:253.
48. Ibid.; Butler's testimony, *JCR,* 2:21.
49. Porter's testimony, *JCR,* 2:89–96; *Butler's Book,* 790–91.
50. *Butler's Book,* 796, 808; Weitzel's testimony, Porter's testimony, *JCR,* 2:75–77, 92; Butler to Grant, Jan. 3, 1865, *ORA,* 42, pt. 1:967.
51. *Butler's Book,* 808; Butler to Porter, Dec. 25, 1864, *ORN,* 11:250.

TWENTY-TWO

Fort Fisher Falls

1. Weitzel's Report, Dec. 31, 1864, *ORA,* 42, pt. 1:986.
2. Glisson's Report, Jan. 1, 1865, *ORN,* 11:333.
3. *New York Times,* Dec. 31, 1864.
4. Huse to Porter, Dec. 31, 1864, *ORN,* 11:351–52; Weitzel's Report, Dec. 31, 1864, *ORA,* 42, pt. 1:986.
5. Porter to Welles, Dec. 26, 1864, *ORN,* 11:258.
6. Guest's Report, and Truxton's Report, Dec. 27, 1864, ibid., 11:330, 334; Lamb's Report, Dec. 27, 1864, ibid., 11:367.
7. Logs of *Colorado* and *Minnesota,* ibid., 11:296–97, 304.
8. Weitzel's Report, Dec. 31, 1864, *ORA,* 42, pt. 1:986; Butler's testimony, *JCR,* 2:23.
9. Quoted in West, *Second Admiral,* 283.
10. Porter to Welles, Dec. 26, and Butler to Porter, Dec. 25, 1864, *ORN,* 11:258, 250–51; Grant to Butler, Dec. 6, 1864, *ORA,* 42, pt. 1:971–72.
11. Curtis's Report, Dec. 28, 1864, *ORA,* 42, pt. 1:982–83; Gragg, *Confederate Goliath,* 90, 92–95.

12. Porter to Alden, Dec. 26, and Alden to Porter, Dec. 30, 1864, _ORN,_ 11:317, 318.

13. Porter to Butler, Dec. 26, 1864, ibid., 11:252; Butler to Porter, Dec. 27, 1864, _ORA,_ 42, pt. 3:1086.

14. Porter to Welles, Dec. 26, 1864, _ORN,_ 11:259.

15. Howell et al. to Porter, and Porter to Welles, Dec. 27, 28, 1864, ibid., 11:290–91.

16. Porter to Welles, Dec. 29, 1864, ibid., 11:263–65.

17. Porter to Sherman, Dec. 29, 1864, ibid., 11:388–89.

18. Grant to Porter, Dec. 30, 1864, ibid., 11:394.

19. Gragg, _Confederate Goliath,_ 96; _JCR,_ 2:29; Porter's General Order No. 77, _ORN,_ 11:401.

20. Grant to Sherman, Dec. 6, Grant to Halleck, Dec. 15, Sherman to Grant, Dec. 16, 27, and Halleck to Sherman, Dec. 16, 1864, _ORA,_ 44:636, 715, 727–28, 728–29, 820–21.

21. Grant to Terry, and Grant to Porter, Jan. 3, 1865, _ORN,_ 11:404, 405.

22. Grant to Terry, Jan. 3, 1865, ibid., 11:404; Faust, _Historical Times Illustrated,_ 748–49.

23. Porter to Grant, Jan. 3, 1865, _ORN,_ 11:405–6; Grant's testimony, Feb. 11, 1865, _JCR,_ 2.51–56.

24. Porter, _Naval History,_ 710–11; Porter to Welles, Jan. 17, 1865, _ORN,_ 11:437.

25. Porter to Welles, Jan. 17, 1865, _ORN,_ 11:437; Terry's Report, Jan. 25, 1865, _ORA,_ 46, pt. 1:396.

26. _ORA,_ 46, pt. 1:396–97; Porter to Welles, Jan. 17, 1865, _ORN,_ 11:437–38.

27. Lamb, "The Defense of Fort Fisher," _B&L,_ 4:647, 649; Anderson to Hoke, Jan. 12, 1865, _ORA,_ 46, pt. 2:1044.

28. General Order No. 78, Jan. 2, 1865, _ORN,_ 11:425–27; Special Order No. 8, Jan. 3, 1865, ibid., 11:427.

29. Parrott to Porter, n.d., and Belknap to Porter, Jan. 17, 1865, ibid., 11:462, 464.

30. Lamb, "The Defense of Fort Fisher, _B&L,_ 4:647.

31. Ibid., 647–48.

32. Porter to Welles, Jan. 14, 15, 1865, _ORN,_ 11:433, 434.

33. Terry's Report, Jan. 25, 1865, _ORA,_ 46, pt. 1:396–97.

34. Porter to Welles, Jan. 15, 1865, _ORN,_ 11:434.

35. Lamb, "The Defense of Fort Fisher," _B&L,_ 4:648–49.

36. Bartlett to his sisters, Jan. 18, 1865, _ORN,_ 11:527. Detachments from other vessels are listed in 468–586 passim.

37. Porter's Landing Orders, Jan. 15, 1865, ibid., 11:429–30.

38. Bartlett to his sisters, Jan. 18, 1865, ibid., 11:527.

39. Whiting to Bragg, Jan. 15, 1865, _ORA,_ 46, pt. 2:1064; Lamb, "The Defense of Fort Fisher, _B&L,_ 4:649–50.

40. Lamb, "The Defense of Fort Fisher, _B&L,_ 4:650.

41. Bartlett's letter to his sisters, _ORN,_ 11:527–28.

42. Robley D. Evans, _A Sailor's Log: Recollections of Forty Years of Naval Life_ (New York: Appleton, 1901), 86.

43. Lamson to Rhind, Jan. 16, 1865, *ORN,* 11:450–51.

44. Ralph J. Roske and Charles Van Doren, *Lincoln's Commando* (New York: Harper & Brothers, 1957), 261–62; Cushing to Porter, Jan. 17, 1865, *ORN,* 11:560.

45. Selfridge to Porter, Jan. 17, and Parker to Porter, Jan. 16, 1865, *ORN,* 11:477, 499.

46. Breese to Porter, Jan. 16, 1865, ibid., 11:446–47.

47. Lamb, "The Defense of Fort Fisher," *B&L,* 4:651.

48. Ibid.; Radford to Porter, Jan. 16, 1865, *ORN,* 11:461–62.

49. Terry's Report, Jan. 25, 1865, *ORA,* 46, pt. 1:399; Blackman's Report, Jan. 16, 1865, ibid., 46, pt. 1:425.

50. Bartlett to his sisters, Jan. 18, 1865, *ORN,* 11:529.

51. Log of *Vanderbilt,* Nichols to Welles, Jan. 17, Porter to Pickering, Jan. 15, Berrien to Pickering, Jan. 18, and Pickering to Welles, Jan. 31, 1865, ibid., 11:456–57, 519, 520, 522, 613.

52. Proceedings of Court, Jan. 21, 22, 1865, *ORA,* 46, pt. 1:426–31.

53. Return of Casualties, ibid., 46, pt. 1:405; *ORN,* 11:443–44n; *B&L,* 4:661; Gragg, *Confederate Goliath,* 235–36.

54. *ORN,* 11:441n.

55. Porter to Welles, Jan. 15, 17, 20, 26, 1865, ibid., 11:434–35, 440–41, 444–45, 457.

56. Stanton to Terry and Porter, Jan. 16, 1865, ibid., 11:458.

57. Grant to Stanton, Jan. 4, and Butler to Army of the James, Jan. 8, 1865, *ORA,* 46, pt. 2:29, 70–71. Butler's attitude toward and opinion of Porter can be traced through the general's *Private and Official Correspondence,* 5:437–650 passim.

TWENTY-THREE

Mr. Lincoln and Admiral Porter

1. Porter to Welles, Jan. 17, 1865, *ORN,* 11:441.

2. Porter to Welles, Jan. 20, 1865, ibid., 11:619–20; Scharf, *History of the Confederate States Navy,* 489.

3. Porter to Fox, Jan. 21, 1865, Porter Papers, New York Historical Society.

4. Porter to Welles, Jan. 20, 1865, *ORN,* 11:444–45; Faust, *Historical Times Illustrated,* 748.

5. Resolutions of Congress to Porter and Terry, Jan. 24, and Lincoln to Porter, Feb. 10, 1865, *ORA,* 46, pt. 1:402, and *ORN,* 11:459.

6. *Butler's Book,* 1126–28.

7. Log of *Malvern, ORN,* 11:740; Porter, *Naval History,* 727; Grant to Schofield, Jan. 31, 1865, *ORA,* 46, pt. 1:44–45.

8. Porter to Welles, Feb. 12, and Temple to Bailey, Feb. 21, 1865, *ORN,* 12:16–17, 34–35.

9. Log of *Shawmut, ORN,* 12:37; Porter to Welles, Feb. 22, 1865, ibid., 12:45; Porter, *Incidents,* 278.

10. Grant to Welles, Jan. 24, Fox to Grant, Jan. 24, Parker to Welles, Jan. 26, and Porter to Parker, Feb. 14, 1865, *ORN,* 11:635–36, 637, 645, 658.

11. Welles to Radford, Jan. 24, and Welles to Porter, Jan. 25, 1865, *ORN,* 11:639, 702; Welles, *Diary,* 2:252.

12. Welles, *Diary,* 2:255; Notes on Joint Committee, n.d., David D. Porter Papers, LC; Fox to Berrien, Mar. 14, 1865, *ORN,* 12:66.

13. Log of *Malvern, ORN,* 12:175; Grant to Lincoln, *ORA,* 46, pt. 3:50.

14. Porter to Grant, and Grant to Porter, Mar. 26, 1865, *ORA,* 46, pt. 3:173; Porter, *Naval History,* 794.

15. Grant to Porter, Mar. 27, 1865, *ORN,* 12:84.

16. Porter, *Naval History,* 79; Sherman, *Memoirs,* 2:324–28.

17. Porter to Fox, Mar. 28, 1865, Porter Papers, Navy History Section, New York Historical Society.

18. Porter, *Incidents,* 285.

19. Soley, *Admiral Porter,* 444–45.

20. Quoted in West, *Second Admiral,* 292.

21. Porter, *Naval History,* 796.

22. Porter to Ronckendorff, Apr. 1, 1865, *ORN,* 12:95.

23. Log of *Malvern,* ibid., 12:176; Porter, *Naval History,* 796.

24. Grant, *Memoirs,* 2:459–60; Porter, *Incidents,* 288–91.

25. Stanton to Lincoln, and Lincoln to Stanton, Apr. 3, 1865, *ORA,* 46, pt. 3:509.

26. Log of *Malvern, ORN,* 12:176; Porter, *Incidents,* 294–95.

27. Porter, *Naval History,* 798; Soley, *Admiral Porter,* 449.

28. Porter, *Naval History,* 798.

29. Porter, *Incidents,* 283–84, 319.

TWENTY-FOUR

The Postwar Years

1. Welles to Porter, Apr. 28, and Porter to Welles, May 1, 1865, *ORN,* 12:129, 132.

2. Dana M. Wegner, "Commodore William D. 'Dirty Bill' Porter," U.S. Naval Institute *Proceedings* 103 (February 1977): 40–49.

3. Soley, *Admiral Porter,* 452; Porter to Fox, Mar. 28, 1862, *Fox Correspondence,* 2:95.

4. Welles, *Diary,* 2:321, 353, 360; Park Benjamin, *The United States Naval Academy* (New York: Putnam, 1900), 261–63.

5. Benjamin, *Naval Academy,* 263–83; Welles, *Diary,* 3:103.

6. *Navy Register,* 1865, NA; *Navy Register,* 1866, NA; Welles, *Diary,* 2:562–63.

7. Coletta, *American Secretaries of the Navy,* 1:356, 363–64; Charles O. Paullin, "A Half Century of Naval Administration in America, 1861–1911," U.S. Naval Institute *Proceedings,* no. 301 (March 1913): 1223.

8. Coletta, *American Secretaries of the Navy,* 1:365, 369.

9. Paullin, "A Half Century of Naval Administration," U.S. Naval Institute *Proceedings,* no. 300 (February 1913): 749; Soley, *Admiral Porter,* 460.

10. Paullin, "A Half Century of Naval Administration," U.S. Naval Institute *Proceedings,* no. 300 (February 1913): 735.

11. *Annual Report of the Secretary of the Navy, 1874* (Washington, D.C.: Government Printing Office, 1875), 198–202.

12. Paullin, "A Half Century of Naval Administration," U.S. Naval Institute *Proceedings,* no. 301 (March 1913): 1223, 1238.

13. *Annual Report of the Secretary of the Navy, 1880* (Washington, D.C.: Government Printing Office, 1881), 70.

14. *Congressional Record,* VII, 1952.

15. In 1898, after the Battle of Manila, George Dewey became the third admiral. Vice Adm. Stephen C. Rowan was the same man who as a lieutenant in the Coast Survey had an altercation with Porter that almost resulted in a duel. Soley, *Admiral Porter,* 465.

16. Soley, *Admiral Porter,* 465. Lloyd Lewis, one of Sherman's biographers, wrote *Sherman, Fighting Prophet* (New York: Harcourt Brace, 1932).

Bibliography

MANUSCRIPT SOURCES

Essex Institute, Salem, Mass.
 Banks (Nathaniel P.) Papers
Henry E. Huntington Library and Art Gallery, San Mateo, Calif.
 Farragut (David G.) Papers
 Fox (Gustavus Vasa) Papers
 Porter (David Dixon) Papers in the Eldridge Collection
 Welles (Gideon) Papers
Library of Congress, Washington, D.C.
 Butler (Benjamin F.) Papers
 Fox (Mrs. Gustavus Vasa) Diary, Blair Papers
 Lincoln (Abraham) Papers
 Porter (D. D.) Collection, "Letter Book U.S.N.A."
 Porter (David Dixon) Papers, 1842–64, Includes his "Private Journal of Occurrences" and a volume labeled "Memorials of Rear Admiral David D. Porter, U.S.N."
 Porter Family Papers
 Sherman (William T.) Papers
 Welles (Gideon) Papers
National Archives, Washington, D.C.
 Cushing (William B.) Diary

Naval Records Collection and Navy Register
   Porter (Benjamin H.) Papers, Records of the Bureau of Naval Personnel
Naval Records and Library, U.S. Navy Department, Washington, D.C.
   Appointments, Orders, and Resignations
   Officers' Letters, Mississippi Squadron
New York Historical Society, New York, N.Y.
   Porter (David Dixon) Papers, Naval History Section
U.S. Naval Academy, Annapolis, Md.
   Porter (David Dixon) Letter Books, Nos. 1 and 2
Lower Cape Fear Historical Society, Lower Cape Fear, N.C.
   Robbins (John Davis) Manuscript, "The Second Battle of Fort Fisher,"
   in McEachern-Williams Collection

NEWSPAPERS

Baltimore American
Baton Rouge Daily Advocate
Cincinnati Daily Commercial
Congressional Globe
Harper's Weekly
New Orleans Bee
New Orleans Commercial Bulletin
New Orleans Daily Crescent
New Orleans Daily Picayune
New Orleans Daily Delta
New Orleans True Delta
New York Herald
New York Times
New York Tribune
New York World
Richmond Daily Dispatch
Richmond Examiner
Philadelphia Inquirer
Philadelphia Press
Vicksburg Whig
Wilmington Daily Herald
Wilmington Journal

OFFICIAL RECORDS

Annual Report of the Secretary of the Navy, 1874. Washington, D.C.: Government
   Printing Office, 1875.
Annual Report of the Secretary of the Navy, 1880. Washington, D.C.: Government
   Printing Office, 1881.

The Fort Fisher Expedition: Report of the Joint Committee on the Conduct of the War, 38th Congress, 2nd Session. Washington, D.C.: Government Printing Office, 1865.

Journal of the Congress of the Confederate States, 1861–1865. Reprinted in Washington, D.C., in 1904 as *Senate Document No. 234, 58th Congress, 2nd Session.*

Minutes of the Proceedings of the Courts of Inquiry and Court Martial in Relation to D. Porter. Washington, D.C.: Davis & Force, 1825.

Official Records of the Union and Confederate Navies in the War of the Rebellion. 30 vols. Washington, D.C.: Government Printing Office, 1894–1922.

Official Report Relative to the Conduct of Federal Troops in Western Louisiana, during the Invasion of 1863 and 1864, Compiled from Sworn Testimony, under Direction of Governor Henry W. Allen. Shreveport, La.: News Printing Establishment, 1865.

Proceedings of the Court of Inquiry Relative to the Fall of New Orleans, Published by Order of the Confederate Congress. Washington, D.C.: Government Printing Office, 1862.

Report of the Joint Committee on the Conduct of the War, 38th Congress, 2nd Session. Vol. 2. Washington, D.C.: Government Printing Office, 1865.

Reports of the Naval Engagements on the Mississippi River Resulting in the Capture of Forts Jackson and St. Philip and the City of New Orleans, and the Destruction of the Rebel Naval Flotilla. Washington, D.C.: Government Printing Office, 1862.

Senate Executive Document No. 62, 34th Congress, 3rd Session, 1856–57. Washington, D.C.: Government Printing Office, 1857.

U.S. Department of the Navy. *Annual Reports of the Secretary of the Navy.* Washington, D.C.: Government Printing Office, 1821–1948.

War of the Rebellion: A Compilation of the Official Records of the Union and Confederate Armies. 130 vols. Washington, D.C.: Government Printing Office, 1880–1901.

PRIMARY SOURCES—BOOKS AND ARTICLES

Adams, F. Colburn. *High Old Salts.* Washington, D.C.: Government Printing Office, 1876.

Alden, Carroll S. *George Hamilton Perkins, U.S.N., His Life and Letters.* Boston: Houghton Mifflin, 1914.

Ames, Adelbert. "The Capture of Fort Fisher, North Carolina, January 15, 1865." In *Personal Recollections of the War of the Rebellion,* edited by A. Noel Blackman. New York: Putnam, 1907.

Ammen, Daniel. *The Atlantic Coast.* New York: Scribner, 1883.

———. "Du Pont and the Port Royal Expedition." In Johnson and Buel, *Battles and Leaders of the Civil War,* 1:671–91.

———. *The Old Navy and the New.* Philadelphia: Lippincott, 1891.

Bacon, George B. "One Night's Work, April 20, 1862: Breaking the Chain for Farragut's Fleet at Forts below New Orleans." *Magazine of American History* 15 (1886): 305–7.

Badeau, Adam. *Military History of Ulysses S. Grant.* 3 vols. New York: Appleton, 1868–1881.

Baker, Marion A. "Farragut's Demands for the Surrender of New Orleans." In Johnson and Buel, *Battles and Leaders of the Civil War,* 2:95–99.

Bartlett, John Russell. "The 'Brooklyn' at the Passage of the Forts." In Johnson and Buel, *Battles and Leaders of the Civil War,* 2:56–69.

Bartlett, Napier. *Military Record of Louisiana: Including Biographical and Historical Papers Relating to the Military Organization of the State.* New Orleans: Graham, 1875.

Basler, Roy P., ed. *The Collected Works of Abraham Lincoln.* 9 vols. New Brunswick, N.J.: Rutgers University Press, 1953.

Beale, Howard K., and Alan W. Brownsword, eds. *Diary of Gideon Welles, Secretary of the Navy under Lincoln and Johnson.* 3 vols. New York: Norton, 1960.

Bee, Hamilton P. "Battle of Pleasant Hill—An Error Corrected." *Southern Historical Society Papers* 7 (1880): 184–86.

Belknap, George E., ed. *Letters of Capt. Geo. Hamilton Perkins.* Concord, N.H.: Evans, 1886.

Blair, Montgomery. "Opening the Mississippi." *The United Service: A Monthly Review of the Military and Naval Services* 4 (January 1881): 37–40.

Boynton, Charles B. *The History of the Navy during the Rebellion.* 2 vols. New York: Appleton, 1867.

Brown, George W. "The Mortar Flotilla." In *Personal Recollections of the War of the Rebellion, Delivered before the New York Commandery of the Loyal Legion of the United States.* Vol. 1. New York: New York Commandery, 1891.

Butler, Benjamin F. *Autobiography and Personal Reminiscences of Major-General Benj. F. Butler: Butler's Book.* Boston: Thayer, 1892.

———. *Public and Private Correspondence of Gen. Benjamin F. Butler during the Period of the Civil War.* Edited by Jesse A. Marshall. 5 vols. Norwood, Mass.: privately published, 1917.

Cooper, James Fenimore. *The History of the Navy of the United States of America.* 3 vols. in 1. New York: Putnam, 1856.

Crandall, Warren D., and Isaac D. Newall. *History of the Ram Fleet and the Mississippi Marine Brigade.* St. Louis: Buschart Bros., 1907.

Dana, Charles A. *Recollections of the Civil War.* New York: Appleton, 1898.

Davis, Jefferson. *The Rise and Fall of the Confederate Government.* 2 vols. Richmond: Garrett & Massie, 1938.

Dewey, George. *Autobiography of George Dewey, Admiral of the Navy.* New York: Scribner, 1913.

Evans, Robely. *A Sailor's Log: Recollections of Forty Years of Naval Life.* New York: Appleton, 1901.

Farragut, Loyall. *The Life of David Glasgow Farragut, First Admiral of the U.S. Navy.* New York: Appleton, 1879.

Gilman, J. H. "With Slemmer in Pensacola Harbor." In Johnson and Buel, *Battles and Leaders of the Civil War,* 1:26–32.

Grant, Ulysses S. *Personal Memoirs of U. S. Grant.* 2 vols. New York: Webster, 1885–86.

———. "The Vicksburg Campaign." In Johnson and Buel, *Battles and Leaders of the Civil War,* 3:493–539.

Hill, Frederic S. *Twenty Years at Sea, or Leaves from My Old Log Books.* Boston: Houghton Mifflin, 1893.

Homans, John. "The Red River Expedition." In *The Mississippi Valley, Tennessee, Georgia, Alabama, 1861–1864.* Vol. 8. Boston: Military Historical Society of Massachusetts, 1913.

Howe, M. A. DeWolfe, ed. *Home Letters of General Sherman.* New York: Scribner, 1909.

Irwin, Richard B. "The Red River Campaign." In Johnson and Buel, *Battles and Leaders of the Civil War,* 4:345–62.

Johnson, Robert U., and Clarence C. Buel, eds. *Battles and Leaders of the Civil War.* 4 vols. New York: Century, 1887–88.

Jones, J. B. *A Rebel War Clerk's Diary.* 2 vols. Philadelphia: Lippincott, 1866.

Jones, James P., and Edward F. Keuchel, eds. *Civil War Marine: A Diary of the Red River Expedition, 1864.* Washington, D.C.: U.S. Marine Corps, History and Marine Division, 1975.

Kautz, Albert. "Incidents of the Occupation of New Orleans." In Johnson and Buel, *Battles and Leaders of the Civil War,* 2:91–94.

Kennon, Beverley. "Fighting Farragut below New Orleans." In Johnson and Buel, *Battles and Leaders of the Civil War,* 2:76–89.

Lamb, William. *Colonel William Lamb's Story of Fort Fisher.* Carolina Beach, N.C.: Blockade Runner Museum, 1966.

———. "The Defense of Fort Fisher." In Johnson and Buel, *Battles and Leaders of the Civil War,* 4:642–54.

Lockett, Samuel H. "The Defense of Vicksburg." In Johnson and Buel, *Battles and Leaders of the Civil War,* 3:482–92.

Lossing, Benjamin. "The First Attack on Fort Fisher." In *The Annals of the War,* ed. Alexander K. McClure. Philadelphia: Times, 1879.

McClure, Alexander K., ed. *The Annals of the War, Written by Leading Participants North and South.* Philadelphia: Times, 1879.

Moore, Frank, ed. *The Rebellion Record: A Diary of American Events.* 12 vols. New York: D. Van Nostrand, 1862–69.

Morgan, James Morris. *Recollections of a Rebel Reefer.* Boston: Houghton Mifflin, 1917.

Nicolay, John G., and John Hay. *Abraham Lincoln: A History.* 10 vols. New York: Century, 1909.

Osbon, B. S., ed. "The Cruise of the U.S. Flag-Ship *Hartford,* 1862–1863, From the Private Journal of William C. Holton." *Magazine of American History* 22, no. 3, extra no. 87 (1922): 17–28.

Paine, Albert Bigelow. *A Sailor of Fortune: Personal Memories of Captain B. S. Osbon.* New York: Doubleday, 1906.

Parker, James. "The Navy in the Battles and Capture of Fort Fisher." In *Personal Recollections of the War of the Rebellion Read before the Military Order of the Loyal Legion, Commandery of New York.* Vol. 1. New York: New York Commandery, 1897.

Parton, James. *General Butler in New Orleans.* New York: Mason, 1864.

Porter, David. *An Exposition of the Facts Which Justified the Expedition to Foxardo.* Washington, D.C.: Davis & Force, 1825.

———. *Journal of a Cruise Made to the Pacific Ocean in the U.S. Frigate* Essex, *1812–1814.* New York: Wiley & Halstead, 1822.

Porter, David Dixon. *Incidents and Anecdotes of the Civil War.* New York: Appleton, 1885.

———. *The Naval History of the Civil War.* New York: Sherman, 1886.

———. "The Opening of the Lower Mississippi." In Johnson and Buel, *Battles and Leaders of the Civil War,* 2:22–55.

———. "Secret Missions to Santo Domingo." *North American Review* 128 (July 1879): 616–30.

Robertson, William B. "The Water-Battery at Fort Jackson." In Johnson and Buel, *Battles and Leaders of the Civil War,* 2:99–100.

Russell, William Howard. *My Diary North and South.* London: Bradley & Evans, 1863.

Sands, Benjamin Franklin. *From Reefer to Rear Admiral.* New York: Stokes, 1899.

Scharf, J. Thomas. *History of the Confederate States Navy.* New York: Rogers & Sherwood, 1887.

Scott, Winfield. *Memoirs of Lieut.-General Winfield Scott, LL.D., Written by Himself.* New York: Sheldon & Company, 1864.

Selfridge, Thomas O. *Memoirs of Thomas O. Selfridge, Jr., Rear Admiral, U.S.N.* New York: Putnam, 1924.

———. "The Navy at Fort Fisher." In Johnson and Buel, *Battles and Leaders of the Civil War,* 4:362–66.

Semmes, Raphael. *Memoirs of Service Afloat during the War between the States.* Baltimore: Kelly, Piet, 1869.

Sherman, William T. *Memoirs of General W. T. Sherman.* 2 vols. New York: Appleton, 1875.

Smith, Walter G., ed. *Life and Letters of Thomas Kilby Smith.* New York: Putnam, 1898.

Soley, James R. *Admiral Porter.* New York: Appleton, 1903.

———. *The Blockade and the Cruisers.* New York: Scribner, 1890.

———. "Naval Operations in the Vicksburg Campaign." In Johnson and Buel, *Battles and Leaders of the Civil War,* 3:551–70.

Taylor, Richard. *Destruction and Reconstruction: Personal Experiences of the Late War.* New York: Appleton, 1879.

Thompson, Robert M., and Richard Wainwright, eds. *Confidential Correspondence of Gustavus Vasa Fox, Assistant Secretary of the Navy, 1861–1865.* 2 vols. Freeport, N.Y.: Books for Libraries, 1972.

Walke, Henry. *Naval Scenes and Reminiscences of the Civil War in the United States.* New York: Reed, 1877.

Walker, Jennie Mort. *Life of Captain Joseph Fry, the Cuban Martyr.* Hartford: Burr, 1874.

Warley, Alexander F. "The Ram Manassas at the Passage of the New Orleans Forts." In Johnson and Buel, *Battles and Leaders of the Civil War,* 2:89–91.

Welles, Gideon. "Admiral Farragut and New Orleans." *The Galaxy: An Illustrated Magazine of Entertaining Reading* 12 (November 1871): 673–82; 12 (December 1871): 817–32.

———. *The Diary of Gideon Welles, Secretary of the Navy under Lincoln and Johnson.* 3 vols. Boston: Houghton Mifflin, 1909–11.

———. *Selected Essays by Gideon Welles: Civil War and Reconstruction.* Compiled by Albert Mordell. New York: Twayne, 1959.

Williams, E. Cort. "Recollections of the Red River Expedition." In *Sketches of War History 1861–1865, Papers Read before the Ohio Commandery of the Military Order of the Loyal Legion of the United States 1886–1888.* Vol. 2. Cincinnati: Robert Clarke, 1888.

Wilson, James G. "The Red River Dam, with Comments on the Red River Campaign." In *Personal Recollections of the War of the Rebellion, Delivered before the New York Commandery of the Loyal Legion of the United States.* Vol. 1. New York: New York Commandery, 1891

Wilson, James H. *Under the Old Flag.* 2 vols. New York: Appleton, 1912.

Younger, Edward, ed. *Inside the Confederate Government: The Diary of Robert Garlick Hill Kean.* Baton Rouge: Louisiana State University Press, 1993.

Secondary Sources—Books and Articles

Abbot, Willis J. *Blue Jackets of 1861.* New York: Dodd, Mead, 1886.

Ambrose, Stephen E. *Halleck: Lincoln's Chief of Staff.* Baton Rouge: Louisiana State University Press, 1962.

Bauer, K. Jack. *The Mexican War, 1846–1848.* New York: Macmillan, 1974.

Bearss, Edwin Cole. *The Vicksburg Campaign.* 3 vols. Dayton, Ohio: Morningside, 1985.

Benjamin, Park. *The United States Naval Academy.* New York: Putnam, 1900.

Bennett, Frank M. *The Steam Navy of the United States.* Pittsburgh: Warren, 1896.

Boatner, Mark M., III. *The Civil War Dictionary.* New York: McKay, 1959.

Bradford, James C., ed. *Captains of the Old Steam Navy.* Annapolis, Md.: Naval Institute Press, 1986.

Bragg, Jefferson Davis. *Louisiana in the Confederacy.* Baton Rouge: Louisiana State University Press, 1941.

Bruce, Robert V. *Lincoln and the Tools of War.* New York: Bobbs-Merrill, 1956.

Cagle, Malcolm W. "Lieutenant David Dixon Porter and His Camels." U.S. Naval Institute *Proceedings* 83 (December 1957): 1327–33.

Canfield, Eugene B. *Civil War Ordnance.* Washington, D.C.: Government Printing Office, 1969.

Carter, Hodding. *The Lower Mississippi.* New York: Farrar & Rinehart, 1942.

Carter, Samuel, III. *The Final Fortress: The Campaign for Vicksburg 1862–1863.* New York: St. Martin's, 1980.

Caskey, Willie M. *Secession and Restoration of Louisiana.* Baton Rouge: Louisiana State University Press, 1938.

Coletta, Paolo E. *American Secretaries of the Navy.* 2 vols. Annapolis, Md.: Naval Institute Press, 1980.

Cunningham, Edward. *The Port Hudson Campaign, 1862–1863.* Baton Rouge: Louisiana State University Press, 1963.

Davenport, Charles B. *Naval Officers: Their Heredity and Development.* Washington, D.C.: Carnegie Institution of Washington, 1919.

Dufour, Charles L.. *The Night the War Was Lost.* New York: Doubleday, 1960.

———. *Ten Flags in the Wind.* New York: Harper & Row, 1967.

Durkin, Joseph T. *Stephen R. Mallory, Confederate Navy Chief.* Chapel Hill: University of North Carolina Press, 1954.

Faust, Patricia L., ed. *Historical Times Illustrated: Encyclopedia of the Civil War.* New York: Harper & Row, 1986.

Finan, William J. *Major General Alfred Howe Terry: Hero of Fort Fisher.* Hartford: Connecticut Civil War Centennial Commission, 1965.

Fiske, John. *The Mississippi Valley in the Civil War.* Boston: Houghton Mifflin, 1900.

Foltz, C. S. *Surgeon of the Seas.* Indianapolis: Bobbs-Merrill, 1931.

Foote, Shelby. *The Civil War.* 3 vols. New York: Random House, 1954–74.

Geer, James K. *Louisiana Politics, 1845–1861.* Baton Rouge: Louisiana State University Press, 1930.

Gosnell, H. Allen. *Guns on the Western Waters: The Story of River Gunboats in the Civil War.* Baton Rouge: Louisiana State University Press, 1949.

Gragg, Rod. *Confederate Goliath: The Battle of Fort Fisher.* Baton Rouge: Louisiana State University Press, 1994.

Hagan, Kenneth J. "Admiral David Dixon Porter—Strategist for a Navy in Transition." U.S. Naval Institute *Proceedings* 94 (July 1968): 139–43.

Harrington, Fred H. *Fighting Politician: Major General N. P. Banks.* Philadelphia: University of Pennsylvania Press, 1948.

Headley, Joel T. *Farragut and Our Naval Commanders.* New York: Treat, 1867.

Hearn, Chester G. "The Brief But Illustrious Career of the Ram *Albemarle.*" *Blue and Gray Magazine* 2 (July 1985): 25–33.

————. *The Capture of New Orleans, 1862.* Baton Rouge: Louisiana State University Press, 1995.

Henry, Robert S. *The Story of the Confederacy.* New York: Garden City, 1931.

Hill, Jim Dan. *Sea Dogs of the Sixties.* Minneapolis: University of Minnesota Press, 1935.

Holtzman, Robert S. *Stormy Ben Butler.* New York: Macmillan, 1965.

Johnson, Ludwell H. *Red River Campaign: Politics and Cotton in the Civil War.* Gaithersburg, Md.: Butternut Press, 1986.

Jones, Virgil Carrington. *The Civil War at Sea.* 3 vols. New York: Holt, Rinehart & Winston, 1960–62.

Knox, Dudley W. *A History of the United States Navy.* New York: Putnam, 1948.

Lewis, Charles Lee. *David Glasgow Farragut, Our First Admiral.* Annapolis, Md.: Naval Institute Press, 1943.

Lewis, Lloyd. *Sherman: Fighting Prophet.* New York: Harcourt Brace, 1932.

Lewis, Paul. *Yankee Admiral.* New York: McKay, 1968.

Lockwood, H. C. "The Capture of Fort Fisher." *Atlantic Monthly,* May 1871, 622–36.

Long, David F. *Nothing Too Daring—A Biography of Commodore David Porter, 1780–1843.* Annapolis, Md.: Naval Institute Press, 1970.

Longacre, Edward G. *From Antietam to Ft. Fisher: The Civil War Letters of Edward King Wightman, 1862–1865.* Rutherford, N.J.: Fairleigh Dickinson, 1985.

Macartney, Clarence E. *Mr. Lincoln's Admirals.* New York: Funk & Wagnalls, 1956.

Mahan, Alfred T. *Admiral Farragut.* New York: Appleton, 1892.

————. *The Gulf and Inland Waters.* New York: Scribner, 1901.

Malone, Dumas, ed. *Dictionary of American Biography.* 20 vols. New York: Scribner, 1928–37.

McFeely, William S. *Grant: A Biography.* New York: Norton, 1981.

Merrill, James M. "The Fort Fisher and Wilmington Campaign: Letters from Rear Admiral David D. Porter." *North Carolina Historical Review* 35 (October 1985): 461–75.

————. *The Rebel Shore: The Story of Union Sea Power in the Civil War.* Boston: Little, Brown, 1957.

Miers, Earl Schenck. *The Web of Victory.* New York: Knopf, 1955.

Milligan, John D. *Gunboats Down the Mississippi.* Annapolis, Md.: Naval Institute Press, 1965.

Nevins, Allan. *The Emergence of Lincoln.* 2 vols. New York: Scribner, 1950.

————. *The War for the Union.* Vols. 5–7. New York: Scribner, 1960.

Niven, John. *Gideon Welles: Lincoln's Secretary of the Navy.* New York: Oxford University Press, 1973.

Owsley, Frank Lawrence. *King Cotton Diplomacy.* Chicago: University of Chicago Press, 1931.

Parks, Joseph H. *General Edmund Kirby-Smith, C.S.A.* Baton Rouge: Louisiana State University Press, 1954.

Paullin, Charles O. "A Half Century of Naval Administration in America, 1861–1911." U.S. Naval Institute *Proceedings,* no. 298 (December 1912): 1309–36; no. 299 (January 1913): 165–91; no. 300 (February 1913): 735–60; no. 301 (March 1913): 1217–62.

Perry, Milton F. *Infernal Machines: The Story of Confederate Submarine Warfare.* Baton Rouge: Louisiana State University Press, 1965.

Porter, David Dixon. *Memoir of Commodore David Porter of the United States Navy.* Albany, N.Y.: Munsell, 1875.

Pratt, Fletcher. *Civil War on the Western Waters.* New York: Henry Holt, 1956.

Reed, Rowena. *Combined Operations in the Civil War.* Lincoln: University of Nebraska Press, 1978.

Roman, Alfred. *The Military Operations of General Beauregard in the War between the States, 1861 to 1865, Including a Brief Personal Sketch and a Narrative of His Services in the War with Mexico 1846–8.* 2 vols. New York: Harper & Brothers, 1884.

Roske, Ralph J., and Charles Van Doren. *Lincoln's Commando.* New York: Harper & Brothers, 1957.

Silver, James W. ed. *Mississippi in the Confederacy.* Baton Rouge: Louisiana State University Press, 1961.

Sloan, Edward W. *Benjamin Franklin Isherwood.* Annapolis, Md.: Naval Institute Press, 1965.

Strode, Hudson. *Jefferson Davis, Confederate President.* New York: Harcourt Brace, 1959.

Summersell, Charles Grayson. *The Cruise of the C.S.S. Sumter.* Tuscaloosa: University of Alabama Press, 1965.

Turnbull, Archibald Douglas. *Commodore David Porter, 1780–1843.* New York: Century, 1929.

Walker, Peter F. *Vicksburg: A People at War, 1860–1865.* Chapel Hill: University of North Carolina Press, 1960.

Warner, Ezra J. *Generals in Gray: Lives of the Confederate Commanders.* Baton Rouge: Louisiana State University Press, 1959.

Wegner, Dana M. "Commodore William D. 'Dirty Bill' Porter." U.S. Naval Institute *Proceedings* 103 (February 1977): 40–49.

West, Richard S., Jr. *Mr. Lincoln's Navy.* New York: Longmans Green, 1957.

———. "The Relations between Farragut and Porter." U.S. Naval Institute *Proceedings* 61 (July 1935): 985–96.

———. *The Second Admiral: A Life of David Dixon Porter.* New York: Coward-McCann, 1937.

Williams, T. Harry. *P.G.T. Beauregard: Napoleon in Gray.* Baton Rouge: Louisiana State University Press, 1954.

Winters, John D. *The Civil War in Louisiana.* Baton Rouge: Louisiana State University Press, 1963.

Index

About the Author

Chester G. Hearn is a retired manufacturing executive whose interest in the Civil War and naval warfare is of long standing. A resident of Potts Grove, Pennsylvania, he has written numerous articles for *Civil War Times Illustrated*, *Blue and Gray Magazine*, and *America's Civil War* and is the author of four books including *George Washington's Schooners*, also published by the Naval Institute Press.

The Naval Institute Press is the book-publishing arm of the U.S. Naval Institute, a private, nonprofit membership society for sea service professionals and others who share an interest in naval and maritime affairs. Established in 1873 at the U.S. Naval Academy in Annapolis, Maryland, where its offices remain today, the Naval Institute has almost 85,000 members worldwide.

Members of the Naval Institute support the education programs of the society and receive the influential monthly magazine *Proceedings* and discounts on fine nautical prints and on ship and aircraft photos. They also have access to the transcripts of the Institute's Oral History Program and get discounted admission to any of the Institute-sponsored seminars offered around the country.

The Naval Institute also publishes *Naval History* magazine. This colorful bimonthly is filled with entertaining and thought-provoking articles, first-person reminiscences, and dramatic art and photography. Members receive a discount on *Naval History* subscriptions.

The Naval Institute's book-publishing program, begun in 1898 with basic guides to naval practices, has broadened its scope in recent years to include books of more general interest. Now the Naval Institute Press publishes about 100 titles each year, ranging from how-to books on boating and navigation to battle histories, biographies, ship and aircraft guides, and novels. Institute members receive discounts of 20 to 50 percent on the Press's nearly 600 books in print.

Full-time students are eligible for special half-price membership rates. Life memberships are also available.

For a free catalog describing Naval Institute Press books currently available, and for further information about subscribing to *Naval History* magazine or about joining the U.S. Naval Institute, please write to:

Membership Department
U.S. Naval Institute
118 Maryland Avenue
Annapolis, Maryland 21402-5035

Telephone: (800) 233-8764
Fax: (410) 269-7940